D1496280

INSIDE KNOWLEDGE

INSIDE KNOWLEDGE

INCARCERATED PEOPLE
ON THE FAILURES OF
THE AMERICAN PRISON

DORAN LARSON

NEW YORK UNIVERSITY PRESS

NEW YORK

NEW YORK UNIVERSITY PRESS
New York
www.nyupress.org

© 2024 by New York University
All rights reserved

Please contact the Library of Congress for Cataloging-in-Publication data.
ISBN: 9781479818006 (hardback)
ISBN: 9781479818044 (library ebook)
ISBN: 9781479818013 (consumer ebook)

This book is printed on acid-free paper, and its binding materials are chosen for strength and durability. We strive to use environmentally responsible suppliers and materials to the greatest extent possible in publishing our books.

Manufactured in the United States of America

10 9 8 7 6 5 4 3 2 1

Also available as an ebook

CONTENTS

PREFACE

THIS is a book of witness testimony. Selected and arranged primarily from the largest and first fully searchable digital archive of nonfiction essays by currently incarcerated people writing about their experience inside prisons across the United States, the writing you will read here presents what we might hope is the beginning of an effort at truth and reconciliation regarding this nation's unprecedented experiment in mass incarceration. Such an effort must begin with the truth, and the most hidden truth is that borne by witnesses behind prison walls.

This is not a sociological study. It is not a legal or policy argument, though it carries implications for social science, policy, and legal practice. The archive of essays this book draws from was not born from a plan to test a hypothesis or to support a preformed position on legal confinement. In the fall of 2009, I had been running a writing workshop inside Attica Correctional Facility for three years. Among men serving decades-to-life sentences, we read and discussed their insights into law, justice, friendship, violence, regret and remorse, day-to-day coping, basic human decency and its absence, as well as the full range of issues workshop members witnessed daily inside a maximum-security prison with a well-deserved reputation for staff-on-ward violence. To understand whether these writers' experience was shared by other imprisoned people or peculiar to Attica, I enlisted a research assistant to send out a call for first-person, nonfiction essays by currently incarcerated people writing about their experience inside. That call led to the publication of seventy-one essays from twenty-seven states in a collection titled *Fourth City: Essays from the Prison in America*, published in 2014. That title reflects a prison and jail population larger than all but three American cities. More importantly, the work submitted reflects a collective experience as cohesive as we would expect from citizens writing of life in New York, Los Angeles, or Chicago. The writing of people held in US prisons, as chapter 1 will describe, is strikingly consistent over 230-plus years of the prison's history. It also consolidates space. The issues it evokes today are as though reported from one location despite spanning state and facility boundaries and at numbers never before imagined.[1]

From among the first 45 (of 154) essays received for *Fourth City*, eleven categories of subject matter emerged and persisted into the final organization of that book. Take the state names off these essays and one could hardly tell they were not from a single, hidden metropolis.

The deadline for *Fourth City* passed in the fall of 2012, but essays just kept coming. Once invited, incarcerated people would not give up the chance to report what they had experienced from birth to arrest, arrest to prosecution, and over collective millennia under lock and key. They literally broke beyond the limits of book publication, forcing the creation of an online platform: the American Prison Writing Archive (prisonwitness.org). At this writing, the APWA hosts over five million words of prison witness, and it grows on average by around seventy essays each month, or by nearly twelve volumes the size of *Fourth City* each year. The archive currently hosts 3,300 essays, representing forty-eight states, over four hundred prison facilities, and over one thousand authors. Unlike work in the book, this writing is not edited. It is posted exactly as it arrives. (Thus readers will note, in the lines quoted in these pages, the uncorrected traits of writing from a population either badly or otherwise underserved by formal education.) Over the course of the next three years, the APWA—which I now co-direct with faculty at Johns Hopkins University—stands to triple in volume.[2]

These essays are not simply data points gleaned from a series of check-off boxes or pre-scripted interviews. Writers describe life at home and in their communities before incarceration; they report on addiction and mental illness and poverty, as well as encounters with police, jails, courts, and all dimensions of prison experience, including staff relations, carceral demographics, food, medical, and other profit-making services, psychological degradation, personal maturation, remorse, sources of hope, friendship, solitary confinement, parenting from inside . . . and, most recently, COVID-19 negligence, illness, and death. Rather than generating graphs or charts, readers can search the Archive by keywords, self-identified author attributes (ethnicity, religious identification, age at conviction, etc.), states, and by layering these facets.

While the work of scholars, journalists, and activists has regularly confirmed, informed, and broadened my views on mass incarceration, those views continue to spring primarily from my work directly with, and my reading of the writing of incarcerated people. Readers who wish to cross-check the trends in prison witness that I state or imply are warmly encouraged to go directly to the American Prison Writing Archive to search and read for themselves.

INTRODUCTION

WHY PRISON WITNESS MATTERS

I N 1974, on the cusp of the American prison's expansion toward its current mass scale, Justice William O. Douglas wrote that "people have the right and the necessity to know not only of the incidence of crime, but of the effectiveness of the system intended to control it."[1] Popular media, political debate, and high-profile cases have made parts of this system the stuff of daily conversation. Arrest, charging, and courtroom procedures are practices of which most people feel they have at least some cursory understanding (however ill-informed they may in fact be). But TV dramas, news segments, and much of public debate often end at arrest, arraignment, verdicts, or sentencing. The criminal legal system narratives we witness day to day typically conclude with a suspect handcuffed and pushed into a squad car or escorted from a courtroom, yet far from prison gates.

The purpose of this book is to continue that story line while allowing its living subjects to unmask its myths. Narrated by witnesses who can testify to the most hidden intricacies of its daily workings, *Inside Knowledge* allows readers to learn from imprisoned people what America's unprecedented experiment in mass-scale incarceration looks and feels and smells like from inside. It is not a flattering portrait. Imprisoned people with the courage and wherewithal to document what they experience make clear that today's prisons not only degrade and debilitate their wards. They defeat each of the missions we have traditionally asked prisons to fulfill: rehabilitation, containment, deterrence, and even meaningful retribution. These purposes are foundational to legitimizing the existence and operation of prisons, to rationalizing the policing and court systems that feed them, and to locating incarceration's place within democracy. If the mass prison actively defeats its own rationales and justifications for being, then rather than using them as the cardinal reference points in public debate about mass incarceration, we would do better to direct that debate to the mass-scale damage prisons mete out upon individuals and communities. Such a redirected debate, as the voices gathered in this book suggest, can redirect (and dismantle) thinking about the future of incarceration itself as a method of securing not only legal order but a constructive, equitable form of justice, one that serves all people and communities, rather than pitting citizens outside against those inside in a struggle that degrades everyone concerned.

Incarcerated people today are ready for this renewed debate, and they know the stakes of their testimony. They know that every detail they convey must counter the fog of misinformation produced by popular media, a multibillion-dollar prison industry, lawmakers beating the drums of law and order, and the perceptions of a public, in legal scholar Jonathan Simon's words, "whose infatuation with incarceration depends on deep ignorance as to its fundamental effects."[2] What prison witnesses reveal is a confined social order made up of people who, even when accepting their culpability, reject the destructive practices that their acts have triggered: "I did something wrong, I deserved to go to prison," writes Brian Nelson after twenty-seven years inside. "But I didn't deserve to be tortured."[3]

Our punishments teach profound lessons. They simply are not the ones we might like to believe are taught inside either a democratic nation claiming to respect human rights and dignity or an institution intended to control crime. What incarcerated people report is that our prisons do not punish so much as they simply damage human beings, rendering them less capable of reintegrating into life outside;[4] we then blame their failures on their lack of moral character. But as one imprisoned California writer observed in 1970, "To determine how men will behave once they enter the prison it is of first importance to know that prison. Men are brutalized by the environment—not the reverse."[5] Fifty years later, a woman who served years in solitary confinement in New York State suggests that little has changed: "Yes, the public is safe for that time [while in prison], but now you have this menace who is developing a shitload of other problems. It's like taking a dog, putting it in a cage and mistreating it for years, and then letting it loose in a playground with children. It's going to act exactly how you'd expect it to act."[6] From Tennessee, a letter addressed to "American Justice" concludes, "I thank you for the pain and unforgettable experiences American Justice. I thank you for creating a beast."[7]

These voices join a history of prison testimony nearly as old as the nation itself. For over 220 years, incarcerated people have been producing a shadow canon to the famously unruly public texts of American literary history.[8] This better-known canon presents facets of a nation so profoundly pluralistic that we take up each day—as fresh as at our founding—the question of just what we are and what we stand for. Meanwhile, imprisoned writers have built, year by year, decade by decade, a literary corpus that tracks the evolution of an institution that translates all of our most noble arguments about values, beliefs, justice, and the rule of law into steel and stone and concrete, into education or torture, into conditions for redemption or utter degradation. What legally confined people write of today offers haunting echoes of what others have written since 1799. That few know this is no accident, since "the prison is," historian Dan Berger writes, "a living archive, steeped in a denial of the histories it confines."[9] And yet people behind bars have documented the steady, dis-equalizing thrum of human suffering that underlies American claims to blind justice, equity, and the rule of law. These messages are not simply from *in there*. They unearth the silent foundation beneath the social and legal facts and culture that Americans call *here*.

Whatever images we like to project upon them, imprisoned people see what prisons do, to whom, and to what effects. When they write, they bear witness to how our claims to meting out justice and respecting the rule of law, to seeking equity, and to protecting public safety serve as a façade masking torturous isolation, arbitrary violence, death by curable disease, and the hourly chipping away at minds and hearts and spirits in environments so "intrinsically pathological" that even the keepers suffer killing effects.[10] Imprisoned people see cells and recreation yards and mess halls filled with the mentally ill, the indigent, and the hopeless who have been abandoned by job markets and the failing civil services of a society that for over fifty years has preferred to police rather than to assist the poor.[11] They also see the resilience of human beings who may be hardened but refuse to be crushed by their circumstances. Meanwhile, from outside, we project upon the prison's opaque walls assumptions and images that reflect less what imprisoned people are or what our prisons do than convenient flatteries to the free public's sense of moral righteousness and superior merit. Our prisons have turned Plato's cave inside out: it is those inside who see the true forms of our criminal legal practices, while those outside thrill and tremble before the carnival of shadowy monsters cast across small and large screens.

This book allows readers to hear the remarkably unified chorus coming today from among writers held in over six thousand spaces of involuntary confinement.[12] It offers a reality check to our beliefs about the differences between the caged and the free, about law, its enforcement, and public policy regarding crime and punishment. Writers inside testify to the full range of problems they witness not only in prison but on their paths there. While this book gathers those texts that directly address our founding rationales for holding human beings inside spaces of willful deprivation, the archive of prison witness that this book draws upon includes testimony about broken homes and communities, gang involvement, addiction, mental illness, policing and court practices, abuse by prison staff, medical negligence, sexual assault, unhygienic food, and the full spectrum of challenges that men, women, and nonbinary people face in environments committed to punishment. This book selects witness to just one set of issues: how prisons succeed or fail at filling their four cardinal missions. There are many more issues that incarcerated writers address, and many more books that could and should be organized from their work.

Americans recognize that mass imprisonment is a problem. There is near consensus (91 percent of respondents in one survey) that America's criminal justice system "needs fixing."[13] We rarely imagine that the people inside might be among the most valuable assets and agents in charting a new path. What they tell us is not always easy going. These writers know that the public has been programmed not to credit their testimony. The resulting will to inform us of the truth is by turns desperate, angry, pleading, appalled, frustrated, and outraged. Yet the longing to be heard and the will to foment fundamental change saturate every word of the messages inside the bottles that manage to reach the outside.

The United States has the largest incarcerated population—nearly two million—and the highest rate of imprisonment on earth.[14] This is not due to our rates of crime but to how we responded to rising crime from the 1960s up to 1993, when crime began a steady decline, and then despite over a quarter century of steadily sinking rates of offense.[15] Fifty years ago, lawmakers—ignoring evidence that prisons were themselves incubators of social failure and continued lawbreaking—made the politically opportune choice not to address the causes of crime. Instead they embarked on an inter-partisan and race-fueled tougher-on-crime-than-you arms race.[16] This race exploded an imprisonment rate that was higher than that in many countries but nothing like what we see today, into what one critic has called "the greatest public works project of our time."[17] By dismantling welfare-state services and turning their remains into vectors of surveillance, America built what critics have called a penal or carceral state based not only on the harshening of punishment for crime but upon the de facto criminalization of homelessness, mental illness, poverty, and addiction; this proceeded alongside tougher policing of the markets in drugs, guns, and persons that sprang up in the employment deserts created when deregulation sent union jobs overseas.[18] That electoral arms race and its rhetoric calmed until very recently (with crime statistic upticks since COVID-19 lockdowns). Sentencing reform is the buzzword of the day, resonating across the political competition that once fueled a prison building binge.[19] Even prison numbers have started to drop. But this is not because we have become a kinder and more forgiving nation. It is because sinking crime rates sapped the political kick of "law and order" politics, because of hard-fought grassroots struggles against mass-scale incarceration (led largely by those most likely to be the victims of crime), and due to the simple exhaustion of state budgets. While national political debate becomes more polarized by the day, mass imprisonment is denounced on the left as a human and civil rights crisis, lamented in the middle as a costly national tragedy, and criticized on the right as a simple waste of taxpayer dollars on an institution that long ago grew well beyond any arguable human and financial cost-effectiveness as a means of securing public safety. And yet incarcerated people themselves are no less demonized, no less thought of as animals that just need whipping. Many Americans believe that prison conditions are indeed harsh. Many also believe that the best way forward is to make them even harsher.[20] Meanwhile, imprisoned people remain our primary witnesses to the carceral city that the carceral state has founded. They see the real effects of our punishments: "You create Spartan conditions, you're going to get gladiators."[21]

One aim of this book is not only to present prison witness but to stand as a warning. Changes in national mood, political rhetoric, and even the statistics, however laudable, will not bar us from continuing on this path now or from resuming it in the future. What might do so is a glimpse of the human faces behind the numbers. Imprisoned people's testimony is as compelling in its condemnation of incarceration as a practice of crime control as slave narratives were in condemning slavery as a machinery sold to the public as a civilizing force. They are also effective in turning numbers back into people.

Behind popular caricatures of the imprisoned, their sheer numbers have rendered them mere units in a mass. Individual minds and hearts are largely indecipherable. Incarcerated writers bring forth a body of testimony that extracts singular persons and experiences from state data piles; at the same time, their words resonate across state borders, thus revealing an untapped, national reservoir of critical insight whose bracing waters might refresh national conversation about the human costs of trying to cage our way out of crime and about a continuing state of penal apartheid. As noted, these writers present a case that is at once as unified and particular as might come from testimony to life in New York, Los Angeles, or Chicago—only one of which is larger in population than the total number of those living under some form of custodial supervision.[22] They write from deeply personal experience, and they have much to say about who and what we are as a people who have embraced years of pain and suffering as the measure of justice. Incarcerated writers make clear that the sentences our courts mete out are only the door charge to the punishments they experience. What is added occurs behind a veil of law that does not protect the public. It merely protects from public view the malign neglect by those who profit—financially, politically, or professionally—from the population of a major metropolis churned through manufactories of pain. This, writes Kenneth E. Hartman, a man who spent thirty-eight years inside, "is a system that produces failure as a matter of course, that pretends to protect the mass of society, and that destroys whole communities in its voracious appetite."[23]

Who and what has stood in the way of spreading the views of those incarcerated today? Walls and razor wire certainly help. But material barriers could not silence a population just smaller than Chicago's without the aid of courts that regularly defer to prison administrators to determine what constitutional rights incarcerated people are allowed to enjoy.[24] Steel and concrete alone could not silence such a population without the combined interests of everyone who profits from a multibillion-dollar criminal law industry.[25] This is an industry whose public support and budgets might be questioned were incarcerated people to gain fully human faces in the minds of voters and taxpayers. On the front lines of obscuring the lives of the confined, ratings-hungry news broadcasters, so-called reality TV, and the producers of film and television dramas reduce complex human beings and circumstances into cartoonishly simplistic fables about law's enforcers, criminals, victims, and procedures.[26] We see this from the ringing courtroom scenes of *Law & Order* at a time when only one in forty criminal cases ever goes to trial (the rest disposed of by prosecutors whose plea deals carry the threat of decades behind bars should a defendant have the means and temerity to seek a jury trial),[27] to the latest carefully staged episodes of *Lock Up*.

The testimony gathered here argues explicitly and by implication that the popularly consumed dramas of individuals facing proportionate consequences for their individual acts are merely the sales pitch, the barker's script obscuring the mass-scale disappearance, in Bruce Western's words, of whole "demographic categories."[28] We measure such punishment by stretches of time. Yet "ex-felon" is a brand as deep and indelible as those formerly burned into the palms and brows of lawbreakers, while a single day inside can demand life-or-death decisions.

The United States was founded in part on a rejection of branding, the pillory, death for minor crimes, and other barbaric criminal punishments characteristic of a tyrannical state; today, we see the equally disturbing effects meted out by other means. As scholar Colin Dayan writes, "We are permitted to fracture the mind in the way that we once broke bones."[29] Plenty of bones are still getting broken, and they are broken in the name of a public that sees too bright a line between criminal offenses and its own implication in what happens to their perpetrators.[30] That bright line obscures a prison that its inhabitants reveal as an index to mass social, civil, and criminal legal system failure. This book's focus on testimony to the American prison's defeat of rehabilitation, containment, deterrence, and retribution charts just one set of paths through an institution that disserves both the city within and the nation without. This book will explore how we have used prisons to contain the effects of such a wide range of social ills, for so long, and subjected their wards to such a predictable range of mistreatments, the witness of those we confine has become the witness of a people with a history as long as the nation. Given the equally extended history of carceral censorship, it is important to clarify how such writing reaches us.

Like those outside, the writers inside prisons are themselves a subgroup, if even more selective among a population plagued by high rates of illiteracy.[31] The work of this subgroup is narrowed drastically again as it seeks a path into print. If manuscripts do manage to broach prison walls, in seeking public exposure they face agents, editors, and writing contest judges who apply standards of literary quality and market appeal that deny platforms to a community disproportionately marked by the failures of public education. What work does reach print is vitally important, and the editors, presses, and organizations that take this risk should be applauded for mounting even a select counterforce to popular misinformation. This book will occasionally draw upon such traditionally published texts. Its major source of witness, however, will be the American Prison Writing Archive (APWA), a digital archive of nonfiction essays by people writing about their experience of prison, criminal legal involvement more broadly, and the lives that preceded their arrival in prison. None of this work is edited or polished. In practice, it is not even selected. The APWA accepts, scans, and posts—exactly as they arrive, accompanied on the site by transcriptions of handwritten texts—all the essays submitted by incarcerated people willing to write about their criminal legal system involvement.[32] Writers inside need only a few stamps and writing materials to reach a global audience. This has made possible a breadth and living depth of documentation of the human experience of incarceration impossible before the digital age.

At the end of her best-selling book *The New Jim Crow: Mass Incarceration in the Age of Colorblindness* (2010), legal scholar Michelle Alexander writes, "Isolated victories can be won—even a string of victories—but in the absence of a fundamental shift in public consciousness, the system as a whole will remain intact."[33] In 2016 political scientist Marie Gottschalk seconded Alexander's conclusion and implied where that shift might begin.

The slave narratives of the antebellum period, which graphically rendered the physical pain that slaves suffered and made it widely visible, helped to propel the abolitionist cause. Today, what happens in prison stays mostly in prison, making it harder to draw connections in the public mind between justice on the inside and justice on the outside. The ability to identify with an offender—or not—is a key predictor of why people differ in their levels of punitiveness. The invisibility of the millions of people behind bars has made it extremely difficult to alter the negative portrait that members of the general public have in their heads of people who have been convicted of a crime. They are simply prisoners and criminals. As such, they often are denied their humanity and any right to democratic accountability, much as slaves were in the United States.[34]

The testimony of enslaved and formerly enslaved people affected public awareness by actively countering southern propaganda that presented the enslaved as the happy beneficiaries of paternal white masters. This book hopes to do for readers today what slave narratives did for readers before and after the Civil War: to allow us the chance to read, from their own hands, the testimony of a population wrapped in popular myths and lucrative misrepresentation, and bound by socially destructive policies and practices that pervert the ends of law and justice. My hope is that these writers effect what they clearly intend, Alexander's proposed "fundamental shift in public consciousness" regarding an institution that has become both one of the nation's largest employers and a crucible for debates on public mores, law, race, and justice.

With thinking about prisons now changing its tenor, it is long past time for incarcerated people to join this debate. By helping us to measure the human costs of the current legal order, they can also aid in guard-railing our progress toward a more humane future. A more civil conversation about how to address crime was relatively easy while crime rates were dropping and state budgets strapped.[35] But as the COVID-19 years have shown, change these circumstances, and we are quick to backtrack. Ideally, prisons will grow drastically smaller and thus be enabled to become more constructive, or merely benign as they shrink out of existence. Even before that wished-for day arrives, though, we need to block the path that has led to a city in cages. We need to listen to the

testimony of those inside this prison city if we are to effect a fundamental shift away from public acceptance of incarceration as our default
response to crime, as well as to poverty, mental illness, joblessness, and
addiction. On the basis of that testimony, we may be able to bring some
humility to outside speculation on what works and what does not, welcome the people who know the system best into the conversation, and
thus begin to address the mass prison's concrete human effects. We need
not like or sympathize with these writers. But it is at our hazard that we
fail to listen to the choral dirge echoing today from inside this nation's
living tombs of justice.

Clinical research and global comparison make clear that punishments are more harsh the greater the social distance—real or
perceived—between those who determine the punishments for crime
and those upon whom these decision makers believe this punishment
will be meted out. Punishments are mildest in the most racially and
socially homogeneous nations, where voters and legislators are able to
relate to the lives and circumstances of those most likely to be locked
up.[36] Today, a yawning chasm stretches between American voters
in comfortable white suburbs and the urban neighborhoods of poor
people of color, a fact reflected in differences in views of the American criminal legal system as a whole.[37] Sociologist Michelle Brown
writes, "Only by diminishing both the mystery and the fantasies of
punishment may we begin to elaborate the shared bond between the
punisher and the punished and the complicity and responsibility of
'distant' community members in the infliction of pain."[38] The writing
of incarcerated people is the most practical means by which substantial numbers of those inside and outside can meet and thus at once
measure and diminish the distance between our respective positions,
not merely as "voters" and "lawbreakers" but simply as human beings.
This is not simply charity to the incarcerated. We need to know what
imprisoned people report of the effects of the actions and inaction of
those who support—through taxes and votes—the lawmakers and police, prosecutors and judges and prison officials and staff who decide
how much institutionalized pain our safety is worth, at what cost, and
to whom. Transformation of penal policy and practice will require taking seriously what imprisoned people can tell us about the effects of
those policies and practices.

My first task will be to place the meeting between the readers of this book and the witnesses found here into historical context. Chapter 1 will offer a history of the rise and varying rationales of the American prison, accompanied by the remarkably consistent testimony of people held there, from the end of the eighteenth century up to this moment. Chapters 2 through 5 begin with brief discussions of relevant current research. Thereafter, each compiles a small anthology of prison witness to the prison's defeat of each of the aims we sanction prisons to fulfill.

Chapter 2 gathers testimony to the ways in which incarceration today fails to mete out meaningful retribution, the one end that even the harshest prison critics claim that it does in fact deliver. Chapter 3 presents witness to how profoundly our prisons have abandoned rehabilitative ends and to the many, ingenious, and inspiring ways that incarcerated people rebuild themselves, entirely on their own, in collaboration with other incarcerated people—most often in direct resistance to prison practices—as well as in the rare instances when effective programming is offered. Chapter 4 gathers testimony that describes the ways in which incarceration at mass scale does less to contain convicted people than to spread and perpetuate harm among their children, families, and communities, and damages their prospects for becoming contributors to each upon release. Chapter 5 presents testimony that even when incarceration does deter criminal perpetrators from the desire to commit new crimes, it also renders them less able to desist from crime by hobbling their ability to gain footholds in legitimate economies; incarceration damages individuals and the communities where they return, thus making further crime more likely even despite reformed intentions. The concluding chapter considers the potential rewards of reading prison writing *as* a witness literature; it suggests ways in which mass-scale prison witness might yield new resources for building a more just criminal legal system and thus a more whole and inclusive society.

Our carceral city holds people and ideas and desires as complex as those to be found in any other major metropolis. But this is the only city in America built to achieve fixed goals that we claim make ours a safer and more sustainable society. Every voice—no matter its intent or mood, and no matter its culpability for actions of the past—bears relevance to assessing how well this walled city achieves those purported, multibillion-dollar aims.

The larger question for this book is how might we reassess law, crime, punishment, and justice, and the triggers between them, in the face of the testimony of those who know them not as abstractions or a cascading series of "shoulds" or policy speculation (which have historically led to wide-scale disaster) but as lived experience in the body, mind, and spirit. Other nations whose policies and regimes have strayed from an inclusive embrace of their own people have faced such daunting questions and come out stronger. They have done so by way of international trials and by creating public venues for voicing truth and seeking reconciliation. If we are to reach that point in the United States regarding mass incarceration, we must take seriously the fact that incarcerated people, whatever their crimes, are the primary witnesses to what incarceration is and does, to whom, and to what ends. Readers might feel no obligation to read this witness; but if we ignore it, we shun the "right and the necessity" that Justice Douglas claimed belongs to all of us.

In the most hopeful future, our prison population will begin to shrink at a rate and over enough time to confirm a substantial change in the pattern of a half century, marking a return to our traditional place among international norms. But we will not have conclusively left mass imprisonment behind until, like many of our peer nations, we settle on a collective skepticism about whether placing people in cages makes those inside or outside any safer today or more whole tomorrow. Whether readers agree or disagree that such skepticism is needed, one thing is clear: We have never invited all the affected parties to the table. My hope is that the witnesses in this book will convince readers that we must.

1

THE PRISON AS IDEA AND PRACTICE

U NDER British rule, branding, placing criminals in the pillory, and hangings had been public spectacles intended to deter crime (including political revolt) by impressing upon the public the dread power of the sovereign. American independence had been argued on claims of the natural rights and dignity of all citizens and against the arbitrary, terror-inducing power of monarchs.[1] Little wonder that the Constitution and five of its ten original amendments (IV through VIII) explicitly limit state powers against criminal suspects and convicted people. The rights that the signers claimed were self-evident and divinely endowed were those of (white male) citizens thought capable of self-regulation and deserving freedom from arbitrary search or arrest, excessive fines or bail, cruel and unusual punishments, or denial of due process of law and a speedy trial by jury. In the new republic, more enlightened punishments were virtually obligatory in order to mark a break from the past. "The history of the United States," Michele Tarter and Richard Bell note, "and the history of incarceration have been joined in a fundamental way ever since." In turn, as H. Bruce Franklin observes, the writing of imprisoned people constitutes "something close to the center of our historical experience as a nation-state."[2]

Yet equally long-standing is the rift between ideas of what prisons should deliver and what the incarcerated experience. Then as today, as Jevon Jackson writes from a Wisconsin prison, "This animal, this beast that I live in, thrives on the illogical and irrational impulses of its wavering political objectives."[3] The testimony of incarcerated people today echoes that of the past because the prison's history of proclaimed purposes and discordant human effects has merely been amplified in the mass prison of the present. Understanding that history will help us to appreciate both what precedents we set and the history we continue by including the testimony of the confined in our debates about prisons, imprisoned people, and the concrete effects of incarceration today.

SILENCING THE SUBJECTS OF LAW'S VIOLENCE

One practical problem surrounding public displays of the bloody power of kings and colonial governors was that crowds often turned these scenes into sites of real or threatened revolt. The suffering of the condemned gave crowds occasion and reason to jeer at authority.[4] Americans attempted to temper these scenes by putting the condemned to menial and shaming roadwork. But bystanders could still hear these workers' stories and extend their sympathies. The condemned themselves were often drunk and prone to carry out robberies and other crimes upon those travelling on the roads they were supposed to repair. Onlookers' sympathies lessened repugnance to crime or dulled those sympathies by repeated exposure to suffering; and the capacity for sympathy, contemporaries believed, was the essential bond of any republican society. Kill that capacity and public virtue, morality, and community itself would dissolve.[5] To protect the public's sensibilities (and avoid its ire), prison walls would stop all such "affective exchange," blocking "sympathetic identification" with lawbreakers.[6]

But how to break such exchange and yet deter crime?

On March 9, 1787, Dr. Benjamin Rush presented to Benjamin Franklin and others a proposal for taking criminal punishments behind walls. A signatory to the Declaration of Independence and the new nation's most eminent physician, Rush spoke from a belief that a true, republican nation must devise rational methods for treating even its lawbreakers. Convicted people would be subjected to regular labor, silent reflection, and instruction, as well as physical punishments.[7] This mix, as well as official struggles between humane reform and punishment, would characterize thinking about penal practice forever after. Rarely would any penal facility, let alone states or the nation, settle exclusively on one or the other. Such running "contestation" would at once mark penological thinking, and appear rather academic in the face of the testimony of people held inside.[8] In Rush's plan, such methods—especially the most benign—would not be divulged to the public. Instead, the prison would be surrounded with the kind of gothic mystery that was the literary rage of the day: dark approaches up winding mountain roads and gates whose groaning would echo from overhanging cliffs. The result? "Children will press upon the evening fire in listening to the tales that will be spread from this abode of misery. Superstition will add to its horrors, and romance will find in it ample materials for fiction, which cannot fail of encreasing the terror of its punishments."[9] Deterrent terror would be relocated from the public gallows and into public imagination.[10]

Rush's prison would be split between practice and fantasy, between flesh and imagination, and that divide has continued for over two centuries.[11] Today, however, we often find such bipolarity reversed: prisons that claim to serve the public good, and that many view as insufficiently harsh, host such debilitating conditions and release their wards under such strict supervisory restrictions that 70 percent are unable to avoid arrest, and 46 percent are back in prison within five years.[12] "Few other institutions," Michelle Brown remarks, "encounter such a radical and momentous divide between their physical realities and cultural imagination."[13] Public policy has been driven by mere "caricatures" of those inside,[14] and this is no accident. Prison walls were built to keep the public outside as well as to keep convicted people inside. Their written testaments would also be more easily suppressed.

Execution sermons, including criminal confessions transcribed and edited to suit the purposes of clergy, were a popular offering of the colonial press. Cotton Mather, the most eminent Puritan divine of his day, used these occasions to teach the wages of sin and healthy fear of God's judgment.[15] Such texts became so popular that publishers began to solicit confessions directly from the condemned, thus removing clerical safeguards.[16] Once placed behind walls, however, criminal punishments "would be public only through the mediation of textual representation," and that representation controlled by prison officials.[17] Predictably, such reports assured the public that the first penitentiary experiment on Philadelphia's Walnut Street was a site of "reforms [that] were enlightened and humane" while surrounding the condemned in mystery.[18] Walnut Street boasted clean living spaces and workrooms. When it quickly became overcrowded and filthy, and those inside grew restless, got drunk, escaped, or languished in idleness, the solution was not to reassess but to take the "separate system" to its logical end.[19] If criminals could be a bad influence on the public, how much worse for each other? Men and women began to be transferred to Eastern State Penitentiary, a mammoth structure that would hold each ward in unbroken isolation.

In the belief that spatial design was key to reform, Eastern's very stones were the expression of a penal theory. Closed in upon themselves, the condemned would see reflected in those stones the material evidence of their guilt.[20] While blocking the influence of incarcerated people upon one another, Eastern State brought all the damaging effects we see among the estimated forty-one to forty-eight thousand people held in extreme isolation in the United States today, including long-term psychological and emotional damage.[21] These effects were witnessed by Charles Dickens—who had spent much of his childhood locked inside congregate debtors' prisons—while touring Eastern in 1842. The faces of the condemned, he wrote, "had something of that strained attention which we see upon the faces of the blind and deaf, mingled with a kind of horror, as though they had all been secretly terrified. . . . Parade before my eyes, a hundred men, with one among them newly released from this solitary suffering, and I would point him out."[22]

Eastern's administrators had been sure that the famous author would report glowingly of their methods. When Dickens's words hit print, rather than reassessing their methods, officials scrambled to counter a public relations disaster. They reinterviewed the men and women whom the author had spoken with; they claimed that he could not understand what managing such a population required. They also quickly introduced education and instruction that would make good on the good work they had claimed to deliver.[23] As in future years, the prison would make reforms only after embarrassing reports or legal pressure came from the outside. Where Walnut Street and Eastern succeeded was in silencing their wards. There is little direct testimony from either facility, for good reason.

THE IMPRISONED SPEAK

One of the few writers to reach the public from this era, Patrick Lyon, describes conditions commonly reported by incarcerated people today: too little and often rancid food, disease, severe limits on reading materials and correspondence, arbitrary punishments, and idleness. Unlike the prison's advertisers, Lyon warned that "such a disregard to justice would, or might certainly have an effect to cause a revolution in this country, and I drew several inferential remarks relative to the bastille of Paris." His conclusion is prescient of testimony from US prisons today.

Advocates . . . cannot believe that such treatment is exercised on the prisoners. . . . When it can be proved, that a prisoner some time back, was starved and disfigured by the rats; and I suppose those advocates cannot deny that a keeper can at pleasure take the unfortunate women out of the west-wing, and keep them in the cells—for what purpose I suppose may be easily guessed at. A man taken to the cells for God knows what . . . and kept several months on half a pound of bread, and a quart of water every 24 hours, until he is so weak that he has been known to knaw the plaister from the walls, and could not stand to evacuate his urine. After such a reduction, the unfortunate and some-times innocent victim, is conducted to the sick room and breathes his last: and if it is asked what he or they died of, it is answered . . . any thing but the real thing. . . . Why rail at the rack or the inquisition, if similar methods are pursued, to extort by means of force, the frantic exclama-tions of suffering innocence, for the purposes of self-condemnation.[24]

The supporters of the separate system at Walnut and Eastern attempted to deny and to appease their critics: presaging official defenses raised today, they insisted that it was imprisoned people, not prison design or administration, that were to blame. They could not hide the fact that theirs was the most expensive response to crime ever conceived.

To the north, New York State commissioned a prison intended to alle-viate unbroken isolation and to relieve the public of imprisonment's ex-cessive costs. Auburn Prison and the Auburn Plan would initiate penal schema, rationales, and exploitative opportunities that would dominate US prison building for the remainder of the century, spread across Eu-rope (in competition with the separate system), and continue to shape prison thinking and practices to this day.[25] It would also spawn a genre of first-person witness that continues to be produced at this moment.

To counter both the damaging effects and high costs of solitary con-finement, Auburn's authorities arranged for inhabitants to be celled alone at night but work together by day in industrial workshops on contracts held by private, for-profit manufacturers. To counter the bad influence of convicted people upon each other, authorities enforced a regime of silence by whipping, hanging men by their thumbs, and a nineteenth-century version of waterboarding.[26] When out of their cells and workshops, men were closely shackled to each other, forcing a machine-like lockstep. Like slavery, this industrial prison "was a labor system managed by terror."[27]

Notwithstanding exceptions like Patrick Lyon, prison authors had found ready publishers only for tales of criminal exploits or edifying confessions. Authors such as William Coffey (1823), John Maroney (1832), Colonel Levi S. Burr (1833), Horace Lane (1835), William Joseph Snelling (1837), and James Brice (1839) deepened the genre of the "prison exposé" largely by financing their own books and pamphlets.[28] These authors—all writing of their time in northern prisons—aimed neither at excitement nor moral instruction (though the latter, they often claimed, could be gained incidentally). Their stated intent was to document existing practices, and, by implication, to transform the incarcerated into primary authorities on those practices. As slave narratives were doing more widely and eventually more effectively, they sought to turn the objects of legally sanctioned dehumanization into its most credible public witnesses. In Jennifer Graber's characterization of antebellum prison exposés, she writes that, "like narratives intended to expose audiences to the horrors of slavery, intemperance, domestic violence, and prostitution, the former inmate accounts pointed out that the lawful suffering of many of America's inhabitants stood in stark contrast to the nation's ideals and religious character."[29]

In *Inside Out; or, An Interior View of the New-York State Prison* (1823), William Coffey describes starvation meals, medical malpractice and neglect, brutal or overly lax discipline, and the corruption of prison officials and staff.[30] None of these issues is unfamiliar to incarcerated people today. Neither is William Snelling's observation in 1837 that true criminals are only one of the types of people the prison holds. Snelling calls the Boston House of Corrections (so called "with a very small degree of propriety") "a receptacle for idiots, madmen, sots, vagabonds, and malefactors of every description."[31] His warning resonates today, when half a million people, never having been tried or convicted, languish in jails simply for the inability to pay bail, and countless others—unable to afford a strong defense—serve sentences handed down without benefit of jury: "Judges of the police court," Snelling warned, "be careful how ye confound misfortune with infamy."[32]

This confounding is made concrete in Austin Reed's recently discovered 1859 memoir, *The Life and Adventures of a Haunted Convict*. Reed was a Black man held in New York State juvenile detention in childhood, and in Auburn Prison starting at age thirteen. His story reads much like the life histories of countless people locked up today: a father lost in the author's childhood, resulting poverty, an itinerant life on the streets that leads to trouble with the law. After an escape, Reed is returned to the New York House of Refuge, where boys are whipped with cat-o'-nine-tails, or "cats," which tear flesh from their bodies. Reed's book presages recent studies that claim that prisons do less to control crime than to brand a social subclass of criminalized people.[33] Of the 800 men held in Auburn Prison, Reed knows 150 from the House of Refuge.[34] They work in ten different industrial shops, making everything from combs to tools to textiles. Reed blames his fall on "follow[ing] the high road of vice and crime" and on the hardening effects of incarceration itself.[35] Locked up from childhood, Reed scoffs at a keeper's threat of being whipped with the cats. "I have had them sunken deeper in my back than ever you dare to sink them."[36] Yet the child's heart has yet to be beaten out of him: on the next page, when a keeper notes that he knew Reed's father, Reed "gave away to a full flood of tears."[37] As happens too often today, the child, seemingly beaten out of the convict, survives in all his emotional vulnerability beneath a web of scars.

Behind the threat of corporal punishment, Reed describes the daily regime of micro-control of bodies for which Auburn was famous, a system seemingly designed to drive men to madness or rebellion.

> When marching, we must keep close together, with our arms folded and our heads to the right, our heads bowed and our eyes a looking at the ground. When sitting at the table, we must keep our arms folded, our heads bowed, with our eyes directly down on our dishes before us, not allowed to touch a knife or a fork or to unfold our arms until the bell rings as a signal for us to eat. Must not pass a piece of bread or meat or potato from one man to another. . . . It makes no odds how bad your companion may want it . . . for if you do, off comes your shirt, and less than a minute's time you are suffering under the pains of the cats.[38]

Such restrictions, forced labor, and hair triggers to tortuous punishments have a predictable effect. As one departing man tells the author, "If I am hard, I have been harden within the walls of a gloomy prison, and if I am cruel, I have learnt it within the walls of a gloomy prison, for 'sthere where cruelty, pain, shame, and misery dwells."[39] This sentiment is echoed by Sebastian Richardson after spending 2010 to 2012 in a federal prison in Pennsylvania: "You come out with a lot of anger, and they create that."[40]

Like Lyon, Coffey, and Snelling, Reed struck blows at a system that, from the founding, had been a key element in what Rebecca McLennan calls "the structure of legitimating fictions of American social order more generally."[41] Whatever the fictions that prison advocates want to spread, prison witnesses reveal each reform's failure and subsequent reform and failure as the systolic and diastolic movements at the center of American penal practices—what Michel Foucault aptly calls this "detestable solution, which we seem unable to do without,"[42] a system that should have been particularly detestable in a nation that boasted both Christian piety and respect for personal dignity.[43]

Yet by midcentury, the Auburn Plan was the norm. Most incarcerated people outside the South were, like their enslaved contemporaries, working for private concerns, their treatment similarly handed over to their production masters.[44] While no institution dehumanized its subjects as did slavery (or so meticulously legalized that dehumanization), a disproportionately Black incarcerated population suffered many similar conditions. Prison guards were paid directly by private contractors. Both the enslaved and imprisoned suffered the whip (among other methods) as the enforcer of authority's power, as a driver of profit, and as the material sign of the existential inferiority of those on the whip's receiving end (a fact of which Reed is intensely aware).[45]

Under these circumstances, the profit-minded contractor, like the slave master, came to shape every facet of prison life: food rations, grounds for punishment, and staff loyalties. Unlike the enslaved, imprisoned people, if they survived, would someday walk free. But the very procedures by which prison sentences might be shortened or lengthened became subject to the contractor's efforts to raise revenue and depress costs.[46]

Convicts might not be made better by confinement—and officials were openly disdainful of the idea that moral reform of imprisoned people was even possible—but they could be made profitable.[47] This system continued unhindered until free world laborers became more widely organized, gained political power, and agitated against private prison contracts as a source of unfair competition and as the very incarnation of the "wage slavery" that industrial capital sought to protect with its bloody suppression of work stoppages and strikes.[48] One obstacle to labor reform in prisons, however, was the Constitution: "Neither slavery nor involuntary servitude, *except as a punishment for crime whereof the party shall have been duly convicted*, shall exist within the United States, or any place subject to their jurisdiction" (emphasis added). So reads the now notorious Thirteenth Amendment, which simultaneously wrote slavery out of and into US law.[49]

Much has rightly been made of the use of this clause to allow de facto slavery to continue after 1865 under the South's convict leasing system, which continued as late as World War II by one account,[50] with remnants today in unpaid or underpaid chain gangs, fire crews, industrial state-use production, and provision of state services.[51] This system permitted southern sheriffs to round up newly freed Black people, convict them of breaking laws created specifically to be enforced against free Black people, and hand them over for court fees or lease by former slave masters and others. Rather than the considerable investment they once made to buy an enslaved person, those who leased convicted people incurred only the fees, leasing rates, minimal food, shelter, and clothing. The operating philosophy was "One dies, get another."[52] "As with chattel slavery before it," Robert Perkinson writes, "convict leasing took hold—surviving countless efforts at abolition—principally because it made men rich."[53] Former slave plantations and industries could literally order up cheap labor from the local sheriff, who could round up men and women on charges such as vagrancy (wandering without money), loitering (standing still without money), or insubordination to whites.[54] What David Oshinsky writes of this system locates it as the prototype for today's profit- and employment-rich mass incarceration.

> From its beginnings in Mississippi in the late 1860s until its abolition in Alabama in the late 1920s, convict leasing would serve to undermine legal equality, harden racial stereotypes, spur industrial development, intimidate free workers, and breed contempt for the law. It would turn a few men into millionaires and crush thousands of ordinary lives. . . . Prisoners became younger and blacker, and the length of their sentences soared.[55]

Indeed, this system explicitly sought to produce the effect we see from mass incarceration today: not to control crime, since the behaviors that turned Black people into felons were largely criminalized by policy,[56] but to control, impoverish, disenfranchise, and socially disable targeted Black populations.[57] Some of the very same lands where enslaved people once worked became state-run prison plantations that continue to operate today.[58] Indeed, any history of prison labor up to the present moment could properly root itself not in the progressive hopes gone unfulfilled in the North, but in the unbroken continuum from slavery to today's prison factories and farms. As one imprisoned man testified, echoing his enslaved ancestors, "Day after day we looked death in the face & was afraid to speak."[59]

What is less well understood is that the Thirteenth Amendment's exception was also a boon to the industrial prisons of the North, granting license to continue brutal and degrading business as usual: practices that the courts protected on the premise that, had incarcerated people desisted from crime, they would not have lost limbs and suffered other injuries in the course of forced work.[60] Also like slavery, the industrial prison spawned a witness literature that revealed the workings of this legally sanctioned system while presenting the condemned as fully human beings capable of documenting their conditions and thus of lodging protests against it.

As H. Bruce Franklin writes, when industrial prisons "shed much of their early pretense of being places of reformation and became frankly acknowledged as places of cheap mass production, . . . literature by convicts became increasingly a form of protest literature against the brutality of prisons."[61] Subjected to beatings and torture—without even lip service to rehabilitation—these writers increasingly saw themselves not simply as a gathering of individual lawbreakers, but "as a new subclass in society, prisoners,"[62] a view deeply felt among incarcerated people today.[63]

Gerald Toole's 1862 exposé of labor conditions in Connecticut State Prison, Franklin observes, was one of the first literary works set on a factory floor.[64] Like Reed and writers in the second half of the twentieth century, and unlike Lyon's, Coffey's, and Snelling's portraits of damaged *individuals*—Toole frames prison workers as a faceless class *en masse*.

In the shop there were about thirty men whose pale, emaciated looks showed that the very life blood was being worked out of them. They were all working at boot making. The coffers of unblushing contractors are filled from the labor of these poor convicts who work from dawn to dusk.[65]

Toole's exposé evidences the spread of the Auburn Plan. His portrait of the conditions of violently enforced industrial slavery in Connecticut repeat point-by-point what we find in Austin Reed's 1859 manuscript: No system for grievances but brutal punishment for infractions as slight as speaking to another imprisoned person, retaliation for any complaint, the use of the lockstep, the water bath, and a pecking order of sadistic keepers. Unlike Reed, a Black man so inured in childhood to physical abuse that he can suffer and finally pass out of Auburn, Toole is condemned to hang for stabbing the warden before he could whip Toole to bloody shreds once again. Yet Reed's and Toole's depictions of incarcerated people *as* a people, as a class created by unequal opportunities, dis-equalizing legislation, and uneven enforcement of the law, are joined; both have gained wider purchase among writers in the age of mass incarceration, particularly those who live and comment on the racial currents of imprisonment today. Such writers echo W. E. B. Du Bois's 1903 observation about southern criminal justice, that "it was not . . . a question of crime, but rather one of color, that settled a man's conviction on almost any charge."[66] Slavery's criminal justice legacy is now national; it followed the Great Migration of freed Black people out of the South and into northern and western cities built on racial segregation among other modes of legally enforced inequality.[67]

At the turn of the last century, however, the imprisoned people whose writing reached the public were generally white, and while they noted incarcerated Black people when they encountered them, their major theme was the Venn overlap between poverty and criminal conviction, as in this passage from Jack London, continuing a theme struck by Patrick Lyon, William Snelling, and Austin Reed, and equally true today.

The tramp is one of two kinds of men: he is either a discouraged worker or a discouraged criminal. Now a discouraged criminal, on investigation, proves to be a discouraged worker, or the descendent of discouraged workers; so that, in the last analysis, the tramp is a discouraged worker. Since there is not work for all, discouragement for some is unavoidable.[68]

Poverty continues to mark most people sent to prison. Many are then paid nothing or paid nickels per hour for mandatory labor.[69] Progressive Era prison uprisings and work stoppages, as well as organized labor's work from outside, added to growing public disapproval of privately contracted penal labor, which New York State outlawed in 1894.[70] Dread of dangerously idle convicts resulted in retooling to produce goods for use by the state (as continues today), as well as offering academic and vocational education, since these could be set up relatively quickly.[71] Yet the reports coming from inside remained consistent with reports that had emerged earlier. Slavery-like conditions continued, both on northern factory floors and on penal plantations, though now serving states or counties rather than private interests. But this only demonstrated again the chasm between publicly stated intentions and rationales, and the conditions that incarcerated people experience. The difference between working in killing conditions for the profit of private companies or to save costs for the state was likely lost on the imprisoned laborer. The fact that prisons cheated these restrictions, forcing imprisoned people to manufacture goods with labels that attributed their labor to free world workers, was not.

On the outside, first-person memoirs and reports on prison life found in Progressive America one of the most welcoming audiences they had ever enjoyed: from Jack London's damning exposé of his time in the Erie County Jail after a thirty-second hearing for vagrancy (1904), to the 1912 memoir of anarchist and would-be assassin Alexander Berkman, to Kate Richards O'Hare's *In Prison* (1920), a study of the barbarous practices, social outcasts, and political crusaders that fill a women's prison where she was held after a conviction for speaking out against the First World War under the notorious Espionage Act of 1917, to fellow Espionage Act violator Eugene Debs's 1927 *Walls and Bars*, which both echoes and anticipates prison witness to the necessary symbiosis between capitalism and incarceration. These writers made clear that the encouraging experiments carried on by Progressive Era reformers had not made prisons elsewhere less brutal, less debilitating, less corrupt, or less lethal—in large part because those reforms were seated in the eugenicist belief that redeemability, and thus susceptibility to rehabilitation, was determined by race.[72] These books and others presented the condemned as neither the threats that occupied public imagination nor the "manly" citizens that reformers claimed to produce.[73] They presented what American prison writers have always presented: the human casualties of unaddressed poverty, mental illness, addiction, selective enforcement of the law, racism, and the seemingly ineradicable symbiosis between these conditions and their willful exacerbation, as London describes, inside unregulated spaces of confinement.

Befriended by a more experienced convict, Jack London writes of becoming a "hall man," violently controlling others and working his "graft" after guards hand off responsibility for keeping order to confined men themselves. If men are not thugs or thieves when they enter the Erie County Pen, they quickly become both if they hope to survive.[74]

In Alexander Berkman's 1912 memoir, we see a prison where there is not the slightest pretense of reformation, only onerous factory work whose products—as in Kate Richards O'Hare's report[75]—are falsely labelled to mask their prison origin. Berkman's roster of penal depredations echoes those of the 1830s and of writers today: staff corruption, arbitrary punishments, lethal medical negligence and malpractice, inadequate diet, filth, and physical and sexual assault by staff upon incarcerated people and by the incarcerated upon one another. Berkman debunks (yet again) the seemingly deathless myth of the "criminal type"—a person internally and naturally prone to crime—in the face of men and women who come to prison from lives of poverty, shattered homes, and other social and emotional deprivations.[76] Berkman condemns the

> presumption of "science" that pretends to evolve the intricate convolutions of the living human brain out of the shape of a digit cut from a dead hand, and labels it "criminal type." Daily association dispels the myth of the "species," and reveals the individual. Growing intimacy discovers the humanity beneath fibers coarsened by lack of opportunity, and brutalized by misery and fear.[77]

As well as documenting his own physical and mental degradation, Berkman's memoir presents a series of sketches of convicted people and conversations with them that exemplify the crushing effects of imprisonment.[78]

What Berkman and other imprisoned writers reveal is that the number of people who need to be quarantined for the sake of public safety is a fraction of the number that prison employees, political fearmongers, and blood-hungry media need the public to believe. Prisons are violent, as London testifies—echoing William Coffey and Austin Reed and anticipating George Jackson and writers today—because they incubate violence by degrading incarcerated people. "By the workings of the prison system," Kate Richards O'Hare writes,

> society commits every crime against the criminal that the criminal is charged with having committed against society. . . .
>
> We send thieves to prison to teach them not to steal and rob and all prison life is thievery and robbing. The fundamental theory of prison management . . . is to "break" [imprisoned people]. And "breaking them" means to rob them of every shred of self-respect, initiative, will, intelligence, and common decency.

She concludes that "every existing prison should be abandoned as soon as possible," thus previewing by ten years the conclusions of a 1931 commission that found that prisons served none of their stated missions, including securing public safety.[79] US socialist leader Eugene Debs found in prison, once again, more a corral for the desperately poor than for miscreants. The running theme of *Walls and Bars* (1927) echoes ideas and implications in O'Hare, London, Reed . . . back to Patrick Lyon: "The prison is cornerstoned in the misery, despair and desperation that poverty entails," an institution that, in turn, is "an incubator for crime."[80] Thus "capitalism needs . . . prisons to protect itself from the criminals it has created."[81] Another early prison abolitionist, and like Berkman unveiling the myth of the criminal type to reveal people criminalized for being both poor and human, Debs, like abolitionists today, takes as his goal to "abolish the social system that makes the prison necessary."[82] If the incarcerated have broken the laws of a profit-driven nation and prison rules, it is because such acts are respectively necessary to their survival outside, and to retaining their humanity once inside.

This brief heyday for prison writing, like Progressivism itself, would not last. The Depression brought yet another lockdown, partly in response to the rise of organized crime under Prohibition, partly in response to the very successes of the writers of the teens and twenties. Bruce Franklin asks, "Did [prisons] also fear the lines of communication being opened between the prisoners inside the walls and the millions of angry people on the other side?"[83] Yet books by the incarcerated and formerly incarcerated did appear during the Depression. Most sensationally, Robert E. Burns's *I Am a Fugitive from a Georgia Chain Gang!*, published in 1932 and adapted to the screen in the same year, describes Burns's time on a Georgia prison work crew. Though the state had outlawed convict leasing in 1908,[84] Burns reports brutal conditions inside a prison stripped of any pretense of betterment of white or Black men. His shackles riveted into place and his labor leased to the county, Burns works on crews where he must ask permission even to wipe sweat from his brow; discipline includes beating with leather straps that rip away flesh, the wounds never treated. Like Lyon and Snelling, Burns compares prison practices to those of the pre-revolutionary era: "The chain gang is simply a vicious, medieval custom, inherited from the blackbirders and slave traders of the seventeenth and eighteenth centuries, and is so archaic and barbarous as to be a national disgrace."[85]

No less revealing was the anonymously authored *Female Convict* of 1934, the chronicle of a woman raised in squalid poverty in Chicago. The author sees her brother thrown out of his job in an auto parts plant due to automation, and then kicked out of the house by a drunken father for losing his job. It's a short path for her brother into prison, and then for the author into the streets and sex work to feed the family. The author sees again the organic connection between poverty and crime.

> Gangsters! They are grown as naturally in the alleys and gutters of our slum neighborhood as mosquitoes grow in a swamp. Now when I pick up a newspaper and read of one more noble crusade against gangsters, I smile—and understand. To whip up a crusade against gangsters is as lu-

dicrous as to organize an army of mosquito swatters while the swamp-
lands where they multiply are left untouched.

Society makes gunmen and then gets excited when their guns go off.[86]

This lesson finds its confirmation in counterpoint to *So I Went to Prison*,
the 1938 work of Edna O'Brien, a woman who successfully made her way
in the men's world of stock investing until the economic crash caught
her short. These books by women underline, respectively, the seamless
continuity between poverty and prison and the jarring discontinuity
between prison and the white middle class. These writers present, once
again, portraits of people driven by desperation to criminal acts, or who
see their acts criminalized because they are poor, and who become the
objects of corrupt and sadistic guards, and of other incarcerated people
in environments that do less to curb criminality than to demand it in
order for them to survive.

After World War I, a penology that touted efforts to form citizens into
successful workers gave way to simple control of growing prison populations. This new managerialism, combined in 1926 with toughened sentencing, offered a preview of the rise of mass incarceration in the 1970s
and 1980s: prison numbers grew to a point where management was all
anyone could hope to achieve, and several bloody riots presaged later
prison uprisings. Yet after World War II, and continuing through to a
fifty-year low in incarceration rates by 1972, US prisons—in professional
intention at least—came closer to the founders' ideal of a therapeutic
prison, and on a wider scale, than at any other time in American history. Visitors from other countries came to study US penal methods.
But whatever the official intentions, incarcerated people see what they
see, which rarely lines up with the claims of prison administrators or
the ideals of theorists (all of whom regularly engage in battles for domi-
nance).[87] One of the many ugly ironies of the present moment is that
theory and practice now align tightly: prisons deliver the pain and suffering that the public has been led to believe that incarcerated people
deserve, that is all that works, and that prisons should in fact mete out.
The change in direction is a lesson in how prisons can serve as registers
of collective sentiment.

Many changes came to the United States as a result of New Deal
policies and the emergence of the nation as an industrial titan after

World War II. One of these was a profound public faith in professional expertise, the sciences, and government itself as an engine for bettering the lives of the American people. No less so regarding penal policy, many states and the federal government enlisted sociologists and other experts to design prison regimes "that would seem distinctly modern and progressive."[88] This was in part due to wartime prison-industrial production, which "soared" as incarcerated workers manufactured military supplies, gave blood, and even bought war bonds. Surely people acting on such patriotism deserved a second chance.[89] There was also bipartisan understanding that politicians should leave prison policy to experts. Academic studies of prison culture in the 1950s had "a real influence on correctional management thinking and the broader governmental discourse about prisons in the 1950s, 1960s, and 1970s."[90] This separation of prison decision making from populist sentiment—whose collapse would become a major driver of mass imprisonment—allowed evidence-based research to take the lead: "The bipartisan approach that the major political parties adopted, and the sense that penal policy and crime control were largely technical matters best left to the professionals and practitioners, were further expressions of this trust in the credibility that professional groups then enjoyed."[91] David Garland claims that "the word 'punishment' all but dropped out of the official vocabulary of modern penal policy, as did the expressions of passionate outrage that it traditionally entailed."[92] But official policy, once again, rarely translates into effective, let alone wide-scale change in practice. Garland himself later admitted that the penological field "is composed not of fully settled practices and firmly established policies but rather of competing actors and ongoing struggles." A study from 1950 concluded that living even in progressive prisons "increases the criminality of the individuals they hold."[93]

This is not to say that the public was fundamentally opposed to retribution. In fact, a familiar sleight-of-hand met public perceptions. Harkening back to Benjamin Rush's plans for more humane prisons that would still allow public imagination to create horror shows, prison officials did not mind telling the public that prisons were about meting out the pain criminals deserved, while also—at least in theory—working to provide rational and constructive treatment. As Garland notes,

This gap between "bark" and "bite" permitted the system to appear responsive to public demands for punishments while tailoring its real impact in a way that liberal professionals deemed more appropriate. So long as the system was not scrutinized too closely, and its internal workings were not fully understood by outsiders, it could simultaneously avoid public criticism and empower expert decision making.[94]

More recent critics, studying regional punishment regimes, however, offer important qualification to Garland's readings of this national trend in "penal welfarism."[95] Mona Lynch and Heather Schoenfeld, assessing prison development in Arizona and Florida, respectively, find that the rehabilitative ethos was never fully embraced in these states, or across the sunbelt more generally, and then only briefly and in pitched contention with retributive traditions. As the populations of these states grew, along with their conservative political sway, they became leading models and engines of the next phase in penal thinking and practice.[96] We might say that Garland presents the plurality position after the Second World War, while these sunbelt regions' unceasing penal harshness foreshadowed emergent national trends. That is, rather than being driven by any fixed national consensus, various authorities, in different states and regions, even different facilities, carried more or less sway in the face of their methodological opponents.[97]

Meanwhile, even in those states that embraced progressive, evidence-based methods, the gap between public perception and practice continued. The writing from inside in this period does reflect more progressive administrative intentions. It also represents such thinking's failed efforts. Caryl Chessman's four books (1954, 1955, 1957, 1960) chronicle the life of a man whose taste for fast cars, women, and money went unhindered by stints in juvenile and prison detention. (No one died in Chessman's crimes, yet he was executed in the gas chamber after a wait of nearly twelve years. His books brought his case international attention, including intense scrutiny of American death penalty jurisprudence.) Malcolm Braly's 1967 novel *On the Yard* depicts men in San Quentin holding make-work white-collar jobs, limited to remedial education, and attending bitterly ineffective group therapy sessions when they are not exploiting or killing each other. The one truly competent therapist quits after seeing that he is helping no one: "A prison is a nearly impossible setting for any therapeutic program."[98] Those who do read and study for personal improvement are viewed as aberrant or elitist among other imprisoned men. Braly's panoply of psychologically and emotionally damaged characters dwell inside a prison that does less to address their conditions than to offer opportunities for their unmet needs to be turned against themselves and one another, while prison officials are presented by turns as hapless, progressive, or brutal. Confined during the same decade, poet Etheridge Knight presents prisons as dungeons for Black people. Among his damning portraits of the damage meted out in a period of purportedly benign prisons, Knight memorializes imprisoned children, generational Black abjection, and a rebellious champion named Hard Rock reduced to slobbering idiocy by the bleeding-edge methods of electroshock and lobotomy.[99] Albert Woodfox, writing a half century later, recalls less clinical methods as guards beat prisoners with baseball bats.[100]

Yet whatever the failures of this era, there were at least aspirations to help incarcerated people. By the late 1970s and 1980s, however, there had risen what psychologist Craig Haney calls a "punishment wave," which

> hit with such force that it has ripped us from the ethical moorings that once held this punitive system in check, kept us from straying beyond the moral outer limits of state-inflicted pain, and ensured that the course we set as a society for our crime control policy was guided, among many other things, by some minimal humanitarian considerations.[101]

What happened?

The tense balance Garland describes between benign penal philosophy and harsher public sentiment persisted into the early 1970s. What upset this balance was history, politics, and their combined work of opening criminal justice policies and practices directly to the evidence-resistant influence of public emotion stoked by politicians ready to exploit racially fueled fear and vengeance. The factors weighing in here were many: rising crime; skepticism about the efficacy of the rehabilitative efforts that writers like Braly and Knight ridiculed; "law and order" rhetoric fueling a decades-long tougher-than-you-on-crime arms race between Republicans and Democrats; mandatory minimum sentences; overseas job flight that created employment deserts across poor communities; wars on poverty, crime, and drugs that militarized the police; an exponential growth in the number of felony charges brought by prosecutors; and the growing political clout of prison staff and police unions, as well as the rising sway of the sunbelt states that continued in their harshly punitive habits . . . all of which would lead to unprecedented growth in the prison and jail population just after it had hit a half-century low, a low—and a record of failure—that had convinced many observers that prisons might and should cease to exist.[102] The result was overcrowding that would make even the best intentions impossible to enact.

The steps toward unprecedented levels of legal confinement, however, had begun some years earlier, and were as racialized and lock-stepped between Democrats and Republicans as the movements of the men inside Auburn in Austin Reed's day: from Kennedy to Johnson, Johnson to Nixon, Nixon to Ford, Carter, Reagan, Bush, and Clinton, "apartheid planning" and "apartheid sentencing" transformed even state social services into branches of criminal surveillance, turned urban streets into war zones, and turned the police (and many social workers) into the prison's de facto field recruiters. Practices and methods often attributed to Republicans simply fulfilled the aspirations of earlier administrations.[103]

These influences converged at the criminalization of young Black men. Liberals pathologized the legacy of slavery to conclude that they just couldn't help themselves, so hardened by poverty as to be indifferent to legitimate opportunity.[104] The right saw an incomprehensible threat. The consequence has been people and neighborhoods that are, as Reuben Jonathan Miller notes, "overpoliced and under-protected."[105] At the same time, amid ongoing struggles between rehabilitative and retributive thinking, reform-minded programs allowed young men and women to read and educate themselves about a system that had slated them for disposal. One ironic result, as formerly incarcerated criminologist John Irwin writes, was that the prison "inadvertently contributed to mounting criticism of itself by promoting a prison intelligentsia."[106] Part of what would frighten white Americans into adopting enforcement practices that led to a renewed war by the criminal legal system against poor people of color was that several widely read writers among this new intelligentsia identified with the Black Power movement (writ large), which helped to organize and politicize incarcerated people as never before.[107]

With his 1965 *Autobiography*, Malcolm X opened this new era in prison witness. Echoing Austin Reed and unlike the history of white writers who reported the shock effect of discovering lawless practices and degrading conditions inside prison walls, Malcolm X unveiled the prison as a vital organ of white supremacy. It was this discovery that initiated the transformation of street hustler Malcolm Little into Malcolm X—a renaming that announced an understanding of prison as the evolution of slavery after Jim Crow. Under the tutelage of Nation of Islam leader Elijah Muhammad, this metamorphosis is complete: "I still marvel at how swiftly my previous life's thinking pattern slid away from me, like snow off a roof. It is as though someone else I knew of had lived by hustling and crime. I would be startled to catch myself thinking in a remote way of my earlier self as another person."[108] Half a century later, Deshawn Cooper reports of an older man telling him upon his arrival in prison in 2014, "Remember what Malcolm said. . . . Prison is the Black man's university."[109] Malcolm X spoke from the experience of a highly progressive Massachusetts prison that had planned to be just that, though not to the political ends that he turned it.

In the *Autobiography*, Malcolm X famously describes copying over an entire dictionary in order to gain the vocabulary and language skills needed to write to Elijah Muhammad. Though the son of an activist, Malcolm Little only turned away from drugs and acting out haphazardly against his confinement once he began studying Elijah's vision of the prison as a system not of crime control but of control of Black men. Facilitated by Norfolk's well-stocked library, Malcolm Little transformed himself into Malcolm X, one of the most powerful and charismatic speakers for the NOI. The NOI, moreover, was not simply one organization among others working in the 1960s. It was arguably the most effective group ever in bonding incarcerated people across states and facilities and thus became a driving force behind litigation that would set precedent and spawn a movement for prisoner rights in the same years when the Warren Court was turning the protections laid out in the Bill of Rights, defending criminal suspects and incarcerated people, into actual legal precedent. NOI efforts to secure a host of religious and civil rights—which crossed over prison walls—"set in motion a string of legal decisions that ended the courts' long-standing 'hands-off' stance toward prisoners."[110]

Malcolm X's *Autobiography*, and his fearless public persona after release, would be an inspiration to the political self-education of other imprisoned Black people. As Etheridge Knight wrote after Malcolm X's assassination by rival Black Muslims (after he chose a more moderate path), "You rocked too many boats, man. / Pulled too many coats, man. / Saw through the jive. You reached the wild guys / Like me."[111] Another of these wild guys was Eldridge Cleaver, working on essays from California's Folsom Prison in the same year that Malcolm X's *Autobiography* was published. Just two years after the 1966 founding of the Black Panther Party, Cleaver's essays were collected into a widely read book, *Soul on Ice*, in which the author lodges eloquent, damning, or bitterly bemused criticism of white power and of white envy of Black culture and sexuality, and in which he excoriates the way in which Black men must sacrifice their masculinity in exchange for peace. He also reports crossing barriers of self-understanding, admitting that once he confronted his crime of rape, he lost all self-respect.

> My pride as a man dissolved and my whole fragile moral structure seemed to collapse, completely shattered.
> That is why I started to write. To save myself.
> I was very familiar with the Eldridge who came to prison, but that Eldridge no longer exists.[112]

The images that Malcolm X and Cleaver present of men breaking down their pasts, rejecting them, and then rebuilding from scratch might well have appealed to Cotton Mather, Benjamin Rush, and the early theorists of the penitentiary. As Caleb Smith documents, the idea of such spiritual death and resurrection was the base upon which the early American prison was founded.[113] In passing, Cleaver also notes the circumstances in which these changes took place: he lives in an honor block, where men with clean prison behavior records enjoy extra privileges; he is a member of a Gavel Club, Toastmasters, a panel of men who oversee radio access, and we see him in a classroom. But no manner of privileges or programs can erase what he sees day to day. He grows aware, like X, "that what had happened to me had also happened to countless other blacks and it would happen to many, many more," while "the prison authorities were both uninterested and unable to help me."[114]

At the same time that Malcolm X and Cleaver undertook the kind of self-transformation that the penitentiary's founders had imagined, they gained a frontline grasp of how—echoing Austin Reed—the institution itself worked not to reform but to mark poor people of color as second-class citizens. As many other imprisoned people have learned, and as the writers among them have documented, reform inside prisons is work that the confined must do for themselves, often in spite of practices carried on even at the high mark of rehabilitative thinking. Progressive programs could neither distract Malcolm X and Cleaver from the racial turbulence beyond prison walls, nor mask their lived experience among other Black men caught up in a system of penal apartheid. Michael Meranze observes that, even in the eighteenth century, while officials could control the material practices of early punishments, they could never control the meaning taken from them.[115] Imprisoned people always see the institution's concrete effects on those inside and draw their own lessons. By reporting what they saw and how they interpreted it, Malcolm X, Cleaver, and others presented images of prisons and incarcerated people from which prison critics on the left and right would draw reasons to pursue (unwittingly on the left, wittingly on the right) the most recent of the seemingly unending "new" penal philosophies. Another Black man's life and writing from prison would help to close this era of seeming concern for rehabilitation.

In 1961 George Jackson began serving a one-year-to-life sentence for a $70 gas station robbery. In 1970 Jackson published *Soledad Brother*, a collection of letters to family, friends, his lawyer, and political allies. In his letters Jackson struggles, often quite bitterly, to distance himself from a mother and father who raised him to keep his head down and out of trouble. In prison, Jackson read Mao, Marx, Che, and Engels. Thus deeply politicized, he documents his efforts to make himself into an efficient tool of a coming revolution, learning to live with less sleep and less food, and without emotional attachments. An active political organizer of Black men inside, and implicated with two others in the murder of a prison guard, Jackson writes reports that seem to come from a foxhole, since he was under constant threat of racist attacks by officers and their aides among imprisoned whites. The transformation that Jackson undergoes, like that of Malcolm X and Cleaver, is both a choice and a reaction to the circumstances that confront him and many others.

> This [concentration] camp brings out the very best in brothers or destroys them entirely. But none are unaffected. None who leave here are normal. If I leave here alive, I'll leave nothing behind. They'll never count me among the broken men, but I can't say that I am normal either. I've been hungry too long. I've gotten angry too often. I've been lied to and insulted too many times. They've pushed me over the line from which there can be no retreat. I know they will not be satisfied until they've pushed me out of this existence altogether. I've been the victim of so many racist attacks that I could never relax again. My reflexes will never be normal again. I'm like a dog that has gone through the K-9 process.[116]

Prison transforms Jackson, but once again not as his keepers might hope. Rather than lament this defensive training, Jackson embraces it: as he writes to his mother, "I feel no pain of mind or body, and the harder it gets the better I like it."[117] He sent an inspiring message to other incarcerated Black men and a warning to their guards, a message rooted in the prison's very lack of mystery for a young Black man. Like Malcolm X and Cleaver, Jackson sees that

> Blackmen born in the US and fortunate enough to live past the age of eighteen are conditioned to accept the inevitability of prison. For most of us, it simply looms as the next phase in a sequence of humiliations. Being born a slave in a captive society, . . . I was prepared for prison. It required only a minor psychic adjustment.[118]

In his writing and in death, "Jackson emerged as the translator of the discontent that had been growing inside prisons."[119] (Even today, mere possession of Jackson's writing can be used to charge incarcerated people as gang members.)[120] Recognizing his slave heritage, he is determined never to bend. Jackson not only terrified prison officials with his charismatic organizing and embrace of revolutionary violence, he modelled the Black man who could not be broken. In *Soledad Brother* he provided the handbook for anti-colonial resistance to prison regimes: "Men who read Lenin, Fanon, and Che don't riot, 'they mass,' 'they rage,' they dig graves."[121] Jackson's politically opportune implication in an officer's murder, his bloody killing inside San Quentin amid a purported escape attempt, and the later acquittal of both of his co-defendants—in addition to the brilliance of his writing, the mass sales of his book, and his death's part in precipitating the Attica Rebellion just weeks later—turned him into two radically distinct icons: a martyr for the left, a chilling harbinger for the right. In his death—along with the deaths of five other men, including a prison officer—he struck such deep fear into prison officials that the rise of today's supermax prisons has been traced to that day.[122] Jackson's letters have served for fifty years as a primer on the racial dynamics of prisons, their radicalizing effects on young Black men, and, for many of his inside readers, on how to survive prison.

The Autobiography of Malcolm X, Soul on Ice, and Soledad Brother recast in racial terms a virtual trope of such writing since the days of Patrick Lyon: prisons are less about crime control than about controlling the poor. This was the message taken up by the left, which critiqued rehabilitation programs for measuring success by how deeply caged people imbibed white liberal values.[123] For the right, these texts and a spate of bloody prison uprisings were proof that prisons were too soft and rehabilitation wasted on people who did not recognize the legitimacy of police, courts, or (white) law itself. Expressing the convictions of the left and exemplifying the attitude that the right condemned as inherently antagonistic to legal order, Angela Davis wrote from Marin County Jail, "We can't expect justice from a repressive judicial system and I'm sure that an exclusively legalistic approach to my defense would be fatal. So what we have to do is to talk about placing the courts on trial."[124] Historians, legal scholars, and others have since corroborated Davis's belief that American legal practices never have been equal across the line of race.[125] At the time, statements such as Davis's confirmed to white Americans that Black radicals were hardly more receptive to reform than the string of serial killers—for example, Berkowitz, Manson, Bundy—that helped fix public perceptions of lawbreakers (once again) as different not only in circumstance but in kind.[126] This belief quickly translated into punishing practice: longer mandatory minimum sentences and more life and life-without-parole sentences, the reduction or elimination of grants of parole, the return of chain gangs, and legislation and Supreme Court decisions that drove back the defendant protections and prisoner rights precedents of the Warren Court years, as well as the very possibility of jury trial.[127] Both cause and effect, popular media reflected public sentiment: the legal heroics of defense lawyer Perry Mason gave way to Dirty Harry blowing .45-caliber holes through suspects.[128]

The racist shift to the right in American politics, court decisions, and crime policy did not come coincidentally in the twilight of civil rights activism. As Vesla Weaver documents, "The graveyard of civil rights legislation was the same place where crime bills were born."[129] Those who felt themselves the losers amid the advances of the civil rights movement (the white right: Goldwater, Wallace, and Nixon only the most obvious among them) changed the topic of concern. They saw civil rights activism and called it urban disorder, clearly coding race-neutral language to turn Black freedom struggles into a symptom and harbinger of civil breakdown. Civil rights, they insisted, were secondary to the right to law and order. The achievements of the civil rights struggle were redirected under the boot of the criminal legal system; and this occurred as that system spread its tendrils into civil society and civil engineering, schools, welfare agencies, immigration control, and a broadly cast net of probation, parole, and an exploding prison population—in short, a fully armed carceral state.[130]

Rather than addressing the roots of crime, which grew in the same soil of poverty, addiction, and despair that prison writers had been naming for nearly two hundred years, "a massive and concentrated expansion of state violence . . . emerged to fill a social policy vacuum."[131] This was only possible because of hundreds of years of the criminalization of Blackness inside a nation where "the relative severity of punishment is intimately related to racial perceptions of crime."[132] Confinement—the only punishment sanctioned by courts—was no longer enough; "the time in prison . . . [became] a time for more punishment."[133]

Acting on the belief that big government was always the problem, Ronald Reagan accelerated the work of his predecessors to shred the welfare safety net, suture its remains to police control, and thus grow a penal state that came down harder and harder on those who fell through.[134] These policies continued and expanded under George H. W. Bush, Bill Clinton, and George W. Bush, and they resumed as openly racist platform and policy prescriptions in the campaign and administration of Donald Trump. While other government services were subjected to massive cuts, blank checks were handed to a system of what one legal scholar calls "governing through crime,"[135] giving prison building and salaries—and police acting as militarized street-level judges, juries, and executioners—priority over public health and education.[136]

Riding the populist punishment wave, legislators ignored evidence that harsher sentences and conditions only make incarcerated people less able to get footholds in law-abiding society and more prone to re-offend. They lengthened sentences on the premise that harsher consequences would deter crime before it occurred, based on the assumption that each perpetrator, in each instance, was "a lightning calculator of pleasures and pains" able to weigh acts and consequences in the often split-second decisions that precede crime.[137] These policies ignored research and what incarcerated writers had been reporting for centuries: crime and other desperate acts are fostered by desperate conditions.

This was, again, a thoroughly inter-partisan effort. Lyndon Johnson's Law Enforcement Assistance Administration sent federal support to states and local police paid further to execute Nixon's initial salvo in the war on drugs. Joe Biden joked about the number of crimes he had added to those eligible for the death penalty,[138] New York governor Mario Cuomo added more prison beds than all of his predecessors combined, California governor Jerry Brown oversaw changing the Department of Corrections' mission from rehabilitation to punishment, and Bill Clinton signed off on laws (even as crime rates were going down) that lengthened sentences for minors and adults, and made it nearly impossible for imprisoned people to seek redress from the courts for unconstitutional conditions inside prisons. He cut federal funding for successful higher education programs for imprisoned people, mandated that those held in federal facilities receive only the minimum amenities that would pass constitutional scrutiny, and made the formerly incarcerated ineligible for the dwindling welfare supports that might help them (and their children and families) reintegrate. His tough-on-crime rhetoric also offered explicit blessing to a state-prison building boom that saw the construction of more prison cells than under all presidents combined since and including Richard Nixon. His successor, Republican George W. Bush, as Texas governor and president, made Clinton look like a prison-building amateur.[139] Rarely has Jeremy Bentham's observation, offered a decade before the initiation of the Walnut Street experiment, proved so true: it is human nature to apply more and excessive rather than fewer or milder punishments—a fact that has now been translated into multibillion-dollar, tax-funded public policy.[140]

Over two hundred years after the inception of the founders' radical humanitarian experiment—one tied directly to the creation of a liberal republic—it was now national practice to operate prisons as concrete warehouses for poor people of color. A marginal employment sector became what we see today: one of the nation's largest employers (and a mainstay against rural white unemployment), and a major enforcer of social inequality.[141]

These changes required a transformation in the public images of convicted people: no longer as people who had erred and could be helped, but as people who were nothing more, and capable of no more, than their crimes. Anne-Marie Cusac reminds us that "only a few decades ago, Americans saw the essential nature of the criminal as separable from the criminal act. Now the crime is the essence of the criminal."[142] In the absence of this distinction, Norwegian criminologist Nils Christie writes, "with the offender seen as another breed, a non-person, a thing, there are no limits to possible atrocities."[143] Sentencing is no longer about enacting rehabilitation but about quantifying pain. That the degree and duration of pain itself are measures of justice is a belief that, in the past, had driven the very tit-for-tat cycles of vengeance and vigilante violence that the laws and courts were created to stem. Political scientist Marie Gottschalk, among others, suggests one thread of how we took that step back toward a premodern sense of justice. She documents a victim rights movement that rose up quickly and stridently against Warren era prisoner rights.[144] Victim advocacy created unlikely partnerships between (white) women's groups seeking serious responses to sexual assault,[145] conservative advocates for Old Testament retribution, and prison staff unions.[146] Courtrooms became "morality play[s]" weighing the pain that perpetrators deserved by the pain that victims had suffered.[147] Rather than serving as the neutral arbiters between victim and perpetrator, intended to yield socially constructive responses to crime, courts became the fulcrum of leverage for personal vengeance.[148] The result, Gottschalk remarks, is that "the judicial system is judged primarily by its capacity to serve as a vehicle for the expression of private rage, grief, compassion, or mercy, rather than by alternative measures that consider the needs of victims, offenders, and society more broadly."[149] This is a system, moreover, that disserves, neglects, and actively harms the most common victims of crime—poor people of color—due to what Lenore Anderson convincingly documents as a "hierarchy of harm"; only those least likely to be crime victims benefit from protections created "in their names" while motiving harsher criminal justice practices for others—practices that hurt and even criminalize victims and exacerbate the very kinds of trauma that precipitate crime.[150]

Yet in the same years that vengeance took the lead, incarcerated writers' books appeared in print in numbers never seen in the past. Among the nearly 1,000 titles listed in H. Bruce Franklin's bibliography of prison-born works from 1798 to 1988, more than one-third (332) were published in the years 1970 to 1979. One event whose aftermath helps to explain this burgeoning of public interest, even as prisons moved toward unmitigated retribution, was the Attica Uprising of 1971.

Three weeks after George Jackson's death in San Quentin, men inside Attica—across race lines—wore black armbands to mark his passing and maintained a terrifying silence in the mess hall. From September 9 to 12, men took over a quarter of that prison, held officers as hostages, and demanded rights and reforms, many of which were so basic that their absence shocks common decency. The standoff ended on September 13, in a massacre caused by then Governor Nelson Rockefeller calling in state troopers, ending what had been peaceful if tense negotiations in the bloodiest confrontation of Americans since the Civil War.[151]

Thirty-nine men without firearms, including hostages, died in the massacre under a fog of tear gas and barrage of gunfire from state troopers and Attica guards. Gross mistreatment and torture of incarcerated men ensued for days after. This was a watershed moment, and, like George Jackson's killing, it shed in two diametrically opposed directions. For the left, Attica exposed the inhumanity and brutality of prisons subject to virtually no public oversight.[152] Jackson and the dead inside Attica became martyrs and icons of resistance to state violence.[153] Imprisoned people appeared as the vanguard witnesses to what state power was capable of doing to US citizens and especially to people of color. On the right, Attica became the sign of a prison population dangerously inspired by Black militants, and an exemplary threat to prisons across the country; the massacre, in turn, was cast as a defense against "the destruction of free society."[154]

The irony of the 1970s was that while prison administrators, politicians, and much of the public became convinced that the answer to crime was simply to lock up more poor people for more years, others read imprisoned people's letters, essays, memoirs, and poetry as never before. The nation's largest publishers, long- and short-lived small presses, as well as scholarly and literary journals printed this work.[155] A sampling of titles from this decade offers some sense of the intents and appeals of inside reports from incarcerated people: *Break de Chains of Legalized U.$. Slavery,*[156] *The Caged Collective: The Life and Death of the Folsom Prison Creative Writers' Workshop,*[157] *Captive Voices, Echoes off the Walls III: An Anthology of Literary Works,*[158] *Death Row: An Affirmation of Life,*[159] *Getting Busted: Personal Experiences of Arrest, Trial, and Prison,*[160] *If They Come in the Morning: Voices of Resistance,*[161] *Latitude Pain, Longitude Anger,*[162] *Look for Me in the Whirlwind: The Collective Autobiography of the New York 21,*[163] *My Light Comes Shining: Women's Writing from Albany County Jail,*[164] *Soledad Prison: University of the Poor,*[165] *Monkey off My Back: An Ex-Convict and Addict Relates His Discovery of Personal Freedom,*[166] *Who Took the Weight? Black Voices from Norfolk Prison,*[167] *Dig the Nigger Up—Let's Kill Him Again,*[168] *A Flower Blooming in Concrete.*[169]

According to Franklin's 1989 research, the 1970s saw more prison publications than had appeared in the first seventy years of the century. Yet just seventy-nine titles appeared from 1980 to 1988; while short-lived anthologies and single-author books appeared from small (or micro-) presses, annual titles from major houses fell into single digits.

What happened?

Cultural attitudes changed. The 1980s were not the 1970s. As progressive momentum waned, a conservative resurgence sapped support for defendant and prisoner rights while crime rates continued to rise. White flight from urban centers continued and the social distance between middle-class whites and poor people of color widened. The disconnection between majorities of voters who elected lawmakers and those against whom longer, harsher sentences would be enforced grew more profound. Incarcerated writers no longer represented people in the grip of excessive state power, or a revolutionary vanguard, but simply the "types" of people that popular media and politicians insisted were irredeemable predators. As Franklin notes of "the repression that was to build during the 1980s and 1990s," "Creative writing courses in prison were defunded. By 1984, every literary journal devoted to publishing poetry and stories by prisoners was wiped out. New York State led the way in mounting a legislative attack on prison writing with its 1977 'Son of Sam' law." This law and those of other states, barring imprisoned people from being paid for their work, was sold as protection for crime victims; "the real purpose," Franklin writes, as in past periods of repression, was "to keep the American people in the dark about the American prison."[170] The handful of anthologies appeared from small presses with limited runs and short lives in print.[171]

The single-author books that were published tended to be by those whose notoriety preceded imprisonment, such as Patty Hearst and Jean Harris, formerly incarcerated authors like John Ehrlichman and G. Gordon Liddy, and novelists who had established records as writers before 1980 such as Edward Bunker and Nathan Heard. These were the same years in which the United States locked in an expansion of prison populations beyond American and global precedents.[172] The imprisoned were becoming the stuff of statistical analysis rather than singular human beings whose stories could tell us something about the people inside and the nation that caged them. And publishers had suffered a rattling chill.

In the Belly of the Beast (1981), by Jack Henry Abbott, is a book edited from Abbott's letters to writer Norman Mailer. Abbott was a man held so long in detention facilities, from such a young age, that prison had become his only credible home. He was, as he called himself, a "state-raised" convict. Abbott is among the most searing and articulate writers about pain and long-term solitary confinement in any nation's literary canon. What Mailer and the public failed to recognize is that the book and its author were driven by a terrible paradox. As Abbott writes,

> I cannot adjust to daily life in prison. For almost twenty years this has been true. I have never gone a month in prison without incurring disciplinary action for violating "rules." Not in all these years. . . .
> . . . I feel that if ever I did *adjust to prison*, I could by that alone never adjust to society. I would be back in prison within months.
> Now, I care about myself and I cannot let it happen that I cannot adjust to freedom. Even if it means spending my life in prison.[173]

The punishment Abbott incurred for not making that adjustment so damaged him that he also could not live outside. Mailer advocated for and won Abbott's release. While living in precarious circumstances, Abbott was trotted to parties among the New York literati; his prison-bred instincts flared after a minor argument with a restaurant worker. He stabbed the man to death, fled, was recaptured and convicted, and later committed suicide inside New York's Wende Correctional Facility.[174] What glowing reviews in the *New York Times Book Review* and *Time* magazine missed was what every page of Abbott's book announced: As tragic as it was that the juvenile and adult prison systems had twisted the soul of a man as brilliant as Abbott, the system had in fact done just that. In the aftermath, one message did come through to publishers: no matter how powerful the writing, take on prison books at your risk. American incarceration had become an industrial-scale machinery for grinding up bodies, minds, and souls; recidivism rates proved its success as a manufactory of tragedy. Abbott's letters amplified the sounds of that machine. Mailer arranged them into a dirge so fascinating in its detailing of human suffering that readers (including Mailer) missed their running theme.

Over the four decades since *In the Belly of the Beast* was published, books written by those who have experienced incarceration have often been authored by people who appear safe from repeating Abbott's history: writing from exile, about conversion to a philosophy of peace, on sentences ineligible for parole, or because they have already been living successfully outside at the time of writing.

Assata Shakur's 1987 autobiography, *Assata*, looks back over the author's maturation into Black political consciousness and revolutionary activism from the 1940s until her escape from prison and exile in Cuba in 1979. Chapters describe her arrest on charges of shooting a New Jersey state trooper, repeated beatings and harassment by police while in the hospital, medical abuse, jail time, and a series of trials (with more beatings in court) that repeatedly failed to convict her and her co-defendant. These chapters alternate with ones depicting a child and adolescent and young woman developing the political education, skills, and motivations that brought her to revolutionary activism. Shakur repeatedly presents scenes of herself imbibing the racist ideas and internalizing the racist attitudes of her culture and then going through a process of demystification, in which these errors are unmasked as the work of a white supremacist culture committed to the degradation of Black people. Shakur not only describes but models an ongoing process, a way to live a revolutionary consciousness, one that must constantly inscribe critique inside itself.[175] This is shown in moments when Shakur embarrasses herself for naively believing that Lincoln led the Civil War for the freedom of Black people and that the Vietnam War was pursued in defense of democracy, and for using the word "black" as a curse. Shakur appropriates as she inverts the founders' intention to create penal spaces that would inspire repentance and rebirth into model citizenship; her story offers an autobiography of revolutionary rebirth after the fall into the errors that a racist nation ingrains into its Black inhabitants. In *Assata*, jails and prisons and courtrooms make open and explicit the white supremacy that rules life outside. She reports a conversation with one of the many Black women imprisoned with her in New Jersey.

> "You'll be in jail wherever you go," Eva said.
> "You have a point there," i told her, "but I'd rather be in a minimum security prison or on the streets than in the maximum security prison in here. The only difference between here and the streets is that one is maximum security and the other is minimum security. The police patrol our communities just like the guards patrol here. I don't have the faintest idea how it feels to be free."[176]

Her treatment grows even worse after she becomes pregnant while she and her co-defendant are in insolation (removed from the courtroom for insisting on politicizing what is transparently a trial of their political allegiances), and later gives birth, in shackles. *Assata* depicts the emergence of a Black feminist and of Black feminism as an ineradicably intersectional experience. She makes evident what has been confirmed by other incarcerated women since: the sexual exploitation and abuse that mark the majority of imprisoned women's lives before arrest are continued behind bars,[177] while Black women's experience is by definition opposed to any comfortable compliance with the norms of a racist, sexist nation. The result is that prisons, rather than suppressing revolutionaries, are their incubators, as Assata proclaims in a Fourth of July broadcast echoing Malcolm X, Jackson, and Davis.[178]

The early 1990s saw a sudden and precipitous drop in crime rates. This was a widespread phenomenon, reaching across nations with vastly different methods of seeking public safety and responding to criminal acts.[179] Yet the US prison population continued to rise, due in large part to Clinton era crime policies and the license they offered to states.[180] Under the administration of the so-called "first black president,"[181] the broad public was blithely on board with becoming the sponsors of the earth's largest race-based social experiment in the imprisonment of a nation's own people. In these years, prison critics could hardly have invented a more ideal embedded reporter than a respected Black journalist.

Mumia Abu-Jamal was a well-established print and radio reporter at the time of his arrest in 1981, and he continued his work once condemned to Pennsylvania's death row for the alleged murder of a police officer. This purported crime meant that this seasoned writer would receive no accommodation from the system, at the same time that, though only twenty-seven at conviction, he brought to prison a full thirteen years of experience as an anti-racist activist, former Black Panther, and later president of the Philadelphia chapter of the Association of Black Journalists.[182] Abu-Jamal continues to file online radio pieces via telephone, and he has produced what are undoubtedly the most extensive and important bodies of journalism, critical analysis, and opinion ever produced from inside prison walls.[183] His best-selling 1995 book, *Live from Death Row*, collects radio pieces along with previously published essays. Given his notoriety (not least as a suddenly discontinued NPR commentator), the book was published by a major press.[184] Abu-Jamal is able to connect his direct experience of incarceration and the stories of the men and staff around him to the longer arc of US colonial and racial history, Supreme Court decisions, and continuation of crime policy as political gaming. His writing is steeped in a mordant irony, seated in a journalist's commitment to facts. In one piece he writes about men on death row betting on court decisions.

> By viewing every decision through the prism of politics, I never lost a bet—even in the cases where the jailhouse lawyers claimed to have the law on their side. There is, of course, no satisfaction in such victories: every bet won has been a case lost; every case lost a step closer to death.[185]

In a passage from a *Yale Law Journal* article, Abu-Jamal writes of a notorious Supreme Court decision that at once admitted that the death penalty's application is demonstrably racist, yet claimed that the court could not grant the request of a Black man appealing his capital sentence.

> McCleskey's claim . . . it was rejected out of fear. . . . Justice Powell noted with alarm, that "McCleskey's claim, taken to its logical conclusion, throws into serious question the principles that underlie our entire criminal justice system." . . .
>
> What does happen, in this America, is the cheapening of Black life and the placing of a premium upon white life. As Justice Brennan's eloquent dissent in McCleskey argues, the fact that this practice may be customary does not make it constitutional. To do justice, one must consistently battle, in Brennan's words, "a fear of too much justice."[186]

Abu-Jamal's legal case continues to be fought in the Pennsylvania courts even as he brings his case against mass incarceration to the court of public opinion.[187]

A very different tone pervades Jarvis Jay Masters's 1997 *Finding Freedom: Writings from Death Row*. This book begins as a series of vignettes that are by turns comic and tragic as Masters encounters veterans and new jacks in San Quentin and grows accustomed to its culture. Each scene carries a lesson, about life, about life in prison, or simply about the wisdom and madness that prison breeds in men born into struggling lives and condemned to years of legalized deprivation: from a man searching for his ankle-tall pet rat and another who carries on elaborate conversations with magazine pinups of women on his cell walls, to the last conversation with an old friend before the friend is stabbed to death, and the final words of a young man who expresses his envy of his dead victim the night before he commits suicide. In the book's second suite of essays, Masters recounts receiving visits from a highly respected Tibetan monk. As Elijah Muhammad did for Malcolm X, Masters's mentor transforms his student; but rather than becoming a political activist, Masters becomes a force for peace even as he weighs his responsibilities as the "Lone Buddhist Ranger" in a place where attempted peacemaking can get a man killed.[188] In the final passage of the book, Masters articulates a sentiment that, openly or by implication, pervades the history of prison witnesses seeking to pull themselves out of both public fantasies and statistics.

> I want to leave my writing behind for when I am gone and the question of who I was enters people's minds. If I am executed, there will be some who believe I deserve it. But those who want to make sense of it will see, through my writing, a human being who made mistakes. Maybe my writing will at least help them see me as someone who felt, loved, and cared, someone who wanted to know for himself who he was. My writing will hopefully show those people they could easily have been me.[189]

Beneath the documentary efforts to expose conditions more destructive and degrading than the public can grasp, prison writing seeks to present the minds and hearts of wholly human beings, capable of understanding and responding to more than state-sanctioned suffering.

A similar implication pervades Native American activist Leonard Peltier's *Prison Writings: My Life Is My Sun Dance* (1999), a collection of Peltier's poetry, essays, memoir, and political history. Peltier presents his personal struggle embedded in that of his unbending people against colonialism's deracination of their life and culture. He calls the Minnesota State Penitentiary an "Indian finishing school"—the same that bred other leaders of the American Indian Movement. When he first enters, he discovers that he is well-known among Native people; he suddenly feels at home and passes on a pack of cigarettes, "and they got passed down from one cell to the other, each guy taking a couple of deep drags and passing it on. We all had a collective smoke, and in a way a collective prayer."[190] Like Black writers before and since, Peltier makes plain that each imprisoned person of color stands witness for others, both inside and out.

Jimmy Santiago Baca's 2001 *A Place to Stand* traces yet another cultural lineage. Lauded in the press and the winner of the International Prize, the book covers Baca's rough life before, during, and after the challenges of entering prison as an illiterate young Latino man, "giving the reader a 360-degree view into the ways in which mass incarceration is not only a matter of crime-and-punishment, but a cyclical and persistent issue that plagues generations of low-income communities around the country."[191] Baca's transformative moment comes when the young man secures a collection of poetry. Baca emerged to become one of this country's most respected poets and a chronicler of how white hegemony, immigration policy, prisons, and poverty create the toxic mix of influences that shape the lives of Brown people in a country that reduces race issues to Black and White. Baca also echoes the two hundred-plus years of prison writers that preceded him—and particularly those who, like him, gained literacy and became writers inside prison walls, and in writing found themselves.

> Language gave me a way to keep the chaos of prison at bay and prevent it from devouring me; it was a resource that allowed me to confront and understand my past, even to wring from it some compelling truths, and it opened a way toward a future that was based not on fear or bitterness or apathy but on compassionate involvement and a belief that I belonged . . . despite the dehumanizing environment of a prison intended to destroy me.[192]

By 2009, as crime rates continued to sink, the national prison population saw its first plateau and slight decrease. This was, though, a very mixed picture: New York's prisons held 63,300 persons in 2006; ten years later, that population stood at 52,245, and it has since dropped to under 35,000.[193] Incarceration rates (per 100,000) in Oklahoma and Arizona continued to rise through 2014. From a national peak of over 700 per 100,000, the rate stands today at 629 per 100,000.[194] One constant is that the racial dynamics of incarceration remain grossly lopsided everywhere. Black versus white incarceration ratios stand at 4.8 to 1.[195] These statistics make evident that white privilege affords not only protection *by* law's enforcers but protection *from* them.

Such protection is not, of course, complete. Written from his then twenty-eight years of incarceration in California, Kenneth E. Hartman's memoir, *Mother California: A Story of Redemption behind Bars* (2008), looks back from the perspective of a man who was, like Jack Abbott, state-raised. After stints in juvenile detention and being sent to state prison in 1980 at nineteen, Hartman witnessed firsthand the explosion of the prison population from numbers on par with the rest of the world to the United States gaining distinction as the world's imprisonment leader. His book is a history of that era and of his own growth from an aspirant to a circle of white prison gang elders called "the fellas" to a committed, inside prison reformer. Hartman describes the unceasing race war, "an orgy of bloodshed and chaos," that was Folsom Prison in the 1980s. Body counts regularly made the local news, and prison officers, rather than trying to control violence, operated like yet another prison gang.[196] After a chance phone conversation, Hartman met a woman with whom he would fall in love and marry, and who would, once weekend visits were allowed, have his child. Hartman initiates an experimental Honor Yard that rewards men for good behavior rather than solely punishing them for bad; and all this at the same time that prison staff become more brutal, conditions more dehumanizing, and, predictably, the prison more chaotic and violent. Hartman's book is a 197-page demonstration that, as he writes elsewhere, "the trouble with prison is prison."[197]

Anthologies of prison writing confirm Hartman's caption and have mounted a vigorous publication history in this millennium. Joe Lockard records twenty-two such collections since 2000, while many others have never reached distribution beyond a writing program audience. He writes that "prison anthologies can be understood as non-sequential guides to the cumulative injustices that percolate through US society, as disordered readers of prison culture hidden in plain sight."[198]

Continuing single-author books make up an eclectic list, including Jarvis Masters's second book, *That Bird Has My Wings: The Autobiography of an Innocent Man* (2009), an eloquently sober portrait of the foster care system, the damage it metes out, and a life condemned to death. Piper Kerman's 2010 *Orange Is the New Black*, covering a single year in prison in Connecticut, is no doubt the most widely read recent book on prison due to its popular television spin-off. The book's electronic avatar has the virtue of nearly unprecedented screen representation of fully humanized, three-dimensional prison characters. Dwayne R. Betts's *A Question of Freedom: A Memoir of Learning, Survival, and Coming of Age in Prison* (2010) makes evident that even a kid from a solid home, one who has academic potential and ambitions, can, if he is Black and ventures too far from home and makes a bad choice that transpires in a few minutes, lose his youth to prison. Susan Rosenberg's 2011 *An American Radical: A Political Prisoner in My Own Country* starts with the author's part in a famously disastrous attempt to rob a Brink's truck to secure money for Black revolutionaries and follows her as she continues her political work inside despite the efforts to isolate her and other political activists. In *Concrete Carnival* (2016), Danner Darcleight offers deftly written scenes of the absurdities, desperation, and stolen opportunities encountered by a white college graduate trying to make willful deprivation better for himself and often for those around him. In Shaka Senghor's *Writing My Wrongs: Life, Death, and Redemption in an American Prison* (2016), the author writes of his life on the streets and dealing drugs in Detroit. In prison he finds a sense of purpose in writing and helping others, then in working outside helping young people to avoid his path. Former CIA operative and torture-regime whistleblower John Kariakou's *Doing Time Like a Spy* (2017) presents a man who, however noble his crime, and in stark contrast to prison texts that offer sympathetic images of incarcerated people, seems to feel little but disdain for the men and officers who surround him as he revels in his ability to put things over on them. In *Becoming Ms. Burton: From Prison to Recovery to Leading the Fight for Incarcerated Women* (2019), Susan Burton offers a jail and prison memoir that is less about incarceration as such than about the paths in and out. We follow her from a childhood of poverty, shifting hopes, sexual molestation and gang rape, to her son's killing by an LAPD vehicle (an incident never acknowledged by the police). This death starts her descent into drugs and repeated lockups, and then to a life devoted to helping recently released women—an effort both so fraught and so successful it would take her to *The Oprah Winfrey Show* and the White House. Albert Woodfox's *Solitary: Unbroken by Four Decades of Solitary Confinement. My Story of Transformation and Hope* (2019) recalls the epic labor of surviving decades in solitary confinement in Louisiana's notorious Angola State Prison on a murder charge that was transparently laid upon him and his Black Panther comrades for their political beliefs. In recalling a sojourn in a New York City jail (where he was first introduced to the Panthers), Woodfox unravels the comfortable assumption that Americans in the North and West enjoy, that southern prisons are qualitatively worse than those elsewhere in the nation.

> Prison is prison. First you figure out the routine, which doesn't take long because every day is the same. Then you learn the culture and how

to play between the lines. . . . At any prison there is a pecking order. The strong rule over the weak, the smart over the strong. All the threats, games, manipulations, stories, and the bullying were the same in the Tombs, overseen with the same kind of cruelty and indifference by the prison administration.[199]

Also from Angola, Quntos KunQuest's novel *This Life* (2021) follows an aspiring prison rapper as he learns the harsh ropes of prison on his way up through a competitive culture of rap-verse face-offs. Marlon Peterson's *Bird Uncaged: An Abolitionist's Freedom Song* (2021), as its title suggests, includes powerful passages of polemic amid the life story of a young man convicted of robbery and discovering—like many before him—that prison is simply the too-familiar innermost cage in which Black lives are made to matter less. "Incarceration," he writes, "is the direct result of white people believing they needed to dehumanize every-thing Black in order to prosper."[200] The son of Russian Jewish immigrant intellectuals, Daniel Genis offers a book-strewn tour of New York State prisons in *Sentence* (2022). Locked up for robberies to support a junk habit, Genis offers details, characters, and anecdotes that underline just how *un*familiar imprisonment feels to the white middle class, incisively recording a kind of wide-eyed prison tourism. Another white writer and former addict, Keri Blakinger, chronicles her stay in New York jails and prisons in the manner of the award-winning journalist Blakinger has become since release. *Corrections in Ink* (2022) traces Blakinger's career as a figure skater, bulimic, college student, drug dealer, and addict. Regularly remarking on the privileges denied her prison-mates, she witnesses—nearly two centuries after William Snelling—that prisons remain

> mostly filled with people who are troubled, not terrible—and those who are didn't usually start that way. . . . Locking hundreds of traumatized and damaged women together and threatening them constantly with additional punishments is not rehabilitation. It is not corrections. It is not public safety. It is systemic failure.[201]

What many of these recent books have in common is a focus not simply on the conditions of imprisonment but on the way prison can serve as a hellish testing place for strong and determined personalities. These writers commit their lives to warning others off their earlier paths, improving conditions inside, ending mass incarceration itself, or providing the tools for a second chance for other formerly incarcerated people. They are also marked like all who preceded them: by their very capacity to tell their stories while thousands of others are crushed, endlessly recycled through or quietly and irreparably damaged by legal confinement.[202]

Several of the titles above have been published by major presses. This may well be because, after crime started to drop in the early nineties, until quite recently, national conversation about prisons took yet another turn. Nearly thirty years of steadily falling crime rates sapped tough-on-crime rhetoric in all but the most extreme spheres;[203] the 2008 recession squeezed state and federal budgets bearing the weight of locking up many more people than needed to secure public safety; and most recently, the coronavirus pandemic has placed pressure on states to release more people from the hottest virus hotspots in the nation.[204] Today, talk of sentencing reform and reentry support is both widespread and bipartisan.[205] Yet the old divide across prison walls persists. Little of this renewed conversation has translated into concrete changes inside penal institutions.

The two hundred-plus years of disconnection between intentions and practices have not suddenly healed. Prisons remain willfully secretive institutions, in large part because they are destructive not only of imprisoned people but of the social fabric itself.

Centuries of shifting purposes and messages continue in public images of incarcerated people, and in the wide gap between what courts intend and what prisons deliver. At the same time, imprisoned writers continue to offer a strikingly consistent testamentary record, now—with the advent of digital platforms—at a scale never before imagined. Yet as in the past, this is a testimonial record driven by the commitment to inform a mystified public about conditions and people the incarcerated see daily inside houses of punishment that warehouse not only a few committed outlaws but the mentally ill, the sick, and the hopeless. Their language and style may have changed since the days of Patrick Lyon, William Coffey, Austin Reed, Gerald Toole, Jack London, Kate O'Hare, and a Female Convict; yet the prison's witnesses stand as ready today to turn the prison inside out, and thus to show the American public what it has sought to hide from itself. What distinguishes today from the past is the sheer breadth of the will to bear witness, and what is revealed when prison witness is gathered in mass.

The source of prison witness that stands behind this book and continues the history we have traced, the American Prison Writing Archive, does not just hold a large body of readily searched testimonials. What readers can explore constitutes a new quality and depth of prison witness.

The history we have traced in this chapter has been one of published work. These are texts that managed to escape prison censors, and then find a way through the equally formidable gatekeepers of agents, editors, and commercial and nonprofit publications.[206] Through the APWA, incarcerated people need only a few stamps and writing materials to reach a global audience with work that is posted as exactly as it is received.[207] This allows a level and breadth of prison witness unimaginable before the digital age. The APWA includes cries for help scratched out in the unceasing light of isolation cells, political diatribes, autobiographies, policy critiques, detailed plans for reform, documentation of staff and peer abuse, memorials for friends and family, and the many other genres of writing from which the testimony in ensuing chapters will be gathered. The only hard limit that the APWA states is that "all submitted essays must draw on first-hand experience."[208] Among essays by writers in prison today and since 2009, readers can check the claims and sentiments of any one writer against dozens of authors in distant states and facilities, allowing us some grasp of what imprisonment is as a national experience. After more than two centuries, the APWA continues, broadens, and deepens insight from the receiving end of American criminal punishment, unveiling punishment's most intimate and visceral human effects.

This book seeks to introduce the voices of incarcerated people into the national conversation about what prisons do, to whom, and to what real effects. It seeks to unveil an institution that purports to contain, punish, and reform incarcerated people while deterring them and others from committing further crime. What we will read is wide-scale evidence that US prisons actively defeat all of these purposes and are much more effective in imposing psychological, emotional, and social degradation. Yet we will also read of how incarcerated people manage to rise to remarkable acts of resistance, persistence, and reconstruction.

The writers gathered here should sober our notions of what legal punishment means in practice. They should move readers to reconsider the very language of retribution, deterrence, containment, and rehabilitation once readers see what becomes of these aims—as they have become for over two centuries—behind prison walls. These witnesses should convince readers that when they look to prison professionals, lawmakers, or academics for guides forward, they should also want to bracket these proposals until they can be checked against the enormous human, intellectual, social, and moral capital that the United States— encouraged by many of these same professionals—has elected to lock behind prison walls.

2

DEFEATING RETRIBUTION, FIGHTING ACCOUNTABILITY, MANUFACTURING "MONSTERS"

> You just want to beat me, beat me, beat me, punish me, punish me, punish me. And then expect me to come out of prison reformed. At some point I'm just going to become what you expect me to. I'm gonna become that monster.
> —SOLO, MICHIGAN

> Just so we're clear, the law says the punishment for being convicted of a crime is the prison sentence. But the law enforcement community sees the prison as a place to inflict terror and abuse upon its prisoners until all hope for humanity is lost.
> —ROBERTO CARRASCO GAMEZ, ARIZONA

T H E witnesses in this chapter make evident that, if prisons deliver any of retribution's purported ends, it is the most primitive,[1] satisfying the vengeful desire among the public to feel that lawbreakers suffer,[2] a desire that Plato compared to the insanity of "lashing a rock."[3] Retribution is assumed to drive American imprisonment.[4] Yet whether one believes that retribution should be measured as just deserts, embraced as an intrinsic good, valued as an act of social equalization, as a deterrent, or simply as an expressive act, all such debate rings naïve, cynical, or ill-informed before the voices of those on its receiving end.

The testimony gathered here reveals a system in which the legalized pain imposed or institutionally tolerated inside prisons is so widespread and generic, and sentencing—retribution's only legal measure—so arbitrarily allotted, the connection to any single criminal act can appear as opaque to the punished as the minds and hearts of the punished are to those who support these measures from outside prison walls. "Penal harm—that is, the actual pain of punishment as experienced by individuals and groups—varies least by what partisans most value: the 'message' of punishment."[5] The imprisoned reveal a machinery of human degradation that can cause incarcerated people to lose any sense of their own humanity and deny that of other imprisoned people, simply as the costs of survival.[6] They testify to spaces where each relay in the circuit assumed to be charged by meaningful retribution is disconnected: between crime and punishment as a communicative act intended to wake the criminal perpetrator to the consequences of specific acts; between punishment and the incarcerated as chastisement of the person the perpetrator was at the moment of that act; and between the incarcerated and the returning citizen as a method of making convicted people reflect on their pasts and bring their future behavior within social norms.

Retribution's defining aim, accountability, is often the last thing incarcerated people discover, and they do so only *if* they can cut through their own dehumanization, and then through resentment at arbitrary and unregulated cruelty. What they witness is not the result of any retributive rationale but the institutionalization of vengeance,[7] a system that assumes that in every moment an incarcerated person lives without suffering, justice ceases to be served.[8] Seated in the testimony of people incarcerated today inside a mass system regularly characterized as entirely retributive, this chapter questions whether retribution is, in any coherent sense, possible. And as John Gardner writes, echoing Solo, Roberto Gamez, and many others quoted in these pages, "Once the moral difference between intended effects and known side-effects [of punishment] is denied or suppressed," then moral doubts arise about the entire criminal legal system.[9]

Some philosophers of punishment might claim that what effects retribution has on the punished are beside the point if we embrace retribution as a moral end in itself.[10] Few will argue, however, that the retributive arguments made by policy makers, victim rights groups, judges, prosecutors, staff unions, and the public do not assume that the punishment meted out must be felt by the perpetrator as a direct response to their criminal acts. A convicted person, once confined, must identify with the person they were outside in order to acknowledge that it was their actions for which punishment is being imposed. Yet imprisonment aggressively severs life inside from life outside. In its American forms, it breeds resentment of state control, of social norms, and of law itself; and simply as the cost of survival, it forces incarcerated people to adopt socially destructive values and behaviors, often to the point of erasing their ability to recognize themselves as the same people who entered prison. From inside prisons purported to deliver proportioned retribution, writers describe manufactories of indiscriminate personal and social disaster.

Retribution is meaningless if it is not felt by the person who committed the crime it intends to punish. But testimony to the effects of incarceration unveils the destruction of what we assume of personhood itself, once articulated by John Locke as requiring the simple ability to attribute past actions "to the present self by consciousness."[11] The incarcerated testify to seeing their past selves and acts placed at an unbridgeable remove from what prison makes of them. Their very self-images as human beings can become precarious.[12] What their testimony makes us appreciate is that meaningful retribution assumes not simply poetic justice, but a direct, causal sequence attaching a crime to imprisonment, imprisonment to reflection, and reflection to changed behavior—a sequence that assumes that the criminal perpetrator survives as a coherent identity able to feel the consequences of past actions as the consequences of *their* own actions and thus ones in need of reform.[13] We would not, for example, tolerate convicted people paying proxies to suffer their punishments. But since the courts and Congress have hardened prison walls, amputating the punishing hands from any more reasoning parts of the body politic,[14] the result is a prison where the statements above by Solo and Gamez are typical and mark a fundamental difference from the conclusions even of past studies that have found the effects of imprisonment at odds with its accepted goals.[15] What is the meaning of retribution if it so dehumanizes the punished they cannot recognize the people they were when sentenced?

It might feel good to cause harm to someone who has harmed others. But if that person does not believe that such harm is linked to the harm they have caused, it will be felt simply as an arbitrary, willful, and capricious assault—traits commonly attributed to the most repellent crimes.[16] In a state-funded environment, such actions will be viewed as grounds not for reflection or repentance but for resentment of law's enforcement and the social order the voting public might hope that incarcerated people would be chastened into constructively rejoining. For all the talk of just deserts served up at the ends of courtroom dramas, argued for inside practicing courtrooms, touted in electoral campaigns, and regularly underlined by the moralizing of local crime reporting, what is felt inside prisons is often something monstrously different. The very recognition of the self may be one of the toughest achievements for incarcerated people. As Andrew Jackson Smith writes from an Alabama prison, among the "aid[s] in continuing the values and purpose in one's life, the single most important factor may be the preservation of identity itself. This marks one's success in not succumbing to all the intrusions upon the mind in prison."[17]

I begin by marshalling testimony to the defeat of retribution because retribution is the penal rationale that even the harshest prison critics assume is in fact achieved, and because understanding retribution's defeat sets the grounds for understanding the defeat of the prison's other accepted ends.

BREAKING THE CRIME-PUNISHMENT CONNECTION

We have seen the factors that transformed the public perception of the person convicted of a crime from one capable of change into a person beyond the reach of rehabilitation. The public was convinced—and penal policy was legislated as though—people committed crimes because they made reasoned, cost-benefit choices to do so or from the inability,[18] among the mentally ill, to choose otherwise.[19] The result was that, as Bryan Stevenson observes, lawbreakers shrank in public discourse into their crimes: "'criminal,' 'murderer,' 'rapist,' 'thief,' 'drug dealer' . . .—identities they cannot change regardless of the circumstances of their crimes or any improvements they might make in their lives."[20]

In this light, punishment is less something meted out against an individual for a discrete act than an existential state: in public and much of official perception, punishment exhausts the identities of imprisoned people, who contain no possibilities other than their capacity to suffer. It is as though the perpetrator's ghost is sentenced, rendering the living and evolving person a moot being. In turn, prisons appear intent to make any change that does occur a change for the worse. Writing from an Indiana prison, John Vance describes the erasure of the confined person's internal sense of an identity larger than their worst act.

Incarceration can destroy the values and sense of self-worth of even the strongest person. . . . John disappears and only an "offender" remains. . . . Labels are reductionist. They define complex human beings in the most simplistic terms possible. For the prisoner, the sum of the person is reduced to the violations of the law for which they have been convicted. The label is so strong that the criminality of their behavior ceases to be what they have done and becomes what they are.[21]

Jamel Lamont Brown writes from New York, describing conditions that cause a break between the person who committed the crime and the effects of punishment.

The stress is unbearable, the loneliness in constant violence becomes a part of everyday life. The heart becomes cold and bitter. Human compassion is at a all time low. Each day spent in prison transforms each individual into something it takes years to deprogram yourself from.
     . . . I speak from personal experience. I was 17 when I arrived in prison today I am 42 years old and have been in prison close to 25 years. Prison is a place of lost souls, self hatred and sadist behavior. A place where men look like men, act like men but aren't men. Prison is a place of evil reincarnated, human suffering, where everyone has a knife or razor blade and walk around with a chip on their shoulder.[22]

From California, Willie Bailey III sees himself as "worthless and unwanted to the world. I am no longer a human being to society."[23]

Testimony to the hardening and dehumanization that John Vance, Jamel Brown, and Willie Bailey experience helps us to measure the distance between crime and the effects of legally sanctioned punishment. Their crimes adhere to them like unignited napalm; prisons provide the spark, charring their identities to the point of unrecognizability.[24]

While sentences unprecedented among modern nations were intended to "send a message" to lawbreakers, their effect on the convicted can be a message that few outside anticipate. A person who *is* their crime is an abstraction, a theoretical construct. Yet someone survives to register what remains, to measure the distances between the crime, punishment, and what time inside might yield. Daniel Perry writes from Oregon.

When a punishment drags on for years it stops being punishment because the point of why we are to learn our lesson, is lost. We understand what we did was wrong, but most of us know what we were doing was wrong in the first place, and still made the choices we made.

Honestly prison stopped being punishment after my first year back in because I no long care why I am here. Once a person stops caring about what the punishment is then you have to ask the question did we get the result we wanted? To me anyone with a brain knows how to help make a person better. You teach them, give them the tools to be something different. Work skills, trades, education and you "kill em with kindness." Yet the mindset is hard time will fix them. The only thing hard time does is takes the humanity out of being human. It takes basic human feelings like loving, caring, compassion, will, and empathy and turns them into weakness. People take those feelings and turn them into, hate, anger, rage, resistance, because weakness is preyed upon in prison.[25]

While time and prison conditions can detach crime from punishment inside any single confined person, when incarcerated people look around them, they see evidence that court-imposed sentencing is equally detached from the crimes committed. Again, Daniel Perry:

There is no uniformity in the way crimes are dealt with. One person in a big city could rob someone at gunpoint and get 5 years with good time. The same crime 50 mins down the road turns to 15 years no good time. Really all the states looking to save money should just fire all the judges because it's the DAs handing out the sentences, then to add insult to injury most public attorneys are in bed with the DAs and also don't like fighting cases because they don't want a loss on their record, so what do they do? They talk people into deals by scaring them with extortion. If you don't take this deal you'll get the max time. And what's sad is if you do fight in court and lose you will get the max time. It's all or nothing and your betting with a attorney who now is mad at you for wanting to put up a fight. You think he wants to really help you now?[26]

In a report from California, Robert Morales confirms the effect of what Perry describes.

The dismal news is that my old friend, Anthony Alvarez, now eighty three years of age, still continues to languish in a dungeon cell. He was sentenced in 2002 to sixty one years to life. He was sentenced to a slow lingering death for the crime of residential burglary.[27]

Irma Rodriquez remarks of women confined for nonviolent crimes "incarcerated with people who have committed murder. It's like one pit. Everyone's thrown into one pit."[28] Robert Saleem Holbrook recalls from Pennsylvania how he "started to question why the white kid received 5 to 10 years for the same role in a murder I received a Life Without Parole sentence for—why did the white man that murdered a childhood friend of mine in 1989 by penetrating his skull with a tire iron receive only 5 years probation."[29]

We know that what Perry, Morales, Rodriquez, and Holbrook report is a fact: race matters at sentencing.[30] It matters even more because race closely tracks poverty, and poverty and race combined create a slick protective coating that allows poor people of color to slide from street to prison without benefit of the costly legal protections that people of means can afford to stop that slide, or receive shorter sentences when they are sent to prison. Incarcerated people witness in their blocks and mess halls and on recreation yards the results of a system of affirmative penal action for poor people of color, the indigent, the uneducated, the mentally ill, addicts, and untreated survivors of childhood abuse.[31] After thirty-three years of life inside, Kenneth E. Hartman's report from California confirms how well imprisonment tracks such lifelong deprivation.

Most prisoners are uneducated, riddled with unresolved traumas and ill-treated mental health problems, drug and alcohol addictions, and self-esteem issues far too often bordering on the pathological. The vast majority has never received competent health care, mental health care, drug treatment, education or even an opportunity to look at themselves as humans. Had any of these far less draconian interventions been tried . . . no doubt many of my peers would be leading productive lives. We internalize the separation and removal, the assumed less-than status, and hold up the idiotic and vainglorious pride we pretend to, like clown's make-up, to hide our shame. In the end, the vast majority of us become exactly who we are told we are: violent, irrational, and incapable of conducting ourselves like conscious adults. It is a tragic opera with an obvious outcome. *Nothing else works* is not a statement of fact; it is the declaration of an ideology. This ideology holds that punishment, for the sake of the infliction of pain, is the logical response to all misbehavior. It is also a convenient cover story behind which powerful special interest groups hide.[32]

The incarcerated know that sentence lengths bear a weaker relationship to crime than to some unwritten algorithm factoring in race, financial means, location and culture . . . all tossed into the mixmaster of laws and mandatory minimum sentences that, as critic Rachel Barkow points out, have for forty years been based not on evidence of what is effective for addressing crime but upon public cries to respond quickly to the most sensational cases.[33] The laws then formed are often grossly indiscriminate: the person who "strikes out" with a third felony shoplifting charge gets the same twenty-five to life as those who strike out on rape or assault.[34] Through felony murder laws, the person who drives a friend to a location (even unknowingly) where that friend commits armed robbery or murder gets the same punishment as the person who carried or fired the gun. "The unlucky," Barkow writes, "are placed in the same box as the malevolent."[35]

Once inside prison walls, the literal severing of crime from the punishment begins by rendering the punished themselves generic. Uncounted prison writers describe entry into prison as what it obviously is: stripping away traits of identity other than that of "criminal" and "prisoner." From Missouri, Jameel Sykes offers a trope of narratives from prisons, asylums, death camps, and every other scene of involuntary detention, the scene of processing in, followed by learning the rules—no matter the crime that brought you there—of prison survival.

> Upon my arrival to prison I was met with a big sign that read, leave all your hopes and dreams behind. I didn't pay heed to the sign at that time, but as time wore on that sign would become more and more prevalent in my mind. First you are unloaded from a bus and shortly thereafter the dehumanizing process begins. You are made to strip naked with a hundred other inmates, sprayed with bug spray and then placed in a shower on top of each other. After that they strip you of

your dignity by herding you naked down a long hall where hundreds of other inmates whistle and cat call at you. Lastly they issue you a inmate number and a uniform identical to everyone else's, essentially stripping you of your identity. Once this is done you are placed in a six by eight cell with another inmate and a new kind of education begins. Quickly you learn that only the strong survive, you have to be tough physically, but even tougher mentally. Mistakes can get you hurt, sometimes even killed. Those of us who are not violent swiftly learn it. If you are capable of feeling emotion, you eventually lose that ability, you can't afford to have it. Men become animal, predators preying on those who are considered weak. Principles are lost, values are rejected, morals become non-existent.[36]

And nothing here, of course, is specific to the writer or their crime. Retribution is dispersed wholesale. From Texas, Lincoln Allen Keith describes a scene from his intake, confirming in a moment of contrast the willful and generic emotional sterility of confinement.

They began to call us out by name, four at a time, and pointed us to a counter where several guards were seated to inventory our property, arbitrarily deciding what we would or would not be allowed to keep. As the female guard asked me a few basic intake questions, she became aware of my New Mexican accent. Having already made her own comments about my "punk rock hairdo" and not getting a rise from me, she decided to focus on my accent and resorted to racist comments in an attempt to further demean me. "It says here you're white. Why you talk like a Mexican? You a wanna+be Mexican or what?" She turned and said something to a gray-headed sergeant who was standing nearby and he stepped up to the counter beside her. He looked at my intake file for a moment and shocked me when he looked up at me and, in a genuinely kindly manner said, "You have a life sentence? You're just a kid. That's a long, hard row to hoe. Take care of yourself, son." Before handing my shoes and property over to me and walking away. There is not much more disconcerting than a display of sympathy or kindness when one has come to expect nothing but cruelty. While I had borne the ridicule and harassment of the other guards, this unexpected show of humanity came perilously close to bringing me to tears.[37]

The irony is that the generic and normalized indifference, ridicule, and cruelty suggested by Keith's unpreparedness for a moment of human concern were fomented in large part by a movement to make punishment more specific to each convicted person. Prison sentences and their lengths expanded in part in the name of victim rights that gave an unprecedented place to the specific nature of the pain presented by specific individuals demanding commensurate pain and suffering in specified perpetrators.[38] The politically opportune claim that justice is served only when a victim's pain is matched by a convict's pain (the most private and incommunicable experience that human beings endure)[39] helped to push longer and mandatory sentencing. The result was that confinement facilities grew to such a size that everything experienced inside would be dictated by the instrumental necessities of running a system too large to attend to the differences between convicted people or their offenses. Less a system of just deserts than of generic reduction, prisons have become something even more disturbing than the "total institutions" that Erving Goffman's classic study called asylums, hospitals, and prisons two decades before the rise of the mass prison.[40] Kenneth Hartman evokes Goffman's work even as he describes a gulf between crime and punishment that Goffman never envisioned.

> After more than three continuous decades living inside the confines of these nightmarish places, I cannot even dream my way back out. My unconscious mind is imprisoned no less than my tattooed skin. Prison is a total experience, as the wholly accurate truism holds. . . . The gulf between here and there is vast. The physical and social construct that is the modern institution has resulted in the creation of a separate world called prison, populated by inmates who have no individual identities— inmates who wear the same clothes, have the same haircuts, and have become blurred versions of every other inmate. In essence, the whole of society becomes the unnamed, mostly unwitting, co-conspirator in the creation of edifices dedicated to the suffering of fellow human beings.[41]

Even if we assume that satisfying the wishes of victims is indeed a legitimate goal of state-sanctioned punishment, the result Hartman and others see stands directly at odds with research suggesting that victims are most satisfied when the punished communicate back that punishment has successfully taught them to change in ways that confirm social norms of proper behavior. In lieu of such communication, victims will seek harsher punishments while securing no more satisfaction.[42] The uglier irony behind reports of how prisons strip away identities such as those of Jameel Sykes, Lincoln Allen Keith, and Kenneth Hartman is that no one asked what crime survivors actually wanted or needed, and—other than in rare, experimental programs—prisons explicitly block communication between victims and perpetrators.[43] As Danielle Sered points out, the only choice offered to crime victims is incarceration or nothing. When crime survivors were asked what they want and need, they overwhelmingly preferred rehabilitation, preventative investment in job training and treatment, and just about anything but incarceration.[44] Lawmakers and prison-staff unions used victims' capacity for public expressions of pain (not their capacity to make decisions) to transform lawbreakers into nothing but their capacity to suffer. In turn, lawmakers, law enforcers, and prison profiteers secured votes, jobs, and industry returns. The result is a system whose disasters are multiple and that successfully shatters any retributively meaningful links between crime, crime victims, and the court-sanctioned punishments meted out for crime.

BREAKING THE PUNISHMENT-PUNISHED CONNECTION

Incarcerated people see sentences determined less by crime than by demographic categories. They are then crowded into institutions that seek to render them generic versions of one another, at a scale that makes impossible any discernible ratio between crime and the penal conditions they endure. Yet even with the crime-punishment connection broken, we must assume that—even if rendered generic—the pain and suffering they experience remains their own. How can punishment not be felt by the punished? What indeed *is* punishment if the punished cannot feel it?[45] As the testimony in this section suggests, punishment meted out by courts according to the law offers cover for a regime that often forces the punished to abandon the capacity to feel that punishment.

Prisons cannot make real the myth that victim suffering can be meaningfully or proportionately translated into the suffering of incarcerated people. The American prison can, however, so amplify pain and suffering that the harm it produces obliterates the personality of the human being against whom the public might have intended to mete a proportioned retribution. Inside American prisons today, the connection between state-sanctioned punishment and the punished is commonly broken. As Kenneth Hartman and Daniel Perry observe, most incarcerated people know that the actions for which they have been convicted were wrong; yet the conditions they face can silence the communicative relay even between retributive suffering and the person who committed a criminal act. As Colin Dayan remarks, incarceration can leave a person "shorn of personality"; a person is rendered extinct, "drained of self-identity." Prisons mete out "state-sanctioned degradation . . . propelled by a focus on personal identity, the terms by which personality is recognized, threatened, or removed."[46] The people supposed to *get what they deserve* and thus to learn accountability often cease to exist, transformed not into penitents but into strangers to themselves, adapted solely to a struggle for survival against prison staff, other incarcerated people, and a culture of willful deprivation. And this alienation is on top of the fact that, in Danielle Sered's words, "prison lets people off the hook," since "for all the ravages of prison, it insulates people from the human impact of what they have done."[47]

When the incarcerated do manage to retain, regain, or simply refer to human feelings and responses—if only to report their deterioration— retribution (let alone remorse) is often not the first thing they feel impelled to document. Much more common are testaments to the arbitrary brutalities of prison itself, the resentments it generates, and the wholesale transformation of personalities in adapting to this environment. The testimony of incarcerated people from across the nation is consistent and mutually enforcing: In order simply to survive, whether or not they engaged in violence in the past, and whatever their feelings about their past acts, the imprisoned must rise to the level of violence and indifference to the pain of others, and to their own, that the prison demands. As in the experience of Kate Richards O'Hare, incarceration in the United States is boot camp for lying, theft, manipulation, physical assault, and the struggle to endure willful dehumanization. Incarcerated people can become strangers to themselves. "Everything I swore I wouldn't do," Victoria Sanchez testifies from California, "I ended up doing!"[48] From Michigan, Robert Cannon Jr. underlines the numbing that incarcerated people must impose upon themselves while enduring imprisonment.

I cannot spell out gentleness because nothing in prison is gentle. I cannot show kindness because in my world kindness is weakness and to be weak is to invite more hurt. I dare not exhibit love because the wolves of my world would rip it to bloody shreds. I cannot bring forth and demonstrate my loneliness or hunger because they have become a bone-deep ache that even I cannot reach to soothe.

While other young men my age grew up watching fat babies grow into healthy youngsters, I grew up watching healthy youngsters having their guts and minds twisted and ripped, and being turned into emotional cripples. . . .

Don't pity me; Understand me. Understand me and the way I changed when they stripped away my identity and self-respect; changed day by day after being treated like an idiot child and forced to live with every type of human derelict . . . changed by the indignity of being forced to scurry about like a mindless fool every time a voice barked or a bell rang, changed after never being able to escape the uncaring or hostile eyes of my cellmates while living in a human fish bowl where one can't even squat on the toilet without an audience.[49]

Stephen Long writes of the emotional disconnections that California prisons demand.

To psychologically contend with being treated like a domestic animal is to learn to cope with constant frustration. One way of accomplishing that is by lowering one's expectations of any type of fortune. The process of self-neutering your enthusiasm requires a process of getting indifferent to life. Becoming insensitive to your state of well being and contentment. . . . Barriers. One is forced to build barriers around their feelings, act as though everything is "fine." Slowly and steadily a prisoner creates a figment of themselves, a sort of nobody-anybody status. A trademark-less being. A puppet-zero.[50]

At the same time that prisons offer the very drivers of violence (isolation, trauma, attacks upon self-worth) that criminal violence stems from in the world outside,[51] absorbing the blunt trauma of American imprisonment can overwhelm consciousness. Writing from one of Alabama's famously violent prisons, Donald Hairgrove offers a portrait of how prison does its damage.

> The exasperating taste of my world, devoid of any emotional nourishment, is gradually overpowering. Bleak and colorless walls; insipid, disgusting meals and phlegmatic, time-worn daily routines stacked upon unacceptable overcrowding, which creates senseless haphazard violence over unadulterated trivial issues and, of course, the irrational guardian harassment all collaborate to numb my faculties. In tiny surreptitious doses anesthesia is dripped into my heart—a formerly complacent heart that is slowly beginning to resemble my dreadful surroundings. An ache settles somewhere deep inside of me, pain linked to the realization that something once deeply cherished has been stolen from me during my outrageous two plus decades of incarceration. Years of sensory deprivation has withered my ability to respond with anything resembling an emotional reaction. Like an ancient tree, gnarled and wizened by time and nature's elements, my heart has grown rugged and callused. A hard price extracted by the dehumanizing environment I am forced to survive in.[52]

Connecticut writer John Russel Bossé describes feeling his humanity reduced to a memory.

> Lately I feel like I'm suffocating. Each minute of every day is a slow asphyxiation. The worst death sentence in this country is being buried alive in prison without hope. . . . I know that in me there must be a human being beneath all this agony. It is a faith belief.[53]

From inside a Georgia prison, Eric Martin Hassel echoes John Bossé's passive awareness that he is losing himself.

> After more than 10 years of continuous incarceration, I am slowly losing the will to re-enter a society that has abandoned me. Contemplating this is a symptom of institutionalization—I am cognizant of this fact while unable to do anything to alleviate the downward spiral I'm currently experiencing.[54]

"Prison," writes Jevon Jackson from Wisconsin, "is a cruel, neurotic tiger that is bent on destroying you."[55] "Prison," for Pennsylvania's Christopher Balmer, "is one tremendous nightmare."[56] Angel Ayala has lived that nightmare inside the California prison system.

> Lately I've been seriously deteriorating. . . . At times I get this very primal urge to attack the walls, attack my captors, and try to run free. . . . Sometimes I'll go days without leaving the cell, without eating or showering, just paralyzed over the mattress and staring at the walls and having bad dreams. Or I'll go days unable to sleep, tackling ten projects at once, punching the obscene walls, talking to myself and having hallucinations and wrecked with anxiety. In desperate lapses I'll hang from a sheet around my neck for a moment, or cut a vein open.[57]

Writing from Pennsylvania, Lee Whitt states the case more briefly: "Cells may be designed to hold a person, but the end result is that they starve the mind and lead to mental damage that, at times, is beyond repair."[58]

Incarcerated people in the United States report witnessing their own metamorphoses beyond recognition, and the subsequent emergence of alien identities that can do no one good. The punishments sanctioned by courts, prosecutors, and lawmakers and embraced by the public echo back from the exteriors of prison walls, satisfying a collective will to vengeance, while inside, whatever message they intend is muted by prison officials who, free of accountability, create or tolerate conditions that incarcerated people must numb their senses to survive. Critics have noted that criminal justice is largely a local matter, a national quilt of states made up in turn of thousands of counties and jurisdictions.[59] And yet first-person witnesses offer evidence that the American prison is less a quilt than one perpetually degrading organism whose DNA crosses the boundaries between individuals, penal facilities, and states.

W. E. Roberts writes from Ohio.

> Prison is a poisoned environment. It leaves no one untouched. It seeps into the pores like mustard gas. It fouls the very air we breathe, polluting it with anger and hatred and bitterness. It creates unseen lesions on our souls, damages our being, eats away at our minds until we have

no choice but to shut down all emotion or risk self-destruction. One cannot "care" for another in here, it is a weakness pounced upon by those who prey on misery, a liability that brings the danger of attack, physically or otherwise. To be safe is to be callous, to save one's self is to become ruthless and aggressive. Prison rips away our humanity and forces cruelty down our throats and into our words. It fills us with psychic bile, a caustic fluid that splashes uncontrollably on all who come in contact with us. It is unforgiving. We cannot see it as it happens and are shocked when our families and loved ones recoil in fear. It is the nature of this place—to eat or be eaten—a reflexive reaction to anything which threatens survival. . . . It has robbed me of all I once cherished as good and honorable: sensitivity, compassion, patience, generosity. I have been bludgeoned into unwanted submission and cheapened by its coarseness, boot-heeled into the mold of a lesser human being. . . . No one thrives here. No one benefits.[60]

Roberts's words represent many writers who deplore their conditions and what these conditions are doing to their psyches. Oregonian Jacob Barrett notes that these effects can be experienced without conscious recognition; the result is a sense of placelessness. Prison, he writes,

drains your sanity without you realizing your mind and ability to rationally interact with the world slips away like water swirling down a drain. Before you know it you are looking into the bottom of the empty sink of your mind. Prison is a half death, a withering of the soul where the core of your humanity is reduced by the state as a matter of law and policy; my otherness and worth defined not only by my overseers but measured by my adherence to the "convict code," a "cultural tyranny," imposed by my fellow prisoners, which was in turn imposed on them. On one hand I am an object of the state, property that is told when it can speak and act, and on the other I am a man who has a desire to find value in his life in a culture that isn't mine at its core and which doesn't want me. A borderland—not one, but both.[61]

Held in a California prison, Ebony Delaney describes the debilitating coping methods used by trans women. She writes in resistance.

We are constantly reminded that once we were sentenced, we no longer mattered, and that no one cared. We are told that none will reach out to help; that once the Judge banged the gavel, we became property. With no regulations or oversight from the "outside world," the staff and inmates thrive and perpetrate unthinkable horrors. Many of my trans sisters fall into a state of depression where they are pumped full of psychotropic drugs. Many adopt attitudes of self destructive behavior. They fall victim to the whims of those who lurk in the shadows and wallow in the mire of investigation and manipulation. They allow themselves to become wrapped in the arms of these defilers. They quietly become addicted to the false sense of security they feel from these vampire soul suckers. They become addicted to drugs, alcohol and sex. They find themselves prostituting and "turning tricks" in order to either sate their drug addicted appetites, to be able to eat and fall asleep with a full stomach, or simply satisfy their addiction to sex which they mistakenly equate with love. Many have no one from the outside world to support them. . . . Yet, I also know that our voices need to be heard, and since I have this opportunity to do so, to not do it would be a travesty. No, I desire to shout from the mountain top. I wanted to scream into the universe that yes, we do matter![62]

From the Tennessee Department of Corrections, James Africa describes what retribution, so called, has left of himself, an "unrecognizable Dr. Frankenstein like creation."

After it has incapacitated my rights. After it has incapacitated my mind. After it has incapacitated my heart. After it has incapacitated my soul. Until I have no power. Until I have no will. Until I have no reason. Until I have no conscience, nor feelings, or individuality. Until I have no potential to not only survive the challenges of the day to day struggle to adjust and fit in outside the prison walls, but also to even so much as love myself enough to care. What I mean is that by the time that one too many Frankensteins are unleashed upon society after long enduring the post traumatic stress disorder like effects of extensive solitary confinement, and the state of Tennessee takes notice in some form of an impulsive, irrational, unprovoked criminal act, that we have nothing left of our humanity but our instincts, it will already be too late.[63]

Under the name Prison Vitality, a man held in Texas describes the mental break forced by the prison's ability to convince incarcerated people that the titles "human" and "prisoner" are mutually exclusive.

> Playing the role of Beast is easy—a disposable person, subhuman, monster . . . it's all the same. It's an easy role to play because it's the label I've been wearing for almost 20 years. Playing the role of Man, a genuine human being, is becoming increasingly difficult as memories of civilization fade, and I become more cemented within my incarcerated reality. . . . Ah to be a human being again! Worthy of respect and affection, capable of dignity and contribution, to have a valuable life. . . .
>
> Thousands of hours of relentless indoctrination eventually took their toll upon my resolve and mutated my psyche. Every day, society and its warders treat me like scum, and I find that sometimes I treat myself the same way. I had never wanted to be anything but a human being . . . didn't even know I could lose the distinction. I've worn many labels in my life: child, student, lover, sailor, husband, father, and countless others, but none of them had rendered my existence as absolute as "prisoner." For the longest time I fought, I stayed a loner and pursued skills that might help me cope with the free world when the courts reversed their mistake and set me free. But it never happened and even if it had, I think it's impossible to escape institutionalization after a period of time and still survive prison. The only way to adapt to such a harsh environment is to give yourself to it completely and forget about the choices or value you once possessed as a real person and leave behind the free world. Two decades passed, and I've basically stopped fighting the stigma society and the state have placed on me and made the adjustments necessary to live here. I accept that by society's standards, I am disposable. Yet forgetting society for a moment as they have done me, do I truly believe in my own heart that I'm worthless? Depends on the day, I guess. On a beastly day I am trash, a pathetic rag, pure shit. But on a good day—when I'm feeling particularly Homosapienish, when I play the role of Man—I see myself as a bit

worn but perfectly usable fabric, valuable enough to be hung neatly and lovingly against the wall.[64]

Imprisoned people resist the dehumanization that so many writers document. When this happens, it's virtually always a fight against seemingly impossible odds, a fight joined out of the desperate will to latch onto the few internal or external resources that pass within imprisoned people's reach, as K. D. Welch, writing from Nevada, makes evident.

> When you're shunned, viewed & or treated as unimportant or worthless, where & or how do you or an individual male/female gain self-esteem? Placed inside places like this maximum facility & constantly treated with disdain hostile belligerent cruel and unusual punishment day and night with all objections towards you to destroy you mentally, emotionally and physically literally with sounds, language, actions, tactics et. al = pain, misery, hate, leads to self-destructive destructive outlook towards and unto any and all things! With no outside meaningful connection, love and or vital support, prison life routine becomes one's all and all else becomes unknown. . . . I live and exist in spiritual sphere and fight to hold on to heart w/ love joy peace while resisting hate, anger and slew of many negatives! Focusing to maintain mentality, strength, will, identity and future hope. . . . Only meaningful hold/grasp is in Jesus Christ. All hope, dreams and reality future plans based on Christ. . . . I pray, study, pray and wait for better times.[65]

These writers record the changes that prison—not remorse, not accountability, nothing that retribution might be thought to inspire—has rendered inside themselves and the obstacles that stand in the way of resisting that change. From Colorado, Jeremy Pinson describes his forced metamorphosis from prey into a predator who has to be kept in isolation to protect others.

> Inmates decided to sexually assault me by beating me relentlessly until I submitted to the rape. This went on for months and the kid in me died. My soul left my body, my heart turned to stone and the blood in my veins turned to ice. . . . I was once a sweet kid who was merely a petty thief. It was the penal system that taught me hate, violence and deprav-

ity. By taking who I was and subjecting me to the very worst of human nature I was evolved against my will into what I am today. . . . As for me I stopped living long ago. While my heart still beats my mind is a dark void inside which lies horrible thoughts. . . . I do not know what will become of me but I fear it will be terrible for me and for many others. I am broken beyond repair.[66]

Writing from South Carolina, Amy Benjamin offers testimony to how, even without the kind of violent assault that Jeremy Pinson describes, and even when incarcerated people seem able to take advantage of constructive programming offered inside, a despair that short-circuits retributive messages is never safely at bay.

I was a model inmate doing my best to atone for my crime and pay my debt to society. Editor of the prisons newspaper, a member of the hospice team, active in the greyhound rescue program, I thought these activities insulated me from the emotional problems that plagued most of the population. My life was as different from Laura's [a recent suicide] as it could possibly be. Two years later I was proven wrong when an officer emptied a full can of pepper spray through the flap in my lock up door while I stood on the sink trying to cut my wrist on the fire sprinkler. I hadn't eaten or drank anything in nine days. My own girlfriend was in the cell next door loudly urging me to kill myself. I am proof and testimony that if you do enough time and allow yourself to become lonely enough you will turn to whatever outlet you can find to ease that loneliness a little. If you are addicted and obsessive by nature, as I am, then that addiction and obsession, left unaddressed, will transfer itself to whatever target is available. Be it starving, bingeing, exercise, purging, sex, self mutilation, I've engaged in them all obsessively during the past years.[67]

The dissolution of even the best resolve and traits of character occurs in many forms inside a major metropolis in cages. Jeremy Pinson's metamorphosis is representative of many taking place in prisons across the nation, while men and women like Amy Benjamin find themselves self-destructing. Andrew J. Smith, quoted briefly above, writes of the personality traits best suited to survival inside.

Inmates in state prisons quickly learn to adopt a protective behavior which must include threats of violence, apathy for others, and above all a self-centered focus. In fact, those that profit most and fare best in prison are the narcissists and sociopaths who enter already with a disdain for others and a genuine inability for compassion. Psychologically normal inmates must mimic the . . . behavior consistent with personality disorders. And at some point, habitual activities/behaviors stop being something performed by one's self and instead become the "self," that is the identity of the person, what naturally characterizes the individual.[68]

No judge sentences people to assault, transformation into predators, rape, or diminishment of personhood. The only punishment sanctioned by courts is time inside. Yet in prisons where even sentences for non-violent crimes can be longer than the years indicated by "life" in other countries,[69] where we measure court-mandated pain in decades, in centuries, in death-by-incarceration, time itself becomes less a matter of calendar days and weeks, months and years, less a measure of retribution deserved for a discrete act, than an infinite, state-sponsored horizon of human dismantling.[70] Accountability is not only missing from this ever-receding horizon; it is pushed over the edge, as Texas writer Darrel Limbocker suggests.

Prison is a place where you write letters and can't think of anything to say, where you write fewer and fewer as time goes by. Finally you stop writing altogether . . . because you receive few or none in return. . . . It's a place where you find gray hairs on your head, or where you find it starting to disappear. It's a place where you get false teeth, stronger glasses and aches and pains that you never felt before. It's a place where you grow old before your time . . . and you worry about it, sometimes a little, sometimes a lot. Prison is a place where the flame in every person burns low, for some it goes out, but for most it flickers weakly, sometimes flashing brightly, but never to burn as bright as it once did. . . . It's a place where you lose respect for the law because you saw it raw, twisted and bent; ignored and blown out of all proportion to suit the people who enforce it. You're guilty because of skin pigmentation, being in the wrong place at the wrong time, poverty, your innocence is for naught!!! It's a place where you strive to remain civilized, but you lose ground. Then you realize the change that has taken place within yourself, in your heart and soul. The reflection in the mirror becomes a constant reminder of what you now recognize of the stranger you've become.[71]

Such strangers are not the people who committed crimes; they are the remainders rendered by isolation, brutality, and hopelessness. In the world outside, we may not like growing old, but we are compensated by moments of joy, of care, of gratification, and the freedom to honor the milestones of births, deaths, marriages . . . Without such markers of time's rewards, time is marked only by unceasing loss. Time fades the ruse that the punishments endured were ever intended to affect the person punished in any way other than to disappear them from life itself, as Linda Kay Stermer writes from Michigan.

Once you have done ten years, if you had young children, they no longer look forward as much to seeing you. They are busy with sports, friends, school and other activities. If your parents were already elderly, you're blessed if they can still visit. Visitors are more often outreach or religious visitors just so you can have a visit with someone from the outside world, or get food from the visiting room and get out of your cell. You are more reliant now on your prison relationships because outside relationships are nearly nonexistent. If you came in young, you are now grown up. You've lived through regret, loss and are still waiting for rehabilitative programming. The courts sentenced you to a long time in order to make you learn a lesson, but you have likely learned that prison is not interested in your becoming rehabilitated. Your rehabilitation will only happen through your own efforts, your incentive.

Once you have been here for twenty or more years, it is unlikely that you still have anyone on the outside that helps provide for you or even visits. Not only have you suffered loss from your family in the world, but the family that you have created in prison begins dwindling. Some have gone home, others are elderly and can no longer visit you in the yard. Some have expired and others are getting close to it. You will never attend a funeral and have a little time or outlet for grief. If you are fortunate enough to be released, you will leave the only "family" you have known for years, only to have no family left on the outside, to go to. The biggest lesson that you have learned in your years of incarceration is that Michigan discarded you when you were sentenced, they never expected you to improve yourself and they never expected you to walk its streets again.[72]

Incarcerated writers know the power of prisons and their supporters to dress up the walls surrounding spaces of willful degradation as retributive bulwarks for the public good. From behind such facades these writers reveal retribution's defeat by generic punishment, forced estrangement from one's identity, and adaptation to spaces that demand cruelty and the abandonment of hope. Punishment and the punished are less parts of a narrative of justice than spark and fuel in the immolation of human souls.

BREAKING THE PUNISHMENT—RETURNING CITIZEN CONNECTION

If retribution serves any greater end than satisfying the public that it has expressed condemnation of certain acts, that end should be people forced to reflect on those acts, and thus resolved to (re)adapt to civil norms. In the testimony that follows, we see not only reiteration of the prison's ability to break connections between crime and punishment and punishment and the punished; we see how prisons facilitate the failure of three-quarters of those released to avoid returning within five years.[73] As Donald Hairgrove writes,

> I look for-but cannot find, the man I was once. Sometimes I stand staring at my disparaging reflection, like a wondering child, of the man I have become. A man that struggles daily with the fading ability to feel the tenderness of the life I once knew. I see a man, whom if released at this moment, would go out these prison gates as ill equipped to live in the free-world of today-as the fool whom entered prison over two decades ago. Not from concern of being confined again, but from the loss of being able to respond to sentimental tenderness. . . . Inside these confines of misery I have only learned it is prudent to prey on the weak, to fight savagely when provoked and to show only the manipulating face of cooperation to those whom are in authority.[74]

Even the best intentions for transformation can be crushed by adaptation to prison. In an essay addressed to "American Justice," Billie Gomez of Texas describes what has happened to him despite his initial hopes.

> [At] no point during my incarceration did I begin my prison sentence with the intentions of assaulting other prisoners and/or "Correctional Officers," in fact I wanted desperately to change my life and to become rehabilitated, however after observing young men being raped, assaulted, humiliated and broken by both prisoners and prison staff, I came to the conclusion that I would rather kill and/or be killed than end up becoming a victim of your tactics and peers. After observing a young man get burned to death by his own so called "brothers" over a few packs of cigarettes, I realized that if I wanted to survive in this world which you skillfully created, that I would literally have to go numb and become an animal myself.[75]

Such statements reveal the effects of an era in which, as Craig Haney observes, "we now celebrate rather than merely tolerate or even lament official cruelty and the infliction of pain."[76] Derrick Starks observes how the culture of cruelty inside California prisons consumes their wards.

> Being engulfed in prison politics 24 hours a day can really break you mentally. It can take you over the edge, past the point of no return. It's like falling down a bottomless pit. There's nothing you can do. It's a freefall and gravity forever has you. I stood at the edge of an abyss and stared into it. I was in complete submission to the gang-prisoner lifestyle. I was a prisoner in body and mind due to the indoctrination and reinforcement by prisoners and correctional officers alike. I was labeled by my peers. I was labeled by the system. The thing is, I accepted those labels because I allowed others to define me and dictate my actions.[77]

Prison labels and adaptation are pounded into mind and body, scarring people who must then work against all odds to live successfully outside. Robert Mark Pitts reflects on a question asked by another man about what he most fears in the transition from New Hampshire convict to free citizen.

The truth is, I fear the resentment for the world that being in prison has instilled in me. And that I won't be able to always keep that resentment under control. I no longer think of myself as an individual, but as a member of a group of mindless non-humans who are deemed as worthless evil people. For years I've been beaten and mentally abused to indoctrinate me into this mindset.[78]

All of these writers witness effects in themselves that make the reflection, attitudes, and behavioral change that we might hope retribution would inspire more difficult than when they entered. Recalling his impending release from a North Carolina prison, Phillip V. Smith II recounts a moment that suddenly released the man prison made of him, attacking a man who slighted him.

Some foreign force charged me—a rage that I'd never known. I punched him until my knuckles were raw and swollen and it hurt me to strike him more. I did not feel human. I was a rabid animal in the wilderness snarling as he clawed at his prey. Dom was not a person to me within that moment. He was the anger I'd been feeling since my bid had begun. He was those two men that had stolen my lock and laughed at me. He was an officer that told me not to talk in the chow hall, when to wake up, go to sleep, eat, watch TV—he was the mountain of my anger come to a bloody head. I did ten days in the hole that time.

When I had time to think about it, I felt like a coil that had once been wound too tight and was now released and relaxed. It was a strange experience to feel on edge for close to a year, then find peace only after an act of rage. It was strange and disheartening. It was not my nature to hurt people. I had not hurt anyone while committing the crimes that had landed me in prison. This foreign feeling of rage was new to me. I was forced to confront a side of myself that I never knew existed and wished had remained hidden within the catacombs of my unconscious psyche. . . .

Prison is a breeding ground for Violent minds. It imposes a need for brutality, giving an ordinary person the motivation to be violent in circumstances when their back is against the wall and they feel that they have no other choice. Because I'd fought Dom, my prison sentence was extended another two months. I was released from prison on a brisk winter morning with $3.36 in my pocket. I had no clothes except for the prison garments on my back. I had no place to sleep for the night. Homeless and hopeless, I did not last long. Less than a year later I was back in prison serving a life sentence for murder.

. . . The public continues to speculate about why recidivism percentages are so high. No one ever stops to think that how people are treated in prison is the biggest contributor to that problem. If you lock someone up, beat them or allow them to be beaten, then release them into the world with no means to support themselves other than the criminal education they received behind bars, what other outcome could you expect?[79]

What we can expect is what Uhuru B. Rowe also sees in the neighboring state of Virginia.

With the transition of the penal system away from an environment which prioritizes reform, treatment, education and rehabilitation towards a more punitive, exploitative, and dehumanizing form of imprisonment, most people are unaware that the torture, abuse, mistreatment, and dehumanization of incarcerated people exacerbates our antisocial personalities, attitudes, and behaviors, which increases the odds that we'll commit new crimes against unsuspecting citizens and return through the ever revolving doors of incarceration.[80]

From West Virginia, Francis L. offers details of the psychological changes prison forces upon its wards, the staff culture that evokes these changes, and the struggle to cling to life itself. L. does not explicitly mention his fears about release; like so many others, he finds his whole attention occupied by survival, thus filling the mental space where we might hope that reflection and the resolve to rejoin the free world might evolve.

Barbarism, brutality, depravity, assault, murder, and other extreme acts of violence, along with an over-all dehumanization of the mind and spirit are mere par for the course associated with incarceration and prison environments. . . . The first time you witness a fellow prisoner beat with hands, feet, or the wielding of a blunt object, literally senseless to the point where if they ever wake from the coma the trauma caused, their faculties of mind are never again the same, at that point you become ultra-aware of your surroundings. It is a sort of functional hyper-vigilance and practiced paranoia. The realization that you won't be protected by staff becomes apparent. That duty is yours alone. . . . That is when your survival instincts begin to hone themselves to fine-tuned efficiency. . . . The arts of self-defense, and the craft of weapons manufacture from seemingly innocuous items become second nature and in time you are able to produce them with skill and artisan quality.

. . . Contrary to the popular belief in the stereo-typical archetype assigned to the incarcerated individual, not everyone found within a prison environment are animals. Yet honestly, some are. The majority of whom wear government issued uniforms. For these individuals it is not enough that the inherent features of an institutional setting are oppression, repression, and depression. Most view prisoners as deserving the harshest treatment imaginable. . . . No unethical treatment is off limits. It is not uncommon for prison guards to abuse their authoritative position at every available opportunity. . . . Most utilize it as a platform to subject incarcerated men and women to their personal, racist dispositions, ideologies, and skewed world views. Racism, as a form of abuse and psychological torture is ever present within the prison system.

. . . The total sum of psychological strain on a prisoner is immense. The mental burden near intolerable. There is truly no way to cope, nor mechanism to reverse, repair, or repress the continuous bombardment of brain altering damage caused by full immersion into a prison environment. . . .

. . . One simply endures and hopes that he awakens from the nightmare before the succubus completely devours his soul.[81]

While Francis L. and others document the effects of a constant battle with other incarcerated people and staff, C. F. Villa, writing from California's notorious Pelican Bay State Prison, reports on the changes that occur in him in solitary isolation or the Special Housing Unit (SHU): spaces of extreme social and sensory deprivation, a condition to which nearly fifty thousand people are subjected on any day in the United States,[82] and in too many cases for months, years, even decades.

His description is one of many that convey the debilitating effects on people who will someday be expected to resume lives outside.

> The ability to hold a single good thought left me, as easily as if it was a simple shift of wind sifting over tired, battered bones. There's a definite split in personality when good turns to evil. The darkness that looms above is thick, heavy and suffocating. A snap so sharp, the echo is deafening. A sound so loud you expect to find blood leaking from your ears at the bleakest moment. The waking is the most traumatic. From the moment your bare feet graze the rugged stone floor, your face begins to sag, knuckles tighten, flashing pale in the pitch of early morning. The slightest slip in a quiet dawn can set a SHU personality into a tailspin: if the sink water is not warm enough, the toilet flushes too loud, the drop of a soap dish, a cup . . . in an instant you bare teeth, shake with rage. Your heart hammers against ribs, lodges in your throat. You are capable of killing anything at this moment.[83]

"Prison," writes Travis Cunningham from Wisconsin, "tends to remove those simply human attributes and instead replace them with an abysmal, diabolic, malicious nature, essentially turning a slightly flawed individual into a tyrant."[84] From a Connecticut prison cell, Patrick Lexis comments, "I came into prison a whole human being and I am leaving as a deeply fractured human being."[85] "You come in precarious," Stephan Darris writes from Colorado, "and leave malevolent."[86] Or, as Massachusetts writer Karter K. Reed notes, "People do not live in prison, they die . . . slowly."[87] "Honestly to allow my mind to conform to the desired patterns of the Department of Corrections," James Lawson-Wilson writes from Florida, "would be a sin against God, and if you don't believe in God, then it would be more in line with abandoning any morals or standards you hold yourself to as a member of the human race."[88] From California, Josef Michael Jensen's essay surveys the damaging effects of incarceration, attending to how resentment of the prison's conditions delays introspection we might hope retribution would evoke.

> My life in prison has taught me many things. I learned to magnify all of my anger and fear. I learned how to harness, those very powerful emo-

tions into the energy necessary to perpetuate the chaotic, unpredictable and very dangerous environment in which I found myself. . . .

Everything that I learned at that crucial time pointed to factors outside of my self. It's hard to be angry at yourself for the state in which you find your life, especially when you have the world to blame. . . .

Psychologically the experiences one has in prison are counterproductive to bringing order to your life and beginning the long journey towards understanding the implications of your life, as you have lived it, as it is and as it could perhaps be. . . . Prison life is being physically, emotionally, mentally and socially contained in an area no bigger than your standard full size bathroom. It is living in that ten by twelve foot bathroom with another man at least eighteen hours a day. It is washing your clothes in the same water in which you defecate. It is living in a state of constant frustration and agitation. . . . It is the heightening of all of your senses and the dulling of all your emotions. It is the abandonment of the capacity to love, to have compassion and to care about other people. It is the relentless murder of your humanity. The culture that survives in prison destroys your ability to see any hope. . . . It is a state of affairs which only serves to fuel our anger, our frustration and our hatred. . . .

"Abandon all hope ye who enter here." These words which appear above the gate of Dante's Inferno describe the only way to ensure your mental survival. Once in prison we find fear and anger. A slow burning hatred for the system that has abandoned us manifests in frustration, violence and inevitably our sense of hopelessness. . . . You have to abandon all that is socially productive, if you haven't already. You have to abandon all which is sane and rational. . . . You must consciously abandon 10,000 years worth of civilization if you are to survive the onslaught of your own humanity upon your existence.

. . . From a prisoner's perspective, prison is death in stasis. It is living while being dead. . . . As someone who has been there, I understand why our lives fuel the hatred we feel towards the authorities. I understand the frustration we feel towards being told we need to conform to a system which abuses us and kicks us when we're down.[89]

Nowhere in this system is accountability featured, except as a pretense for staff and other incarcerated people to engage in acts of cruelty.

When true accounting does take place, it can be attributed to the efforts of incarcerated people: having first proven themselves capable of violent indifference to human life and suffering, they must then begin the self-exploration required to rediscover the parts of the human beings that remain despite the prison's demands. Yet even after this work is done, they also know the indifference of prisons to their efforts. From Michigan, with a series of rhetorical questions, India Porter implies the inconsequence of her efforts at self-transformation for a life outside, suggesting that, in this system, hope itself is presumptuous.

> I am a woman who believes that she has made some bad decisions. Learned everything I could from my bad decisions and willing to do everything I can to never make decisions like the ones that caused me to come here. Am I wrong for wanting a second chance at life as a free woman while I am still young? Am I wrong for believing my life matters enough to deserve a second chance? And that I am capable of returning back to society, living a normal life and have such a strong desire to use my experiences and lessons learned to do good in my community?[90]

Porter's frustration is representative of the desperation that confronts those whose reflective labor will not be recognized by prisons or parole boards that refuse to acknowledge growth beyond crimes or convictions. This is growth that must be battled for inside boot camps in dehumanization—a fact as obvious to the incarcerated as it is opaque to those outside.

In Aeschylus's cycle of tragedies, *Oresteia* (458 BCE), King Agamemnon sacrifices the life of his daughter, Iphigenia, in order that the gods might turn the winds to carry the king and his troops to the Trojan War. Upon his return, his wife, Clytemnestra, murders her husband to avenge their daughter. Their son, Orestes, avenges his father by murdering his mother. He flees, harassed by the Furies. No further murder ensues because one of the earliest courtroom dramas in Western literature spares Orestes from becoming yet another victim of lethal vengeance. This cycle of plays champions the rule of law as a neutral, collective agreement against retributive vengeance.[91]

The writers cited here represent hundreds of thousands of others who see and hear, smell and taste and feel the corrosive effects of spaces where the institutionalized will for retribution has created mass-scale dehumanization masquerading as justice. Behind the force of lawmakers pushing race-fueled calls for vengeance in the name of crime victims, funded and enabled by a $180 billion criminal justice industry, justice has retreated by nearly two and a half millennia.[92] The mass prison's dismantling of the connections between crime and punishment, between punishment and the punished, and between punishment and the returning citizen has defeated what we might imagine retribution achieves. The scale of the generic and irrational pain that incarcerated people feel renders prison a lesson to the incarcerated in their own capacity to numb emotion and abandon moral sense. The effort to retain their humanity marks the imprisoned as virtual miracle workers within this dystopian environment.

Incarcerated people testify to the grinding on of a machine built to produce human failure, a machine that routinely thwarts the efforts of incarcerated people to reform their own thinking and actions. Rehabilitation is, after all, simply bad for a business sustained by the recycling of human misery. Rehabilitation, transformation, and reform do occur inside prisons and inside incarcerated people, but such change takes place only with herculean struggles against the currents of prison policies, practices, and culture. When imprisoned people do succeed in self-examination and transformation, they do so due to their own hard labor. "They always talking about how prison rehabilitates you," says a man imprisoned in Louisiana. "Prison don't rehabilitate you. You have to rehabilitate yourself."[93]

That work entails facing formidable obstacles and enacting small miracles.

3

DEFEATING REHABILITATION, PRISON RESISTANCE, AND TRANSFORMATION

> Because really, prison isn't designed for you to leave, it's designed to keep you. And I don't care what anybody says, you don't go in there to get better. Only the strong survive, and you have to fight to get better, and you have to fight and win.
> —SHERI DWIGHT, CALIFORNIA

> Everything starts with a thought. I am what I think I am. The prison conveys a non-verbal thought that I am unworthy and unredeemable, but I resist that.
> —DAVID JONES, TEXAS

THE gap between theories of a rehabilitative prison and what incarcerated people witness has rarely narrowed. The era often touted as taking up the rehabilitative charge most seriously led to rehabilitation's nearly wholesale rejection—even ridicule[1]—for a policy of containment and willful "penal harm."[2] This harm, as we have seen, is at once so profound and generic that it breaks the communicative bonds of meaningful retribution. We might well debate the borderline between punishment that admonishes and instructs, and punishment that diminishes and debilitates, but prison witness testimony documents a history of human degradation that has metastasized into a defining national industry.

It might thus seem redundant to marshal testimony to the absence of rehabilitative programming in US prisons today. Why gather witness to an absence? The reason is that incarcerated people can tell us not just what is missing, and why they think that is, but what they are doing every day to forge ahead with the project of self-transformation. They describe the work of maintaining their humanity and enacting self-transformation. They describe the few facility-run and many more volunteer-run programs that are truly effective, and they offer recommendations for change. If a rehabilitative prison were possible, they suggest what it might look like.

The following testaments may also be the most damning of American complacency with prison practice. They speak directly to the sleight-of-hand that much of the public has bought for over two centuries in order to live in comfort with the damage meted out in the name of public safety.

For nearly as long as we have claimed ourselves a nation, Americans have assumed two things about prisons: they should punish lawbreakers, and they should make lawbreakers into better people. We have rarely questioned how any single environment can do both, how cages can heal, how people hired to keep prisons secure can also make them curative, or how administrators can at once satisfy public fear and any hope for human transformation.[3]

The schism between theory and practice has persisted in part because alleviating public fear of lawbreakers and avoiding political backlash for appearing "soft on crime" have commonly taken precedent over vaguely articulated ideas about what good prisons might do, other than offer theatres of retributive containment.[4] What has greased a broken system into continuing operation is ingrained racism, classism, and moralizing that have erased worries about the rights or dignity of largely poor, nonwhite people who have been convicted. Any residual qualms have been salved by the belief that all convicted people deserve punishment, or by taking moral comfort in the assumption that incarceration is, in the end, good for those inside. The public, in effect, has accommodated spaces without legal accountability by resting astride the same unbridged divide that runs between prison practice and its boasted mission.

The lie of just deserts is seated in racism and resentment—in public imagination of what "those people" deserve. It hardens and embitters us and turns us against the best principles that founded the nation. When stories of inhumane actions, unjust sentences, rates of recidivism, and evidence of dehumanization do reach the public, the comforting lie of rehabilitation sets the background for temporary moral discomfort, even outrage, before settling back into simple dismissal as exceptional instances.[5] Incarcerated people are inoculated against the lie of just deserts simply by knowing themselves, the circumstances of their crimes, and their peers. But as we will see, in their expressions of shock, confusion, anger, and often desperate questioning in the face of what prisons either do or fail to do, the witnesses in this chapter present poignant examples of the depth of the rehabilitative myth in the American psyche. Even the poorest and most hyper-policed believe that prisons *are supposed* to be about reform.[6]

After years of reading and talking with men on Tennessee's death row, philosophy professor Lisa Guenther offers an assessment of the public service such men provide, suggesting one reason why any rehabilitative ethos disappeared half a century ago with hardly a word raised in objection.

> Their job is to provide a concrete illustration of evil, to contain this evil within a single body, and to allow themselves to be flushed out of the world through the apparently painless and humane procedure of lethal injection. By disappearing behind the mask of the villain, the monster, the cold-hearted killer, the death row inmate slips a sedative to the audience, allowing us to fall asleep at night knowing that our families are safe and that justice has been done.[7]

Living inside California prisons, Michael L. Owens sees what Guenther sees, as well as what we all stand to gain simply by being honest with ourselves and acting accordingly.

> Our country's prisons are not just the dumping ground for our nation's offenders. Prisons are, in a very real way, the psychic repository for our hatreds and shames; the place we can dump all of our loathing for what We find despicable in ourselves. By now most of us are aware that the US is the leading incarcerator of all time. We must somehow come to see our prisons as places to confront and heal our demons, instead of warehouses in which to hide them.[8]

This chapter is largely about the work of healing that incarcerated people are not waiting for others to authorize, fund, institute, and enable. It is about what's wrong, and it's about resisting dehumanization. It's about the labor of rehumanization and self-transformation, and what would obviate the need for the former and empower the latter. It's about answering Thomas Mott Osborne's question, "Shall our prisons be scrap heaps or human repair shops?"[9] with an answer Osborne might have entertained: That depends on whether we will listen closely enough to enact what the human beings inside have indicated they need.

The lie that prisons can be rehabilitative gave rise to the Progressive Era innovation of the indeterminate sentence: with sentences such as George Jackson's one year to life for a gas station holdup, prison time was determined by the opinions of prison staff, administrators, and parole boards, rather than by sentencing judges. Convicted people would be released when they were deemed ready by those writing prison records and by the politically appointed members of parole boards. This system assumed that whatever rehabilitative programs were in place were accessible, effective and adequate, that staff records were objective (unaffected by race, politics, or personality), and that parole board members appointed by politicians were not working primarily to protect those politicians from the potential fallout of headline recidivists. The indeterminate sentence was forward-looking, humane, and delusional. At their best, as Gresham Sykes observed in 1958, such sentences were "calling for an operation where the target of the scalpel remains unknown."[10] Julilly Kohler-Hausmann writes of the critics of such sentences, "They charged that cloaking these oppressive functions with benevolent, therapeutic rationales shielded their true operation but also legitimized them."[11] Rehabilitation programs, rather than lifting people up, cast a threat: they sorted the "corrigible" from the "incorrigible," the latter to be confined indefinitely and heavily determined by race. This judgment was also weighted by class, and by the political, religious, and cultural beliefs of the imprisoned and their keepers. "Although the commitment to rehabilitation was a central ideological column that supported the criminal justice system," Kohler-Hausmann writes, "these programs were sustained more by their usefulness to politicians and prison authorities than by their ability to fulfill their promise"; "the indeterminate sentence's ability to adjust to an individual's unique circumstances was its most innovative, promising feature. In practice, it produced what appeared to many prisoners as uneven and arbitrary administration and the antithesis of justice."[12] As one incarcerated man testified, parole board members were indifferent to behavior records or achievements: "They want prisoners who are conformists, whose spirits have been broken. What they can't take is a man with pride."[13] As bad as indeterminate sentences were, the alternative has accelerated prison numbers to those we see today: mandatory minimums tie the hands of judges who might fit sentences to the circumstances of crime, and they obviate personal assessment, leaving rehabilitation to the convicted. The testimony of imprisoned people can point us toward prisons that see most of their wards only once, allowing prisons to shrink in the direction of vanishing, even as they begin to proffer hope.[14]

Though she writes about men condemned to death, Guenther concludes with an observation that resonates across every state and federal facility: "There are countless prisoners on death row who are working harder than we can imagine to transform themselves and to build a meaningful sense of community. We could learn a lot from these people if we weren't so determined to kill them."[15]

REHABILITATION'S FAILURES: RATIONALES, PERSONNEL, RESPONSE

In *Golden Gulag*, Ruth Wilson Gilmore documents how California's prison system was transformed from one of the most progressive in the nation into a site for absorbing excess capital and labor. Her work describes what has occurred across the nation: prisons have become a major tax-supported industry and one of the nation's largest employment sectors.[16] Incarcerated people have seen this change from inside; they regularly describe an industry whose interests would be subverted by making people better. Marquis Gilliam writes from Wisconsin, "I often find myself wondering what these wardens are really thinking and why nothing is changing. Well I guess if things start to change for the greater good they wouldn't have jobs."[17] In Ohio, "the prison system knows exactly what it's doing," writes Nicholas A. Hale, "by not informing its customers of living right because they would be out of business and that's not ideal."[18] Oklahoman James Bauhaus agrees: "The game of 'justice and corrections' is to ever enlarge their pool of victims-slaves, never to diminish it. Despite any high-sounding programs they may pronounce, no bureaucracy willingly cuts its power or shrinks its size."[19] Amanda C. Gatlin writes of a Tennessee prison where "I became like an animal being fed through a fence. . . . Having to fight for my right to exist and never completely succeeding. I'm only a number in this maximum security hell. I wish this would end, but they wouldn't get their payday, would they?"[20] Ricky Pendleton writes from West Virginia, "I think rehabilitation is a propaganda word used by the lawmakers to cover their motives. Exploiting the inmates in a business venture. How do I cope in a place like this, by being warehoused in a prison like a produce with an item number?"[21] Arkansan Daniel Hagen writes what he believes stands behind talk in his state of helping imprisoned people: "The guise of rehabilitation is a funnel by which the A.D.C. sucks allocated money from the state legislature and federal government sources—the taxpayers."[22] From California, "Prison officials . . . have no concern on how we live in here," Manitas writes, "so long as their 8 hour shifts pay. Overtime or lockdown just means more pay. . . . Entering prison isn't going to make a difference. Prison is just being buried alive."[23]

Paul S. Johnson sees in California a wider story played out across the nation: "Cops only go after the poor & homeless. Were easy targets for them. They can physically & mentally abuse us and not be fired, in fact usually there promoted, for there abuse! We are treated like zoo animals as prisoners, and rehabilitation is a joke." He lists the range of criminal justice job sectors that rehabilitative efforts might threaten: "from politicians, courts, law enforcement, guards, medical staff, down to construction workers who mass build these modern day hell holes!"[24]

From Michigan, Charles Brooks Sr. describes a system whose limited rehabilitative offerings are so antiquated, restricted, or expensive, they might as well not exist at all.[25] From Wyoming, Michael Flores laments that the absence of effective programming perpetuates the current system.[26] From Florida, James Lawson-Wilson writes that

> if more men and women were to leave prison a more productive and law abiding citizen, whom could act as a role model for our youth heading down the same path . . . then the prison complex would virtually collapse under its own burdensome weight. . . . Call me a cynic, but . . . the system is not broken, but a well-oiled machine that is doing exactly what it was designed to do, keep the beds full.[27]

Pennsylvanian Burl Corbet sees how the public will to punish overreaches the will to reform.

Many of these rehabilitative courses and programs were conceived during an era of relative prosperity. But when the public learned the many hidden costs of mandatory sentences and the attached bureaucracies that attend them like flocks of glutenous seagulls pursuing a garbage scow, they demanded reductions in everything except the number of incoming prisoners.[28]

Incarcerated people see a system both so cynical and financially self-perpetuating, finding the resources to make positive changes inside themselves must be pursued in the face of environments that teach disrespect for the very system touted as a bulwark against social disorder. Enysia Rosado testifies from Connecticut to the need for incarcerated people to take a stand for themselves.

> Personally, prison has zero resources to rehabilitate and mend a broken person. As women we need to learn how to maintain a healthy lifestyle without abuse, neglect and abandonment. When will the system learn to help us instead of mistreat us? Seems like they never will, because this is a however many dollar industry. As long as the door keeps revolving with unhealthy beings these unfit prison conditions will remain. This includes the mold in our rooms or the brown water we're suppose to drink. It's deplorable! Never mind the inhuman 20-24 hours a day in a less than 8x10 cell. As proficient individuals we need to learn how to change ourselves, in spite of the odds. We shall stand up for what we believe in and empower others.[29]

James Barstad writes from Washington State.

> The prison has taught me nothing that will assist me if and when I am able to go home. Their only concern is that I do the time. I can waste away in the yard playing cards if I want to. The State has these "evidence-based programs" that they always want to promote. . . . They only tested in five prisons. The professor who made the program stated that his findings were not even completed yet, and that it was not meant for a prison setting. . . . The real "evidence" is that the State will be able to get some federal funding to promote the program. That is the bottom line. The only programs I have found in prison that I think are worth

anything at all came from volunteers. They are not promoted (sometimes even deterred) by the State and cost the taxpayers nothing. The State will then only admit that there is "anecdotal evidence" that these programs work. They will not recognize any true evidence that does not pad their pockets. They know that education will prevent people from entering prisons, but they still spend seven prison dollars for each education dollar.[30]

Whether explicit financial motives can be documented among prison administrators, lawmakers, or staff, we should be alarmed and take heed of the fact that the prison's inhabitants see such motivations as the primary cause of their degrading conditions. Held in Texas, Mary Ann Jalomos sees the same cynical math.

The mental, physical, emotional & spiritual stress a person goes through is compacted by the fact that TCDJ does not truly want to help an inmate get on the road to rehabilitation. Their job is recidivism. Can't make money if they work with the inmate/offender to make a better life for themselves by making better decisions in life.[31]

Ineffective, tax-funded programs are a problem most would condemn. Programs can also virtually announce themselves to incarcerated people as mere time fillers. April Dawn Pineda writes from California.

I sit in my 10 by 4 concrete cell with a blue steel door, with no visibility out a purposely fogged out window, (so we can't see the sky, for what reason I do not know) with a hatch for our meals in a maximum level 4 unit locked down for 23 hours a day to the beat of commercials, banging, clanging and screaming at all hours of the day. I'm at Elmwood Correctional facility in Milpitas California and have been in maximum level security ever since I've banged on a door without stopping back in 2014. My behavior has been what it can only be back in these remote, forgotten parts of the jail, muted and subdued, yet I am denied from our classification to down class, although I have completed the only two programs they allow back here several times over, meaning I complete the same "cycle" of material to receive a certificate . . . then, upon the end of that program, we just begin at the same never ending cycle again,

over and over, just like the commercials, TV shows, CO's and their attitudes picking favorites and bringing their petty jealousies and feelings
to work.[32]

Nashay M. Ziegler-Wurtz describes what goes on behind the mission
statements for South Dakota prisons.

> Women offenders here have very few resources and services available
> for them to re-entry. A big credit this prison once had was the IMT
> program (Intense Meth Program). Ten years ago, this program was
> praised for having a very high success rate for drug offenders. Now this
> program is non-existent. Judges all over South Dakota sentence women
> here to complete this program that no longer exists due to no staff. We
> currently have only one chemical dependency counselor that juggles
> intakes with one other part time gal along with the only running class—
> MRT (moral recognition therapy). The mental health staff employed is
> just as slim, with only two mental health counselors, no secretary, and
> a director that just resigned on the spot. For a prison with a popula-
> tion of roughly seven-hundred women—I'll let you guess the number
> of women who actually will benefit from any help behind the walls of
> my current correctional facility. I am a statistic; I am one of the many
> women here that was sent to receive classes, programming for rehabili-
> tation, and treatment. Instead I have sat idle, seeking my own rehabilita-
> tion through my own efforts and luckily having the resources to become
> the first inmate incarcerated in this correctional facility to take college
> courses. I'm sure this is just one of many facilities that portrays in their
> mission, value and vision statements that they strive for "practices that
> maximize the opportunities for rehabilitation for offenders . . ." when in
> reality resources and services available are non-existent for us.[33]

Michigan writer India Porter laments a similar absence of programming
aimed at successful transition back into the free world. She writes for
thousands of others, eddying in dead time that might be used to prepare
people for successful reentry.

> Why doesn't this "Department of Corrections" have any type of pro-
> gramming to help me deal with the issues that have caused me to of-

fend? There is no sexual abuse groups for victims, there is no insight and accountability available, nothing for an assaultive offender until you are one year within your earliest release date. I have been incarcerated for 13 years now, and I do not qualify for any groups or programs that promote rehabilitation until 2026. According to the Department of Corrections stipulations I have to spend another 11-12 years just existing. There is no computer literacy training, when everything in society is computer based. After being locked up for 13 years, the world I knew before I came is very different from the world right now, I am going to leave one day and prison is doing nothing to help me prepare to eventually re-enter society. Because of inmate mail policy, I cannot purchase a book that would at least give me basic instruction on how to operate and navigate on-line. I am not allowed to purchase books on business or real estate. I am a person who wants to change positively in every way I can. It is extremely hard for me because I feel "trapped" in an environment that doesn't promote or support that change. When I wake up in the morning my options consist of: Do I get up and sit in the activity room all day and play cards or table top games? Or do I hang out on the yard or gym? or maybe I'll stay in my cell all day, since because of over-crowding issues I'm only allowed 2 hours of activity room usage a day? Every day I feel that I am here just existing.[34]

Many incarcerated writers point to staff attitudes and physical conditions whose perpetuation conveys just how little society believes imprisoned people and any efforts at rehabilitation are worth. Fredrick M. T. Pearson writes from South Carolina of the psychological reaction this sets off.

The environment and conditions of the prison system builds resentment. You first hate your conditions. Then you hate your society for allowing such conditions. And finally, you start to hate yourself for falling victim. And the man who hates himself has no interest in reforming himself. In the South Carolina Department of Corrections ("SCDC") rehabilitation is not a priority. It's all about custody & control. . . . When the officer approach your cell, he is hostile and unnecessarily aggressive. The smells are of bad hygiene, decay, and mold. . . . Your provoked by staff. Treated worse than most people treat their animals. . . . Trying to do the right thing is so hard, because the staff imposes so many obstacles for the prisoner who wants to better himself. It's nothing to hear an officer say something like, "you dont deserve nothing," or "we waste our tax money on yall, for what? Yall are not meant to be in society."[35]

Best-selling author Shaka Senghor recalls from a Michigan prison, "I had been working every day to better myself and learn how to resolve conflict through the proper channels, but I realized that rubbed a lot of officers the wrong way."[36] SKS Heruglyphx Maga Neteru writes from a state he chooses not to name.

> Correction/rehabilitation cannot be genuine where DOC is not leading by example, where officers are behaving like overseers, brutes, thugs, goons, ruffians, and mercenaries for the state, which automatically and guaranteeingly grant unlimited impunity for all atrocities against prisoners. Genuine correction/rehabilitation cannot start with the prisoners, it must begin with the DOC.[37]

From Wyoming, Steven A. DeLogé offers a broad overview of how far we stand from where we could be, and the shift in thinking needed to start that movement.

> We could get back to the place where we value our citizens as worthwhile human beings and focus on rehabilitating them as productive members of our society. We could stop paying employees just to show up and get actual return on our investment. We could let our prison system become a self-sustaining factory of rehabilitation, rather than an overpriced dog kennel that churns out anti-social and angry miscreants. We have become a society that has little or no concern for its most valuable resource—its citizens. Our judges, prosecutors, police forces and citizens all seem to agree that if a person runs afoul of the law, that person has forfeited the right to be human and deserves to freeze to death in the dark while being brutalized by fellow convicts.[38]

Paul J. Kiser reports from Kansas on how security staff training negatively affects prison atmospheres where imprisoned people must find the means to change themselves.[39] Kareem Davenport sees the thinking that underlies the removal of rehabilitative programming and the attitudes of staff in Illinois. He articulates again a common perception of the public consensus that has allowed American prisons to go so wrong.

> The purpose it seems now is to put you in prison to undergo inhumane conditions and deprive you of your humanity and place in society. We are looked at as heathens, barbarians, not worthy of society, menaces, a burden to the world, and meant to be left in a cell to die. . . . A man is shot down by an officer it is a national outbreak. An inmate beaten to death by a gang or officer in prison, no one cares. No one has any emotion about it, if any feeling at all society feels as if the inmate deserved it. This is the opinion, without even knowing a single fact about this man.[40]

The desire for treatment, training, and education is widespread among incarcerated people. Those desires are met by systems that have decided in advance that nothing works, and staff who have adopted that attitude.[41] The result is predictable, as Cesar A. Avila writes from California.

> When I ask if I can be transferred to a prison where my rehabilitation needs and wants will be met, I'm laughed at. . . . I'm a hungry person that wants to be versatile in a positive way once I re-enter the real world. According to the staff here, though, my petitions to assist me in my journey of self-transformation are a waste of time and money. Do you know how that makes me feel? Hopeless, angry, resentful, depressed, bitter, and anxious are a few of the emotions I experience on a somewhat daily basis. I do what I can to stay mentally, emotionally, physically, spiritually, and intellectually strong, making the best out of nothing. There's times when I wish I could be in a classroom and be called upon by a professor or instructor so that I could show time invested in me is not in vain. . . . My way of thinking and doing time productively can be found among other inmates in other prisons, it's not just me.[42]

From Texas, sentenced to life in prison for a crime committed at the age of fifteen, Meagan Adams writes that in the past 16 years many things have become clear and many lessons have been learned. Among the things I've grown to see clearly is the fact that prison is not meant to rehabilitate. Prison is punitive at best and dysfunctionally abusive at worst. Somehow the children, like myself, have to wade through the muck and chaos of prison to figure out who we are and how we'll rise above. Sadly, I've seen many young people lose their true essence to conform to the dysfunction of their surroundings.[43]

Open antagonism, inadequate training, indifference, incompetence, and aggression among security staff are not the only challenges people face in seeking transformation. L. Mack-Lemdon writes from Michigan that the ethos of security affects the attitudes of trained professionals as well.

RTP [a mental health program] is mostly ran by corrections officers who, for the most part, are not properly trained in the mental health field and the "real" mental health staff, although they perform the task, have so greatly adopted the attitudes, behaviors, characteristics, and personality of corrections that it further denies the mentally ill of an authentic therapeutic environment. In other words, most MDOC "CLIP ON" agencies, such as health care and mental health, are more concerned with custody and other MDOC related matters rather than with the professionalism of their own occupation.[44]

Confined in the Colorado Department of Corrections, Tommy Lee Dean describes the danger of blocking his desire for change.

It's hard enough for me to change without the additional discouragement from my captors. . . . I feel like no matter how hard I keep trying to do something positive, they don't want me to achieve such positivity in my life, which leads to me wanting to show them just how negative it can all get.

He goes on to describe the story of a man, released straight from solitary, who went on a crime and murder spree: "From what I understand, Evan was as well trying to pursue positive goals at one point. He wanted to take college courses. . . . But, how bad do things have to get before punishment is replaced with true rehabilitation?"[45]

Jon R. Morgan describes an Illinois system in which rehabilitative programs are disappearing, pushing hope beyond reach.[46] In Mississippi, Joseph R. Dickey sees not punishment suited to individuals or their behaviors, but a "one size fits all approach," leading to "people getting out with no experience of why one does what is right."[47] Vincent Calamia is held in a federal prison in New Jersey; he notes that, even when programs do exist, they are often inaccessible to those who need them most.[48]

New York writer Dean Faiello reflects many of these views as he describes the paucity of helpful program offerings, the slim chances of getting into those that do exist, and the profound help offered by the unpaid volunteers and volunteer programs that give their time to incarcerated people. He also writes of the challenges of enacting unaided self-transformation, and the inspiration he gets from a man imprisoned for over half a century. Like many incarcerated people, Faiello finds his steadiest supports not in a system that calls itself correctional, but in other incarcerated people and outsiders who give their time from a simple sense of human decency.

> The parole board wants prisoners to take drug abuse and anti-violence programs before granting them freedom. Yet Attica's waiting lists for those programs hold over two thousand names. Some men have been incarcerated for more than twenty years before getting the opportunity to take State mandated programs. . . . I was incarcerated for eight years before being granted the opportunity to participate in a State drug program.
>
> . . . I've received no vocational training whatsoever. . . . For nearly four years, I've worked toward a two-year degree in a college program. Embracing change, I attend Alternatives to Violence Project workshops and meditation sessions.[49] . . . I visit the prison library. The newspapers are weeks old. . . . When I arrive at the school building that houses the library, most of the classrooms are dark; the desks are vacant. . . .
>
> As I watched Richie patiently create a sylvan scene with watercolors, I had no doubt that he has undergone a transformation. . . .

After fifty years in prison, he is a college graduate who worked at Attica's vocational shop making memorial plaques for Corrections Officers who have died. After a religious epiphany, Richie converted to Quakerism and attends prison Quaker meetings every Friday night. He mentors young men who have just arrived in prison, and teaches them artistic skills. When I was taking a college art class, he helped me with a charcoal and pencil portrait, patiently demonstrating the technique of chiaroscuro. When I had nothing to read because the prison library was inaccessible (closed nights and weekends), Richie lent me books. I read about meditation, Buddhism, the Quakers, and Viktor Frankl's theory of logotherapy—finding meaning in life. . . . In *Man's Search For Meaning*, Viktor Frankl wrote that prisoners need a reason to get up in the morning, that such purpose provides the motivation, the will, to survive prison, to overcome the daily suffering and humiliation. . . .

Attica employs 585 Corrections Officers, but only one Counselor for the Alcohol & Substance Abuse Treatment program. In view of the fact that eighty percent of crimes involve the use of alcohol or drugs, such a lack of drug treatment programs is myopic. . . . How can rehabilitation take place when those yearning for change, for education, have few if any opportunities to participate in programs, to find seats in classrooms. Fortunately, compassionate volunteers from neighboring communities come to Attica on a regular basis to help prisoners embrace transformation and adapt to change. At night, Attica's chapel often resounds with music as Protestant Volunteers lead men in hymns and chorals. Catholic priests teach Bible classes where men read holy scripture and reflect upon passages and verses. . . . Although I remain a Catholic, I attend lectures on Buddhist philosophy, Protestant services and Quaker meetings as a guest—a traveler seeking alms and enlightenment. . . . While counting breaths, I meditated, letting anguish and hostility escape through the steel casement windows and be absorbed by fat clouds reflecting a tangerine sunset.[50]

Closing out this section, from his perspective in Utah, Tom J. Orton offers the facts that belie the public-facing claims about imprisonment's rehabilitative mission.

We teach felons to:

1- Be responsible by taking away all their responsibilities.
2- Be trustworthy by disbelieving most everything they say.
3- Be non-violent by injustice, abuse of authority, and putting them where hostility surrounds them.
4- Be kind and loving by demeaning them & subjecting them to cruelty & hatred.
5- Stop being a tough guy by putting them where tough guys are most respected.
6- Stop exploiting others by exploiting inmates having medical needs, making phone calls to loved ones & their purchasing of commissary, books & music CD's usually at higher than retail prices.
7- Be independent by making them reliant upon us & by incessantly telling them what they can & cannot do or threatening with write ups.
8- Be vital contributing members of society by labeling & isolating them.
9- Have a sense of self worth by breaking their spirit & destroying what's left of their self esteem.
10- Move forward by constantly reminding them of their past.
11- Be productive by depriving them of jobs & education opportunities.
12- Make better choices by making every decision for them.
13- Be rational in their thinking by often providing ridiculous answers, illogical rules, policies & procedures.
14- Be individuals by mass punishing & using a cookie cutter or, "one size fits all" approach, especially towards inmates in any kind of treatment.
15- Be merciful by refusing to have compassion for them.
16- To have integrity by being less than honest about our motives & responses to their legitimate questions.
17- To get help for their problems by discounting or negating their feelings & punish them further from their confessions of "coming clean."
18- To be respectful by being rude & insolent towards them all, even those who've shown civility towards us.
19- To have a strong support group of good, productive & well-rounded citizens in the community by unnecessarily frustrating their visits, phone calls, mail, money, property, jobs, housing, etc. at every turn from anybody trying to be supportive.

20- To have realistic expectations & to be rational in their thinking by enforcing illogical unreasonable rules, policies & procedures.

21- To stop their criminal behavior by oppressing them & subjecting them to a state of being or condition where "The fox is guarding the hen house."

22- To make proper use of the established system by ruling against them at every grievance & either taking away their privileges or moving them to a more restrictive living area to gain compliance.

23- To trust in the legal system by only giving justice to those with lots of money &/or influence, & who can afford a powerful attorney.

24- To maintain hope for a good future by telling the public they are monsters who can't be trusted & should not be hired, or allowed to advance to better positions. And that's if they're ever let out in the first place.[51]

Orton's list represents what incarcerated people experience, and either sink beneath or rise to resist and overcome in prisons in every state and federal jurisdiction. Yet many imprisoned people manage to do the work that prisons will not aid: to retain or restore the sense of their own humanity, transforming their thinking and behavior, despite the environments in which they live.

RESISTING DEHUMANIZATION, PURSUING SELF-TRANSFORMATION

In order to resist dissolution of identity and hardening of heart and mind, incarcerated people must find within themselves the resources to maintain their sense of humanity. It rests upon the imprisoned to make themselves better than what the prison would make of them.

After a young man is killed inside the facility where he is held, A. Whitfield reflects on the change he has wrought in himself and the labor of maintaining that change despite the ethos inside a New York State prison.

> Most conversations center on who did the stabbing and how much time he might get in the box.
>
> We identify with the perpetrator rather than the victim, even though the victim is one of us. It scares the hell out of me to think this. . . .
>
> I can't help but wonder how awful those last few moments must have been for the man I killed. (I have long since accepted responsibility for

the act.) The thought is repugnant to me, and I tell myself with conviction and sincerity that the creature I was then is not the man I am now. I am more of a human being for detesting and condemning my actions, yet less of a human being for having committed the act.

I struggle. Transformation is difficult in any environment, but in prison the helplessness and hopelessness can be overwhelming. . . . And I have to face the fear that my newfound concept of what it is to be human is an illusion, that it is fostered by mistaken beliefs, that I will be forced to confront obstacles too large for me to overcome, and not have the moral strength to sustain my humanity. I'm scared I'll wake up one morning to look in the mirror and see the monster that was once me staring back, ready to devour me. . . .

. . . Soon I'll hear the dull, metallic clunk-clank signaling the opening of the cell gates for the evening rec', but I won't stir. . . . In the last few years I venture from my cell less and less. Watching other men pass, sliced up by the bars of my cell, I know that I won't find the solace I seek by walking circles around the prison yard.[52]

Like A. Whitfield, many incarcerated people struggle to shore up inner resolve. Others rebuild through self-education. In "Finding Freedom inside of Prison," Stacy Shaw links his awakening in a Missouri prison to educating himself in the history of collective Black struggle.

In retrospect I was just as much a slave to the system as my beautiful ancestors were slaves to "White America" hundreds of years ago. . . . Perusing through the cathartic story of Malcolm X strongly motivated me to begin the journey of self-education; hearing about the stalwart expeditions of Marcus Garvey imparted in me the necessary wherewithal to lead towards ethical prosperity. . . . All that I have spoken on thus far can be summed up with one thought: I have truly found the meaning of "FREEDOM" . . . Until we as people take the time to get to know who we truly are, where we came from, and where we are trying to go, we will remain in a bottomless pit of nothingness.[53]

Shaw climbs out of that pit by situating himself among others, if only through reading. Among witnesses who find themselves reduced to numbered versions of each other, to "puppet-zero[s]," replicated at mass scale, becoming fully human is often discovered in scenes of simple connection with other human beings—connections that prison environments seem built to break. Any bond with another human being affirms one's humanity and resists becoming a faceless statistic. George Whitham recalls the unlikely friendship he formed in Massachusetts with a man named Billy, born into a family as violently abusive as his own, and condemned like himself to die in prison.

> For the first time in my life [after a close friend outside died], I felt a kind of pain that no pill could relieve. It was my good friends here who propped me up and carried me through the toughest period of my life. Billy was right there every inch of the way; without their help I don't know where I would have been. I did contemplate suicide, but I was smothered with love from Billy and my friends. Not once did the prison give a rat's ass. . . . It was a group of men who society deemed unworthy to be on the streets who nursed me back into a functioning human being.
>
> [On Billy's deathbed] I gave him a hug. I didn't care what the others thought. Love and compassion are not common sights in this place. While I was hugging him I whispered that I hadn't been able to comfort him and ease his pain. In a soft whisper he said, *You've been a good friend.* . . .
>
> In the years since Billy's passing much has happened. . . . I finally recognize myself as a caring human being who's not just a con number or a statistic. I now try to help others as Billy helped me.
>
> The prison system still grinds its slowly turning wheels. . . . There is one thing the system never figured on, and that was that one of its occupants, one of its numbers, would become a human being who feels and cares.[54]

Michael Arreygue writes of the support he found inside a prison cell in California, where friendship helped him to "realize alot of things about myself and became a better person."[55] Corey J. Richardson embraces his identity for the first time after he falls in love inside a Kentucky prison.

> He said before he left that I had changed him forever. I felt the same, and still do. After having truly been loved for the first time in my life, I

found that I was finally proud to be myself without reservations; I was glad to have been born gay, and maybe now I could find real love once upon my release.[56]

Arizona writer Levert Brookshire III describes "developing my leadership skills and the ways in which I use them, to influence others" as intrinsic to his ability to "resist that 'psychological' hold over me and keep taking my mind in the direction I want to go."[57] Louisiana writer Albert Woodfox documents the bond between himself and two fellow Black Panthers who, largely due to their solidarity, survived decades of solitary confinement: "Behind the pain, the betrayals, the brutality, and the disappointments, Herman, King, and I existed somewhere, unhurt and together."[58] Confined in Maine, Arline Lawless documents her return to herself through the generous goading of other incarcerated women.

> Some women here are still in segregation because they can't handle all the [staff-induced] stress here. I was one of those women, only I was not put into segregation. I just stayed in my room and never came out except for meds and sometimes meals. . . . I was going to sleep my bid away. This worked for almost 2 years. However, there were some women here that I am so glad to have met, just wish that it were under different circumstances they would come to my door and bang on it and yell, "You get out of that bed right now and you come out here and play spades with us." I can tell you that that really boosted my confidence that there were women here that actually gave a shit about me.[59]

Although finding moments of communion with other incarcerated people can serve as a path to reclaiming one's humanity, privacy is also a scarce resource inside prisons packed with people living in planned deprivation. Such spaces so turn people against one another that moments of quiet separation can be as valued as human bonds. Alabaman Donald Hairgrove finds in private acts of writing a means of humanization.

> Only in written words have I found my way of doing time. Writing for myself as well as for others, depending on meager support from loved ones, have I survived, but my only escape, my only privacy has

come from my written words. With a pen I am allowed the liberty to say, to express—"TO FEEL," and when the words are thrown away or destroyed, forever banished by fire, then there can never be reprisal for my rebelliousness. Thereby I will have been in touch, through my pen and paper, with contumacy or tenderness and whatever strength that is within me . . . and I have survived.[60]

Josef M. Jensen reports that, in California prisons,

the daily events on any level-four prison yards are enough to drive a sane man insane. . . . You don't have the time for self-reflection or the luxury. It wasn't until I "locked it up" that the atmospheric noise sub- sided enough to allow me to hear my own thoughts and the recrimina- tions of my conscience.

He goes on to articulate what he has learned from such quiet moments: to honestly face lessons from the past in order to change his thinking in the present. This is an achievement that the founders of the penitentiary hoped to realize, and that today's prisons appear designed to interrupt.

I have spent the last twelve years of my life thinking about what I have done yesterday to get me where I am today. . . . This has become an almost religious practice. Trying to find the subtle ways things are con- nected, how they have affected events years, decades later has become like a ritual I perform as part of my obligation to remember the past. It is an obligation I owe the past; that I owe to what has happened. It is just something I do almost unconsciously in those quiet moments when I can still my mind long enough to disentangle myself from the exterior noise of the world around me. . . .

Being honest about my past and what I have done is very hard for me. I have done things in my life that I am not proud of, things that I would take back, or undo if I could. If we are to understand who and where we are in our lives, we must admit it all to ourselves, and then others. We must do so with all of the accompanying fear and trepidation that accompanies such honesty. Honesty is rarely an all at once kind of thing. There are some things that you just can't be honest about until you are honest about others. You have to walk the minefield very carefully disarming each piece of the past in turn until you have a clear path. . . . Find new meaning, and new significance in old and familiar ideas, experiences and beliefs. . . . I was scared to admit these things, especially to myself. What makes it worse is that even if I had been willing to peel back the covers of my life, I didn't have the eyes to see what was there. That would be something I would need to develop and nurture as I went. . . . Honesty is a powerful thing, a life changing thing. Honesty has the power to dissolve the self doubt and lack of understanding that allows despair and hopelessness to creep into our lives; to destroy the shadows in which the monsters of self loathing, self hatred, misery and anger hide.[61]

Benjamin Rush could hardly have written a better outline of what prisons should achieve; Josef Jensen got there only by rejecting and finding moments of mental separation from his environment. Shariff Ingram writes from Pennsylvania, like Josef Jensen, about not only surviving in prison, but resisting its dehumanizing effects: "For those who know me, they commend me for not letting these places destroy me. To still be holding onto my sanity, still trying to better myself whether I get out or not, not allow these places to turn me into an animal like they do so many others."[62] Such testament to the labor of resisting the prison's debilitating effects is commonly explicit, when it is not implied, as in Christopher Balmer's advice from Pennsylvania: "View yourself as worthy and your future will be worth creating."[63] Laura L. Purviance gives neither advice nor instruction from California; she simply states what she faces, her hope, and her resolve.

I'm uncomfortably aware of the psychological control games and policies I must live under, and I don't want to be an institutionalized ward of the state for the rest of my life. I like to believe I'm not a disposable human being. I want to prove I'm so much more than the worst moment of my life, so I do my best moving forward, living my amends.[64]

Enysia Rosado offers assessment, advice, and encouragement. She too sees that prison presents a horrible opportunity to challenge one's worst fears and vulnerabilities.

Little to nothing good comes from being jailed. Fortunately for me I am at a point in my life where all I want to do is change. I refuse to continue being a product of my environment. Not everyone is at a stage in their life where they're willing to change. . . . A lot of us have trauma and trauma affects everyone differently. . . . You too can change your life. . . . When you fall or fail, gather your broken pieces and begin to remold and reshape. We're all works of art in progress.[65]

This sense of responsibility to take what they have learned from their experience and help others, directly in opposition to the prison's effects, is common among those who have managed to grasp their full humanity despite all that prisons can do.[66] In offering advice, these writers draw maps of their own paths to restored hope. The next step is to move beyond humanization, to self-transformation. The results of this work are the signature products of resistance to prisons that thwart constructive ends.

A truism of recovery literature is that the subject of recovery must want to change. That desire often comes at the point when all excuses have been exhausted, when the addict or alcoholic or reckless gambler has devastated their own and others' lives. Whether or not drugs, alcohol, or other addictions led them to where they are, many people feel they have reached bottom once they have been locked up, making them seemingly ideal subjects of recovery efforts.[67] Yet what incarcerated people report is a system that systematically misses that opportunity, piling ridicule onto people in whom the work of self-assessment and transformation is thus all the more remarkable. Writing from Missouri, Sheldon D. Bush understands that no one will help him but himself, that responsibility for change rests solely on his own shoulders.

I'm a person that made a mistake, but all they [staff] see is the mistake that I've made, every day they talk to me and treat me less than a repeat con man. They look down on me and stretch their holy laws and rules to the fullest extent, trying to break me and every other offender, instead of trying to reform me. But, then again I have to be the one responsible for reforming me. I have a golden chance, and I'll do everything that I have to do to set an example for me. Nothing will change unless I put in a positive effort to make a difference.[68]

Keith Burley, held in Pennsylvania, knows that freedom of mind will not come from the institution but in rising above it.

> Our ability to recognize the truth is a form of freedom necessary for growth and development. Being able to find strength in one's moment of weakness is the catalyst of change. To triumph over ones trials and shortcomings regardless of time and place is a freedom of which even the most valuable of jewels pale in comparison. For when one recognizes truth, he is not plagued by the dis-eases of doubt and delusions. So he becomes free in accordance to what the word "freedom" denotes; even if walls confine him!!![69]

From Wyoming, J. D. Frandsen describes anger to the point of madness that arbitrarily imposed solitary confinement can induce. He describes struggling with aimless thinking and self-recrimination. Yet he goes on to describe how

> profound clarification of the mind through focused meditation is absolutely obtainable in any environment, even one that reeks of urine and sadness. . . .
>
> After arriving, I clean the parking space sized cell as best I can and set up a comfortable practice space. Blankets and bedding are sometimes provided, but most of the time these are withheld for days, or weeks. I do some light stretching to get limber. A quick splash in the sink then I'm ready to sit. Once the screaming and banging blends into a tolerable white noise, I focus on my breath. The abrasive ego dissolves and my internal dialogue shuts off like the flipping of a switch. A wave of genuine peace, wellbeing and unconditional love surrounds me, envelops me, permeates my soul and resonates through the bricks, the barbed wire and throughout the infinite reaches of the universe. In this place, where psychosis and mental breakdowns are so common, I have found a peace unlike any other. No one can ever strip away my true identity as a being of infinite loving light. Meditation practice pushes me toward the path of knowledge and an altruistic objective. It leaves me in a state of heightened awareness that is absolutely divine. This prison is my home, I belong here. My physical self maybe ensnared, but my spirit is free, and I am truly content.[70]

While the love Frandsen articulates wells up from within, the key factor in Abraham Hagos's transformation inside a Colorado prison was also not anything done for him between prison walls but his sense of responsibility to those outside. As is so often the case, his idea of what rehabilitation requires has been wrested from many years inside.

> It is important to understand that rehabilitation is an ongoing process. It's like a stream that flows on and on through different sceneries and environments. . . . On a personal level, for me, after almost 17 years in prison, I have a clearer perspective on life, family, friends, society and most importantly myself. When you can honestly admit to yourself the wrong you have done, whether it was to a friend, family, the community, wife, children, a stranger, whoever it was to that's when rehabilitation really begins. . . . The key elements for me that caused me to change my thought process was my family and my true friends. By realizing how my incarceration has affected them so negatively has provided me the core reason for me yearning for change. . . . The key is to unlock the psychological, physical, emotional restraints that we place upon ourselves. Once we achieve that we will truly begin the rehabilitation process.[71]

When such self-determination is in force, often directly in the face of prison practices and culture, incarcerated people find paths to change that no court, prison official, or penologist is likely to imagine. Confined inside a New York State prison, Intelligent Allah reflects on how taking on the formidable challenge of committing to a vegan lifestyle in prison, where the mainline diet features unnamed meats and processed foods, has transformed his sense of self and purpose.

> Becoming a vegan was inextricably linked to my maturing from the reckless 17-year-old teen that entered prison in 1994 into the responsible 34-year-old man I am in 2010. I discovered discipline through overcoming my appetite. I began applying this trait to suppress my temper, resolve conflicts and excel in other aspects of my life like education and exercise. Learning of the environmental and moral implications of an animal-free diet helped foster my growing empathy for people I had hurt. I had rarely considered the feelings of people who were

not my friends, because I had been desensitized to violence within the 5.5-square miles of the crime-infested streets of East New York, Brooklyn where I was raised. But Veganism helped me develop a worldview that entails my understanding and concern for how my actions—dietary choices and otherwise—effect our environment and other beings in our global community. I became a man determined to reclaim his humanity by embracing all life.[72]

For many incarcerated people, the commitment to self-transformation comes from simple disgust and exhaustion with what they witness of the prison conditions and the behavior of staff. William Smith Bey reports on the brutal staff abuse, medical negligence, vermin, and feces-covered walls he has seen, as well as the obstacles faced by ex-felons once released in North Carolina. Far from crediting any state-sponsored program, he attributes his self-transformation to taking a political stand, with "the 3rd Party Black Panthers," a group committed to raising voter awareness to elect lawmakers who will "make, pass, or enforce laws and statues that effect your everyday life to how you get treated in prison to how you get treated in society as well."[73] Robert S. Holbrook has also found his bearings through political activism, and he has faced the costs for this turn. After years of unfocused acting up that got him kicked out of seven Pennsylvania prisons, Holbrook drastically changed his behavior.

But in the eyes of the D.O.C. the behavior I was engaging in was far more serious misconduct. . . . Challenging the injustice of the so-called criminal justice system, writing articles and pamphlets exposing the injustices of prison and most serious in the eyes of the D.O.C articulating a perspective of prisoners and prisons in opposition to the false perception of prisoners and the need for prisons the D.O.C. is articulating to the public. . . . Despite the repression and personal difficulties imposed by the D.O.C. in the end the transition from "public enemy" to "enemy of the state" has been worth it and I have no regrets other than I wish I had made the connection between the drug trade and the government's failed war on drugs and the transition prior to coming to prison as a juvenile offender. Life is about transitions and transcending one's limitations and sooner or later, for better or worse, we all make or miss the transition that will define who we are and most importantly choose to be. No longer will the state define me. I will dare to define myself.[74]

SKS Heruglyphx Maga Neteru confirms what Robert Holbrook writes: "The first thing a politically educated prisoner learns is the fact that no one can correct/rehabilitate him but himself, through genuine self-criticism. This cannot and will never come from DOC. The politically educated prisoner is an out-law."[75] Neteru and Holbrook thus echo Malcolm X, George Jackson, Assata Shakur, and a host of others who located their political bearings in pitched opposition to the experience of imprisonment in America; these writers substantiate Jack Henry Abbott's observation that "a political outlook . . . is one of the inevitable products of suffering inside prison."[76]

Self-education and transformation can be political, spiritual, philosophical, dietary, or take many other forms. In every case it enables a more comprehensive grasp of the narrative trajectory of one's life. Part of this can be a result of the simple process of aging and maturation, despite the prison's tendency to infantilize its wards.[77] The assault on the senses and identity in US prisons makes this process both more difficult and clearer to view once achieved. The writers who describe their progress in positive directions virtually all write of shifts in thinking and perspective carried out so that the ugliness inside prison walls ceases to limit their horizons. James Same writes of an instance in which this crossing was literal, modelled by a glimpse of a doe and her offspring through the chain link and razor wire surrounding a West Virginia prison.

> The "mama" doe was leading the three younger fawns in a spurt of energy, as if they were discovering the world for the first time. . . . It is true, I can't come out of my cell and housing unit jumping and leaping. I can approach each new day with spiritual and emotional excitement. It is not an automatic attitude, but requires making a new decision every morning in your heart and mind. . . . When my vision is blurred by things going on in my life with other inmates and family concerns, causing me to see no good things in my life and in my day. . . . But after a prayer, or maybe just stopping and taking a deep breath, I can see more clearly now. The blurred vision clears up, the stinking thinking

doesn't smell anymore and I am ready to smile and be a part of my world again. Prison life is often foggy, but hold on, when the Sun comes up it will clear your vision.[78]

Jamil Hayes writes of the choice he has made to change his perspective and seek a path of constructive change so that, even while in prison in Georgia, he can become a counter to the problems that surround him.

> You can decide to do hard time. Instead of bettering yourself you don't sign up for educational classes. Instead you surround yourself around men who have also given up on themselves. . . . Doing your time like this takes no effort but will land you in bad situations like lock down or worse high max or death row. I started my time off the wrong way. Now I'm changing the way I think because what you think gives birth to your actions. . . . No matter where you are or what your dealin with, you can always have a positive mindset. . . . I had to stop sayin poor me an start thinking what can I learn from this? How can I use my experiences to help others? . . . I now motivate others to think positive. . . . It takes nothing to give up. But it takes a strong mind to be positive through the negative. To be a light in the darkness. It'll take you a long way. So what I'm saying isn't for coping in prison only, but in life period.[79]

Profound self-searching is needed to achieve the kind of positive thinking that Jamil Hayes advocates. In writing a letter to himself as a child, Californian Dennis J. Sierra measures the distance he has come and exemplifies the kind of self-reflection required for incarcerated people to become better than the obstacles in their past lives and prison conditioning.

> Dear Dennis,
> I am writing to the child who was abandoned by mother and father, the kid who lived with fear of the next unknown, who had feelings of longing for mom and believing that someday she would return. . . .
> You remember the quiet peace of solitude mixed with fear when you ran away from the torment of the foster-system, the child predators, the authoritative parenting, and the cold walls of institutions. You kept yourself partially sane by the belief that your mother would someday

find you and take you away from the seemingly insidious world that you lived in. Through all of the pain of your memories, you still see the child, skin bronzed by the summer sun, innocently playing hide-and-seek with your friends. The boy who loved to pretend to be Speed Racer, the child who loved to listen to the music of the Beatles and Elton John, the kid who loved to play the flute and the recorder, go hiking in the forest, swimming in the ocean, just being a kid. Dennis, you survived the foster-system, your drug addiction, prison, and most importantly, you survived your own self-destruction. You have learned to seek a higher purpose, to find empathy where you could not. . . . By understanding the feelings of anger and resentment are at times caused by being abandoned, shamed, and rejected, you empathize with people and understand the human condition. Remembering your past has helped you develop into the creative and compassionate person you are today. You are known by some to be a person who heals and not hurts others, and has a way of inspiring peace. Now it's time to forgive you. You have revisited the child you once were only to find the man you were destined to be.[80]

A plunge into self-reflection and changes in thinking often move incarcerated people to new ways of acting. For others, new action brings a change of mind. Tony Enis writes of taking up painting with the help of another man on death row in Illinois.

This kind and decent man agreed to teach me how to paint. . . . I began by learning how to do landscapes and seascapes. They quickly became my favorite subjects. My teacher told me this was the way I would learn how to mix and create colors. It would also give me an understanding of blending and brushstrokes, and prepare me for my eventual jump to other subject matter, such as still lifes and portraiture, etc.

. . . I was turning a blank piece of canvas into something more. I was creating with my own hands. There was something extremely fulfilling and liberating about that.

I was often my harshest critic when it came to my painting . . . but I knew it had arrived so to speak, when an officer asked me if I intended to sell this particular seascape I was working on. It took everything in me to temper the pride and excitement I felt at that moment. I also felt a resurgence of self-worth that my time on death row had been slowly and steadily chipping away at.

That self-worth peaked when, for the first time, I was able to tell my then-wife and my family—"No, you don't need to send me any money right now"—because I had sold a painting. And although financial independence was my initial motivator, that soon became a convenient by-product of a creative fire that had been lit within me and continues to burn brightly to this day.[81]

Incarcerated people like Tony Enis cling to whatever opportunities for growth, education, and self-transformation come within their reach. This is true whether these are offered through the help of other imprisoned people, the work of self-education, volunteer offerings, or the rare instances of effective facility programming. James L. Griffin, held in Connecticut, writes of becoming an addict by age eleven while raised in a house where every other member of his family had been removed by jail or child services by the time he was thirteen. He details both the utter senselessness of his sentencing and the many ways he worked to make prison work for him as nothing else ever had. In his list of facility-run programs and how they helped him, he provides a segue into testimony to the depth of appreciation that imprisoned people express when effective programming is made available.

By age 15 I was facing life in prison. I wasn't even the guy who committed the murder. . . . The trigger man got only 25 for shooting, killing, robbing and kidnapping someone. A recent juvenile bill cut my sentence down to 27 years. I have been inside for 20. I have spent more time behind bars, than I have in the outside world. But I have not given up. I never will. While incarcerated I earned inmate status for model behavior, encouraging other inmates to change. I received my G.E.D. which taught me how to deal with discipline and focus. I completed Tier 2 which taught me how to gain control of my addictions. I completed the People Empower People program which taught me how to communicate, manage conflicts and stress in my life. I completed anger management, which taught me how to channel my anger and refocus it in a positive way. I have worked in the institution kitchen where I learned about the importance of teamwork, accomplishing a job, and making good decisions. I completed the Business Education Vocational Training program where I learned keyboarding, word processing, spreadsheets, records management and accounting. I completed the Commercial Cleaning Vocational Education Program with proficiency in every subject. I received a Unified School District #1 Outstanding Achievement Award, as well as numerous offender work performance reports. . . . I have lived in a cell for 20 years. That can break a man. But as you can see, I have worked to better myself during this time. I have learned to work well with others while also being able to think for myself. I am not the same anti-social kid who DCF [Department of Children and Family Services] left in a terrible home environment. I am a strong positive person who can do great things in society.[82]

From such descriptions we can infer the kinds of programming that would change the trajectory of lives despite being relegated to decades inside factories of suffering. The imprisoned know what they need, where state-sponsored offerings fall short, as well as when state and volunteer programs are effective. Their recommendations could provide the road map toward constructive policies and practices. The final segment of this chapter gathers testimony to what prison witnesses have seen work and their recommendations for changing lives.

WHAT WORKS

Prisons today are backward-looking institutions.[83] Incarcerated people are viewed as little more than the threatening remainders of their worst acts, even when those acts unfolded decades earlier, and when they were children. When incarcerated people see helpful programs, they do not ignore but build from the lessons of the past, toward visions of more constructive futures.[84] The consensus of testimony from imprisoned people is that these facilities stand squarely in the path of positive growth, offering fodder for bitterness and resentment rather than spaces for self-searching. It is thus all the more remarkable that imprisoned people do find the initiative to transform their thinking, behavioral, and even emotional habits. It is also understandable how appreciative they are of programming that speaks to them. It is bracing to read incarcerated people's witness to what has worked for themselves and others, giving the lie to claims that nothing works to change incarcerated people.[85] This testimony also makes clear what most outside readers don't realize: much of the reformative work carried out in American prisons is the result of the time and effort of thousands of unpaid volunteers and organizations across the nation, giving up their time and directing their resources to the benefit of confined people.[86]

Such volunteers include those who facilitate AA/NA meetings and religious study (beyond the duties of staff clergy), the faculty of college-in-prison programs (some paid by their home institutions or organizations, some not), and individuals who lead meditation, creative writing, and other non-credit courses. Understanding which programs are provided by state facilities and which by volunteers is important for assessing the landscape of prison programming. For this reason, I have added the abbreviations "vtr" and "fcty" in brackets to distinguish volunteer programs from programs run and staffed by prison facilities.[87] If I could not identify a program source, I have added the abbreviation "ukn" for unknown.

John Robert Sweat's essay from Tennessee describes common stops and starts toward one of the most widely called-for offerings among incarcerated people: higher education.

> Going to prison after the dust settled, I was placed in school [fcty], I wasn't that far from leaving high school, so school knowledge was still fresh in my mind. I took the first G.E.D. test offered me and passed. The teachers . . . made me a teacher's aide. When the opportunity presented itself, I continued my education. The state offered college courses [vtr],[88] I learned a great deal and almost had enough credit to earn an Associate's degree. When politicians heard that prisoners were getting college educations, our Pell grants were cut off, so ended my scholastic endeavors. Anything else was me picking up a book and educating myself out of desire. . . . I took several classes called Alternative to Violence Program (A.V.P.) [vtr]. . . . The class spoke to me, I understood its origins and the material, because I had lived it. . . . It was teaching people to be stronger than their emotions, how to basically overcome their "selves." . . . It's the few souls you do reach that matter, those souls that can go back into the world and live their lives, building a future for themselves, to live, to love, to work, building a foundation. Our A.V.P.

classes were shut down, the state took it and let it die, due to the lack of state volunteers to back us. The program lost its ability to reach inmates that have lived this material and can make sense of it.[89]

People like John Sweat recall college courses supported by federal Pell tuition grants—before Congress and President Bill Clinton made incarcerated people Pell-ineligible in 1994.[90] Since then until 2023 (when Congress agreed to renew Pell eligibility), those fortunate enough to be admitted to the few remaining college programs were supported largely by private foundations and individuals. The three-decade hiatus in full-scale federal support ignored the fact that college classrooms in prisons offer more than education. They can serve as foundations for transformed thinking and hope. Adam Roberts works as a teaching aide in the Cornell Prison Education Program (CPEP) (vtr), at Auburn Correctional Facility in New York. He describes the program's effects.

We work on homework . . . and discuss the readings. . . . But perhaps where I've been able to add the most value are the instances of coaching, motivating, or mentoring. When, for instance, Leap . . . remarked, "I'm doing life; thesis statements can't help me," I talked to the men around the table about the myriad academic opportunities I'd thrown away in my formative years, how education allows one to make better choices of what to focus on, while improving the quality of one's life. Plus, I noted, I'm doing 25-to-life, just like Leap, and learning is how I make the most of my time rather than getting high in the yard. . . . Zach, Leap, and Umar nodded along as my argument crescendoed, then redoubled their efforts on the text. . . . While I'm certainly no objective observer, CPEP fills a basic need that is not met by the prison's official programs that dole out mandatory rehabilitation in one-shot, ten-week courses. We connect with professors and undergraduate teaching assistants who voluntarily enter a place most people only dream of escaping. Their teaching provides the shared frames of reference that facilitate lasting connections to the marketplace of ideas. . . . I have heard how students elevate the nature of the dialog of those non-students around them, who, in turn are incentivized to stay out of trouble and practice writing so they can pass the yearly entrance exam. In providing positive outlets that the criminal justice system has abandoned, CPEP creates students who are altering the course of their lives, something they can pass on to their children.[91]

Writing from Indiana, Mick Whitlock describes how higher education evokes self-searching, resisting the process of "prisonization"—the narrowing of horizons such that incarcerated people perpetuate destructive prison culture.

> For these [prisonized] individuals, a life of crime is a given and a return trip to prison is guaranteed. As my understanding of the prison system grew, my personal goals and ambitions were solidified. I enrolled in college [vtr] at the first opportunity. . . . By focusing my full attention in a positive direction, I was able to ignore the negativity that surrounded me. . . . I simply vowed to do my very best and take it one class and one assignment at a time. I soon found myself leading class discussions and tutoring other students. My age and numerous life experiences proved to be incredible assets. At the end of the semester I had accumulated a perfect 4.0 grade point average and had made the Dean's List. Attending college was the greatest transformational experience of my life. Not only was I gaining knowledge about the subjects I was studying, I was gaining insight into myself and my behavior. I stopped trying to justify past actions and personal failures. I came to the realization that the only thing I could do about my past was learn from it. I began to fully understand the incredible possibilities that exist within myself and the world. The challenges and obstacles I was facing were made clear.[92]

Sylvia Boykin writes from Pennsylvania. The mother of three daughters, she describes her own history of childhood sexual abuse, and the drugs, alcohol, and childhood suicide attempt she used to blunt or end her suffering—a story that is common among incarcerated women.[93] She also describes the rare experience of state-based programs that have helped to change her life.

> The groups and programs that I have participated in and the training that I have received and continue to get as a Certified Peer Specialist [fcty], enables me to help Women to cope with confinement, overcome trauma, addictions, criminal behaviors and prepare for reentry. . . . I

needed all of the groups and programs that were provided for me. Without them, I would not have been able to improve myself and help others. . . . My counselors [fcty] . . . were there for me when I experienced a crisis or a difficult situation. . . . The staff at Muncy and Cambridge Springs [fcty] truly were motivated to help me to reach my full potential. I am particularly grateful to the organization Kids and Kin [vtr] for helping me with my daughters. The religious offerings at Muncy and Cambridge Springs helped me by encouraging me. . . . I never thought of myself as a criminal while in prison. I identified with being a mother Without her children. When I first entered Muncy, I was able to bond with my daughters with the Wonderful program, Project-Impact [fcty]. This was great. As my daughters grew up, our time together changed. The visits were both very enjoyable, but heartbreaking as well. We cried a lot. I learned how to cope with this sadness by praying. All the while, I couldn't not think about the life that I was responsible for taking. I had to change. I had to change for my daughters and I thank God that to this day, they forgive me and love me.[94]

Jy'Aire Smith-Pennick writes that "when you come to prison, two things can transpire: You can either become a better human being or you can become a better criminal. For my first two or three years inside, it was the latter for me." Facility programming helped him. Crucial here, as it is for Sylvia Boykin and many others, is the quality of personal interactions.

I know now that I ended up in prison because I never addressed my underlying issues—fear of abandonment, lack of trust in others, social anxiety, anger, PTSD and depression. . . .

At Chester, I received drug and trauma treatment.[95] And I noticed early on that the interaction between the guards and the men housed here is very different. Staff in Delaware had refused to interact with the men in a civil manner. Their motto was control and confrontation. At SCI-Chester, a lower-level facility, we speak and laugh with one another. Some of us even shake hands. I think the interaction here is different because most of the guards come from where we come from. They can relate to our problems and know that they could have easily ended up where we are.

This prison also offers a wide variety of programs. I've been able to earn a traffic management certification [fcty], and, through the Certified Peer Specialist (CPS) program, I've learned to support men who are facing mental health problems, drug abuse and other issues. In addition, SCI-Chester's education department [fcty] is a lot more hands-on. We get to interact with our teachers more, and we even have a principal who helps facilitate our learning. I feel like the educators really want us to succeed, and sometimes that makes all the difference.

I've been able to earn college credits through Widener University [vtr]. And the Inside-Out Prison Exchange Program here [vtr] has allowed me to take Swarthmore College courses [vtr]. Sitting in a classroom with professors and students is scary, humbling and exciting. It has changed my life.[96]

Serving his time in Minnesota, Maurece L. Graham comments on the good effects of non-facility programs: "I've seen tremendous adjustments in attitude and outlook by those involved in programs like Power of People Leadership Institute [vtr] and the Alternatives to Violence Project [vtr]. People who complete those programs and stay involved actually hold their heads higher and try to put themselves on a road to success."[97]

We often say that time in prison pays a "debt to society." But how isolation and debilitation behind walls—other than creating jobs and profits—pay anyone back is rarely questioned.[98] Bobby Bostic describes a more literal payback: the Restorative Justice Garden Program, sponsored by the Jefferson Correctional Center in Missouri, contributes fresh produce to those in need. Bostic has witnessed the desire among incarcerated people to contribute directly to communities outside. This work also provides a narrative thread for Bostic's pursuit of personal growth after being condemned to 241 years in prison at age sixteen for a crime that killed no one.

To my amazement I found the peace of mind and tranquility that I craved for right here in this prison garden. . . . With every weed that I pulled out of the garden it felt as if I was pulling an old part of my criminal self away. . . . So as I sat there in the dirt I wondered how could I turn my dirt trouble filled life into something beautiful? . . . I wanted to produce meaning in my life like the nutritious cucumbers, water-melons, carrots and other edibles that we grew in the prison garden. These fruits and vegetables would feed those in need. . . . Now it is 19 years later and I am 38 years old. I look at the garden from my cell and remember my vow. I am proud of my accomplishments since then. . . . I have a paralegal diploma [vtr], received a basic business studies cer-tificate from Missouri State University of West Plains [vtr], and I am currently enrolled in Adams State University to get my Associates of Science degree [vtr]. I have obtained over 50 certificates for complet-ing rehabilitation classes inside these prisons [fcty], started a book club based around rehabilitation etc. . . . Like the garden that dies in the winter and revives itself in the springtime, I got a new life.[99]

Incarcerated people, like those struggling outside, often begin to get a handle on their lives and situations once they can locate themselves within a larger narrative that connects the past with the present and ori-ents the present toward the future, as Bobby Bostic found in gardening. Such narrative schema are found in religion, education, family connec-tions, or secular practices that offer imprisoned people a meaningful horizon. From California, Judith testifies to the power of a program that places "The Lioness Tale" at its center. This allegorical narrative involves "a Lioness who spends her entire life in captivity and yet moves toward the light of forgiveness, acceptance, and love anyhow."[100]

Fellow Californian Steven Lomas writes of the effects of a medita-tion group in prison (vtr). The practice has become a journey of "self-discovery." Motivated by a desire to escape "the crowds and the noise," he has learned through meditation that "to be transformed into a person who genuinely cares for others is the greatest type of self-help."[101] Also held in California, Eve Mazzarella leads women in yoga, and like Bobby Bostic and Judith she finds yet another compelling analog for her jour-ney forward.

Yoga became a means to help others not only to survive, but to thrive in a very difficult environment. . . . Sharing this with others, I have witnessed healing and transformation of many broken and wounded women—beginning with myself. . . . Like losing balance in a pose and then bringing it back, we take ownership, find our center, and recover that which has been lost—our freedom, our reputation and our value. Yoga is a means to restore balance to whatever knocked us off track.[102]

Following a favorable court decision allowing men to practice their Eastern faiths inside an Arkansas prison, Keith A. Deaton started yoga sessions with the help of a volunteer teacher. Like Eve Mazzarella, he seeks to help others.

> In closing, we meditate and read from one of several texts; the *Bhagavad Gita*; *Yoga, a Path for Healing and Recovery*; or other texts.
> The sun shines bright every Wednesday, whether it's cloudy or not. The men in our classes advance in mental and physical discipline, our spiritual values grow. We have a moment of silence for our peers in the . . . yoga studio and their tragic loss—may we be instruments to stop the madness.[103]

When programs like this do work, whether states, nonprofits, colleges, religious organizations, or incarcerated people initiate them, it is often due to the commitment of and direct interaction with particular individuals (incarcerated or free). Imprisoned in Alaska, Diana Waggy contrasts a speech about "God-given destiny" delivered to her and her peers by then governor Sarah Palin, and the dedicated time of a volunteer Zen teacher named Judith whom Waggy first contacted; through meditation, Judith helped her to a grasp of how to cope with her condition.

> Through Zen Buddhist meditation and contemplation, I have learned about myself—all the ugly, dark and scary stuff: the fear, self-pity, anger and deep sadness; and, surprisingly, some good stuff too: a sense of humor, intelligence, compassion and true remorse. . . . I often think, WWJD? Not, what would Jesus do, but what would Judith do? What would be the unselfish thing to do right now? When I think of Judith I always imagine her smiling, dressed as always in blue, and asking me thoughtful questions and giving me helpful advice. . . . Has Judith inspired me? Definitely. Did Governor Palin's speech that day in our gym inspire me? Not really. Of course, Judith has been coming here for eleven years and Governor Palin was here for only an hour. . . . When Sarah Palin speaks to people, she walks out to jubilant

applause. When Judith comes to prison we all take off our shoes, plop down on the floor, and she says, "Okay, let's start with ankle rolls, first the right, then the left." Palin talks about what other people should do. Judith . . . comes to prison and she teaches and loves murderers, bank robbers and chronic alcoholics. Palin mocks others who are trying their best to make positive changes in the world. Judith listens quietly as women such as I selfishly rant about our situation in the world, and then helps us become calm, grateful and willing to comfort others who are suffering. . . . I can tell you that there are Judiths in this world who are making positive changes; men and women who will never give speeches to thousands of people and will never get media attention, but who take a hopeless woman or a hopeless situation and transform them.[104]

Fredrick Sledge praises the time given by volunteer teachers in Tennessee supporting imprisoned GED and college students, as well as the faculty and students from Vanderbilt Divinity School. He asks, "Why educate a prisoner? Simple, so that the prisoner can educate the young generation and better serve the public." He concludes, "I accept the fact that the system is not going to change but it does not mean that for the betterment of humanity that I cannot change. I would rather be a public benefit, and not society's burden."[105] Such change can also be facilitated by prison staff, when they are able and willing. Anthony Brunetti describes two programs that have helped him: a course of study in theosophy and a program started by a prison librarian who has put in the time to bring Brunetti and other men together for creative practice inside a Connecticut prison.

In this program prisoners are encouraged to write and perform original plays as well as classics. It provides me an avenue for positive, creative artistic expression and teaches prisoners—many of whom are antisocial—to learn to cooperate and interact with others in a peaceful and productive way, and build skills which are vital to a successful reintegration into society. Credit for the success and effectiveness of this program must be given to Mark Aldrich the kind, compassionate humanitarian who runs this program and is also the prison Librarian at Garner Correctional Institution. He treats his students like human beings not criminals, a practice which gains respect and should be adopted by more D.O.C. staff to aid in the rehabilitative process.[106]

Any moment when someone from outside the pitched antagonism between staff and incarcerated people comes inside can be a moment that opens the simultaneously stale and tense air of prison corridors. There are also those volunteers whose work does much more. Bev Jaynes writes from Missouri about a theatre program that created a community of people willing to give their time and support.

> Prison Performing Arts theater . . . director, Agnes Wilcox [vtr], travels weekly to the prisons, directing the students in plays by Shakespeare, to ancient Greeks, to contemporary playwrights, including . . . offenders. . . . Wilcox . . . has drawn upon her many contacts in the theater world, with college professors and Missouri's Poet Laureates to invite them to lecture classes on theater and literary history, writing skills, and related subjects. I wish you could be present in the theater class, sensing the excitement in the air, as the students warm up with snappy word-action-rhythm games to shed their prison mode and then do improvisational acting exercises. Together, they take part in the selection of the play they'll perform, reading through scripts in class, discussing the merits of each. . . . Actor's measurements are taken so that PPA staff can scout out costumes to fit them and suit the characters [from] clothing found in second-hand shops and stores. . . . Actors get together to rehearse in between classes at Recreation and friends and roommates help actors learn their lines in the dorms. . . . Sometimes PPA supporters from St. Louis, many of whom are college professors and theater buffs, have chartered a bus to attend. . . . They've watched our growth as actors and poets over the years. . . . I wish you could see into the hearts of these actors and poets, to see their gained self-confidence from meeting challenges and reaching goals, to see their joy in understanding their ability to take direction with self-discipline, to see their bonding and how far they've come together in personal growth.[107]

Ni Nermirttan sees a fundamental shift in staff attitudes in Washington State's Airway Heights Correctional Center, where "a 'Therapeutic Community' model for 'living right' [fcty] is currently being implemented." A key point is that "leadership here is setting the standard as they model open-mindedness, humility, respect, grace, civility, helpfulness, trust, praise, esteem, appreciation, fairness and flexibility." But effective programming, as so many incarcerated people realize, works directly against the prison industry's interests. Given his grasp of penal economics, Nermirttan, understandably wary, hopes for fundamental change in public thinking.

> I struggle with my own cynicism. . . . Will this model be implemented effectively and honorably according to the spirit and goal of its inception, which I understand to be the reduction of recidivism and prison population? "Corrections" is big business. . . . The DOC . . . has ballooned, in recent years, monopolizing upon the fact that Americans are willing to incarcerate more and more of their neighbors and for longer terms than ever before in our history. Will the call for prison reform, and the public oversight of it, be strong enough to resist the economic incentives and forces that keep the system expanding? . . . In order to effect fundamental change in "Corrections" the American people, as a whole, will need to take responsibility for the problem and have the foresight to commit to the development of an effective human resource reclamation program that is not the typical quick fix proposition, but one that is aimed at lasting individual change and long term social benefit. May God help us to do what is right.[108]

We can gather from these witnesses the traits of effective offerings: consistency and longevity, respect, personal connections with people who care, opportunities for basic and higher education, focus on the present and future rather than the past, respect for human dignity, invitations to participate in personal reflection in space as secure and thus distinct as possible from the lockdown atmosphere of prison facilities, meaningful use of time, and offerings that welcome and incorporate input from incarcerated people. Prison witnesses are also able and willing to make their recommendations explicit.

RECOMMENDATIONS FOR CHANGE

If the public, lawmakers, and prison employees were motivated to include the views of incarcerated people in thinking about and running prisons, the descriptions above could become the blueprint for creating prisons that are actually correctional. This chapter concludes with statements that do not simply imply what is needed but describe it, as well as reiterating what is not working now. Several of these voices we have heard before. People who know what's not working, who are enacting self-transformation, and who have seen what the right programming can do, can also describe what could and should be occurring.

From Pennsylvania, Lee Whitt suggests that the first practical step should be simply to recognize how much anger and resentment incarcerated people carry inside them, anger and resentment that stem in part from institutional indifference to who imprisoned people are and what they endure: "With no way to properly vent, sooner or later all the stuff that we are storing inside is going to come out. No controlled flow. Just a straight explosion. . . . There needs to be programs designed around being outlets for guys to unleash the burdens they carry without causing any harm."[109] Mississippi witness Joseph R. Dickey echoes Lee Whitt in recommending "more psychology courses that teaches the prisoners to fix what is broken in them. To fix their families. To vent and share their fears and concerns about their early life that contributed to them being here and how to live life after prison."[110] From Missouri, Zachary Smith calls for full-scale assessment of people's past trauma, as well as current and post-release needs, thus treating the imprisoned as individuals rather than as generic units of a mass population.[111] Michigan resident Daniel Pirkel recommends motivating incarcerated people to participate in programming, and he sees what we all stand to gain by a fundamental change in our thinking about what prisons should do.

> People need motivation as well as the opportunity to change their behavior. As Gershoff argues, reinforcement more effectively changes behavior than does punishment. Everyone knows that we catch more flies with honey than with vinegar. . . . Prisoners should receive training on how to deal with their psychological issues as well as the unique stresses of prison from day one. . . . The US prison system fails to systematically

employ procedures that psychologists have demonstrated to be effective in reducing crime because of its refusal to focus on the potential of rehabilitation. . . . Rather than rejecting people, society is better off helping them. . . . When the most disadvantaged people in our society are lifted up, everyone wins.[112]

Californian Kenneth Hartman articulates an idea that is widely shared among incarcerated people, directly at odds with common public assumptions, and diametrically opposed to a notion that stood behind penal practices at their beginning: that the incarcerated themselves may be among the best resources to their peers and policy makers in charting a better way to operate.

> There is another way to bring about transformational change to prison. It is to include the voices, talents, and experiences of prisoners. . . . Surprising to all not incarcerated, many prisoners apply themselves to the process of personal transformation with a fierceness that only those who have fallen deeply into the mire can comprehend. And we prisoners know prisoners. It is that fundamental and simple. We know what it is like to fail, to be imprisoned, to desperately desire to rise up out of the ashes of our own mistakes. We know what works and what doesn't work. We prisoners also know prison. . . .
>
> I am confident we have lessons to teach, we who have survived this abyss, this darkness outside of view that grows in the collective consciousness, a menacing force.[113]

Darnell Lane, writing from Illinois, offers a broadly insightful assessment of what is wrong, what could help to make it right, and the healing effects of a fundamental shift in our collective thinking about how we respond to trespasses against the current legal order (or to its often arbitrary enforcement). He brings together many of the ideas and recommendations we have seen thus far into a restorative justice vision that, once again, places faith in incarcerated people, as well as in the families and the communities to which they will return.

> As prisons have cut back on most correctional programs and policies, an offender has to look within or to other prisoners with the desire to

transform themselves to useful citizens. Befriending others who have begun the transformation process of being an asset rather than a hindrance to growth, unity, and human decency is a building block in the rehabilitation process. The most honest gauge of an offender's progress is another offender. As a whole, the offender population is more astute, honest, and aware as to what it takes to reform, rehabilitate, and redeem. An offender's family and the relationships he/she values also play a significant role in the rehabilitation process. . . . When institutions encourage family bonding, and the value of both parents raising or having input in their children's lives, changes in the attitudes of offenders are by-products. An offender who is in close contact with their spouse, children, and other family members wants to be a part of a productive family structure. Criminal justice policy and institutions should promote family unity, its value as an ideology. . . .

My argument is not for the complete absolution for an offender's wrongful actions. My argument is for criminal justice policies and practices that promote social awareness of crime and punishment, an understanding of compassion and empathy, a reflection of moral decency, and the humanity of all beings, even and especially those who commit crime.[114]

Mathew Lucas Ayotte's essay from Maine places a particular focus on how his own transformation was made possible by his peers. He also advocates, again, for provision of higher education. In imagining how in-prison, mutual aid might become a regular part of incarceration, he brings us full circle and in an entirely different direction from the earliest American prisons; these sought, above all, to isolate imprisoned people from each other. What Ayotte, Hartman, Lane, Jaynes, and other witnesses clarify is that, in the name of removing the bad influences of convicted people on one another, we also barred and have since ignored or blocked opportunities for them to do each other substantial good.

Peer to Peer Mentorship is an integral aspect of humanizing the criminal justice system by encouraging, while at the same time empowering the persons most effected by the experience of incarceration—those who are serving the time. If men and women were afforded the opportunity to share their life experiences in whatever area of specialization or expertise they might have, a mutual benefit would be enjoyed by all those involved. In this way a person's sense of self isn't diminished but bolstered. We all have roles and various skills that often make up a sense of who we are. Whether it be a career role or family role, everyone has a way of identifying themselves within the scope of the world in which they live. Often it's these very roles that provide our sense of worth. . . . Upon arrest you are manacled, placed in handcuffs, in irons. . . . Stripped naked . . . given a uniform that never fits correctly with bold lettering signifying that you are an inmate or prisoner. By this time your sense of self has been thoroughly undermined. . . . So who are you now? . . . I personally feel so strongly about this approach because it is my experience to have witnessed the benefit of peer driven programs. . . . It has been my good fortune to have the opportunity to participate in the Second Chance Pell Grant Program,[115] which is a program to provide individuals with funding to take college courses [vtr] while incarcerated. . . . One of the main factors for my having gotten involved with the program was on account of encouragement from other men who were a part of the program suggesting that I submit an application. . . . I presently have a 3.79 GPA and am orienting my future around the possibility of working in the Human Service Field. This would have never occurred to me if it would not have been for the encouragement of my fellows. . . . I began tutoring other students and helping out the education staff. I found purpose and meaning in my days, meeting my peers and professors with humility and gratitude for the opportunity at hand. . . . Because I took one step forward onto a path of education my self-esteem and personal self-image grew into a sense of responsibility and a certain amount of accountability to my fellow man and the whole of humanity for being a part of society and a citizen of the world.[116]

When Mathew Ayotte and others describe their volunteer and college experience inside, they record the revelation of work and classrooms where the collective focus is on the future, rather than on past actions that can never be undone. Mick Whitlock points out the dollars-and-cents wisdom of such programming: "An ex-con with a minimum of two years of college has a less than ten percent chance of returning to prison. . . . In Indiana, it costs less to fund an inmate's four-year college education than it does to incarcerate that same individual for six months."[117] Such bottom-line arguments for higher education in prison are backed by the research.[118] More commonly, like Christopher D. Ridley writing of the faculty who came into a North Carolina prison, incarcerated students describe higher education's rehumanizing effects: "In their eyes, we weren't inmates, we were college students. That alone had a huge impact on many of us. A dollar figure can't quantify this lesson in confidence and self-respect."[119] Randall L. Cole, living inside a Tennessee prison so violent it was eventually closed by court order, recalls his first exposure to faculty from outside, what came from an assignment on the stabbing death of a classmate, and the effects on the whole of his life.

> We expected [faculty] to be fearful of us and limited in their interaction. To our surprise, they treated us like normal people and clearly had a lot of expectations for the success of the class. . . . Our teachers made it clear. We weren't being *forced* to learn and failure would be our *own* fault. That was a simple but powerful lesson for everyone. Education was there for us, but we had to *earn* it. . . .
>
> I wrote a poem about . . . [a classmate's stabbing death] and was forced to examine my own self and the fact that I had killed someone. . . . I had to be honest with myself about the terrible impact of violence and accept responsibility for the things I had done. I was starting to feel and understand the power of education. . . .
>
> As my thinking changed, my behavior did also. I stopped associating with people who used drugs and broke the rules. Most of my own bad habits disappeared and I began to feel calmer and more in control of my life. Most importantly, I had learned to think for myself and to *trust* my thoughts and decisions. I learned to respect the rights and opinions of others, and my relationship with my family improved greatly. All these changes happened slowly, but they were a direct result of my education.[120]

Daniel Pirkel calls for more support for a college program run through a Christian college in Michigan that he sees "transforming the prison culture."[121] While we know that any exposure to college courses while incarcerated reduces recidivism rates,[122] prison witnesses like Cole and

Pirkel focus on how higher education can transform the whole student. At a time when the utility of humanities courses is under critical scrutiny outside,[123] Mikhail Markhasev, from California, suggests that such courses are what can most profoundly serve imprisoned people.

> When introducing the philosophy courses on active gang yards, it is a powerful testimony of doing things differently in a place where a strict gang structure enforces the tenets of the convict code. . . . The first work we read this semester was Plato's Apology of the Death of Socrates, a philosopher who was executed for doing what was right. Socrates refused to wrong others or respond with violence. . . . Even after two millennia, the voice of Socrates echoes in a most unlikely cave. . . .
>
> Availability of a philosophy degree may not be the cure for criminality, but it is definitely a pathway toward healing. . . . The possibility to major in philosophy provides the prisoner a sturdy staff to help him along the way. After all, especially in prison man is reminded that he is a being in search of meaning.[124]

New Yorker Deshawn Cooper's essay about college in prison points to how much studying inside is like college work outside: late nights, seemingly impossible assignments, the headache that is statistics. He also describes having textbooks locked down, and all of his possessions tossed amid a cell search. His implicit formula for rebuilding the self, diminished by crime and incarceration, includes five crucial elements.

> Perhaps the experience I most share with traditional college students is the sense of pride and accomplishment one feels when graduating. My chest swelled, my head tilted further towards the sky, and my shoulders squared firmer with every step I made towards the podium to receive my degree from the [Bard] college president, Leon Botstein. And like they do for traditional college students, the tears that streamed down my grandmother's face told me everything I needed to know, for reasons that differed greatly from my campus counterparts: *I am capable of doing something good.*
>
> In all, my experience as an incarcerated college student has been a six-year tour that continues to challenge me to use both imagination

and experience to reach beyond myself, yet draw all the intensity possible from the self to reconnect with what was lost in the streets at such
a young age: Hope. Faith. Compassion. Humanity. Community.[125]

What Deshawn Cooper lost is not easily regained in prison. Despair and
hopelessness are always in good supply. Cooper, like all other incarcerated people lucky enough to enroll in college classes, let alone graduate,
is a winner in the prison higher education lottery. Congress has agreed
to restore Pell eligibility for incarcerated people. If these programs maintain quality standards for content and delivery, they will yield all the aid
that past and current enrollees describe and for which the nation should
be thankful.[126]

As needed as it is, restarting higher education in prison is just one
facet of the kind of holistic metamorphosis that prison witnesses envision. Some years ago, given the ugliness of American prisons, I
wondered what incarcerated people would imagine as its opposite, a
Beautiful Prison.[127] This led to a collection of speculative and descrip-
tive essays by imprisoned writers and scholars both inside and out. One
contributor, philosopher Drew Leder, made the topic into a semester-
long discussion for a class of men in Maryland. Leder then wrote up the
men's deliberations and conclusions.

> We decided to move away from the language of the "beautiful prison";
> a number of the men suggested discomfort with the term after years
> spent in harsh and unaesthetic environs. In fact, it provoked some bit-
> ter laughter. Prisons, they agreed, could be places for soul-searching
> and self-transformation . . . but not *beautiful*. One man launched into a
> description of the *enlightened* prison, and it met with general agreement
> when I proposed that as an alternate title. What if prisons were not like
> the dark cave described in Plato's Republic: chained men, cut off from
> reality, consigned to watching shadows on the wall? What if, instead,
> prisons were places of, and for, enlightenment? . . .
>
> The enlightened prison, we concluded, would embody the following
> five core attitudes: *hope, growth, recognition of merit, individuality, and
> community*. . . . In the absence of these attitudes, you have the "endark-
> ened" prison. This type of environment, all too often characteristic of
> current-day institutions, embodies the opposite attitudes, which we

termed respectively, *despair, stasis, recognition of demerits, class-ification, and isolation.*[128]

The essay that grew out of this discussion was broken into subsections contrasting the traits of the enlightened and the endarkened prison: concrete reasons for Hope v. Despair, Growth v. Stasis, Recognition of Merit v. Recognition of Demerits, Individuality v. Classification, and Community v. Isolation. The message is clear as a recommendation about current prison practice: Stop doing everything wrong. Provide opportunities for hope by fostering growth and recognition of good actions by individuals treated as such rather than as numbers, and as individuals who, like all other human beings, require an active sense of community in order to become fully alive.

Ken Hartman was another writer involved in this project; he wrote too of the pitched struggle enjoined by trying to think of anything beautiful from inside prisons where he had spent two-thirds of his life.[129] He concludes with similar recommendations, posed as an additional set of binary contrasts from current practice.

> The beautiful prison is characterized by the quality of its treatment of human beings. Respect real and not based on fear but on the recognition of the inherent dignity of even the most damaged. . . . Punishment is never for the sake of inflicting pain and suffering. In the beautiful prison, men and women who have done awful and even vile things are constantly encouraged to rise above their worst acts and rejoin society. This is done because to do any less is to succumb to the basest of human instincts, to fall prey to the worst of what resides in all of us, to become ugly. Restoration, rehabilitation, reconciliation, redemption, resolution—these are the watchwords of the beautiful prison.[130]

The visions of a truly rehabilitative prison offered by prison witnesses are all forward looking. They do not deny the past. Instead, they locate the past *in* the past, as a powerful negative reference for charting progress into peaceful lives inside and then out. No Pollyannas, they are fully aware of the obstacles they face. They advocate for programs that bring people in from outside—through family contact, educational and other volunteer programming—and for restorative justice measures, all in order to snag a lifeline from the world they will someday reenter. For no matter how well intended, designed, and executed are any programs inside prison walls, they all stop short of addressing the conditions in which crime occurs and back into which people will be released. One of the latter conditions, as Lee Whitt suggests, is the image the public holds of imprisoned people—an image that must change before they can be offered an effective second chance. In this he echoes Lisa Guenther and Michael L. Owens and writers we will read on the defeat of deterrence.

> Develop some type of advocacy group that can help shape the public's opinion of ex-felons. The media and society likes to focus on the negative. There are a lot of positive things one can find in an ex-felon if there was a source to help promote these things rather than the negative. . . . Something or someone needs to market the people who have paid their debt to society and want to return to be a member of that society.
> . . . In a society where we are overly sensitive about labels, prejudice, stereotypes and so open about letting everyone have a chance and letting everyone be represented, . . . why do we still judge someone who has been to prison with such a strong stereotype that we think all ex-prisoners are just waiting to commit another crime?[131]

The fear that the world will never think of convicted people as more than their worst acts marks the thresholds both into and out of prison; imprisoned people are never fully forgiven in America. So the labor of self-transformation is just the first leg of reentry into constructive lives outside.

Neither the planned deprivation and willful harms that occur inside, nor the challenges that most former felons face upon release were created by incarcerated people. They were created by misguided or politically opportunist lawmakers and other state and federal authorities overseeing criminal legal practices; by civic failures to address at their source the employment deserts, poverty, failed public education, addiction, violence, abuse, and mental illness that fill the space where hope might otherwise thrive in communities outside; and by a policing and prison industry that today provides a large block of all American jobs and feeds itself on the bodies of poor people[132]—an industry built on the irrational claim that the remedy for crime can be imposed after the fact, by state-sponsored proliferation of harm against convicted people.

We will next see unveiled the myth that prisons contain and incapacitate damage to individuals and communities. We will see this veil raised to reveal how—at the center of all of these failures and feeding them—imprisonment institutionalizes and gives a moral guise to the sources of more problems than it contains. Based on the testimony we have seen already, the only thing successfully contained inside prisons is the full story of what imprisoned people are, and what prisons do to them.

4

CONTAINMENT AND INCAPACITATION'S COLLATERAL EFFECTS

Any ideology that demands the intentional increase in suffer-
ing rather than its diminution can hardly lay claim to justice. . . .
The "Land of the free" has become a society of the caged.
—ASAR IMHOTEP AMEN, CALIFORNIA

No one goes to prison alone; my imprisonment had impacted
my family as though they were sitting in the cell with me.
—SHAKA SENGHOR, MICHIGAN

CHAPTER 1 exposed what incarcerated people have long said about the historical lie that containment facilities are also correctional. Chapter 2 offered witness to what mass-scale containment can do to its wards. Chapter 3 made evident that any constructive results of imprisonment are almost entirely due to the extraordinary efforts by the imprisoned to counter mass-scale containment's degrading and debilitating effects. It would thus be absurd to suggest that American prisons do not contain people convicted of crimes. Imprisonment *is* containment. Such incapacitation stops the truly dangerous from hurting others outside prison walls, while the harm they and the previously nonviolent are allowed or required to inflict upon others inside goes nearly unchecked. What prison witnesses describe is what researchers have since confirmed from outside: no matter how necessary to address immediate threats to individuals and communities, containment also has wider, damaging effects. A legally confined person is the proverbial pebble tossed into a pond: consequences spread in space, time, and suffering often greater than the (often speculative) threat contained and incapacitated by incarceration. When those pebbles are tossed in busloads, ripples become a storm inside families and communities targeted by the criminal legal system. Handheld videos of police shooting unarmed and mentally ill people reveal instances of law enforcement acting as an assault upon public safety. The testimony from inside documents how far prisons' very premise and definitive act violates the rationale that Asar Amen implies and that philosopher H. L. A. Hart states as a principle: "The law should not inflict greater suffering than it is likely to prevent."[1] The question for assessing penal containment is whether, on the whole, it reduces or multiplies suffering.

In 53 percent of cases, when a person is legally contained and incapacitated—no matter how petty or serious their crime—a father or mother is extracted from the life of one or more dependent children.[2] In 100 percent of cases, a family member is removed, along with an active or potential contributor to family income; in their place hangs a cloud of shame, and costs that can sink a household budget that in most cases was already precarious. This is particularly true if loved ones mount the heroic effort to maintain contact and support that both states and for-profit enterprises have made emotionally and financially costly.[3] And because the strength of communities is constituted by the cumulative strength of the families that live in them, in those neighborhoods where the legal extraction of people in their prime breadwinning and family-forming years is most concentrated, and where criminal legal practices most commonly disrupt family cohesion, prison diminishes the very life activities and social forces that most effectively reduce crime.[4] The result, as scholars Bruce Western and Becky Pettit document, is that "the current system is expensive, and it exacerbates the social problems it is charged with controlling."[5] While achieving demonstrably limited and often self-defeating effects on crime,[6] containment guarantees that suffering will continue among people who are neither perpetrators nor direct victims. Penal containment, in short, does less to halt suffering than to institutionalize it on both sides of prison walls.

While increasing harm among family members and communities already in need, concentrated incarceration both deepens that need[7] and perpetuates it among the 2.7 million children of the 1.9 million people held in US captivity.[8] "By getting tough on crime," Susan Phillips and Barbara Bloom write, "the United States has gotten tough on children."[9] Mass incarceration has created the struggling suburbs of a city in cages. Those without young families of their own often become barely supportable burdens upon mothers and fathers and others while imprisoned, at the same time that they are sidelined from exactly those life-supporting events—marriage, parenthood, and work—that are the most effective curbs on criminal behavior.[10] Post-release, now carrying the mark of the ex-felon, they find their chances of participating in those events badly diminished, often precipitating yet more criminal acts, and reducing the community's sense of the legitimacy of the law itself.[11]

While prisons try to contain, they cannot incapacitate prison witnesses from seeing what they see: the burdens their confinement has levied upon their peers, their children, their families, their communities, and themselves. To date, no national archive exists of first-person witness to the immediate or long-term repercussions of imprisonment among partners, families, and communities.[12] Incarcerated people can only offer a partial picture of these repercussions (save for the many, as we will see, who are themselves the children and grandchildren of imprisoned and formerly imprisoned people). Yet their speculation, their grieving, their warnings, and their concerns present an invaluable grounding to the research on imprisonment's devastating effects on families and communities. Together, first-person testimony and the critical literature reveal why it is that the very communities most likely to suffer from crime present the most strident calls for reform, defunding, or abolition of branches of the current criminal legal system.[13] These communities see the "broader corrosion of social bonds" that concentrated incarceration brings to their homes and neighborhoods.[14] This is not, of course, a new battlefront. A struggle for Black civil rights as old as the nation itself and its modern rise in the 1950s, 1960s, and 1970s (both outside and inside prisons), and the largest demonstrations in American history, insisting that Black Lives Matter, have all been precipitated or sustained by the ongoing deployment of extralegal and legalized force against targeted populations. The difference is that there now exists a population of confined people so large that walls and razor wire cannot contain testimony to their experience of American law in practice, and to the wide horizon of its repercussions.

None of this is to suggest that containment inside jails and prisons does not offer relief to the direct victims of physical and sexual assault and domestic violence. On its face, locking people up in order to contain them and thus rendering them incapable of hurting others is a less philosophically ambiguous or speculative aim than retribution, rehabilitation, or deterrence. Taking a serial rapist off the streets surely gives relief to existing and potential victims living in the perpetrator's former vicinity. We cannot suggest that prisons defeat containment while, by its most rudimentary definition, prison *is* containment. We can only begin a comprehensive measurement of containment's effects, however, by seeking evidence of the success of containment's purported aim: to limit and curtail harm. And even while acknowledging their own culpability, imprisoned witnesses describe how containment spreads injury even as it seeks to draw injury's limits.

Imprisoned writers see the prison's containment of the poor, the mentally ill, the uneducated, the unemployed, the addicted, and the despairing who will virtually all be released. They write of the violence to their own minds and against others. They understand how deeply their imprisonment has hurt those they care for most and the communities they know best. They know that direct victims—backed by the state—and perpetrators—missing from families—stand at the center of a widening storm.

CONTAINMENT'S COSTS TO CHILDREN AND FAMILIES

Incarcerated parents' writing regularly counters perceptions of them as hardened to the point of indifference to containment's effects on their children.[15] California writer Julius Kimya Humphrey Sr.'s poem "So I Can Hear You Call Me Father" offers a sense of the longing and hope that imprisoned parents feel.

> From afar, I have watched you rise like the sun,
> so warm and bright.
>
> Wasted opportunities has caused what I hope for to live in your eyes,
> and my dreams to come forth with each breath you take.
>
> Repeated mistakes have scarred my past and wounded my future so
>   bad,
> that the damage may never heal.

Still, I stand looking into the mirror until I find you,
as always hiding behind the lines in my own face.

If not for the joy you have created in your mother's heart,
I would not even know you. So as I slip into silence and listen,
she transforms your evolution into words on a paper,
allowing me to read about someone I love, but for now, can't see.

The possibility of you becoming so much more,
keeps me looking forward to tomorrow, hopeful,
that one day I will find you there.

The setting of the sun fills my heart with so much joy,
I rush to fall to sleep, so I can hear you call me father

With each new day I will always look ahead into the future,
but only in my mind.

To watch you rise like the sun, so warm and bright.[16]

From Texas, Tracy Lee Kendall writes of himself in the third person: "Tracy just wants to show his son love, keep him out of prison, and affirm his potential to achieve his dreams."[17] New Yorker Andrew R. Sumahit Jr. describes how containment can deepen the sense of parental responsibilities even as it bars acting on that sense. Sumahit describes a childhood of constant beatings (so profound that he incurred chronic seizures). He then lived with his grandmother until he was kicked out when child support payments ceased, and next became homeless; finally,

ten days after my arrest, May 13, 2008, my daughter was born. I always promised myself that I'd be the perfect father one day. Now, I feel as if I'm no father at all. Since my daughter's birth, I have only seen her three times, the most recent was October 2008. In March of 2009, I filed my first visitation petition, but was denied because I had not established paternity. . . . After a long process, I proved my Paternity and received the final paperwork two weeks ago. Now, I am preparing to re-petition for visitation. In June 2009 however, my worst nightmare came true. I was contacted and notified that my daughter's mother was on trial for child Abuse and Neglect. I wrote the judge, and was allowed to attend the court proceedings. I learned that my daughter's mother had been hitting my infant daughter. . . . My daughter received a series of three surgeries to repair her arm after falling down the third floor staircase. My daughter's mother pled guilty and received a twelve month A.C.D. [Adjournment in Contemplation of Dismissal] with court-mandated programs. She still has custody of my daughter. Once again, the justice system fails. . . . So far, I have already completed two parenting programs. . . . I gave a presentation on Incarcerated Fathers as my final project for my Inmate Program Associate class. . . . I was twenty-three years old the first time I got answers to questions about my father. I refuse to let my daughter do the same. Every day that passes is one more day my daughter is deprived of the love I have for her. So I spend every day trying to get involved in her life. . . . I choose to be a man; I choose to be a father; I choose to break the cycle.[18]

Tafari Tai, held in Pennsylvania, offers a portrait of trying to parent from inside, echoing Andrew Sumahit's and many others' concerns. He places his story in the wider context of those communities that lose the greatest number of their people to mass-scale incarceration. He also notes the challenges that face formerly incarcerated people struggling to make it outside.

I am the father to a little boy who will be five this year. His sister is about to be six. I have not seen them in three years, and that was only for 50 minutes. My son was only two months when I was taken away from him. . . . My baby's mother seems to miss me less and hate me a little bit more with each birthday, Christmas, Valentine, and graduation that I am not there for. I don't too much blame her. . . . But with no high school diploma and a resume that includes selling drugs, and working in a Riker's Island mess hall, there isn't much chance to make a decent living. . . . I try to remain optimistic and keep close ties with my family especially my son, but he doesn't like to talk to me. . . . On top of that I spoke to my daughter a few months ago and her first words were "Who is this?" . . . It's things like that, that drive a person insane. The way I see it, I have to keep in constant contact with them, that means not losing my phone, or visitation privileges, but the inmates and C.O.'s seems like they're just set to make that impossible. It's like the more you try to walk away the more they tempt you, it's a lose lose in this environment. I just pray I don't kill someone or end up getting killed in this place. My mother and kids don't deserve that. I have calmed down a lot though, it's as if my 4 year old son is helping a twenty eight year old me become a better MAN. Being a father is still awesome to me. It might be because I am in here away from them, but every snowstorm, heat wave, or violence/accidents involving children I hear on the news, I get to worrying about my own kids . . . I tell them all the while, that out of sight never means out of mind when it concerns them and me. . . . It is amazing how corrupt and Machiavellian, not just the penal but the whole American system is, for the lower class, inner-city citizens. . . . If you look at what's in plain view, it's hard to miss . . . mom working two to three jobs nodding off, fighting sleep on the train on her way to work in the morning. Coming home when the sun is down, to cook (sometimes), iron and make sure everything is ready for school, just to get a few hours nap to do it all again. And all this on basically minimum wage. Pops ain't around to the point he's not even missed anymore and the kids in almost every case is left to parent their self. Which leads to drugs, violence, and sex. Now Imagine a neighborhood with eight out of ten kids fitting this category regardless of gender. This cycle just repeats. . . . That is why I am trying to make it home in time to catch my kids before they fall into the ills of the ghetto.[19]

"Incarceration," Ken Sherman writes from Wisconsin, "ruins lives not just of the offender but also of the offender's families."[20] In an essay from Michigan, Larry R. Carter writes,

> Be assured: Prison is a kicking. Prisoners are kicked, and kicked, and kicked. It is a figurative kicking, unlike slavery which was a literal kicking. But it is a "kicking" all the same. And, you are not just kicking prisoners, America. You are kicking children and elderly parents. You are kicking the life out of them.[21]

Romell Winters writes from Illinois, describing the emotional and financial burden imprisonment imposes on families.

One way or another, our crime and eventually incarceration has made our families victims as well. Due to our actions, it has created all kinds of turmoil—emotional, psychological, financial. It may have come as a sudden shock, or it may have come as one more thing in a long series of dealing with us. Either way, our families has been through a lot— shame and guilt because they sometimes don't want to show their face around other people. . . . So in their dark moments, they beat them- selves up for not being a good enough parent. They torture themselves with whether they did the right thing by you. . . . You know how you feel helpless dealing with the legal and prison system right? Well so does our families. . . . They're sick of it all! They've been dealing with fear for a long time. . . . Now there's the fear of what will happen to you behind bars. . . . They're drained, emotionally spent. And sometimes financially as well. The path that leads to prison puts a huge dent in a lot of our families finances. They don't have much left in the emotional bank either.[22]

Linda Field's story from California is that of too many incarcerated women: after she is convicted for protecting her children from an abu- sive partner, those children must then endure the prolonged suffering that comes from the loss of their mother, as well as state and facility mandates that either forbid or degrade the few opportunities for families to try to heal. The toll is particularly harsh on children so young they can see only willful parental rejection.

I came to prison when Sara was seven. She was too young to under- stand 25 to life meant she'd grow up without her mother. Her brother and sister, who were 15 and 12, didn't truly understand. Sara's first visit was traumatic. She spent the day begging me to allow her to stay with me. She promised to be good, never leave my room, and never bother the guards. She couldn't understand why I didn't want her. She sobbed, clinging to me when it was time to leave. Her little arms reached out to me over her grandfather's shoulder, her hands rapidly opened and closed, begging me. I kept telling her I loved her. She was finally out of sight, the dam I had erected broke and I let the flood free. I cried for my children and myself. I cried for every mother and child who went through this. Why didn't the courts understand? They passed a verdict not only on me but my children. My children were abused by their father, orphaned by me, and abandoned by the judicial court system. After 13 years of heartache, we now have a governor who doesn't want to hear any circumstances of why a murder was committed. He believes we should rot in prison. While I cannot justify my actions, no one is beating my children anymore. The state decided family living unit visits were no longer acceptable for lifers, further punishing my children. No longer could we have visits in a little apartment in prison which allowed a pretense of normality. During those visits mothers could rock their children, cook for them, and talk for endless hours. No more can we maintain a thread of parentship with children or grandchildren. Instead visits are conducted in a visiting room with cameras and guards who look at a mother-child relationship as abnormal. We cannot talk about important things because "Big Brother" is watching. The playroom in visiting has few toys, only foam-type blocks. There are no strollers, no high chairs, no outside toys or activities. . . . Our children deserve better. Punish us but not our children. It is time for the state to re-evaluate their treatment of our children.[23]

The image of small children struggling to understand the reality of legal containment runs through many witness narratives. In her autobiography, *Assata*, self-declared revolutionary Assata Shakur describes her child—like Linda Field's, too young to understand theories of punishment and just-deserts—upon arrival and then leaving a prison visiting room in New Jersey. Brought in by her grandmother, Assata's four-year-old child pummels her mother with her small fists.

> "You're not my mother," she screams, the tears rolling down her face. "You're not my mother and I hate you." . . . She calls me Mommy Assata and she calls my mother Mommy.
>
> I try to pick her up. She knocks my hand away. "You can get out of here, if you want to," she screams. . . . "You just don't want to."
>
> I look helplessly at my mother. Her face is choked with pain. "Tell her to try to open the bars," she says in a whisper.
>
> "I can't open the door," i tell my daughter. "I can't get through the bars. You try and open the bars."

My daughter goes over to the barred door that leads to the visiting room. She pulls and she pushes. She yanks and she hits and she kicks the bars until she falls on the floor, a heap of exhaustion. I go over and pick her up. I hold and rock and kiss her. There is a look of resignation on her face that i cannot stand. We spend the rest of the visit talking and playing quietly on the floor. When the guard says the visit is over, i cling to her for dear life. She holds her head high, and her back straight as she walks out of the prison. She waves good-bye to me, her face clouded and worried, looking like a little adult. I go back to my cage and cry until i vomit.[24]

Kentucky writer Corey J. Richardson offers a perspective on the damage done by incapacitating parents from regular contact with children already suffering marginalized lives.

The number one indicator for future imprisonment is having an incarcerated parent or familial role model. In this way, prison is a self-perpetuating reality, like a gene passed on generation after generation.

Incarcerated fathers self-identify as parents, though removed from the family unit, and rank the value of the relationships at an extremely high level. . . . Difficulties maintaining these relationships are obvious. Far-flung and costly travel on already constrained family budgets and limited transportation options, brief visits in tightly-controlled conditions, cards and letters with their intrinsic limitations, and expensive collect calls, all added together do little to keep the family together. . . . The rates of anxiety and depression for the incarcerated fathers and their children are high. On visits to prison, incarcerated fathers ravenously devour the attention of their children, as if they could absorb the lost years of ball games, family outings, and other innumerable shared moments in a one or two hour long visit. The children cling to their fathers as well, with the younger children often attempting to drag their dads home from the visiting area once and for all. I have seen their pained, flustered expressions as they are carried away, reaching out one last time until the next visit, months or years away. Aggressive, hardcore convicts morph into extremely paternal and loving men during phone calls home to their kids. One can hear in their voices a sincere desire to connect on some deeper level with their sons and daughters. They spend hours decorating cards and building crafts to send home, as if these things could substitute for the real closeness and intimacy which they desire. But there is little else to do, and something, anything, is better than nothing.[25]

As Corey Richardson describes, poverty and low-paying jobs among the families of imprisoned people often make journeys of hundreds of miles to state facilities, or thousands in the case of federal lockups, costly in both time and dollars. Yet getting there is just one, albeit long step. Ruth Askew Brelsford chronicles the work required to visit a friend and former student inside an Oklahoma prison.

My alarm is set for 5, but I can't sleep. If something happens and I don't make it by 9:15, they will close the yard for count and I will just be hanging around in the middle of nowhere til count clears. . . . I'm 67 years old and my costume is not the first thing I think about when I get up in the mornings, but it is on Visitation Day. I try to avoid all hassles and all reasons to hold up the line: no zippers on my pants, shoes that are easy to slip off and have no buckles nor heels that might appear to conceal contraband, no underwire in my bra. No scooped necklines, no t-shirts announcing my liberal politics, no open-toed shoes or sandals, no cute little hat to camouflage the fact that I need a haircut. Some of the rules are written; some are not. I don't want to do anything that will hold up the line. We've all got to get in there before the yard closes. . . . Face-to-face time is special and monitored and limited in prison. I close the door quietly and slip out to my car, . . . join hundreds of women all over the state on our way to visit our loved ones in prison in Oklahoma. Many of us have kids in our car, sleepy kids in car seats, grumpy teenagers slumped in the back seat with headphones on their nodding heads. These are our kids we are taking to see their daddies. Sometimes they are our grandchildren we are taking to Visit their moms. There are lots of grandmothers my age raising their daughters' children and making the weekly, or sometimes monthly, trip to visit Mom. . . .

As we, the families and friends, preachers and teachers, children and mamas, park our cars, grab our clear plastic bags of quarters and hurry to the gate, I look at us and marvel at how representative of America We are. We are black, White, American Indian, Latino, Asian. Some of the women are wearing the hijab. . . . In one way, however, we do not represent society at large. As I look around, I realize that we are disproportionately female. . . . Yes, there are men making their way to the barbed wire fence, but mostly there are women. Women with babies, women whose "babies" will not be coming home with them tonight. Women all dressed up and looking as sexy as they can for their men. Women who can barely afford to make the trip. Women with heavy zip locks full of quarters because it takes a lot of quarters to feed a family from vending machines. We joke that there is more than one thief in this visiting room where a bag of chips costs 2 bucks and a stale sandwich will cost upwards of $4. A little prison humor. . . .

. . . This pretty mom has her hands full. . . . She laughs and her pretty eyes sparkle as she watches her boys' daddy roughhouse with them. She is supposed to sit on her side of the table and he is supposed to sit on his side; however, the kids can run and play freely. So the three little boys crawl all over the daddy they resemble so closely while the sullen preteen sits by his mom, cutting his eyes around the room. I wonder as I watch him if he realizes he is in danger of becoming a statistic? Biracial son of an incarcerated parent living at or below the poverty line. I wonder if Mom knows. . . . That's one thing I was surprised about the first couple of visits: no one is yelling at their kids. No one is yelling at each other. No one is pouting. No one is scolding. Everybody is happy. The noise is deafening. Laughter, card-playing, board games, flirting, praying, Bible reading. And I think about that every month: what if the rest of my state could see these families? Could see these men with their loved ones?

Everybody is walking slower as we make our ways back to the parking lot, sun starting its descent. . . . We are all leaving our hearts behind.[26]

Ruth Brelsford is among the fortunate people with the time and means to get to prison. When they do, such visits seek to soften containment's direct damage to children and families, and they make more likely that a loved one's current confinement will be their last. Yet prison staff often seem intent on making things difficult. Writing from Arizona, Nolaw97 describes such instances.

Staff here at USP Tucson seem to get a kick out of persecuting inmates AND their loved ones. My cellie had family come from Florida, to Tucson, Arizona and he told me that they (staff) searched his parent's CAR! They're not driving THROUGH the prison! He also said that they refused them entry because of the clothes they wore. . . . Another friend of mine had just had family come from Maine. They (staff) refused his people TWICE because of their clothing, and had it not been for another (kinder) staff member, who could vouch for the inmate, he would not have had a visit at all. Another friend here had his parents visit, and his 70year old MOTHER was refused because her bra had metal in it. She had to go to buy a sports bra just to visit her son. They came from Texas. . . . What's she carrying, a file? Sometimes these people who work here are as heartless as vampires on a blood binge. . . . Of course, the prison will hide behind the letter of the rules and completely ignore and reject the spirit of the rule.[27]

From Maine, Arline Lawless sees similarly arbitrary obstacles.

Where can I start about the sources of stress in here? There are so many forms of stress from the guards screaming at the top of their lungs to your family not being able to come to see you because they were 2 minutes late for the check in. That is complete bullshit if you ask me especially when your family drives 2 1/2 hours to see you. In fact, there are a few women in here where their family members drive over 7 hours to come and see them and they were denied because they were late.[28]

Kali Yuga Vikalpa, writing from New York, notes of prison staff, "They love to hassle and mock Visiting family members, denying visits and destroying family ties."[29] Shane Bell describes having his four-year-old nephew turned away from a visit in South Dakota, in retaliation, he claims, for Bell filing grievances. He is told that only a biological parent or legal guardian can bring in a minor, though his six-year-old nephew had visited with Bell's parents and he finds that there is in fact no such regulation.

I got the informal resolution response (grievance) back today and it states "Your parents can bring in Carter . . ." No apology or explanation. . . . The damage is already done. I get few visits and when my family spend the time and money to travel across the state to visit me, denying their visits out of retaliation is wrong.[30]

In his best-selling memoir, *Writing My Wrongs*, Michigan writer Shaka Senghor describes how his desire to be present and a credible father to his son turned his life away from criminal behavior; and yet,

> the system isn't designed for inmates to cultivate healthy relationships with people on the outside. Families of loved ones are discouraged from visiting by the invasive pat searches and the disrespectful officers who talk to them like they are children. Then there was the reality that while the majority of prisoners come from Detroit and other parts of southern Michigan, the majority of them are sent up north to prisons in rural areas. This makes it close to impossible for loved ones to visit often enough to cultivate a real relationship.[31]

Shaye E. describes the arduous process of trying to get time with his mother as she was dying of cancer, across the many miles that separate California's major cities from its prisons. In passing, his essay offers glimpses of some of the challenges that the families of incarcerated people face. Imprisonment of a loved one adds yet another burden upon burdened families.

> Six months before my release on my last prison term in 2012, my mother died of brain and lung cancer at 59. Her name was Karen and she gave birth to me, her only child, at the age of 16. I found out about the cancer diagnosis about 8 months before her death during one of the bi-monthly calls I made home to her and my son, whom she had custody of due to my incarceration and his mother's struggles with addiction. Except the call was answered by my aunt. . . . It was, needless to say, difficult to communicate all the heartbreak . . . [what] losing this person would mean to my aunt and my son and myself and everyone who loved my mom into a 15 minute phone call that had a recording repeat "This is a call from a California State Prison" pop up every 5 minutes. . . .
>
> . . . I was in an institution 5 hours away in Central California and asked to be moved to one 40 minutes by car away from my family in

what's called a HARDSHIP TRANSFER. . . . Reality dictated that we try to make my mom as comfortable and happy as possible and visiting her son is what she wanted the most. I wanted it too. . . . She could be brutally honest with how disappointing I was but always let me know how I was loved unconditionally. She traveled to every prison I ever ended up in to visit me, scold me, laugh with me but most importantly, to let me know I mattered to someone. Now, as I tried, as my family, tried, to make the transfer happen, we were stonewalled by the administration. . . . To this day, the indifference of the staff is mind boggling. . . . I think it's worth mentioning that I experienced more human connectivity and compassion from my fellow gangbangers, bullies, robbers and junkies than any of the professionally trained correction and rehabilitation staff. . . . I am truly blessed to have a father and stepmother who not only took care of my mom during her final months but also rented a van, took time off of work and traveled the 5 hours to the prison I was trying to get transformed out of so her and I could visit. . . . She deserved a better son and I used the memory of that last visit with my mom to try to live a life she could celebrate post prison. The memory of losing her though, proved to be a hard one to shake and I again was drawn to heroin addiction and am in prison again for drugs 7 years after her passing.[32]

As Shaye E. makes clear, prison facilities are slow to respond—if they ever do so—to the needs of families at times of pain or death among their free members. Lee Novinger offers a view from Texas of just how callous prisons can be to the needs of people dying inside, who are clearly no threat to anyone. She sketches scenes of a family's worst fears.

Many women are dying here in Carswell that should be home in their final days or months with their families. Less than 1% of the filed Compassionate Relief forms are granted. Because of rooming with an INA (nurse aid) I have listened to the statements of intensely poor care being provided to patients on the 4th floor. Some of these patients I've known well over the years. They do have families that want to share the end of their lives with them. . . . Nearly every patient has been denied Compassionate Release. . . . The warden here candidly states, "If they can dress or feed themselves, they're not going anywhere." "They can die right here." . . . On the 4th floor it's common to limit the number of diaper changes allowed per day, decubitus ulcers are a norm, colostomies are frequent, malnutrition is evident and fractures are highly frequent due to poor nutrition. Patient inmates are spoken to aggressively and cussed at. Professionalism does not exist. How can conditions and staff attitudes be so deplorable? . . . All prisons, male and female, would rather allow inmates to die in prison versus having quality medical care and important time with family members.[33]

When incarcerated people write of the costs of imprisonment to families, they often blend the emotional and financial burdens meted out. Linda K. Stermer writes from Michigan.

You become completely dependent on the people who care about you. More than ever before, you rely on them for all of your financial and emotional needs. . . .

By the time you have served five years, you have become a financial burden on your family. If you have children, you have missed many of the monumental firsts in their lives. Whether it was learning to walk, ride a bike, the first day of school, first date or graduation. Or your parents are becoming elderly and are having major health problems and you cannot be there to help them.[34]

From Arizona, Herukhuti describes the psychological and physical damage prison does to incarcerated people; he then details the ways that states exploit families, as well as observing the repercussions of incarceration on children and communities.

Laws need to be introduced that prohibit the "double-dipping" into the taxpayers pocket i.e. Families of prisoners pay taxes as well as send funds to their sons/daughters, spouses, fathers/mothers. These said funds are not given in its entirety to the prisoners. . . . Percentages are taken out and set aside for the various restitution set up by the state. These are not wages earned by the prisoner and the family is being penalized also (by association) for crimes they did not commit. This adds to the mental degradation patterns set up by prisons. Telephone prices are extremely high. . . . This is meant to isolate the prisoner by destroying communication to the family/world causing emotional distress. The food store prices are equally outrageous. The taxes pay for the food (which is not giving even the required caloric amounts), yet even to supplement the diet, the costs are high, seemingly for pro[fi]t motives more than is necessary. All of these negative prison laws/policies/ guidelines are for the duration of the prisoner's life AND especially the family(s) lifetime (who are equally punished; without justification).[35]

Justin Case writes from South Carolina. Like many other writers able to access studies conducted outside, he takes researchers' statistics as confirmation of what he has experienced.

The Institute for Advancing Justice Research and Innovation at Washington Univ. in St. Louis have factored in the various societal costs of incarceration. Things like lost wages and increased criminology among the children of incarcerated parents, as well as other collateral expenses. Many affected families live beneath the federal poverty line as it is, and are the same families that struggle the most beneath the massive financial burdens of incarceration. Everything from paying bail bonds and raising the children of incarcerated parents, to the cost of prison and jail phone calls and fees to place money on prisoner's institutional accounts. According to the study, an estimated $923 billion in incarceration-related costs are not factored into annual government budgets. Those hundreds of billions of "invisible dollars" are an enormous drain on overall social welfare, and account for more than 90% of the overall cost of incarceration.[36]

New York resident Harold Caprers notes four of the built-in costs to families: "They may even be in debt from sending us packages and money orders, not to mention the fact that they visit us every week, spending money in those vending machines, and excepting our collect phone calls."[37]

From Washington State, Rufus Andrew Phelps III criticizes not only the costs but those behind the financial costs to families.

This state promotes monopolies. They do not allow anything from anyone but access securepak. . . . They do not allow any of these items that we need to be purchased from any other vendor when it comes to typing supplies, shoes, and general items that we need. That way, they can extort us and anyone that try's to help us in my opinion, which makes it really hard on our friends and families every time they want to help us. . . .

I know that I have to be and am responsible for the reason that I am here instead of out in society. . . . I should not have to watch my family be extorted for trying to help me and care about my well being. It seems like the DOC feels that it is their mission to punish not only the prisoners in their charge, but anyone and everyone that has anything to do that might help us that are locked up.[38]

Sebastian O'Neal writes of the costs passed directly to families in Florida.

Inmates use to be given all kinds of sports equipment to use at the rec yard. Now they are lucky to get a basketball and even that has to get donated. Inmates use to be able to have their families buy them packages from stores, where they found the best prices. Now they are force to buy from a company, that charges the highest prices, sometimes for a defective product. Like shoes that cost about $30 in the free world, they charge us $70 and they start tearing up in a few months. We use to be allowed to buy gloves and tobogans to keep warm in the winter. Now they claim they are a security threat and their officers are the only ones allowed to wear them. Inmates use to be issued sweatshirts during winter. Now only inmates with money who can afford to buy them, gets them. Inmates use to be issued boots, but now they are issued crocs, that let their feet freeze in the winter. . . . Even though they are making more money off of inmates and their families, they are doing less for them.[39]

Under the name The American Pharaoh, a man held in Georgia continues O'Neal's list.

The state barely feeds you, but they have food for sale. The state doesn't pay its [incarcerated] workers, but it offers services for a cheaper price to the nation. You can't own a phone here, but they offer collect call services. You can no longer receive packages from family if the items were purchased in stores, but the state offers a vendor your family can purchase items from. Your family can no longer send you money directly to the prison, but they've opened accounts for us through Bank of America and have contracts with JPAY to make sending money possible. . . . Family is no longer allowed to bring food to visitations, but they have vending machines available for your family to purchase food. . . . Each one of these things actually made life more expensive for inmates, made things more difficult financially and physically for parents possibly poverty stricken, and makes the state millions. At the price of harder living conditions for inmates, breeding more violence, deaths, and contraband.[40]

Many of the services O'Neal and Pharaoh describe, including all those through JPay, charge families and their loved ones inside, as Jeffrey Jason Gardner confirms from Virginia: "The family and friends of prisoners are sympathetic and compassionate when they hear of prison conditions such as poor quality food, small portions, poor medical, and dental care. So, these compassionate people send money through Jpay and pay the extortion direct deposit fee."[41] From Connecticut, Peter Padilla describes the mental, physical, and financial burdens on families and the condemned—burdens laid on by the legal system, from probation, to courts, to prisons. He also highlights the gap between public representations and what he has witnessed.

Outside these walls you can look up D.O.C. and they'll show you a clean cell, a good mattress and a pillow. In some sites the picture will even have a T.V. I'm in prison that cell is not here, that pillow is not here. On the outside you can look up the prison menu the portions we're allowed. I can assure you what you read and what we eat is not the same thing and the portion you read we are given is false also. The amount of food grown men are given will not fill a child's stomach. The tactic of the amount of food we're given here is to force you to buy commissary. You have to buy food or you will go hungry and the prices of the items you have to choose from are 3x the price it is outside the walls. This makes your family have to send you money a burden on their shoulders more psychological abuse on you. It cost $205.00 for a "13" flat TV that breaks in a year or so. Items you buy in here for hundreds of dollars you can get at a dollar store out there. Everything you read about in here does not exist in here. There isn't a pillow unless you buy it and the pillow you buy is one of the items made rite here in this jail.[42]

The emotional and financial costs to families come simply from trying to keep their loved ones in decent health and maintain relationships despite exile to distant facilities. Families must also bear the weight of witnessing the operations of a system that never considers these burdens—a system that demands and can break down resilience at every step. Ronald Marshall writes from Louisiana, laying out all the work that the families of incarcerated people must do if they want to see their sons or fathers, daughters, mothers, aunts, or cousins outside again. His essay adds to emotional and dollar costs the resolve families must find to counter the business interests that want to keep the count of incarcerated people as high as possible. He concludes on a note of sober encouragement.

Believe me, trying to get your loved ones off the count when the alphabets, numbers, aggravated circumstances or for profit prison companies are double stacked against them will likely feel as if you and your incarcerated loved ones are being victimized by the criminal justice system, parole board or victim advocate groups. You and incarcerated loved ones will experience severe emotional trauma: anger, anxiety, depression, shame, humiliation, despair, or even spurts of fear at the prospect of death by incarceration. In whichever mind state you and your incarcerated loved ones find yourselves on the incarcerated journey, quitting is not an option when there is a better life for your incarcerated loved ones after release and reunited with the family. So, keep the struggle alive and healthy in your hearts. To struggle is to never know defeat, only progress, and eventually victory. Until your incarcerated loved ones have achieved . . . freedom, continue to strive with them and chant down Babylon, "We're getting our incarcerated loved ones off the prison count."[43]

While Ronald Marshall addresses the work for the families of the incarcerated, Alice G. Bingner, writing from an unnamed state, offers a sketch of the courtroom beginnings of the pains of imprisonment for the parents of incarcerated people.

I could see the top floors of two hospitals from my seat. Is the sickness, suffering, remorse and hopelessness in them worse than that which I felt in the courtroom where I waited for my 16-year-old son to appear? I felt sorry for the mothers in the maternity wards. Their pains currently, in my opinion, were symbolic of a future lived with heartache. . . . The judge, groggy, defeated, bored by the repetitiveness and hopelessness, must have felt especially affected as I was. "You want a court-appointed attorney?" The judge would ask. "You have no job? When did you work last? No savings? No bank account? No source of income to defend yourself with?" I paid indirectly; all the audience and the participants did, because my son and the others who appeared that day had no money, no job, no income. . . . Often a siren shouted "make way" as a stork screamed for recognition. I wondered where those babies would end. . . .

The young, frivolously dressed lawyers that day knew the game being played; as did the youth in the audience and those on the stand. In fact, they may have written the manuscript. What they couldn't know was the ones, who, like my son Barry, would continue committing seemingly petty crimes—not violent but criminal nonetheless—after another and ultimately spend most of their adult years behind prison bars. Their productive years wasted, their children neglected and sadly trending toward a repeat of history.[44]

Yet despite what imprisoned people and outside researchers know about the consequences that devolve from a family member's prison term, these consequences, as Anastasia Bogomolova writes from Florida, are barred from consideration at sentencing in federal courts.[45]

Our prized justice system does not even consider the fact of having minor children when sentencing the parent. This is the law. Thus, 28 U.S.C.S. 994(e), describing the duties of the Sentencing Commission, states: "The Commission shall assure that the guidelines . . . , in recommending a term of imprisonment, or length of a term of imprisonment, reflect the general INAPPROPRIATENESS OF CONSIDERING . . . FAMILY TIES AND RESPONSIBILITIES OF THE DEFENDANT." In other words, during the sentencing of a parent, the destiny of a minor innocent child is not even a factor for consideration. One would think that the rights of a child of incarcerated parent(s) should be protected by the Constitution. Not so. While the rights of "family integrity" are supposedly protected by the 14th Amendment under the due process clause for both parents and children, this "familial right to be raised and nurtured by their parents" is considered not applicable to the children of incarcerated parents: ". . . so long as the detention (of a parent) is lawful, that so-called deprivation of the right to family integrity does not violate the constitution. To rule otherwise would risk turning every lawful detention or arrest of a parent into a substantive due process claim . . . Were a substantial number of young children knowingly placed in harm's way, it is easy to imagine how valuable claims might lie." But you would think that 2.7 million children CAN be considered a "substantial number"! How much more substantial should it get for the justice system to actually notice that the mass incarceration of parents IS hurting their children?[46]

Kenneth Fitzgerald Nixon writes from Michigan of the effects of his confinement on himself, his children, his sister, and his mother.

It's torture to wake up in the morning and it's torture to go to bed at night. It's torture to talk to my kids over the phone, and it's even worse to watch them leave me in the visiting room. I'll never get a chance to see those first words, those first steps their first day of school or there first ball games, my life is literally hell. Since I've been gone two of my close friends have died. One to gun violence and the other to a brain aneurysm. My grandmother doesn't remember who I am or what I look like because she has been diagnosed with full-blown dementia. My mother wants to move out of the state and retire, and my sister refuses to accept a full College scholarship out of the state because they both wanted to stay close to me, hoping that this would be over soon.[47]

Ignoring the consequences for families only makes sense within a narrowly retributive view of sentencing. The following testimony reveals what can happen to incarcerated people's children and continuing generations. It also provides a segue into testimony to how containment can shred the fabric of communities already struggling with the poverty, narrowed job markets, and weak civic involvement that characterize the neighborhoods where incarceration is concentrated and where high incarceration rates deepen such challenges.[48]

In "Like Father, Like Son?," Illinois writer Romell Winters describes the steps from poverty to addiction, gang involvement, and unwanted pregnancy to prison that so often become a generational cycle.

> My story is like a lot of others who grew up the way I did. I grew up in poverty in a single-parent home with four older sisters. My father went to prison when I was very young, so he wasn't in my life at all when I was growing up. Sometimes, I would get letters and birthday cards from him, but that was the extent of our relationship. When my mother lost her job, we moved from a bad neighborhood to a worse one where at the age of 9 I learned about gangs and soon after joined one. By the time I was 12, I was running around the streets hustling, drinking and smoking weed like I was grown. Even though I really wasn't going to school, I was smart enough to manage to graduate to high school. . . . I went to "juvy" the first time when I was 14. When my mom came to visit me there, her words to me were: "You're gonna end up just like your father" which will prove to become true. When I got out of "juvy" four months later, things seemed to get worse at home. We had lost our house and had to live in the shelter for awhile. After months of my mother trying to find us a permanent place to live, she decided it was best for us to go live with relatives in Mississippi where it happens to be where my father was in prison. Shortly after moving there, my mom took me to visit him, meeting him for the first time. It was awkward and uncomfortable. I didn't know what to say or do, and I could tell he was nervous, which only made me nervous. Our second visit wasn't quite as awkward, and all the subsequent visit together grew gradually less difficult. While getting to know my father, I was trying to know myself. During that time, I struggled a lot with identity like a lot of teens of course. I really had no moral support, and my role models were my mother who was now addicted to drugs and the gangs back in Chicago who I felt loved by. Looking to escape the slow and boring life in Mississippi, I rebelled and found my way back to Chicago, picking right back up where I had left off doing: hustling, drinking, and smoking weed. Also during that time I became very promiscuous and ended up getting a girl pregnant whom I really didn't have a relationship with. Right before I was arrested for

this case she gave birth to a boy who since being incarcerated I only have seen him a couple of times. At the moment I hear he's following in my footsteps, but I'm hoping to change that soon. I missed out on seeing my son grow up. I can't rewind time, but I sure can try to make a difference in my own life, so I'll be able to become important in my son's life now that he's going down the wrong path. There is no future for him behind these walls, and I pray to the heavens that I will be granted my freedom and the power to stop the cycle of like father, like son incarceration—I guess we'll find out?[49]

Peter Mehmel chronicles the repercussions for his children of his conviction after a bar fight resulted in a man's death on the night of his son's birthday. Like Assata Shakur, he describes a scene commonly depicted by incarcerated parents: his child's first visit.

He lunged to meet me, hugging tight. His skin was hot, feverish, and he didn't let go after the initial greeting. I searched for an answer to his unspoken plea for an explanation. The small, unadorned visiting room was crowded and seemed to close in upon us. . . . I just held him, fighting back my own emotions. Maintaining a front grew harder as the visit continued. My voice threatened to break. . . . Some things cling and won't let go—like his hug, and how I had to pry his tiny hands apart when the visit ended. Prison has extracted pieces of all of us. Happy childhoods. Bonds between brother and sister. . . . None of us saw the stigma they'd endure. Schoolchildren can be mean. As a convict's kid, there is no acceptable answer to "What does your daddy do?" . . . They saw the pecking order from the bottom and had to fight to fit in where they could. They migrated to the misfit groups. Drug use became abuse. . . . Through no fault of their own, they grew up experiencing prison secondhand. As if that wasn't bad enough, what weighs upon me now—both went to prison themselves. . . . All that I've experienced will be passed on. For over a decade, my son believed that I did not love him. My daughter had her first child at fifteen. Neither finished high school. . . . My grandchildren, all born out of wedlock, never met their grandfather. Both my children went to prison when their children were young—so repeats the cycle that I started. No doubt they too have learned the anguish of restricted space, resources, and actions. They will have no careers, no pension plans, and college is out of the equation. My brother wrote a while back. He told me to sit down because he had really terrible news. Two of my daughter's three children had been killed in a house fire. I sat stunned. I wondered how my daughter received the news in her cell. Did her hands shake like mine? Did she utter prayers to reverse time? No doubt, her distress is much greater than mine. I'm sure it's killing her to be caged while her remaining child is in such need.[50]

Peter Mehmel records the prison history written into his children's lives by a first instance of legal containment. Like Rommel Winters, others write as the children of imprisoned people.

From South Carolina, Amy Benjamin writes a poignant narrative of another three-generation prison legacy. Her essay recalls the night of a friend's prison suicide and the arbitrary humiliation and deprivation that can drive such an act. This leads to reflection on a familial history of containment's domino effects.

My paternal grandmother was a whore. A heroin addict and a prostitute. I have one picture of her that was taken at the Jersey Shore sometime in the 1930's. Neither my father or I look anything like her, though we closely resemble each other. We must look like whoever the trick was that provided our genetic material. This gives me a very random sense of my identity. Like my grandmother, I am also a heroin addict. . . . My grandmother gave birth to my father in prison. . . . After his unfortunate birth my father returned to prison twice more. Once for armed robbery and once for welfare fraud. I was really young when he did that second bid and my family told me he was traveling with the circus taming lions. Why do I begin to believe that my hair and eye color are not the only traits that are genetic? . . . I should have joined the circus. I would have traveled the world and swung from a flying trapeze maybe been shot out of a cannon and lived a life of danger and excitement. When my grandmothers picture was taken it must have been winter because she is wearing a coat. She is smiling and her smile makes her wrinkle her nose. I never saw that picture until I was twenty one years old but when I smile I wrinkle my nose just like she does. Perhaps my identity is not so random as I've believed. . . .

My maternal grandmother sold my mother and my aunt to families in New Jersey. They were three and five years old. They never saw her again until her funeral forty years later and by that point she wasn't answering any questions. I think about my white trash, Irish Catholic grandparents sometimes. . . . My grandmother was twenty one years old and widowed with six children. Why choose my aunt and my mother to sell though? Was that decision as random as the man who sired my father? Who would I have been if the women in my family were never sold? . . . Some years ago I called my aunt from prison and told her I was contemplating suicide. She begged me to find the sweet girl inside myself that she remembered. I'm thirty seven years old now, far from a girl, and whoever that child was I suspect she's long dead. But I do remember that when I was young I wanted to tell stories. I would walk alone with my dog and make up tales about the people I saw. I saw a black haired girl on a motorcycle, the man that sold me candy at the corner store. My imagination has been burned down by time and drugs. All I have left now are true stories. They've festered inside me for thirty seven years, and now on this night so much like another that I recall my conscience demanded that this story be told. On the night Laura killed herself I sleep walked into the bathroom to get a glass of water. When I flicked on the light a cricket with a crushed back leg dragged itself painfully across the floor. I stared at it, dumb and shocked. Where did it come from and how did it get so wounded? It was midnight on the coldest January day in forever. . . . The whole world was locked down and frozen dead. How did this lone and injured cricket make its way here to die in prison?[51]

New York writer Rahasheem Brown offers yet another story of how carceral containment can affect one generation to the next, and laterally, among siblings. He also conveys how concentrated incarceration can transform prison into less of a threat than what outside research has repeatedly characterized as an expected and even aspirational rite of passage.[52]

There were role-models in the hood (neighborhood) from which I hail; very few, of whom, have never been incarcerated. Even fewer have never committed a crime in my presence. When I was young (and looking up to them), they did not &, probably, could not have known that they, indirectly, planted some seed or another in my young mind. . . .

I remember walking past the Schenectady County Jail once, (where several people I know/knew had been and spoke of) thinking "I wonder what it looks like in there?" In the back of my mind, I knew I need not contemplate that for too long, thus, because I knew that I would, eventually, find out. So I abandoned the first thought and began contemplating what I would be doing, to get my name up, (become known and respected [or better fearful]) while I'm there. By this time I had already been to D.F.Y. (the New York State Department of Corrections Services, Division for Youth) for 4 years, in total. . . . While there, I became a better (or worse) and more organized criminal. . . .

My brother, Keith, has been to prison once, back in the 70s or 80s, but has never returned. Aside from myself and him, 3 of my mother's other children have been to prison. . . . My father, who, himself, passed away in prison, bore 6 children. Of that 6, 3 of us have been to prison. . . .

Eventually, [brother] George went to prison. . . . At some point, my younger brother came to Greene while I was there. Instead of being a good role-model to him, I corrupted him even worse.[53]

From New Mexico, Victor Andrew Apodaca Sr. quotes researcher Todd Clear's words in describing both his own and his children's experiences of parental containment.

Clear concluded after a review of evidence, the ubiquity of the prison experience in some poor urban neighborhoods has had the effect of eliminating the stigma of serving time. On any given day, as many as one in five adult men in these neighborhoods is behind bars, and as Clear has written, "the cycling of these young men through the prison system has become a central factor determining the social ecology of poor neighborhoods, where there is hardly a family without a son, an uncle or a father who has not done time in prison." As this rings true in my own life my father was a convict, so I am a convict and my oldest daughter is a felon, and my middle son is a convict that will be receiving a life sentence.[54]

Richard Hall offers testimony to what he has observed in California's San Quentin Prison. He then calls on those related to incarcerated people to lead in the struggle for change.

In 1980 I observed a woman with child inside her who used to visit her husband faithfully while he was housed at San Quentin State Prison. She had a bouncing baby boy, the apple of her eye. Try to imagine how I felt in 1999 when I reported to my prison work assignment and learned that that woman's baby boy had grown up from wearing diapers to end up with me and his father in prison? . . . Always remember one very important thing about prisoners in general. They usually embrace the same exact mentality of the communities they come from. They are also a reflection of, too often, the worst about their own family. I have lost count of how many youngsters I have encountered in here who were not even born when I entered this bottomless pit.[55]

From California as well, a woman who writes anonymously echoes Amy Benjamin, reminding us that prison also affects mothers and daughters. This author's mother was in and out of prison all of the writer's life. Like the children of divorce, she blamed herself for these periods of deprivation, and the essay marks a moment of celebration that is, at best, ironic.

For the first time, I finally had my mother in my life. Granted, we were sitting in the Pen, yet it was what I had dreamed of my whole life. It had finally happened; no one could keep her from me anymore.

It seemed that no matter how hard I tried when I was growing up, nothing was ever good enough to get my mother to stay out of prison. . . . No one could tell me it wasn't my fault, though no one had ever bothered to try. I just knew it had to be that test I took last week and only got a B+. It was the day she was arrested again. Or maybe because Dad said I didn't do the dishes right.

She didn't write because I don't spell good enough. Not because it's easier on her, or because Dad wouldn't let her write.

The worst part is now sitting here, doing life without parole. I was finally given my lifelong dream, a chance to see my mommy. The worst part was hearing her say she came here to be with me. The fact is, that was the benefit but not a cause. Yet the same guilt is alive and strong in me. It only sealed all those childhood beliefs.

I never thought I would hurt as bad as I did the day she walked out of those gates a little over a month ago. . . .

Looking back, I was very blessed for the time I had.[56]

In a third essay from California, Running Water offers a view from the other side of the relationship that Anonymous describes: that of a repeatedly imprisoned parent. Her essay first describes her own childhood and young adulthood. Her father, on the occasions he was present, raped her and beat her mother; her addiction to heroin followed. She was using when she became pregnant amid a gang rape, and then—as a result of stabbing one of her attackers—endured withdrawal behind bars. Released when her son was seven, she stayed clean but was sent back to prison for six years after being caught driving a car "without the owner's permission."

My son Timothy, who is everything to me, is now very hurt and angry with me. I promised him I would not mess up again. You know, sometimes sorry is not enough to tell him. I have to show him.

Timothy was so hurt and angry he would not talk to me; he didn't answer any of my letters. It would be easy to slip back into drugs. It is the easy way out.

After three and a half years I am so happy because recently I got a letter from my son with pictures. My son is sixteen years old. Now I have something to look forward to in getting out of here. He told me I better be out there to see him graduate from high school. But how do I makeup to him these last five years?[57]

These writers make plain: the idea that incarceration contains and incapacitates suffering is as myopic as believing that each convicted person was born from a vacuum, without biological kin, without parental responsibilities. Every act of containment, imprisoned people know, is a violent extraction from a home and a family. Such extractions, in turn, can damage the communities that are the most heavily policed, and the most in need of human resources if they are ever to become strong enough to resist state powers that have chosen to surveil and punish poverty, addiction, and all the other triggers to crime and criminalization.

CONTAINMENT'S COSTS TO COMMUNITIES

Writers inside regularly address the costs and damage that concentrated incarceration imposes upon targeted communities. The cycle we have just seen repeated through generations is not confined to families but spreads across the neighborhoods where such families live. "All my life," Isaiah M. Thomas writes from Minnesota, "I've witnessed this system break up homes and destroy communities."[58] From Michigan, Lacino Hamilton writes of "how caging people for part or all of their lives has removed from the community and the family the abilities to sustain themselves free of state and corporate domination."[59] Michael Rippo comments from Nevada.

> The phenomenon I refer to is America's overcriminalization craze. . . .
> It has created criminals out of honest people and continues to disrupt
> families and communities as enforcement of unrestrained, knee-jerk re-
> tributive and utilitarian legislation tears through disadvantaged classes,
> leaving in its wake mass incarceration and a burgeoning mass of disen-
> franchised citizens—i.e., ex-felons stripped of voting rights and other
> so-called constitutional guarantees. The Blackstone ratio has been innu-
> merably reversed. Now it matters not how many innocent people suffer,
> so long as not one guilty person goes free.[60]

From California, Maurice Harris—in an essay that advocates for formerly incarcerated people to become "peace ambassadors" in their communities—echoes Michael Rippo.

> Locking people up has an especially malign effect on poor urban neigh-
> borhoods, where up to 20% of the male population may be behind bars
> at any given time. Not only do the men come home with diminished
> prospects that hurt the whole community. . . . Their absence weakens
> the family & social networks they need when they come home & hurts
> those left behind. It is no accident that the sons & brothers of men who

go to prison are more likely to follow the same path. These trends help cause crime rather than prevent it.[61]

Timothy J. Muise writes from Massachusetts of a common link in the domino effect of concentrated containment.

In the early 1980's there was a serious overreaction to the crack cocaine epidemic that faced the streets of our urban areas. Tough on crime drug laws removed many of the males from the community for double-digit prison sentences. This forced their children to seek that type of paternal love from each other in the form of gangs. These gangs are responsible for many of the murders on our streets.[62]

Also from Massachusetts, Daniel S. Throop describes prisons as "islands," where people are "surgically" removed into extreme isolation with terrible effects on them, their families, and their communities. He draws his conclusion from the sheer numbers of those contained by prison walls.

The Massachusetts Department of Corrections . . . captains eighteen such islands with a total population of 11,149 human beings. When one factors in all of the families and friendships which were once associated with such a large prison population, the sheer numbers of the socially dead amount to nothing less than state-sanctioned relational genocide. . . .

In the correctional war on crime the friends and families of the incarcerated become collateral consequences, thereby adding to the relational carnage which prison isolation creates. For every single social death that takes place within prisons, a ripple-effect occurs and multiplies the number of casualties beyond the walls exponentially.[63]

A third Massachusetts writer, Darin Bufalino, writes simply that "all agree the system is broken, mass incarceration does not make our communities safer—just the opposite."[64] Jesse Campbell III writes of the "economic slavery" he sees foisted upon communities by the political economy of prisons. His extended essay from Connecticut offers a breakdown of the sources of corporate profits from prisons, the costs to incarcerated people, their families, and communities. As he summarizes, "To profit rather than rehabilitate from the American prisoner is Capitalism. It is the American way to spread that reality at a great cost that we all pay for in the end, not just in taxes but in lives, time, and wasted resources."[65]

While many writers point to the direct financial costs of placing millions of people in legal containment, others list the constructive services depleted by such costs, with predictable community fallout. Robbie Switzer Green writes from North Carolina.

> The state governments are shifting funding from education and highways to pay for construction and operation of these penal facilities. This means that your local schools don't get repaired, potholes don't get fixed, and your community has to raise your property taxes to pay for the incarceration of more prisoners. The real horror of the system is that it is recycling the same people. . . .
>
> If they fail, they return to prison, or end up derelict (abandoned) and destitute (without a home or reg. job and rejected by society) fed and clothed by either the taxpayers or charity. The human wreckage piles up on street corners and accumulates in homeless shelters.[66]

Texas resident Tandy Marshall sees the zero-sum economy of prison building within state budgets.

> The tax payers are paying to build all these prisons to make the wealthy wealthier while kids can't get decent books at schools. While teachers are under paid and the cost of living is going up and people are fighting for higher wages, the federal government is sending billions and billions of tax payer money to support prison profiteers. Our veterans aren't getting the help they need and taxes go to welfare because families are ripped apart and need help.[67]

Ty Evans presents an extensively documented assessment of the costs of mass incarceration as well as a detailed list of steps that might be taken to reduce prison population numbers. His views from Indiana on the social damage that incarceration imposes specify the effects noted by other writers.

A balance sheet contrasting the costs and benefits of incarceration is difficult to prepare because the accounting requires both objective and subjective elements. The objective costs begin with the fiscal burden shouldered by the states. On average, 6.2% of state budgets in 2007 were devoted to corrections. . . . Direct corrections expenses now total $80 billion a year, and the total expenditure exceeds $260 billion once police, judicial, and legal services are included. Virtually no tangible goods or services are produced, rendering the entire system an exercise in lost productivity. Subjective costs include the incalculable harm done to other parts of society. These collateral consequences include the effect incarceration has on families of prisoners—higher rates of divorce, separation, domestic violence, and developmental and behavioral problems among children. Mass incarceration is most acutely felt in disadvantaged communities where poverty, unemployment and family disruption combine to create a permanent underclass.[68]

Michigan writer Alice G. Bingner echoes Ty Evans, stating that "in too many instances an auxiliary cost is State care for the families who are left without a breadwinner for years" and that "the children of convicts are destined to become convicts themselves."[69]

Many writers describe the damage disseminated among communities from the damage done to people while legally contained. They offer a transition to the final section of this chapter, where witnesses speak to their fears when contemplating release back into their communities.

Edward C. Shelley provides an aphoristic summary of the issue, writing from Washington State that "you build the human being, you ultimately build the community"[70]—a statement whose inverse is clear to many incarcerated people, including Idaho resident Mark T. Wayne, who suggests how containment today nullifies its own best effects.

As more young men and women are socialized to the cell blocks and then returned to the streets, the violent subculture of the correctional facility increasingly acts as a vector for crime in our communities. Prisons and jails thus have a dual effect: they protect society from criminals, but they also contribute to crime by transferring their violent subculture to our community once inmates are released.[71]

From Pennsylvania, Richard S. Gross echoes the no-win cycle that Mark Wayne describes: "Prison burdens the entire family, leaves everyone broke, often renders the felon permanently unemployable, and promotes mental illness."[72]

California writer Ivan Kilgore rounds out this section with an observation that locates the destructive psychological effects of incarceration among other institutional failures in communities targeted by mass imprisonment, perpetuating cycles of crime.[73]

When we consider the mass incarceration of Black males, . . . family structures and other social networks in the community are destabilized and crime prone environments are created. . . .

The institutions that prevail here have effectively manipulated our thinking and conditioned us as if lab rats to exist in an environment of extreme poverty and ignorance. As a consequence of the chaos that comes of this, our informal social controls are weakened because daddy either dead or locked-up. And the only religion we practice is self-preservation—kill or be killed—because drugs and guns are sprinkled about as if parade candies. When we look to other institutions it's pretty much the same scenario. America's educational institution creates scores of poorly functioning ghetto youth. In terms of political gamesmanship, the school-2-prison pipeline has been highly effective. Furthermore . . . our incarceration exacerbates these problems. After years, if not decades, of being tormented, humiliated, and isolated from our loved ones, we are extremely insensitive, volatile, embittered, sexually deviant, and shell-shocked having been shot-up by block guns and bombed with explosive canisters of tear gas. Having underwent such treatment, the psychological effect has us foaming at the mouth like rabid dogs by the time we are released back into that other cage—THE GHETTO. As can be expected, we are mad, . . . driven to the point of pure insanity and sure desperation given what this manipulation has created within us. Therefore, by humiliating and brutalizing us as prisoners society stands to increase our potential for aggressive violence. The dope, prostitution, robbery, and high homicide rates affirm this.[74]

CONTAINMENT'S DAMAGE TO RETURNEES

The harms that containment imposes on people who will someday be back on the street include effects of the literal, concrete circumstances inside. In "The Vertical Neighborhood from Hell," Brad Carney offers a glimpse of where he lives in California. Readers who have never lived there can only imagine what dwelling in such an environment for years or decades might do even to the most resilient human being.

There are 45 cells on each of the five tiers, 225 cells on each side of the building, 450 concrete boxes built to house the people who have lost their right to remain in civilization. Each cell is 4.2 feet wide and 11 feet long, theoretically giving the two occupants 49.5 square feet of floor space to live in. However, a 32" wide by 6-foot long metal bunk bed is bolted to one wall, which kills off 35% of the floor space. A toilet and sink decorate the rear of the cell past the end of the bed, occupying that space. This leaves a 22" wide by 9' long area of open floor in each cell, a very narrow walkway that two men cannot navigate at the same time without becoming excessively intimate. . . . Outside the bars, a five-foot wide concrete "freeway" runs the length of the tier. There is zero privacy, ever. Guys will frequently loiter in front of your cell, lean against the railing, stand there and just stare into your cell; frequently smoking cigarettes and talking loudly to their friends who stand there with them. . . . Two gunner's walkways run along the walls opposite the cellblock, circling the inner perimeter of the building. . . . Each guard carries a Mini-14 rifle and a 9mm pistol; he or she is less than 30 feet away from the cells. Posted on the walls are large signs: "NO WARNING SHOTS FIRED IN THIS UNIT." Twin metal staircases at each end of the block provide access to the upstairs tiers. During the periods of "open unit," the flow of prisoners up and down these stairs and back and forth along the tiers is endless, a human ant farm of activity as the inmates scurry to and fro to leave or return to their cells, shower, and frequently go on missions to procure food or drugs or tobacco. Roving vendors cruise the walkways, offering a wide variety of things for sale: stolen food from the kitchen, clothing, linen, canteen items, drugs, tobacco, almost anything imaginable is readily available. The residents of this neighborhood are constantly throwing trash over the railings. . . . The men assigned to clean the walkways do the same thing. During clean-up time, a fine mist of dirt, hair and trash interspersed with large chunks of debris floats down from each tier and flows down into the cells below. Only the fifth tier occupants escape this nasty, airborne miasma. Black mold and fungus line the walls and cracks . . . in the communal showers located at the end of the block. They are accessible for only 4 1/2 hours a day, and there is always a long wait to get in. The water temperature cannot be adjusted, and is frequently painfully hot, almost scalding. . . . There are always about 50 men showering while 25 are drying off and another 50 or so are waiting to get in. The noise level is thunderous, almost painful. The drains often get plugged up, making it necessary to wade through a stream of dirty, soapy, contaminated water to get in or out of the shower. . . . It is not a nice place to live, but none of us who reside here do so voluntarily. We are sent to prison as punishment for our crimes. West Block does a fine job of reminding us of this on a daily basis.[75]

Writer Tshombe Amen, also from California, writes of what such spaces can do to the mind: "I have seen a man's mind so shaken he can no longer speak," effects seen primarily among men "from poor and broken communities." He goes on to question the terrible redundancy of the longest sentences in the developed world: "I have seen a man who's lived forty-plus years in prison for a crime he committed when he was nineteen years old. . . . Yes, he made a mistake which by standard of correction he should pay for but, is the mistake of a teenager worth more than twice their life?"[76] Andrae L. Bridges, held in Wisconsin, echoes Amen's views of the pointlessness of containment for containment's sake and similarly implies the effect on prospects for successful social reentry.

Now here it is I've served nearly 24 years and doing this time has only gotten harder and harder. I'm always on the verge of throwing in the towel and just giving up because all of my efforts seem to be in vain. Having to remain incarcerated is serving me, the community, and tax payers absolutely no purpose. I've completed everything asked of me and some, yet I'm forced to remain incarcerated with no chance of release in sight.[77]

Beyond the direct effects of legalized warehousing, writers inside explicitly decry that they and others will be severely damaged when sent back into the world. Robert Cannon Jr. writes mordantly from Michigan: "When this human meat-grinder spits me back out into the world I'm going to be different from the all-American square-John who has never been to hell."[78] From Washington State, Dewayne L. Harris writes of the sandwiching of the formerly incarcerated between the prison's effects and society's expectations.

> This is the person we mold and create to be turned out into society. A damaged or possibly destroyed human being at the end of his confinement, not the rehabilitated ex fellow human we are led to believe, but a man who has often lost his family and friends and hopes of a future, being returned to an often alien and hostile society that expects him to act in a rational manner in the most irrational situation a man can be thrust into upon being released from prison.[79]

Grey Ghost writes from California: "The lessons that our prison system teaches its residents is how to survive as prisoner, not as a citizen—not a very constructive body of knowledge for us or the communities to which we return."[80] Shakkir T. Mujahid also sees, from Maryland, that "long term confinements and the practice of mental and emotional degradation only creates an economic burden on the correctional system and more dangerous and bitter individual beings released upon our communities."[81] Echoing many of the writers testifying to the damage imposed by prison culture, Christopher Buckham writes from Wyoming of how men's prisons demand emotional hardening that surely disserves successful reentry.

> Scholars have described the prison code as: Suffer in silence. Never admit you are afraid. Do not snitch do not do anything that will make other prisoners think you are gay, effeminate, or a sissy. Act hard. Do not help the authorities in any way. Always be ready to fight, especially when your manhood is challenged. One way to avoid a fight is to look as though you are willing to fight. As a result, prisoners lift weights compulsively, adopt the meanest stare they can muster, and keep their fears and their pain carefully hidden beneath a well-rehearsed tough-

guy posture. The prison code is super-masculinity. Having these characteristics enables both strong and weak minded prisoners to survive their prison terms. . . . Prison rewards manliness and antisocial behaviors because displaying opposite behaviors is to be perceived as the opposite, weak and delicate; or prey.[82]

Held in Alaska, Daniel Rogers sees the kind of people that prisons not only contain but produce: "Inside these prisons people are degraded, sexually demoralized, trained to be co-dependent and subjected to society's worst behaviors. The outcome is a population of human beings that become victim of their own bad choices and a man made disorder."[83] James Lawson-Wilson finds in Florida that the most deleterious effects on people who will someday be released come from those paid for the work of correction.

What I'm saying is, sure there are men in here that deserve to be here, but the culture of brutality and disrespect and lies that permeates the ranks of officers seems to me like a self fulfilling prophesy. They convince themselves that we are dangerous animals, then proceed to abuse us physically and verbally to the point where even a rational man couldn't stay quiet any longer, then when we react, they pat themselves on the back for being right all along. Bottom line is that they need some form of oversight that cannot be infiltrated or corrupted by the intimidation that occurs to everyone who walks into a prison and into their world regardless whether your an inmate or an employee.[84]

Whether they state it or not, all of these writers contribute to a group portrait of the people containment degrades as it diminishes their capacity to rejoin the world outside. "The majority of us are going to walk the streets again, some right out of isolation," Christopher Balmer writes from Pennsylvania,

and guess what? The PA Department of Corrections doesn't care about the possibility of some dude with hate on his mind committing another heinous crime. Some of these prisoners never had a day of treatment during their entire time incarcerated. And they're thrown out to society with not a chance in hell of succeeding. Not only do the prisoners confined to long-term isolation fight with their own problems, they have to fight the (lack of) common sense of men and women who operate these prisons. . . .

People are so focused on keeping us in so we don't hurt someone else. But in the same breath they hurt us psychologically which could have a negative impact on our communities once these people are released from prison.[85]

After enduring the direct impacts of the violent, dead-end world of the prison, people are then sent into communities marked by continuing material need and social marginalization. Little wonder that thoughts of release can be as deeply woven with trepidation as with hope. Tandy Marshall describes the ways that prisons contain people inside their pasts, which are badly misunderstood by the public, thus blocking better futures and doing less to contain than to multiply harm.

There are battered women who were beaten constantly and raped constantly by men who were suppose to love and protect them, and when the abusers turned that violence on the children the woman was put in prison for injury to a child by neglect. What do people see when they do background checks for jobs or apartments? What does parole see? Robbery, murder, child neglect/endangerment and what will these people think? Our police and district attorneys are on a mission to meet quotas and have huge conviction rates. The result is them on crusades to make defendants look like monsters no matter the circumstances. The result is millions of Americans with no faces, only numbers, broken homes resulting in more criminals in a justice system that cares nothing about justice. Mass incarceration makes our society more dangerous.[86]

Carceral containment is never a clean in, then out. All incarcerated people know that their records will work against them for the rest of their lives and that release often results in a quick return. Their fears stretch from what incarceration has done to them personally, to how quickly they will have to muster the resources needed to survive outside, to the circumstances they will find themselves back in again after years away. From an Arkansas prison, B. C. Murray ponders the effects of long-term containment.

I sardonically recall the many times before my isolation where I craved solitude and detachment from the world. Only then, I naively felt, could I find peace I so desperately coveted. Now, with no excuses and a ten-year head start, I will dwell in a society void of family, friends, and acquaintances with only self-spawned encouragement to get me through each day. Whether I am able to generate the fulfillment necessary to justify my continuing to breathe and endure remains to be seen.

The only upside is that without the interaction with others, I alone must judge whether my existence is worth the plethora of challenges I must face as a banished, forever-tainted human being. I can only hope that my self-discernment is objective and fair and takes into account the many obstacles an ostracized and alone man faces in a world where connectivity and conformity trump individuality and where a man's past, as Faulkner says, is not even past.[87]

Ryan M. Moser writes for many people contemplating release without money or a home. He lays out the cycle in which prisons and states seek to contain crime while they also challenge the formerly confined to resist it. Moser writes from Florida.

When a man walks out of prison or jail, many times they leave with only the clothes on their back and whatever small penance the DOC will give them (typically around $50.00 and a Greyhound bus ticket). Some would ask why taxpayers should pay anything to a person whom has committed a crime, or try to help someone who has violated the law. The easy answer is that you're only helping yourselves. A man who leaves prison with no help will, as a first or last resort, choose to commit another crime in order to get basic necessities, and the next crime could be against you. . . . So before we judge and point fingers at the "bleeding heart liberals" who want to lift up and support disenfranchised ex-felons, remember that they may be stopping a crime against you or your loved ones before it happens. . . . The reality is that compassion begets better citizens, and no matter what you do, it will always be up to the individual to change inside and society to change outside.[88]

Held in Michigan, Christopher John Velthuysen contemplates release with palpable desperation.

So, I'm worried for these reasons if I get/receive parole: 1.) Only a GED level education, 2.) No money to survive on, 3.) No place to live (community placement is where I'd live for while on parole 4 years), 4.) no clothes, and 5.) no food. What do I do? These are the main reasons so many former incarcerated inmates commit drug, robbery, theft, etc. crimes, and get rearrested, because they don't have nothing when released from prison! I have the desire, passion, and drive to do good, and I don't want to be another statistic, but I'm going to need a lot of help![89]

In "My Greatest Fear," Jason Daugherty anticipates release in West Virginia, where he too fears "becoming a statistic." He is doing what he can, taking college and substance abuse classes. Yet he understands that "these steps will not guarantee me success upon reentering society." The other fears he describes are quite concrete: How, he wonders, will he gain housing, transportation, and employment—each of which can require already having the others before it can be fully secured?[90]

While Moser, Velthuysen, and Daugherty write of concerns stemming from a lack of personal resources, many others comment on the dearth of resources in the communities they will reenter. For no matter their good motives, no matter how much rehabilitative programming imprisoned people receive, concentrated incarceration negatively affects conditions in the places where most incarcerated people come from and will return. Despite surviving prison with some sense of himself, Tracy Glenn, held in Pennsylvania, writes of his concern for the life and conditions he will meet upon release.

I've found a bit of myself this trip with a new sentence that will soon come to an end, that I do have the skills to be a better person and I do have the capabilities mentally to finish my life on a good note. . . . I do still have concerns about where I'm going when I get out of here and that concern is, I'm going back to the same poverty stricken neighborhood in society where I came from in the beginning. Scary, is what it is to me, adversity lurks and awaits my return. Where I come from difficulty is a normal thing. . . . I come from west Philadelphia, a city with a very high criminal activity rate and one of the highest homicide rates in the country because of that same poverty where struggles for just about everyone is in effect. Pennsylvania's prison system cannot prepare me for this. . . . No program, No halfway house can simulate what's happening where I come from nor can any of those same programs distinguish how to respond where I come from.[91]

The realities Tracy Glenn faces are presented to the great majority of imprisoned people, and he never mentions restrictive and often arbitrarily enforced parole conditions that send about half of released people back to prison.[92] These are conditions they can face even before release. Valjean Royal, who identifies as both trans and Christian, describes from Indiana preparing her required, pre-parole hearing report. George W. Bush gave federal dollars to faith-based organizations, she explains, to aid in prison reentry. But when she seeks a promise of help from a church that will accept both her faith and her identity, she hits repeated dead ends, and these are just one sector of the spectrum of challenges for soon-to-be-released trans people.

> I know from personal experience that for most transsexuals and other gender variant individuals, the process of reintegration will follow a rocky path: their families may not be willing to accept them, finding jobs will be difficult, and the individuals in their old peer groups will be ready to support the resumption of criminal habits.

And these challenges are layered on top of the fact, as she writes, that "both state and federal courts have almost uniformly held that transgendered people are outside the legal definitions and protections of existing anti-discrimination laws."[93]

Nebraskan Connie Gibbs, though serving a short sentence, knows that all the resources she can muster will be needed to reenter her former life. Her essay argues explicitly and by example for more transitional services in and outside prison. Containment can make people into aliens to their former lives, even when those lives provide advantages that very few incarcerated people can access. Programs inside

> cannot build better schools, they cannot treat all the addicts coming out, and they cannot generate homes or enough good jobs to support more than half a million people released each year. The need to prepare these people to return to a society that has become foreign to them is

urgent. This process should begin months prior to release and be maintained after transition out. My observations of how the mind responds to the dehumanization process that begins the minute a citizen becomes an inmate present a vivid picture of how and why "reform" doesn't seem to carry through after an inmate is released. . . .

My own incarceration is only one year, and I have the good fortune of my own home, family, friends, and a job to return to. Yet I still foresee many major, difficult transitioning issues that I will need to face. The most pressing to me is the question: "How will I fit into the space that I left behind since I am virtually not the same person that I was when I left home?" . . . My loved ones have just begun to grasp the depth of the changes that have occurred within me. . . . I believe both my family and I will need help with this transition because the woman coming home is simply not the same person as the one who left. I have the distinct advantage of some pretty powerful supports, which many inmates will not be so fortunate to have. I have been blessed with a keen foresight, and I have an amazing and dedicated therapist on the outside who has worked tirelessly with me throughout my incarceration via letter, homework assignments, telephone calls, and occasional visits. . . . This is not programming offered to me by the system in which I am incarcerated. . . .

I have put together a workable relapse prevention plan that I will utilize on a daily basis. I have been gently guided through strengthening the bonds with my ever-devoted family and friends. I have been able to aide and direct my support group in becoming more familiar with my disease, recovery, and the transitioning process. I am working to prepare my family for the changes that have occurred in me because of the institutionalization and dehumanization that I have experienced. I have also been able to expand my support group with additions throughout the community. . . .

. . . *The way I see it, all who desire this valuable, personalized programming, should have the same potentially life-altering/saving opportunity.*[94]

Finally, if all the challenges described above were not enough, the final two writers in this chapter describe the state of legalized quarantine that the formerly incarcerated must navigate even after release. Ronald Marshall writes again from Louisiana.

> The circumstances of recidivism have pitched camp right outside the prison wall, in communities, in homes, lurking to convert patience into desperation, visions of a good life into chaos and confusion. Once labeled an ex-felon, the label authorizes systematic discrimination in housing, employment, education, public benefits, the denial of right to vote, etc. Felony disenfranchisement is a cruel hand dealt to an ex-felon; its consequences are devastating, influential and designed to publicly humiliate all ex-felons with discriminatory tactics and flunk them right out of society. The label informs the general public, potential employers, institutions of education, landlords, loaners, and government institutions for welfare benefits, that "felons are not wanted here."[95]

Brendon Smith writes from Colorado of post-release social disenfranchisement that harkens back to an earlier era of American racial history.

> The smallest confession of guilt of a state felony has the power to release the same kind or similar wrath of discrimination that was felt in an era of deeply express racial discrimination. . . .
> . . . Once they are released they enter a parallel social universe—much like Jim Crow—in which discrimination in nearly every aspects of social political, and economic life is perfectly legal and large majorities of men in cities across the United States are once again subjected to legalized discrimination, effectively barring them from full integration into the mainstream, while . . . mass incarceration has nullified many of the gains of the civil rights movement putting many black men in a position reminiscent of Jim Crow.[96]

Damaging children, families, communities, and the people who will return to them, containment seems to fail any reasonable cost-benefit test. This is not to say that there are not people who need to be separated from the public for some period of time, or in particular circumstances, to stem further pain to others. But incarcerated people have long witnessed that applying decades of indiscriminate containment is an exercise in the predictable defeat of containment's primary end, to reduce harm—a defeat now practiced at the scale of a national industry.

But what of deterrence? Surely, if conditions and treatment are as terrible as the previous writers have described, prison should make both prospective lawbreakers and those who have served time reluctant to trespass beyond the law's limits. Such assessments rest upon a number of unfounded assumptions, and they ignore—once again—incarceration's concrete effects on individuals and communities.

5

DEFEATING DETERRENCE

DEBILITATION, ABUSE, AND DIMINISHED FUTURES

> The system is set up for failure because inmates are leaving
> prison more criminally minded than when they came in.
> —JENNIFER BATTLES, ALABAMA

> Once the light of hope has been smothered, it's difficult to
> revive it.
> —BRIAN MCCARN, MICHIGAN

I N reading testimony to the prison's defeat of retribution, rehabilitation, and containment, we have previewed the territory for
assessment of its defeat of deterrence. Prisons mete out damage at once
so generic and so profound that it can block meaningful communication of retribution's message; incarcerated people emerge uncertain of
their very sense of identity while confronting the challenge of desisting from criminal behaviors amid diminished opportunities.[1] Although
many imprisoned people make heroic efforts, and by sheer strength
of will resist prison environments to achieve self-transformation and
rehabilitation, such resistance does not fully prepare the released to gain
footholds in the constructive social networks and legitimate economies
that make desistance from crime more likely. In reading testimony on
carceral containment's pernicious effects on children, partners, families, and communities, we glimpse the impoverished landscapes where
newly released people return to attempt to resume or begin (often late
in life) their roles as parents, partners, and members of households and
communities. The destruction wrought by just a few years of legal containment breaks social continuity, diminishes resources, and weakens
human connections among individuals and the homes and neighborhoods where formerly incarcerated people must try to begin their lives

again. Rates of return to prison are indicators of the criminal legal system's degradation of the human and material resources of people seeking new paths to law-abiding lives.[2]

While for forty years lawmakers increased sentences and sentencing standards in the name of deterring crime by *sending a message* to potential lawbreakers, they failed to recognize that few people for whom crime is a temptation watch political press briefings or read the minutes from legislative debates. Few know what the consequences are for their acts before they are apprehended for committing them.[3] Their focus is on avoiding detection, and the certainty of detection—not the severity of punishments—is the major deterrent of new crimes.[4] Equally often, the moments preceding a criminal act are caught up in unfocused need and desperation that appear linked to survival.[5] And whatever their motives and conditions, people who are racially targeted can do little to avoid criminalization. Few of the supposed targets of politicians' messages were listening, and even when they did, chest-beating sound-bites failed to outweigh the deprivations that have been precipitating crime or marking individuals as criminal suspects since long before Philadelphians concocted a new way to address lawbreaking. Given race- and class-targeted policing, sting operations, the pathologizing of crime, suffocating parole conditions, and cold shoulders from employers, communities, and even family members . . . it's little wonder that released people feel the message, *You are not welcome back.*

Tough and mandatory sentencing—a major practical driver of mass-scale incarceration—has consistently been shown to fail at significantly affecting crime rates or to have a deterrent effect either on would-be or formerly incarcerated people.[6] Indeed, by reducing prospects for strong relationships, steady employment, and community connections, prison is demonstrably criminogenic.[7] What deters crime for those who are tempted and for those who have served years inside are the same things that deter crime among people to whom lawbreaking rarely occurs: stable relationships and families, steady employment, and a sense of connection to the community—influences that incarceration decisively ends or severely challenges, and makes harder to (re)establish.[8] "In our frenzy of locking people up," Devah Pager writes, "our 'crime control' policies may in fact exacerbate the very conditions that lead to crime in the first place."[9] What Pager writes applies to diminished access to employment, marriage, and community involvement. An institution that grew to its current scale on claims of deterring criminal acts has been more effective in making desistance from crime more difficult.[10]

In gathering testimony to the prison's defeat of deterrence, this chapter offers a coda to the previous gatherings: if incarceration not only fails to deter but challenges desistance, retribution's message has clearly missed its mark; the defeat of deterrence renders nearly meaningless any state-sponsored rehabilitative efforts that do exist; penal containment that renders desistance more difficult simply relocates crime and crime victims into the future while accelerating community degradation.

The writing of incarcerated people regarding deterrence, then, often echoes testimony to the prison's other defeated purposes. Imprisoned writers testify to trauma and degradation that render people less capable of desisting from crime or of (re)starting constructive lives outside. They describe the causes of such degradation, especially in treatment by staff. They write of how a prison record itself limits their ability to enter into law-abiding lives. And they offer broad overviews of a system that reveals to incarcerated people its motives and methods for enabling their failure.

DEBILITATION, TRAUMATIZATION, LEGALIZED STIGMA

The idea that more punishment produces more deterrence is as old as it is false. As Californian Bobby G. Wheeler observes,

> The more fiercely, the more ruthlessly, the more inhumanely my criminal brethren and I are treated, however legally, the more certain you are to have more victims.
>
> Of course victims should not be forgotten in the quest to capture and deal with their victimizers, but neither should the next victim be forgotten—the one who is going to be raped, maimed, beaten, robbed, kidnapped or killed so long as the vicious cycle of evil for evil and Vengeance for Vengeance perpetuates the revolving-door principle of penal justice.[11]

Imprisoned people feel their mental, physical, social, and employment capacities diminished by their experience inside. Daniel Pirkel writes as much from Michigan: "By emphasizing retribution, deterrence, and incapacitation, prisons create people who are unfit to deal with everyday life."[12] The effect that Pirkel notes is particularly severe in children. People exposed early to violence and other traumatizing events are more likely than others to repeat such scenes in adolescence and young adulthood, often leading to time in prison. In turn, incarceration itself counters everything we might hope the institution would do for young people.[13] Fellow Michigan resident Lasan Bellamy was imprisoned at sixteen.

> Imagine being stuck in a grave you can't escape unless you kill yourself. Only to realize you're too weak. You continue being tortured. Too weak to end it. That's Hell, a justified cruel and unusual punishment. I became an animal. I observed others throwing feces, smearing it on walls, putting it in their mouth to spit on someone, prisoners masturbating on staff, cutting themselves. . . . I picked it up and started doing it too. Monkey see, monkey do. I just couldn't put feces in my mouth or cut myself. Yet, all that destructive behavior was like negative energy at the bottom of a tornado for under those circumstances we were mentally ill and staff are not educated to deal with our insanity. A lot of times even their emotions overcrowded their better judgement, provoking us for entertainment. I was lost completely with no rational mind and out of control.[14]

Meagan Adams writes from Texas: "Children, regardless of circumstance, are still kids. Vulnerable and in need of nurturing. Prison does not solve the problem. . . . It exacerbates and perpetuates the very mentalities which landed the child in the predicament they are in."[15]

Locked up in Wisconsin at the age of seventeen, Curtis Lee Walker describes what so many incarcerated writers document: the effects of such a place on children charged as adults.

> The desire to extract the full adult measure of punishment from the juvenile offender requires that the person be written off from society as having a permanently malignant personality. This despite the fact that juveniles, with their underdeveloped minds and immaturity, will at some point cease to exist leaving behind a more conscious adult who

did not exist at the time of the offense. If a teen is unable to envision themselves in some form in the future, if they are stunted at that age and unable to place proper value on their lives, there should be no surprise that some of them, being deeply entrenched in an environment where violence is commonplace, will end up as perpetrators of that same violence. It should be expected. The surprise should be when a kid grows up in an environment of ever-present violence and goes on in life without succumbing to it.[16]

Sixteen-year-old Birdy describes what she sees inside carceral facilities.

It don't teach you a lesson. It makes you worse, because you start believing what they're telling you. I felt like I was a criminal. Once you get put in the system, you consider yourself a criminal. So when you get out, you think, "Oh well, I've been through it before. Why not again?" I started believing I wasn't gonna be nobody.[17]

Garmon Coats describes a Texas prison population and culture seemingly built to manufacture social dysfunction, especially among the young.

The prisons are spawning ground for racial conflict, rebellion against authority, a breakdown of personal discipline, paranoia, and other things. The fruit of these are violent futures and perpetuation of recidivism. In fact, no longer are the majority of prisoners criminals in the original sense. Most are behavioral problems. And since the States have abolished asylums and mingled their mentally disturbed into prison populations, what eventually returns to society are mean and remorseless criminals. And somehow they demand respect, playing roles gleaned from their criminal idols. . . . This pretense of a baseless version of mob respect works well with ignorant youth who have no wholesome role models. . . . Indeed the more treacherous and ruthless the offender acts, the closer to actual respect he gets. . . . And when blood is smeared on these walls, nothing is getting done but a precursor to vindication. Glory starved misfits commit any sort of outrage in order to be deemed fit for the herd.[18]

Arkansas writer Charles A. Brownell describes how incarceration can render young men "frozen in time": unchanged, immature, and more troubled than when they arrived.

> Imagine being forcefully caged up against your will, attacked, abused, beaten, tormented, and tortured and having to watch all this happen to others for 20 plus straight years! Who would you become and what would you do? Many of the men observed have been incarcerated since the ages of 17 to 21 and have little to no experience in living life in the real world, the "free" world and have probably never held down a real job or paid taxes. So much of that young arrogance and mentality stays with them as they age in prison because they never grew up to maturity in real society. Combine that with years of dealing with sadistic assholes both prison staff and other inmates and this causes them to become hardened, egocentric with a driving need to "prove" themselves, arrogant, and know it all assholes themselves.[19]

For all the help convicted people receive, writes Prince from New York, "They might as well go back to whips and chains."[20] Fellow New Yorker Frans Sital sees the same effects.

> One thing I did learn from this system about this system is, they try to break you in every possible way: instead of trying to build you into a better person than the one that entered these prison gates. Do you think, incarcerated human beings should be placed in a corner, constantly being poked at, heckled, antagonized, mentally, emotionally, physically abused; and then released back into society? Right next door to you and your family!?[21]

Writing from Tennessee, Christopher Hallum details the traumas that have left their marks upon him and that he will carry back outside.

> These scars are me now; a part of my physiological and psychological makeup. . . . A prisoner lies in water, clothed only in a pair of boxers, being electrocuted by a guard's shield. Sounds of screaming and crying. A mentally disabled prisoner, not understanding where he's at, calling out to his mother, is attacked by three guards. Blood is ev-

erywhere. . . . Their "investigation" found that the "retarded" prisoner killed himself. His blood soaked hands had tried to reach through my cell bars, hoping I could save him. . . . Two Crips enter my cell. The skinny one is holding a shank. Mumbling is all I hear coming out of their mouths. . . . Do I sacrifice my physical safety and stand against them? What am I standing for? Shouldn't I use my wits, sacrifice my pride, and get home to the love of my life? She becomes victimized too. I call her to send money electronically to these beasts. . . . Words, what good are words when trying to describe of such things? My body kept the score.[22]

In an essay titled "When All Hope Is Lost," Chanell Burnette observes the effects of prison on women in Virginia.

When I look around at some of these women, my heart breaks for them! . . . Many see no end in sight so they grope around like the blind. Feeling, reaching out for the nearest thing to hold onto; to attach themselves to for help during their helplessness. Their hopelessness. They have simply let go. Have simply lost themselves in the darkness.[23]

A man held in Pennsylvania, writing as Lone Wolf, echoes Burnette's observation.

Death of the spirit occurs many, many years before the actual sentence is completed. This is the true meaning of the phrase DEAD MAN WALKING. We Lifers are real zombies, nothing but modern mummies. At least in ancient Egypt the society waited until a person was physically dead before they were mummified. Today mummification happens to many convicts while they're still alive.[24]

Texan Michael H. Murphy's experience following time in isolation suggests the effect of many of the conditions and treatment described by Hallum, Burnette, and Lone Wolf: release becomes simply another turn in a revolving door that virtually guarantees return.

On August 21st, 2008, I was pushed out a side door of the Walls unit in Huntsville, TX and stepped out of prison for the first time in 10 years.

It was an unbearably hot day made more so by the fact that I had not been exposed to the sun in more than 8 years. . . . This was just the beginning of things I was distinctly ill-prepared for. To truly appreciate why I was so unprepared for unrestricted freedom, you have to understand that I had just spent 7 years in Solitary Confinement; 5 years of that in a "high security" unit which is Texas' answer to super seg. . . . The adverse psychological effects of solitary confinement are well-documented. I didn't realize this. I didn't notice what had happened to me. That's what makes time in solitary so insidious and debilitating. It changes you so slowly you don't really notice the incremental accumulative effects that permanently leave scars on your psyche. . . . Upon release, I found myself unable to function in the modern world. I had none of the skills or support networks that one would typically depend on during the re-entry phase of a supervised release. It wasn't just that the world had changed; I had changed as well. I suffered from, and still do, severe anxiety, frequent panic attacks, confusion, concentration & memory problems, insomnia, and paranoia. I also experienced prolonged periods of despair, black depression, and thoughts of suicide. Much of the time I found myself in a semi-dissociative state. Not fully there. As if the most mundane things my body did were happening to someone else and I were watching it happen. . . . Prior to my incarceration, I was extremely outgoing, the life of the party with friends everywhere. Suddenly I'm the polar opposite. I would unintentionally flinch from normal human contact. . . . I couldn't maintain employment or hold a job. . . . I became homeless, sleeping on couches at first, but eventually lapsing into having to sleep in empty buildings, trailers, and vacant houses. I was extremely unstable, lacking effective emotional control. I ended up flaming out in a drug induced heat stroke on the side of Jacksboro Hwy with a pistol in my waist band. I had gotten the pistol that morning with the vague intention of ending it all. Instead I was arrested for felon in possession of a firearm and sent back to my own private ring of hell, inadvertently leading to the places that had made my life so unmanageable in the first place.[25]

Many writers describe an experience that, far from an effective deterrent, deepens the problems people bring in with them. Richard S. Gross writes of men he has observed imprisoned in Pennsylvania.

I have met thousands of convicts from all walks of life finding that they are not who the media portray them to be. I've met no mobsters, safe-crackers, wheel men, or cat burglars. Instead: addicts, retards, and nut jobs. I meet people who couldn't hang on to a job or a romantic partner. People who couldn't control their addictions or manage their finances. . . . People who couldn't keep it together and fell apart in a desperate, unknowing cry for help. . . .

The overall effect of incarceration is to take those who have problems (poverty, addiction, mental illness, learning disability, etc.), and place them in a setting which is known to not help, or exacerbate those types of problems. The dubious satisfaction of seeing "bad people" punished should not lead us to support a system which is not helping people or preventing future victims.[26]

From Wyoming, Daniel Lee Harris offers an aphoristic summary of practices that defeat deterrence: "You don't teach people how to stay out of quicksand by throwing them into it!"[27] T. L. Maynard, a woman held in Michigan, finds in quicksand a similarly apt image of the struggle to stay sane inside.

I watch as so many slide over the cliff's edge. Thunk, thunk, thunk is the sound a forehead makes against a metal door as blood drips down her face, eyes so blank and empty. Thunk, thunk, thunk. Fully SWATed up they rush the cell to hold her down for a shot. Tied to the metal slab screaming and blood dripping from gaping wounds along her forearms. She's actually bitten chunks out of her own arms. Are those my paths, my choices? Is that how, where I will end when I slip over the edge? Did I ever have a chance? The waves are pulling me under I can't breathe, I can't see or hear. What choice do I have? I let go instead of thrashing out, just floating. I feel, I watch, I listen, and "do" nothing. . . . Like quicksand, the less you struggle to escape, the less you're sucked down.[28]

California writer Ivan Kilgore joins others in documenting the conditions that damage those we regularly claim to want to see emerge as citizens deterred and capable of desisting from crime. He stands among a chorus of writers who cite the attack on character as the most destructive effect of imprisonment; from lived experience, he also lists the carceral disconnections that research shows precipitate failure among the released.[29]

> There's no doubt about it, [prison] will make you more of what you were before you came in, which brings us to the question of rehabilitation. Please! Prison only teaches us to become better thieves, Swindlers and predators. Why so? Take for example, prison labor. The California Department of Corrections . . . doesn't pay but 7-90 cents per hour, if that! After restitution and court fees are deducted, we barely have enough to buy a case of Top Ramen noodles. Most of us don't have family and friends to support us. Therefore the only way we can obtain the things we want and need is by stealing, conning, and preying on other inmates and staff. I need not say that these anti-social behaviors will follow that 90% of us back into society that is to be released. In a nutshell this is what prison amounts to:
> Isolation
> Severing of family and community ties
> Promotion of racism
> Deprivation of genuine social interaction
> Transformation of positive attributes such as trust, honesty, and kindness into points of vulnerability
> Exposure to diseases such as Hepatitis C, HIV, and many others
> Enslavement
> Psychological torture
> Fostering dependence upon others and state welfare programs
> And most noteworthy, stripping one of his dignity

> To our detriment, a significant number of officers misconstrue what they are here for. Generally, they have this attitude to deprive us of something that sustains us even as all else seems to be lost without freedom—DIGNITY. This self-respect and sense of self-worth is the innermost armament of the soul. It lies at the heart of our attempts to maintain our humanness. To be deprived of it is to be dehumanized, to be cleaved from, and cast below, mankind. Dignity, needless to say, is as essential to human life as water, food, and oxygen. As this sug-

gests, the loss of a man's dignity can carry him off as surely as thirst, hunger, exposure, and asphyxiation, and with greater cruelty.[30]

The prison can make its wards not only less able to function peacefully outside but so disconnected from free society as to become unable even to see beyond prison walls. Michigan writer Brian McCarn names this phenomenon.

> Institutionalized is when you're no longer capable of grasping the concept of being free. Although you're cognizant of another world existing beyond the perimeter of the prison fence, you no longer have the ability to envision yourself living in it. The focal point of your world now consists of trivial concerns as what concoction is being served in the prison chow hall, the accumulation of commissary, or what program is airing tonight, and whether yard will be called on time, or some other insignificant mundane activity associated with the monotony of doing time. . . . Once the light of hope has been smothered, it's difficult to revive it.[31]

Amy Buckley describes institutionalization among women held in Mississippi.

> I often look around and it saddens me to see so many women satisfied with their lives here. They are satisfied with disgusting food and filthy conditions, they don't even care when it is 120 degrees in the building all summer long. The majority of them stay so high that nothing seems to phase them. As long as they have their drugs and their phones, and have the run of the building they seem happy. It seems that at some point prison became home for them and that is unacceptable! When and why did they give up and stop fighting for their freedom? They have gotten comfortable and built their own world behind these walls. . . . A world unknown to those who have never been in prison.[32]

Cole Onstad describes what such institutionalization looks like inside an Arkansas prison.

I'm a 44 yr old convict that has spent approx 20 of my years in jail or prison. I have embraced institutional life and became so accustom to it that at times I truly feel at home. Entire seasons have passed without a single thought of the free world or the life I could've had. I've literally went months at a time without a single moment outside, for any reason. . . . The space station, Navy submarine personnel, and the institutionalized (medically or criminally) are the only people I can think of that can exist without the slightest concern about the weather conditions outside. . . .

My incarcerated brethren became my family. Aside from my mom and dad the only people I write or talk to outside of here either recently left or are helping to facilitate my needs while I'm here.[33]

Writing from Illinois, Jay C. Miller provides a vision of the institutionalization of a nation within a nation, and how, behind the façade of deterrence, this inner world combats efforts at self-transformation.

Prison has given birth to Prisontonia: A new and unique culture born and bred on American soil. Like the indigenous Native Americans, Prisontonia may be one of the few cultures to ever originate on this chunk of land. Prisontonia, like the fantasy world of Neverland, also seems to somehow defy the Laws of time. Instead of children never growing old, it is the criminals who remain unchanged. They are stuck in a mental time warp, frozen as they watch time stand by behind the bars and the years pass by outside the walls. This is Prisontonia. . . .

The American prisoner has become our countries modern day scarecrow, left to hang in a cell and dangled invisibly before the masses. You might not physically see these Scarecrow inmates but you know they're there. You understand the symbolic warning their incarcerated lives represent. . . .

The only magic taking place is the fact that a very few inmates DO actually change, they defy nature, swim up a river in a brutal world. Those men are miracles. . . .

I watch [staff] fail to help the prisoners around me every single day. I watched men get warehoused in a human zoo, treated like animals for 10 years only to be released back into the wild once they've lost every skill they needed to survive in it. Every day I see the hollow stare of men who are but the empty shells of a soul that jumped ship and abandoned them long ago. Men who have spent 20 years in a dark cell staring into a T.V. screen desperately trying to escape their bleak existence; hoping to experience just a taste of what it feels to live. They have long forgotten the sensations of life. . . . Most inmates might come and go, but when they come to prison, they adapt. They assimilate into their new culture. They might of stepped into the prison system as Americans, but I can guarantee you they will leave as Prisontonians.[34]

Zombies, lost in the darkness, Prisontonians . . . the human beings whom the prison takes in are sent back out less deterred from crime than inured to violence, dehumanization, neglect, and degradation of personal dignity. California writer Michael L. Owens describes a culture so successful at institutionalization, at fostering immunity to deterrence, and so steeply pitched against personal transformation that those who choose a constructive path become pariahs.

By definition, we the rehabilitated are no longer a recognized part of prison culture. Our only connections of any depth are amongst ourselves. We are distrusted, disliked, and largely shunned by other prisoners and correctional officers alike. We are judged as foils by the former and fakers by the latter. Achieving rehabilitation during the course of one's sentence does not make one immune to the toxic soup of the prison environment. Most often, the opposite proves true. Those who make the decision to sincerely pursue rehabilitation are among the most vulnerable groups found in prison. Having rejected gang association and the protection that comes along with it, we become easy targets for the predatory groups that need have little fear of repercussion. Those who run the prison underworld, and the officers who enable them, suspect us as likely informants simply because we abstain from the usual prison vices. In the violent, chaotic world of incarceration, not many inmates are looking to voluntarily place themselves in harm's way, especially for something as ideologically elusive as rehabilitation.

Those prisoners who have yet to commit to involvement in prison gang membership are watching those of us who have chosen rehabilitation. They see that despite being consistent examples of high moral character, the rehabilitated remain subject to the exact same conditions as the unrepentant. And the unrepentant are acutely aware of it. They understand very clearly that to renounce the culture is to disassociate and thereafter have less influence over the quality of their life. Prime job assignments, choice of cellmate, all the little things that go into determining if you do hard or easy time, all depend on your connections. Not many are willing to surrender that small amount of control in a place that strips you of almost all control. Who would choose that? In many ways, choosing to become one of the rehabilitated is to become subject to a sadistic experience. I've seen men on the path to rehabilitation make that discovery and turn back.[35]

Maine writer James Castrillo echoes Michael Owens: when he tells his peers he's going to class, their jaws drop "as though they had just seen Jennifer Lopez walk through the pod naked."[36]

Tennessee writer Dexter Henderson suggests, once again, that effective programming that might support deterrence cuts against prison-industry interests. He also suggests that change cannot come entirely from within but must engage people and communities from outside.

The issue is not only the fact that we are locked away from our communities, but we are further abused by the institutions we reside in. Lack of healthcare, lack of nutritious food, lack of programs for development, human rights abuses, racist attacks, exorbitant prices for necessities of food and hygiene that causes inmate on inmate violent crimes, etc. All contribute to the deterioration of minds and bodies, often resulting in premature deaths, insanity, and hopelessness that feeds the criminal mentality by many seeking solace in gang activity. This becomes a self-perpetuating cycle of destruction. No one in the community is immune from this disaster. . . . We as prisoners have to take the initiative to combat this destruction. We have to break the mental and spiritual chains that bind us to this destructive lifestyle. But we can't do it alone. The outside support is crucial. The community should know that when prisoners attempt to do something positive, the system attacks them and/or interferes with the work. The reason is simple: if prisoners become productive, intelligent, responsible individuals then the rate of prisoners returning to prison will be reduced which will mean less money for these peddlers of human flesh. They will attempt to isolate individuals and harass them if there is no one on the outside concerned with their plight. The most important need though is the moral support of the community, the love and concern for our plight.[37]

If deterrence is the crown of the four cardinal aims of incarceration—addressing as it does both those who have been convicted and potential lawbreakers—recidivism is its stamp of failure. Yet we continue to effectively trigger re-offense by treating the released as less than other people. A prison record, many imprisoned people know, renders any deterrent effects virtually moot. One of the ways that the community outside can help is simply to assume that any social debt has been paid in full once people have served their time. Imprisoned people know that this is not the case today.

Many writers describe what they will face upon release: life sentences of legalized stigma and discrimination across an obstacle course of social, economic, and housing restrictions that make desistance from crime a profound challenge. In addition to loss of the powerful aids to desistance found in personal relationships, Allen Ramer writes from California of the cyclical nature of the moral and practical effects of the limits placed on released people.

Without believing that upward mobility, dignified work, and good wages are attainable, pessimism towards the jobs market is a natural result. Over time, many find themselves reverting back into lives of crime, seeing it as the lesser of two evils. . . . Because of scant or ineffectual rehabilitation programs in US prisons, criminal attitudes remain fairly intact. Upon release, the same issues that caused their incarceration still lurk beneath the surface, making them particularly susceptible to a recurrence of old behavior. The result of the myriad restrictions on where ex-offenders can or cannot reside—whether based on state law, parole policy, or exclusionary rental practices—is that many find themselves stuck in situations that tax their ability to withstand the Siren Song of illicit activity, such as living in or near areas saturated with high levels of crime and the powerful exertion it has on their behavior. In some cases, ex-offenders are mandated to return to the same county (or city) where their originating crime(s) occurred, forcing them to again grapple with the very triggers and old acquaintances that gave rise to much of the

troubles of their past: even despite having healthier alternatives some-
place else, like living with a responsible family member located in another part of the state. . . . The third leg of this tripartite discrimination
is the disappointing practice of excluding ex-offenders from meaningful
participation in democratic politics. . . . Most states now have laws that
bar ex-offenders from exercising their right to vote. . . . The problem
with discriminating against ex-offenders politically is its ability to dis-
courage healthy community interaction. . . . Political association has a
positive effect in shaping more socially oriented individuals. . . . Taken
together, these discriminatory practices foster attitudes that facilitate
criminal activity. Rather than strengthening social bonds, providing a
sense that future success is possible, and creating conditions conducive
to personal growth, these petty acts of discrimination, no matter how
well-intentioned from a public safety standpoint, actually serve to un-
dermine effective behavioral transitions, making it even more difficult
for these individuals to solidify the resolve necessary for turning their
lives around in positive directions. Ostensibly, we become witness to a
circular pattern: Social backlash caused by crime leads to negative attitudes, which in turn lead to a return to illicit activity. The whole process
then starts anew.[38]

From Texas, Don Cox describes the headwinds of public labels and
assumptions that imprisoned people are released into, as well as their
cumulative, demoralizing effects.

Offenders that do get out of prison are instantly labeled, ex-cons, trash,
lowlife, scumbags, dirtballs, misfits, outcast, career criminals, and etc.
For the most part they despise us. They think that we are 100% worthless, dangerous and in no way capable of changing our old sinful ways.
They are shamed of us afraid of us and would love to forget about us.
Who in the world would want to give a job to an ex-con? We are at the
very bottom of the social ladder. Like the bottom of a well used out-
house with no ladder to get out. Dejected, courage and confidence gets
lost along the way with a mingled blend of not knowing how to get back
on one's feet. . . . Spend 10-30 years locked away in a prison and get out
with no family no friends no help, no job, no money no car, no food or
no clothes and no place to go but back to the streets.[39]

Joseph E. Jones writes of the bleak prospects for the formerly incarcerated in Kentucky: "What rehabilitative programming can be offered to prisoners to strengthen career choice if the career field rejects ex-convicts? Hence, post-release persons end up in minimum wage jobs while attempting to pay rent, buy clothes, and provide for self and family."[40] Mikell McCall writes from Ohio: "Uneducated criminals will continue to break the law. No one will hire them, so they break the law to survive. What is the point of sending a man or woman to prison to be rehabilitated if that person is not receiving the tools they need to enter society and live a productive life!"[41]

Felton L. Matthews Jr. connects the dots from Nevada, linking prison-bred trauma, institutionalization, and violent re-offense.

> When civilians think of Post Traumatic Stress Disorder, they think of Afghanistan, Iraq, Kosovo, or even Vietnam. I do not believe civilian psychologists or doctors consider the fact that the condition could be triggered by hostile prison conditions, excessive gang or criminal violence, or even violent abusive conditions in one's very home. The issue, in my humble opinion is causally related to violent crime recidivism. . . .
>
> These are the questions that run into a convicts mind pending his release, especially on parole: "Where am I going to live?" "Who will hire me, I need a job?" "Will my family help me, take me back?" If you are a sex offender or a guy who has been raped repeatedly, . . . you got even less help or resources. Prison's familiar and comfortable with three hot meals, medical, and a place to sleep. This is "pre-prison release anxiety disorder," and some inmates actually sabotage their release. . . . And this is where P.T.S.D. kicks in. You see, when you come out of prison, you see guys do things that would get him stabbed up or killed. . . . The violence they had to endure or perpetrate in staying alive or at least to discourage rape has become the rule. The system has created them. And instead of fixing them, they rather "warehouse" or destroy them. This is how P.T.S.D. works: You get into an . . . argument, situation, and confrontation and you do not think of violence as a last resort it's your first option. . . . You do not see that stranger or that family member for who they are; and that they are not the ones who did all that to you in prison. You see them as an enemy target who has pissed you off and you unload on them. Do you, my readers, understand this?[42]

STAFF ABUSE

Although most prison staff take the work they do simply for the paycheck—often in otherwise employment-starved rural areas[43]—incarcerated people document the anti-deterrent effects of staff seemingly intent on acting out extralegal ideas of proper punishment, or exercising sadistic whims in spaces free from accountability. Paul Keller writes from the state of Washington that "mistreating, harming, enraging, and inciting of inmates is par for the dreadful course every bit among staff as it is among the imprisoned."[44] New Hampshire resident Michael B. Beverley writes of an uneven three-way split in staff attitudes: a few want to help the people they guard; an equal number see incarcerated people "as a disease of society and so deserving of nothing but scorn and abuse," while the "majority of staff fall in the large middle range." In any case, Beverley writes, "the success or failure of the inmates' treatment is inexorably linked to staff behavior."[45]

Writers like Beverley regularly testify that the crucial first step toward reform and rehabilitation, and thus toward desistance, must be taken by imprisoned people themselves; yet the link between attitudes and behavior of staff and the results of incarceration is noted equally often. Indifference, disdain, abuse, or injury by staff can be the inflection point for yet more crime. No doubt, many staff members simply want to get through their days and get out. Others surely imagine that they are rightful legal agents of retribution and deterrence through the delivery of pain. Yet the message that prison is a place to avoid grows into white noise behind debasement that damages the ability of any of its subjects to shape lives based on rational choices. Writing from Kentucky, Cynthia L. Wallace offers a broad view of the personal and social effects of staff attitudes.

> Staff forget that every human has a breaking point. Each breaks differently. Some internalize and self-harm. Others externalize and hurt others. . . .
>
> Inmates are bullied on a daily basis. Does anyone care? Inmates are mentally abused on a daily basis. Does anyone care? Inmates are treated as if we are something other than human. Does anyone care? All too often, that answer is no. Once placed in prison, an inmate is stripped of

any humanity or dignity. An inmate is a number. A bed. A liar. A thief. Violent. Cunning. Stupid. Underhanded. Manipulative. Those who weren't before they are incarcerated become many of these things during their sentence. What one is treated as, one becomes. And staff treat inmates as all of these. When an inmate tells the truth, they are told they are lying, so they begin to fail to see the point in being honest. Inmates are deprived of basic physical human contact, which is proven to cause depression, deepen depression, and intensify other mental problems. Inmates' children cannot even send them colored pictures. . . . The function of prison is to protect society and to rehabilitate those it houses. Most inmates will eventually be released, but even then they continue to be punished. They are considered unemployable. They are discouraged and outright forbidden from living in many areas. They are not even second-class citizens: they are usually treated as if they were not citizens at all. Inmates are humans. Inmates have made mistakes. But inmates are paying for those mistakes—inmates and their families. It is not the job of the Dept of Corrections to punish. It is the court's job to determine punishment. It is DOC's job to contain, control, and educate. It is their job to demonstrate and teach inmates how to be law-abiding, productive citizens upon their release. Mistreating, abusing, and bullying inmates is NOT the way to accomplish that goal. Mistreating, abusing, and bullying inmates IS the way to continue the cycle of incarceration. The cycle of negativity. The cycle of violence.[46]

Shariff Ingram writes from Pennsylvania, offering details of what he has experienced and a common explanation for why prison practices, rather than serving deterrence, are simply destructive.

For a person who finds himself incarcerated under their [staff] care, you will find they do everything they can to break you physically, mentally. Try to destroy your mind. Snatch away your sanity. Your dignity. Self worth as a man. You are treated as though you are less than human. Abused verbally, physically. So either you become the wolf or the sheep. Either you bow down & submit, or you resist & rise up. You choose to resist, they have other tactics. Isolation, solitary confinement, the hole. Where they treat you even worst. May not feed you, allow you to shower, etc. . . .

The focus is not on deterring crime, nor rehabilitation. That is not the
desire. If a person is able to find some rehabilitation, he has beat the
odds. . . . Instead of help, there will be every attempt made to circum-
vent your efforts & destroy your mind so that if you do leave here, they
hope you come back so they can continue to get rich off you.[47]

Amber Rose describes the recycling of untreated addicts in and out
of prisons and presents a damning assessment of what the Idaho
Department of Corrections (IDOC) is about.

I believe IDOC is in fact furthering addiction on purpose, as well as
contributing to creating new addictions. I feel that if someone would
take the time to look into the officials who are running IDOC, as well
as the contracts that are contracted through Idaho Department of Corrections, they'd find a corrupt system victimizing the lower class, tax
payers, and our families, for money. I'm just one opinion in a world of
billions however, I have a voice and I'm determined to be heard. What
IDOC is doing, and what Idaho is allowing to happen is nothing short
of human trafficking.[48]

Shree Agrawal, writing from Illinois, describes a cycle of violence per-
petuated inside and reaching back outside, all at public cost.

Oppressive treatment of prisoners generates anger and hatred against
prison staff and the government. This accumulation of anger and hatred finds its expression in different people in different ways. Some
prisoners become depressed and taxpayers pay the cost of their treatment. Some prisoners commit suicide. When the family files a wrongful death lawsuit the state defends against it and taxpayers pay the cost
to do so. Some prisoners become violent and injure or kill someone.
Again, the taxpayers pay the cost of treating the injury and defending a wrongful death lawsuit. . . . Staff brutality against prisoners is a
common practice in prisons. One prisoner was beaten so badly that
his left lung and part of his right lung collapsed. The three officers who
attacked him called in the following day claiming work related injuries. Of course, the taxpayers paid the cost of the hospitalization of the
prisoner and the officers' injury claims. . . . As a result of unjust and

abusive treatment by prison staff, prisoners hate anyone in authority. These dehabilitated prisoners are then released into society. They commit new crimes that are often more violent than their previous ones. This provides repeat business to the entire criminal justice system. Innocent people are the victims of these crimes, and taxpayers pay the cost of prosecuting the repeat offenders. The West Virginia Supreme Court in a unanimous opinion stated: "A penal system characterized by retribution or revenge, rather than rehabilitation, can only result in embittered former criminals returning to society to wreak predatory acts upon the community." Cooper v. Gwinn, 171 W. Va 245 (1981), FNI.[49]

Writing from an unnamed state, Anna Vanderford describes desperate measures taken simply to get some time outside a cell. Rather than deterring violent behavior, conditions require it in order to secure a moment of relative reprieve. We can only imagine the strength of will required to live this way and then find the wherewithal to step back into the outside world free of the destructive effects of such treatment.

You have figured out how to get a break from your cell. You smear your feces on the walls. OSHA (Occupational Safety and Hazards Administration) mandates that someone has to clean it up. Ha Ha! The cops have to clean your poo. Oops! You didn't think this out well, as the officers suit up, rush you and put you in four point restraints. Now, they bring a bedpan when you have to use the rest room. Your hand is uncuffed to wipe and/or get a drink, then restrained again. . . . How long can they keep you this way? Isn't there a Geneva Convention or Amnesty international or something?[50]

While Shree Agrawal and Anna Vanderford write of extreme encounters with prison staff, Benjamin Boyce describes just a few of the common humiliations built into prison life in Colorado. In these and so many cases, deterrence is undermined by the undermining of respect for those carrying the authority of law.

The thousands of men who were caged with me were mostly good guys stuck in a bad situation. . . . We were convinced that the penitentiary was a dangerous place full of terrible monsters, but it turns out that the abuse most of us experienced came directly from the system.

No inmate ever forced me to get naked so they could photograph my body, or to bend over and spread my ass so they could look inside me with a flashlight. No inmates ever agreed to feed me, then left me hungry night after night. No inmates ever put their hands on me or took my possessions. No inmates ever uprooted me from one prison and moved me to another without notice. These power moves were monopolized by the system, not the people caught up in it.[51]

Charles Brooks Sr. sees from Michigan the irony of such treatment.

It's amazing to me that the State is trying to "rehabilitate" me from the same types of characteristics they are displaying. Hypocritical? Very. Such is the life of any inmate in the State of Michigan. If you refuse to lay down and be ran over at the whim of any staff member, then you risk being sent as far away from your family as that staff member can arrange.[52]

From Mississippi, Newman N. Kage echoes others while noting the human effects of the seamless continuation of the attitudes of police on the streets to police inside.

We are treated less than human and therefore we become animals. Those who are not animals become one in prison out of a necessity to survive our environment (peers) and because of the treatment received by Correctional officials. Many people experience this mistreatment from Police officers in our neighborhoods & hometowns. We look at the Police as the enemy instead of our allies for good reason.[53]

Incarcerated writers point to staff behavior and personalities as both cause and effect of prison conditions, resulting in the kind of treatment described above. "If you have no heart," Chanell Burnette writes from Virginia, "you're hired."[54] Steven A. DeLogé sees the anti-deterrent effects of staff profiles in the Wyoming DOC.

Who wants to work in a correctional system anyway? There are the rare socially conscious caseworkers or perhaps a person with a background in law enforcement that considers several years as a correctional officer as a stepping stone. But many are unemployable in the private sector due to emotional or skill deficits. Even if you can't function tending to the fryer at a fast food restaurant, you can land a government job with benefits at the local prison. When a large proportion of the Department of Corrections is staffed by these defective personalities, the system becomes arbitrary and irrational. Try reforming good people who have made a serious mistake in their lives when they are subjected to this environment for years on end. Every waking hour becomes a series of grievances and insults. The negativity is like a dark cloud that hovers over the person, and he or she carries it to the streets when they are released.[55]

Timothy D. V. Bazrowx writes from Texas, proclaiming the will to resist the effects of a legally sanctioned system that does not foster deterrence and negatively affects both jailors and the jailed.

The real purpose of my imprisonment, like many others, is not "rehabilitation," not "punishment," or to deter others from committing crime. My incarceration is part of the age-old program meant to reduce me in such a way that I fall into a state of complete submission to my captors. Animals are trained using this method. I, however, do not accept the appendage to my character marking me a beast and therefore reject all state efforts to punish me into submission. That is not going to happen. I am not an animal and I do not acknowledge the state's agents of repression who pigeonhole every inmate as being one and the same due to the unfortunate nature of our circumstance resulting from a criminal conviction. If one allows the evil machinations of the state to take effect it may destroy him altogether, or it could reveal the best he has to offer. Everyone is affected by the state, both prisoner and guard, and no one who lives or works here remains a normal human being, assuming they were normal upon their arrival.[56]

Held in Arkansas, B. C. Murray offers a bitterly sympathetic view of the shortcomings of staff.

So who then benefits more from prison? Regardless of the effects on society and the inmates enclosed therein, one thing is abundantly clear: Prison provides a sequestered microcosm where prison workers can pander to their insecurities and shortcomings in a world where, for a few hours each day, they become everything they ever wanted to be. And when they leave work each day, they return home to look at themselves in the mirror. There they face the same failed ego that admonishes and reminds them that, unlike the detained, prison is only a temporary reprieve from their unfulfilled dreams and discouraging lives they can never totally escape. Thus, realizing then and everyday thereafter that they need prison even more than the men sentenced to live in such a confined artificial world.[57]

From an essay quoted earlier from Mississippi, Amy Buckley continues describing the anti-deterrent effects not only of harsh staff treatment but, where she resides, of the near-total surrender of the institution to the whims of its wards.

> How do the powers that be explain an unsupervised prison? Sure there are officers but they are only here for the paycheck, not to do their jobs. How do they explain the vast amounts of drugs and number of cell phones in this facility? With a shrug of their shoulders I suspect. I am still somewhat in shock because I remember the days of order and control, but those days are long gone. The inmates run the show and the officers are merely paid spectators. Wow! How things change! Of course, in an attempt at control the officers will play with your health, medical and mental health care, keeping you from appointments just because they can. To me, that just shows how weak they truly are and how badly they desire to be obeyed. Unfortunately, they lost the privilege of being in control and obeyed when they began violating the very rules and regulations they were sworn to uphold. What can I say? Such is the insanity of CMCF and the Mississippi prison system, where the women are thrown away and forgotten, left to their own devices in what some of us consider a living hell.[58]

Nevada writer Sabrina echoes Amy Buckley's observations.

> The guards here have a high turn over rate. If they don't quit or transferred, they are walked off for having sex with inmates, or bringing il-

legal things in to women. Alot of the c/o's abuse the authority that they are given by verbally, mentally, and physically assaulting us. I was sent to prison AS punishment, not FOR punishment.[59]

Finally, if change is to occur, Alaska writer David W. Mason claims, it must begin with a change in staff and system thinking.

Just as the minds of the lawless must be changed in order for their actions to change, so too must the minds of those tasked with dealing with the lawless be changed in order for them to adopt comprehensive, non-biased program models that provide real structure and incentives for their charges.[60]

DIMINISHED FUTURES; MOTIVES AND METHODS OF FAILURE

The writers above describe malign neglect, willful irresponsibility, aggression, and other experiences that make incarcerated people less able to desist from crime that will return them to prison. Others draw back to offer wider pans of an institution that thrives on the failure of its wards. In this last section on the defeat of the prison's four rationales, imprisoned authors testify again to the lessons prisons teach about what mass incarceration is really all about.

Californian Bobby G. Wheeler:

Society wants crime, needs crime, and gains definite satisfactions from the present mishandling of it! You condemn crime; you punish us for it; but you need it. The crime and punishment ritual is a part of your lives. You need crimes to wonder at, to enjoy vicariously, to discuss and speculate about, and to publicly deplore. You need us (criminals) to identify yourselves with, to secretly envy, and to stoutly punish. We represent your alter egos—your "bad" selves—rejected and projected. We do for you the forbidden, illegal things you wish to do and, like scapegoats of old, we bear the burdens of your displaced guilt and punishment—"the iniquities of you all." Crime in the news is often a kind of sermon; it is a warning, a reminder of the existence of evil and the necessity for good to conquer. And are not the forces of good gradually overwhelming the forces of evil? All of you want to think so. It is the perennial hope of and for your civilization. Hence the wretched handling of me and my brethren, from beginning to end, is part of a daily morality play—a publicly supported, moralistic ritual enactment, without benefit of clergy.[61]

From Pennsylvania, Reese S. Wilson sees the basic inability of policing and prisons to deter crime after the fact.

> They believe that the longer the sentence the likelier the person will come home—rehabilitated and deterred from committing more crime. . . . Time itself is not going to provide inmates with the employment-and interpersonal skills needed to successfully re-enter free society. . . . Minimum mandatories, often heavily-applied against ethnic minorities and the poor, do not deter crime. Criminals commit crime because they don't believe they'll be caught. They don't think, "I'll get this much time if I do this crime." Criminals don't think about sentences until they're standing before a judge. Whatever sentencing scheme our legislature enacts, it won't deter someone who does not believe he'll get caught.[62]

Fellow Pennsylvanian Steven Lazar shares Wilson's view but goes further into the thinking of would-be lawbreakers.

> The problem is that deterrent sentences have never shown themselves to operate at any level of efficiency. Law Professor John Pfaff drove home this point in his book, *Locked In*, where he remarked that harsh sentencing is of minimum value in the realm of deterring crime, because a characteristic of criminal behavior is impulsivity, i.e. prior to committing crime, many (or most) people are not thinking about the consequences. In cases of violence, it is illogical to believe that the fear of a stiff sentence would halt the actions of a person in an extreme mental and emotional state. . . . Most criminals do not think about the consequences, and if they do, they take the appropriate steps to avoid detection. . . .
>
> On the other hand, take the poverty stricken youth who chooses to sell drugs. . . . The youth is already in a dire situation, and the short term rewards from the risky behavior could potentially have a huge impact on meeting a pressing need. In addition, the consequences of

the conduct if detected would leave him in no worse situation than the one he is already in.[63]

Don White, writing from Arizona, echoes Wilson and Lazar and adds another caption to an ineffective system: "Speaking first hand, criminals don't ponder the penalty for their crimes. They simply count on not getting caught. As far as closure for victims' families is concerned, I doubt there is any such thing."[64]

In addition to failing to account for people not thinking before a crime is committed, or the desperately poor finding an acceptable cost-benefit balance in crime, Virginian MarQui Clardy Sr. notes the failure by those legislating supposedly deterrent sentences simply to convey their message to potential lawbreakers.

Deterring crime isn't accomplished by over-punishing people after they've broken the law; it's accomplished by making people aware of the laws and the full legal ramifications of breaking them before it happens. I can honestly say that I would not have committed those robberies if I'd had prior knowledge of even a fraction of the things I now know concerning criminal justice policies. . . . That alone would have deterred me from even thinking about going down that path. I didn't know that parole had been abolished in Virginia, or that no matter how many rehabilitative, vocational or college courses I completed while incarcerated, how many accomplishments I made, or how much of a model inmate I was, Truth-in-Sentencing would prohibit me from serving any less than 85% of my sentence (which is approximately 29 years). It should go without mentioning that I am extremely remorseful for committing those robberies and for the effects my actions have had on so many people, but I'll mention it anyway. Regardless of the laws, if I could go back in time I would not have committed those robberies simply because it was wrong. But my overall point here is that prior knowledge of the law would've further deterred me from breaking it. Just about every other first-time offender I've encountered in prison has expressed the same sentiment. . . . Judge Thomas intended for my original sentence to be one of those "example sentences" meant to deter others, but it didn't. People didn't stop committing crimes after I was sentenced . . . nor did the local, state or national crime rates drop.[65]

Such statements suggest that the tough-on-crime grandstanding that built mass incarceration is less concerned with curbing crime than with garnering votes. Californian Mutope Dugma describes the self-fulfilling feedback loop facilitated by such public-facing rhetoric.

> Although, the public sector fraudulently believes prisons combat crime, unconsciously the public sector support the breeding of criminality by their votes and tax dollars. The politicians and special interests sell the fraud to the public regarding crime and its deterrent. The public hasn't seen past the fraud nor will they believe the Legislature sponsors social evils that produce criminal activities. The fear and fraud of crime makes the public believe in prisons as an absolute correction. Prisons and crimes serve only the private interest.[66]

The interests that Dugma notes grew up in the same soil plowed by political leaders turning away from welfare-state supports for the poor and toward punitive responses to the effects of poverty.[67] Delaware resident Robert W. Warrington points to the same absurdity that early critics of mass incarceration—including imprisoned people—saw driving so-called deterrent policies: "Any attempt to solve the recidivism problem by altering the conditions of prison—as it is currently designed—without first addressing society's overall structural issues will be like trying to use a lid to keep steam in a pot while a fire rages underneath."[68] From California, Asar I. Amen similarly notes that prisons cannot be a deterrent when they fail to address the base causes of crime and exacerbate these causes' effects.

> Street crime is typically an act of desperation, insanity, drug-induced behavior, or sometimes all three. Making punishments harsher does nothing to prevent crime it serves primarily to satisfy the desire for revenge and retribution. Society believes in this false logic of punishment for deterrence and does little or nothing to alleviate the problems that led to the offense. Anyone who has raised children knows that children do not stop misbehaving merely because they are punished. If we punish a child without nurturing, mentoring, and loving, we create at least a dysfunctional adult and sometimes a dangerous adult.[69]

Alabaman John Gargano writes what should long ago have been as obvious regarding prison practices as are Amen's observations.

> You can not deter future crimes while bypassing the ladder out of the gutter that placed them there, or by placing cinderblocks on the feet of the imprisoned effectively keeping them in the never ending cycle of recidivism. To deter future criminal behavior you must provide the recipe and ingredients to change behavior. Changing behavior does not come from warehousing people like some inhumane puppy mill, and continuing to treat them with little worth. If deterrence is indeed still a driving principle of the criminal justice system, then people need to be lifted up, not kept down. . . . A complete overhaul of this broken system is long overdue.[70]

Such an overhaul would radically shift priorities in criminal-legal policy and in state and federal budgets. Californian Kenneth Hartman describes what we are left with in lieu of such change.

> The policy hawked in the public square propounds that punishment, the deliberate infliction of pain and suffering, is the only answer. On closer inspection, it's merely a remarkably sophisticated bait-and-switch routine played to near perfection. What is never acknowledged openly, but known to everyone in here, is that their punishment program is guaranteed to increase the failure rate of parolees. This increases the numbers held within the tall fences, which also increases the number of guards needed, the amount of money diverted into the prisons and, not coincidentally, away from the social programs that would result in fewer admissions to the dismal empire in the first place.[71]

This dismal empire supports jobs and profits borne on the backs disproportionately of poor people of color and rooted in the racialization of crime.[72] Prisons can hardly be expected to have deterrent effects when their targeted populations face the same obstacles to living law-abiding lives inside and outside prison walls. Two more California writers point to the entrenched racism that not only made mass incarceration possible but holds it in place. Again, Asar I. Amen:

The problem is not just that a de facto police state is ready to descend on Black people at any time, but also, more broadly, that the entire population of African Americans is perceived by the broader society 1) as a potential threat and (2) as unworthy of being listened to when we protest through legal, institutional, or other means. . . . The problem of Black lives not mattering is a problem of meaning that isn't just individual or institutional but structural. It is rooted in what America is.[73]

Kevin Sawyer points to his state as a national example.

The carceral State of California, like others, uses common mechanisms such as branding, zero tolerance and tough-on-crime rhetoric to mask its malfeasance and insidious Jim Crow methods to deal with its 21st Century "negro problem" of those of us who dare to cross the "color line" and other tacit demarcation points.[74]

From Ohio, Rain Man sees the roots of a system that has broken beyond its racial origins, not only offering little deterrent to crime but also narrowing the horizon of possibility for many. Structural racism has spawned structural confinement.

I know most kids in the urban community are getting ready for prison life every day, self consciously or unconsciously. I know this is not just a black people thing and way more people are affected than just blacks. It may have started out targeting blacks. But it backfired and now everyone is affected. Most of the kids on their way to prison, have family and other people they know who has already been to prison and survived, it's becoming normal. Apartment Complexes in the urban Communities are . . . lined up and resemble cell block or prison pods.[75]

Finally, from his position in Illinois, Darnell Lane underlines a number of the running themes and implications in the preceding testimonies.

Shouldn't criminal justice have a humane component that teachers offenders that they are better than any act of crime? That they can learn from their mistakes and choose to be productive citizens in our society? . . .

Even in the face of great resistance we have to be the voice of reason and compassion. We have to place value on every life and believe that even the so-called "incorrigible" are worthy of humane treatment. How can we judge a person as guilty for a wrongful action, and then banish that same person to a facility that is wrong in how it treats the person? That is the proverbial pot calling the kettle black. How can we raise the awareness and conscious choices of an offender if our criminal justice policies and institutions only promote the same negative behaviors and ideas of the offender? Where does the criminal mentality end and justice begin? . . .

The drive to incarcerate, punish, and limit the activities of offenders has often resulted in the elimination of strategies and programs that seek to prevent or reduce crime. With so many ex-offenders returning to prison, it is clear that the punitive incarceration approach to public safety is not working. America needs to promote policies and procedures that are compassionate, humane, and cost-effective to be successful at crime prevention.[76]

Darnell Lane's is just one voice among hundreds of thousands of people who have lived years or decades inside this system, observing the daily damage done to themselves, their peers, their families, their communities, and the moral health of the nation. This is a system so long-standing in US history, and so large and widespread today as to seem to many Americans both natural and necessary and thus inevitable, beyond questioning its social effects or proper place in a democratic legal order. Yet over the course of more than 230 years, this system has consistently produced multifaceted disasters in millions of lives and thousands of communities.

This is not today and never has been a lesson lost on incarcerated people. The difference is that they are now reporting the lessons they have learned in numbers never before imagined. Those lessons are sobering, often shocking, and should chill any commitment to sustaining the status quo. How we might build those lessons into public discourse, research, teaching, judicial decisions, and legislation will be the subject of the final chapter.

CONCLUSION

CHARTING THE PATH FORWARD

> If we don't write our own endings, we hand our pens over to
> the legislators, owners of privatized prisons, and propagators
> of the lies behind mass incarceration. . . . [I write] because my
> experiences are the experiences of countless others. I write
> because there is truth in our stories that cannot, must not,
> be denied: the separation from our families, the toll on our
> loved ones, all the wasted time, the warehousing of our bod-
> ies, and our fruitless efforts to prevail against a flawed reality
> of incarceration. That is the story I dare everyone to acknowl-
> edge. And only people behind bars can tell it as it truly is.
> —DEREK R. TRUMBO

> Allowing our experiences and analysis to be added to the
> forum that will constitute public opinion could help halt
> the disastrous trend toward building more fortresses of fear
> which will become in the 21st century this generation's mon-
> uments to failure.
> —JO-ANN MAYHEW

THE witnesses in this book have laid out their case for the prison's defeat of incarceration's founding rationales. In this way
they help clear the grounds to address what Angela Davis charges is "the
most difficult and urgent challenge today . . . that of creatively exploring
new terrains of justice, where the prison no longer serves as our major
anchor."[1] By charting the human landscapes ravaged by the mass prison,
these writers urge us to turn away from policies and practices that for
centuries have silenced, ignored, and stridently denied evidence that US
penal "justice" institutionalizes suffering and enforces inequality.

There are indications today that laws, attitudes, and practices are changing. At the state and federal level, excessive sentencing is being reconsidered or rolled back. The media is more prone to present sympathetic images of imprisoned people and to investigate disturbing or illegal prison management. The numbers of the incarcerated are going down, however unevenly.[2] Yet a COVID-19 era spike in violent crime has divided camps supporting criminal legal system reforms. This spike has precipitated the defeat of progressive district attorneys, confirming that we have not really turned the corner toward a vision that answers Mariame Kaba's question: "How do we create safety outside carceral logics?"[3] How do we evolve into a society led by inclusive understanding, rather than racial and partisan hatred; where we have rule of law rather than mere regimes of criminalization, and practical aid is as much a given as accountability is a necessity? The stepping off point for such a vision is emerging today from the pens and pencil stubs and typewriters of incarcerated people. These writers mark the true first step on the path toward an authentically just criminal justice system: the recognition that the only monster contained by walls and razor wire is the prison itself.

Scholars outside echo Derek Trumbo and Jo-Ann Mayhew: "To guide politics or policy, the ethics of punishment must confront the real lives of those who are incarcerated."[4] When we do confront the lives and breadth of common stories presented by prison witnesses, we see that simply trimming around the edges of one of the oldest and most profound policy disasters in US history—with roots in the same cultural and legal habits that enabled slavery—is not enough.

Prison witness alone obviously can't directly affect practice. Yet those with the wherewithal to report what they see do much more than debunk the prison's supporting rationales. They urge us to sweep these rationales out of our thinking in order that we might address incarceration's lived effects. Witness to punishment so generic that it makes bitter nonsense of any retributive message also measures the chasm between judicial pronouncements and the damage that such pronouncements initiate. Testament to the prison's anti-rehabilitative practices unveils an industrial-scale institution whose bottom line is its own bottom line. Pointing out the myriad directions in which carceral containment spreads rather than limits human suffering reveals the prison's weight as an anchor of all manners of inequality. Witness to incarceration's anti-deterrent effects makes plain that prisons proliferate crime more efficiently than they curb it. On all of these fronts, imprisoned writers raise a chorus that voices not only the social, economic, political, and cultural policies and habits that sustain a carceral state; they suggest what will be required to reroute us toward the creation of inclusive democracy.

In offering such revelations, incarcerated writers do for incarcerated people what slave narratives did for enslaved people: through representative writers, they dismantle public propaganda about who de-legalized people are, the nature of the regime under which they live, and the disastrous personal and social effects of this regime. They testify to the depth of moral depravation that can be practiced under law even by an otherwise advanced nation, memorializing the lost, and building a bulwark against future policies that might tempt a return to such practices. And they do for those caged in the United States today what witnesses at truth and reconciliation commissions do for themselves and for future generations: they give faces and voices to those on the receiving end of state-imposed violence, making evident the irreplaceable, experiential vision that witnesses bring to any thinking about ways to move forward as they map that future path.

The prison, as these comparisons suggest, does not stand in isolation from other social and civil failures. It is their hidden index. Collectively, the people who write of their lives inside document the full landscape of market-force abandonments, civil and social service breakdowns, and abuses of state power that they have traversed on the way behind prison walls. They map from inside the issues that policy makers speculate about before writing laws they can only hope will either address these issues or simply boost their own political and professional careers. Meanwhile, these crises continue to serve as pipelines into legal confinement and its degradations. To enact radical change, we must first face the crisis, and without the contributions of imprisoned people, we will never chart the full breadth or depth of the ruinous "justice" landscape of today.

Much attention has rightly been addressed to the school-to-prison pipeline: kids in hyper-policed communities and attending the schools most likely to have police officers on campus, when they engage in the common and predictable behaviors of children and adolescents, are criminalized for being kids in public schools. They thus begin to accumulate records that slot them for adult prisons.[5] But there is also a poverty to prison pipeline,[6] a foster care to prison pipeline,[7] an addiction pipeline,[8] a mental illness pipeline,[9] an illiteracy pipeline,[10] a childhood trauma pipeline,[11] and others. Those who write about this experience open new horizons of understanding of how social and criminal justice issues are knotted together. Unraveling these and other such knots will require enabling imprisoned people to help us understand them. If their potential is to be realized more fully, however, their voices will have to be gathered and amplified as never before.

I offer below, first, a description of efforts to grow and more widely disseminate the witness in the American Prison Writing Archive beyond its unprecedented size and to build a national Prison Witness Collective. This Collective seeks to make prison witness not only accessible but unavoidable by journalists who shape much of public debate, scholars and teachers whose work influences thinking and practice, legal professionals, legislators, and a public that both consumes hours of skewed popular media on legal system practices and also votes. I next suggest how the writing of people who know what prisons do and to whom, and know the pipelines that lead there, might offer a reality check aimed at affecting practice. Incarcerated people are writing about systems that implicate or affect every US resident whether they experience these systems directly or live in comfortable complacency with the myths of criminal justice. With their words, often the last resource left to them, legally confined people have started a national reckoning with the institutional shadow cast at this nation's founding. Within this shadow of legally enforced inequality hide slavery's surrogates and the criminalization of social catastrophes that much of the white public has been happy to lock out of sight. If effectively gathered and disseminated, imprisoned writers can help to chart the way into the very light that this nation purported to seek at its beginning.

BUILDING A PRISON WITNESS COLLECTIVE

Two major initiatives are underway to grow the American Prison Writing Archive into a Prison Witness Collective at (and beyond) prisonwitness. org. The first is acceleration of prison witness intake through broader direct solicitation from writers inside US prisons and jails, along with collaborative incorporation of the existing and future holdings of other prison witness projects. The second is expanded dissemination and public engagement with Archive holdings through placement in periodicals, a book publication series featuring guest editors in conversation with incarcerated writers, public archive curation projects, and fellowships for formerly incarcerated writers to bring their insights directly to bear on public awareness.[12]

The aim of the Prison Witness Collective is to make the public aware of what confined people have been for over two centuries: the leading sources of understanding of the human experience of what incarceration and criminal legal practices do to living human beings and communities. The Collective's aim is that when scholars, students, journalists, policy makers, activists, and the public discuss incarceration, they must confront the testimony of those inside. By spreading first-person understanding of the mass prison, the Collective will help to blueprint the dismantling of the prison as we know it today.

What exactly these revelations will unfold is not entirely predictable. What is certain is that various constituencies of readers will find different ways of applying the insights offered by prison witness. Here I suggest what seem to me only the most obvious ways to not only bring prison witness into the mainstream, but also help it permeate public, legal, and academic thought.

ACADEMIA

Much recent scholarship on prisons and the criminal legal system has taken seriously the reports of first-person legal system witnesses on what they have seen and felt. These statements, however, tend to be localized and often—due to the simple barriers to access—do not include broad sampling from currently incarcerated people.[13] Something more is required to build a body of witness literature that bears "the power to suspend forgetfulness and denial."[14]

The writers quoted in this book are fighting the effects of confinement behind walls that enable public forgetting and denial of the humanity of incarcerated people. Scholars can aid in that fight by taking seriously the notion that "big narrative" can join with big data in redirecting criminal legal system thinking, research, and policy recommendations. Big narrative can set broad grounds for dismantling invested public myths that both enable and excuse denial and forgetting. Statistics can be both shocking and sobering. Human testimony speaks to hearts and minds and can precipitate action that can aid in resisting institutional self-perpetuation and the political economy of the prison industry.

Of particular service here will be the work of humanists, with their nuanced manners of reading, as well as humanistic social scientists who are practiced in bringing first-person witness and the numbers into alignment. Such scholars can devise and practice manners of reading and analysis that follow the lead of incarcerated writers while indirectly lending such marginalized writers the authority of their academic titles and affiliations. The manners of reading that such scholars will devise will be many. What this book has presented as one mode of such reading is what I have elsewhere called mid-range or "cellular" reading.[15] This is an approach that neither focuses so closely on individual essays that it misses the resonances with others across facility and state borders, nor draws back so far into digital removes (made possible by computer-aided methods) that it reduces prison witness back to data points, losing the sense and feel of its subject: an archipelago metropolis of distinct individuals.

This is not a new way of reading. Scholars regularly read in this way when writing on slave and Holocaust narratives. We know without having to say that each whipping described by an enslaved person represents thousands. Each memoir of frigid, starving nights in the barracks of a death camp memorializes uncounted others. Such assumptions have not premised the reading of US prison witness due to the simple absence of a broad archive able to demonstrate the coherencies in such work, and because of the ongoing myth of just deserts, which assumes that because individual acts caused these witnesses to be incarcerated, their testimony must remain in a similar state of isolation. This assumption ignores the fact that the United States systemically enforces the law unevenly, and that no matter what acts place people in legal confinement, once there, they become primary, frontline sources of testimony to the experience of this nation's carceral metropolis. These writers write at their risk.[16] When they do, they become irreplaceable to the effort to understand what penal practice is today, what tax- and voting-supported state violence does, and the people it lands upon.

Chapters 2 through 5 of this book are examples of and arguments for this manner of reading. By demystifying the rationales for incarceration as a moral and crime-fighting practice, the APWA authors quoted offer gateways into research on the wide and layered range of topics that incarcerated people address.[17] These are topics among which scholars can seek patterns in testimony on very specific practices and broad overviews regarding how incarcerated people critique state power, how they experience government, and how they challenge and resist institutions. Specific studies might address lethal medical neglect and malpractice, staff sexual abuse of imprisoned women (at numbers that rival reported sexual assault across the entire nation),[18] food and hygiene, psychological coping, the effects of higher education, family visits, pandemic disease, and many other subjects. Broader views might take up the links from abusive homes to addiction, homelessness, and violent crime; the ways that convicted people build and sustain hope; or how the very experience of legal caging engenders political awareness and insight.[19] The writing on these and literally hundreds of other subjects can serve as the bases of evidence for research offered to legal professionals, lawmakers, prison administrators, and the broader public.[20]

By bringing the testimony of confined people into effective unity and solidarity, scholars can present that united front both to the public and to their students. As the Black Lives Matter movement has made quite clear, there is broad, inter-racial awareness—particularly among rising generations—that abuse is engrained in the culture and ethos of American legal enforcement. Faculty can support students by broadening awareness of the most invisible of those under legal supervision.

As teachers, by introducing the prison archive to undergraduate students, faculty can further a generational change in public attitudes, images of incarcerated people, and understanding of American criminal legal practices. With the ease of a few keystrokes, the writing of incarcerated people can be incorporated into the many classrooms that address inequality and racism and their translation into law, policing, and judicial decision making.

The academic study of prison writing as a genre and as a witness literature is relatively new. Virtually all of it is based in traditionally published texts that have been shaped as they pass through the hands of editors and contest judges. The APWA's singular power is its engagement with unedited manuscripts by authors describing lives led inside even as students read them in their dorms, at home, and in libraries. This reading is particularly able to touch college students because so many of these writers were locked up in students' home states and counties when the writers were themselves teenagers.

This work has already begun in classrooms from New Haven to Berkeley, from Houston to Chicago, where faculty are assigning students work in (and often for) the APWA or directing them to the Archive as a source for writing assignments.[21] In my own classes, I have seen students' notions of prisons, imprisoned people, and criminal legal practices transformed. Their ideas of these practices are re-grounded before a horizon on which policing, courts, and prisons appear as mere road signs on the highway from poverty, domestic violence, sexual abuse, addiction, and mental illness and into cages.[22] The testimony of imprisoned people can so jostle students' moral compasses that they come out seeking ways to further understand—and often ways to affect—the underpinnings of this system. As the Archive and Collective grow, they will serve a greater number of students, introducing them to a wider body of incarcerated writers, helping to close the distance created by policy shaped by popular misinformation.

Classrooms should be spaces where students can confront difficult and uncomfortable ideas and information, where they can examine how and why some are granted the mantle of truth or fact, and where they can discuss how and under what authority that mantle is bestowed or denied. The collective testimony of incarcerated people is a rich case for such discussion. It is a substantive and deeply relevant subject in its own right for a wide range of academic studies. It can also serve as an occasion for exploring how the diverse perspectives that make up most higher education classrooms reflect diverse student relationships to criminal legal involvement. Discussion can retain the value and integrity of such diversities while coming to agreements regarding the grounds for further inquiry. Such discussion is vital for young students because criminal legal systems and practice—as at the nation's founding—lie close to the heart of what constitutes American democracy.

THE CRIMINAL LEGAL PROFESSION

> Let every judge, attorney general, district attorney, and juryman at a trial spend a bona fide term in jail, and there would be no more convictions—prisons would end. Every convict and ex-convict knows that.
> —JULIAN HAWTHORNE, *THE SUBTERRANEAN BROTHERHOOD* (1914)

Julian Hawthorne, son of the author of *The Scarlet Letter*, knew prison from the inside. He expresses a sentiment that is indeed common among incarcerated people.[23] The truth that virtually all prison witness conveys is that the charges prosecutors choose and the time that judges give to convicted people are like the numerical dimensions of a water tank: formidable perhaps, but a mere abstraction, blind to the pain and suffering contained and to the labor that incarcerated people (and their families, and their communities) must exert every hour of every day to tread stagnant water for years or decades. Hawthorne is also entirely unrealistic to imagine that any one of the actors he names would ever be required to spend "a bone fide term" inside. What is realistic is that these authorities be expected to understand in substance what legal scholar Robert Cover wrote over forty years ago.

> Legal interpretive acts signal and occasion the imposition of violence upon others: A judge articulates her understanding of a text, and as a result, somebody loses his freedom, his property, his children, even his life. . . . Neither legal interpretation nor the violence it occasions may be properly understood apart from one another.[24]

One of the most problematic contributors to mass incarceration, as noted earlier, was the introduction of the victim impact statement. Such statements bring the human consequences for victims of crime into courtrooms so that those consequences can be weighed in determining punishment. But such statements are one-sided. Legal decisions themselves, as Cover suggests and as incarcerated people testify, bear unstated consequences that resonate and can spread damage for generations among the families and communities that surround convicted people. The least we can expect of legal decision makers is that they work to understand those other impacts and be apprised of the real and potential consequences of their decisions for the human beings on their receiving end.[25] Legal professionals should have a concrete sense of what sentencing to prison will look like for each convicted individual, the people who care for and are cared for by them, and the communities they leave behind and will someday hope to rejoin.

We could begin this effort by building prison witness into legal training, to provide a sense of the effects that unfold from common legal procedures, decision making, and the diligence with which lawyers pursue their daily work and fulfill their public trust. Students who aspire to work in criminal law need a full grasp of the stakes involved in representing or prosecuting defendants—a grasp wider than the zero-sum thinking built into an adversarial system that allots wins and losses less according to guilt or innocence than by financial and demographic profiles.[26] Clinical training, which gives students hands-on experience and provides vital services to the very populations typically underserved by legal experts and courts (and who are subsequently overrepresented in prisons), does much of the work that reading prison witness can aid. But not all law schools offer clinical settings, and many of those clinics cannot accommodate every student who seeks a place (let alone serve every deserving client). These clinics are also necessarily limited to local clients while students may eventually practice elsewhere, including out of state. Reading prison witness cannot replace clinical work (nor should it, since such clinics serve those most in need of help); it could, though, become a modest stand-in for and supplement to clinical opportunities. This would expand students' sense of what lies in store for clinic clients sent to prison, as well as how often the stories they hear in clinical settings are echoed by writers in different counties, states, and regions. Young professionals who aspire to practice in all phases of criminal legal proceedings should gain some sense of the whole, state-sponsored narrative—including its potential and certain violence—in which they will play material parts.

THE PUBLIC

In the introduction to a collection of essays on witness literature sponsored by the Nobel Committee, Horace Engdahl compares the relationship of the witness and their audience to that of the messenger and the chorus in Greek tragedy: "The Chorus attests to the truth of the testimony by expressing grief and horror. To be complete, the testimony requires an answer from the human community."[27] In the great majority of instances, the audience implied by imprisoned writers is a broad one. They present their appeals to the outside community writ large. The urgency, desperation, despair, anger, and outrage they convey are fueled in large part by the certainty that the world outside is as naïve and deluded about prisons and its wards as it is distanced from them. This is evident not only in the excerpts gathered in this book, but by the coherency—the effective solidarity—of writing from vastly scattered states, and in its sheer volume.[28] These writers seek to effect change by broaching the distance between themselves and Americans who have been convinced that the quantity of barriers between outside and inside measures a qualitative difference between people of an existential kind. They suggest that assuming an *us* and *them* effectively criminalizes the difference, and by that act we justify suspension of the most basic of human and civil rights. The writers quoted in this book and across the Archive seek to unveil a self-confirming system that demands the very behaviors that it then attributes to incarcerated people in order to justify their confinement.[29] Such witness counters both institutional and public solipsism regarding crime, justice, and law.

This is a system that has enacted constructive change largely in response to outside pressure brought by public condemnation, such as when Charles Dickens's scathing assessment of solitary confinement sent officials scrambling to provide literacy training;[30] when organized labor (and prison strikes) curbed for-profit contract labor and moved prison officials to offer education as a panic response to the fear of confined people left idle;[31] when dozens of prison uprisings in the early seventies brought reform of basic day-to-day conditions (and tighter lockdowns);[32] after imprisoned people raised recent prison strikes;[33] and in 2018, when Education Justice Project leader Rebecca Ginsburg led a media campaign to restore college library books that had been summarily removed without warning or justification.[34]

From the early republic to the Progressive Era to the age of mass incarceration, the public response to exposure of degrading prison conditions has been inevitably shaped by the times. This is no less so today, with one large exception: those who have some direct experience of criminal legal practices have grown into a full third of the US population. An American citizen today is as likely to have an arrest record as they are to hold a college degree, and more likely than they are to be married or to have served in the military.[35] And these numbers don't include the millions of family and friends whose lives are affected by the arrest or imprisonment of a friend or relative. There exists today a marked nation within a nation, a de facto race- and class-based state of penal apartheid.[36] The potential of prison witness to complete the witness-recipient dyad must be viewed accordingly.

For those who only rarely if ever have contact with the criminal legal system, these systems are often mere media events: in TV and film dramas, online, in newspapers and magazines, and in local and national news broadcasts.[37] With a few exceptions, these sources are market-driven. Despite recent improvements, in the breakneck competition for ratings, sales, and clicks, presenting whole, balanced stories of individual crimes and larger trends in legal trespass is something few of these media can afford or have particular motivation to offer.[38]

Articles and broadcasts that do look inside often exhibit the exoticizing tones of deep sea or space exploration. This makes sense since prisons are secluded and censored spaces. It makes sense, but there's nothing natural or inevitable about it. This "sense" emerges from the broadly unquestioned acceptance that the prison's social function is not simply to keep some people inside but to keep others outside and perfectly unfamiliar with imprisoned faces, voices, and living conditions. There may be penological rationales for keeping people locked up. There is none for wrapping them in mystery—other than a history of creating spaces of terrifying myth, and the desire of the prison industry and its enablers to control the narrative, to veil both the humanity of prison wards and the conditions in which they live. Prisons hold American citizens who are mothers and fathers, sons and daughters and cousins and who bear every other imaginable relationship to people outside. Yet they are presented as the inhabitants of another planet. If socially distanced readers and viewers had a more realistic grasp of what imprisonment actually does and means, to whom, and for what reasons, they might move lawmakers to write policies and support practices more like they would choose for their own errant friends and family. Widespread access to the writing of people living in carceral spaces cannot complete but could begin to effect such change by interrupting a self-sustaining disinformation feedback loop that rarely involves the living subjects of legal practices. Such access could be enabled by widely disseminated prison witness, by journalists and other media producers taking the time to check their work against and include the writing of incarcerated people, and by teaching—as noted—that brings this witness into the classrooms and thus into the homes most removed from the conditions and lives of imprisoned people.

Convincing the sector of the public most often heeded by authorities—monied white voters and taxpayers—may be the most effective way to motivate change. But change initiated by this population alone will likely continue to spin the centuries-long cycle of reform and continuing failure that has resulted in the mass-scale disaster we see today. As Davis and Kaba insist, reform is not only not enough. It continues the growth and legitimizing of things as they are.[39] Real change, the kind of change that might lead in a credibly new and sustained direction, will require partnerships led by those who have been fighting this fight for years: the people and communities who are living the crisis. Important organizations are already pursing this work.[40] The evidence and ideas coming from prison inhabitants themselves can aid the people and communities most directly affected by concentrated incarceration and who are taking the lead in pursuing fundamental redirection. These are the people best able to offer realistic assessments of how to achieve public safety without allowing the purported means to such achievement (police, prisons, social service-based surveillance) to continue to pose yet additional threats and burdens to the very effort to make communities safe. As the activist truism states, *Those closest to the problem are closest to the solution.* People living the current failures—both those inside and outside prison walls—are best positioned to pursue Davis's charge of "exploring new terrains of justice."

If imprisoned writers are successful in evoking "grief and horror" over their conditions, that in itself will be an achievement. To turn those responses into action will require ideas supplemented by research but based in the lived experience of the incarcerated and formerly incarcerated, their families, and the communities that know continuing local problems from their receiving end. Community discussions of the writing of those in confinement could serve as catalysts for devising community-based solutions. What this might mean in practice is public fora for presenting the Archive; workshops where people come together to read and discuss prison witness with focus on specific conditions and issues in order to curate collections of essays and excerpts on these topics with the aim of enabling local, community discussion and aiding future decision making. Adding records of such work to the Archive can help alert readers who are political, legal, and grassroots decision makers.

LEGISLATIVE

Mass incarceration came about in large part because lawmakers made an inter-partisan contest of how selectively they could exaggerate and pathologize Black delinquency.[41] Claims about the so-called first civil right to public safety—pursued through increased policing and imprisonment—sought to secure that right for some by locking up others, trumping policies that might have addressed poverty and unemployment and other root causes of crime. Lawmakers cherry-picked research. They responded to protests fomented by police brutality by growing, militarizing, and effectively immunizing police forces from prosecution. Democrats and Republicans pushed federally backed local policies of criminalizing unemployed Black youth for being poor, Black, and unemployed. Military-grade hardware and tactics transformed wars on poverty, crime, and drugs into an ongoing war against the poor.[42] The views of those most directly affected, the individuals and families and communities living in police states from South Central Los Angeles, to Chicago's South Side, to Brooklyn's Brownsville went ignored, unheeded, or heard only when their words pleased patronizing experts and chest-pounding legislators.

Research on the effects of mass-scale prison practices addresses what is occurring today and how we got here. The question now is how we might gain insight into past failures in thinking and imagination and direct that insight toward a better future. If the writers featured in this book have done anything, they have offered a glimpse into the resources they can offer to that turning. While researchers, lawmakers, and others speculate and debate and fail to hear each other while defending methodological or ideological turf, the people who have lived every phase of the issues argued are, again, actively mapping those issues from inside. Their writing could become a substantial material aid to the *social movements* seeking to reverse and redirect policy and practice.

Incorporating prison witness into academia, legal training and public awareness could bolster opposition to destructive lawmaking, thus joining the efforts of those who have been fighting mass incarceration since before there was such a term. It could aid in a sea change in legislation, thus seeking to do more than temper a half century of aggressively bad lawmaking, pushing toward a committed skepticism that more lockups make anyone better or safer. This will mean understanding that prisons as they operate today are socially destructive even when they hold people guilty of violent crimes.[43]

More lawmakers could first take the ample lessons of the past. They could begin where their colleagues representing hyper-policed and caged Americans begin: from the premise that methods of the past have created an entirely unnatural human disaster whose legacy shapes the daily lives of millions of Americans, and that the work ahead is to unravel and reverse that disaster. They can do this by listening to those living on the receiving end of multiple policy crises. Rather than instituting criminal legal policies influenced or written by police and prison officer unions, victim rights groups, and others who stand to benefit personally, professionally, or financially from caging more people, they could consult with those most directly affected by these policies, their families, and communities. They might thus discover some of the well-known alternatives that cost less and actually address root causes of social distress.[44]

If actors among all the communities and people noted in this chapter make efforts to bring the testimony of confined people forward, this could aid in incorporating their thinking and observations into legislative deliberations. These courageous actors, along with others willing to learn from prison witnesses, either know or will come to understand that "testimony's worst enemy is not silence but the ready-made explanation."[45]

Such ready-made explanations are thick across state department of corrections websites. If the mission statements of American prisons reflected the consensus of testimony of over two centuries of writing from inside their walls, including the testimony of writers today among what is still by far the largest prison population on earth, those mission statements would include the following: *Our aim is to degrade and damage our wards, to test their ability to rise to the level of emotional, psychological, and physical assault that we mete out and allow to be meted out against them, thus assuring that they will be less able to enter peacefully and lawfully back into free society than when they entered our control. To this end, we demand the human and financial resources that might otherwise be directed to addressing the problems out of which we know crime grows.*

No lawmaker or judge would endorse such a statement. Yet it reflects the hard lessons learned by people inside an institution where instances of judicial and legal oversight are the rare exception. At the end of all the arguments about unfairness and abuse in policing and judicial practice, their final repository is an arena of malign neglect. It has been left largely to those who oversee this neglect, to prison administrators—and inevitably to day-to-day staff—to decide what human, civil, and constitutional rights imprisoned people may or may not enjoy.[46] The American public has generally been ready to accept that prisons are pressure cookers—until the pots blow up. In the aftermath, a system of "double government" guarantees that what courts decree as minimum humane conditions, prisons deploy as maximums.[47] Rights are presented to incarcerated people as privileges that can be taken away, becoming added instruments of control and punishment. For their and for the nation's sake, the first civil right that should be guaranteed to imprisoned people is the right to disseminate testimony to what prisons actually do. This is the check needed to counter the effective licensing of dehumanization inside an institution built by its founders to silence those inside.

At its start, the American penitentiary appeared among the most salient proofs of American legal exceptionalism. But after Benjamin Rush had delivered his thoughts, after Ben Franklin's salon broke up on March 9, 1787, that institution would prove most effective in allowing Americans to congratulate ourselves on exceptional thinking by applying blindfolds to the prison's utter failure in practice. Alongside Native genocide and slavery, the American mass prison should stand as a co-equal cause for national shame and humility. It is the only one in industrial-scale operation today, churning out hundreds of thousands of legally sanctioned tragedies concentrated among slavery's children,

Latina/o people, and Native survivors. Yet like formerly enslaved writers of the past—and, like them, despite the death, debilitation, and enervation of many of their peers—writers inside today offer evidence of the very values so often boasted as America's best: dogged persistence, unceasing hope, devotion to family, innovation and ingenuity, principled opposition to and determination to document injustice, and fidelity to a vision of a nation that should make good on its founding promises.

Reading deeply in the Archive reveals that American claims about the pursuit of justice and equity, respect for the rule of law, and the rationales for imprisonment are unrecognizable to those on the receiving end of the practices that hide behind or are triggered by these ideas. They see in practice what Lenore Anderson sees in her work fostering alternatives to incarceration: "the only way to really stand up for the future of public safety is to soundly reject mass incarceration as unsafe."[48] The implications for Americans as a people are as profound as they are disturbing: the spaces called free may be merely the airy distances between the struggling suburbs of an archipelago city of concentration camps—camps we have created in part to silence the witnesses against racist self-assurance, against a legal order that is too often morally indefensible, and who stand, at the scale of a major metropolis, to testify against a legal landscape they reveal as a cratered minefield of lies. The broad public has not yet faced the fact that we have created—in a remarkably short period—an institution that will require a revolution in thinking, leadership, policy, practice, and cultural assumptions as profound as those commonly associated with the national inflection point of civil war. The hope of this book is that a revolution, while required, might be led peacefully when we take to heart the lessons that prisons teach incarcerated people and that they can teach us about the manufactories of pain that have stood for over two centuries as this nation's concrete icons of justice.

ACKNOWLEDGMENTS

THANKS, first and foremost, to the incarcerated and formerly incarcerated writers quoted and cited in these pages. Their words are the marrow and muscle of this book. Foundational to all of my work in and about prisons are the many men who joined the Attica Writers' Workshop (2006–2016), first among them, Adam, Jose, Dean, Jason, Abdullah, Jacob, and John. Their wisdom, humanity, arch humor, humility, resilience, and outrage inform every page of my writing and hover around the words of others I've quoted. Wherever I have quoted them directly, the rest of the AWW circle surrounds them (with personal appreciation and writers' critical eyes).

Next, to everyone who has worked and those who are working now (including dedicated interns past and present and too many to name) to make the American Prison Writing Archive an open venue for all writers inside, at prisonwitness.org. The APWA founders' plaque (if there were one) would include Hamilton College's Janet Simons-Oppedisano, Lisa McFall, Greg Lord, Kathy Kwasniewsi, Tristan Gordon, and Shay Foley. Their efforts have enabled writers inside to show the public just how rich and crucial a source they are of insight into what mass incarceration means in practice.

New York University Press senior editor Clara Platter's generous encouragement, guidance, humanity, and insight gave this book a place and a way to grow, from a bit more than an idea and two rough chapters into a complete text. The press's anonymous reviewers offered pointed and helpful comments and encouragement. Rosalie Morales Kearns served as a thoughtful and skilled copyeditor. Those who gave their time to read the manuscript—including Marc Mauer, Kenneth Hartman, Joe Lockard, Vesla Weaver, and Will Andrews—cannot know how important and reassuring their reviews were. Hamilton College, for the past quarter century, has provided me a professional home that has fed my research, prison organizing and teaching that has been deeply entwined in the evolution of my ideas about prisons and the testimony of imprisoned people. Others have provided essential support over the course of the years of building and disseminating the holdings in the APWA. Thanks to Jonathan Simon, Marc Mauer, Bill Keller, and Valerie Jenness. The APWA advisory board continues to mind the APWA: Jimmy Santiago Baca, Kenneth Hartman, Randall Horton, and Michelle Jones. Tristan Gordon (still) keeps the APWA moving steadily on track. Vesla Weaver—first among folks at Johns Hopkins University as they welcomed the APWA into a new home—is a generous and inspiring thinker, scholar, teacher, comrade, and friend. Thanks to everyone at JHU who works to sustain and grow prisonwitness.org. Kirstyn Leuner and Catherine Koehler have helped me to appreciate more fully what we do when we bring students into the APWA.

The National Endowment for the Humanities, the Mellon Foundation, Hamilton College's Office of the Dean of Faculty and Library, Information, and Technology Services, and Johns Hopkins University have supplied essential material support and human resources to the Archive. Thanks as well to the hundreds of volunteers (on at least four continents) who have given their time to transcribing the many handwritten essays and poems that the Archive receives.

Profound personal thanks to my wife, Jennifer Ann, for her warmth, faith, humor, and unceasing support. Surrounding her, her children—and my much-beloved stepchildren—Julia and Shayne, and my brothers Jon and Eric. Together you give me a home in the world. Thanks as well to the whole extended Larson clan, and to the abiding spirits of our progenitors, Eric and Lola. To Lola I owe whatever spirit of raucous joy I contain. More than to any other person, I owe an instinctive sense of what is wrong with incarceration—and right and wrong everywhere else—to our father, Eric Larson. Rarely in word but always in action, he taught the lesson that dignity, respect, and generosity are owed to every human being, and that to deny these things is a sign of ignorance of the suffering that others have endured. I hope that wisdom is felt in each sentence I have contributed to this book.

NOTES

Preface

1 This is despite the fact that literacy rates among incarcerated people are abysmal. Corey Michon, "Uncovering Mass Incarceration's Literacy Disparity," Prison Policy Initiative, April 1, 2016, www.prisonpolicy.org.

2 The APWA is and will remain an open-access archive, free of paywalls. No fees are charged to its writers, and every effort is made to see that writers are compensated for any for-profit use of their work. NYU Press is a nonprofit entity. My advance has been and any royalties due to me from this book will be redirected to benefit writers inside. Every effort has already been made or is being made to see that the writers quoted in these pages are compensated for the use of their work.

Introduction

1 Pell v. Procunier, 417 U.S. 817 (1974).

2 Jonathan Simon, "The 'Society of Captives' in the Era of Hyper-Incarceration," *Theoretical Criminology* 4, no. 3 (2000): 303, doi: 10.1177/1362480600004003003. As a 2006 report notes at its outset, "Every day judges send thousands of men and women to jail or prison, but the public knows very little about the conditions of confinement and whether they are punishing in ways that no judge or jury ever intended." John J. Gibbons and Nicholas Katzenbach, "Confronting Confinement: A Report of the Commission on Safety and Abuse in America's Prisons," *Washington University Journal of Law & Policy* 22, no. 385 (2006), doi: 10.1525/fsr.2011.24.1.36.

3 Taylor Pendergrass and Mateo Hoke, eds., *Six by Ten: Stories from Solitary* (Chicago: Haymarket Books, 2018), 48.

4 Jose Cid, "Is Imprisonment Criminogenic? A Comparative Study of Recidivism Rates between Prison and Suspended Prison Sanctions," *European Journal of Criminology* 6, no. 6 (2009): 459–80, doi: 10.1177/1477370809341128; Jessica M. Grosholz, "Code of the Prison: Inmate Culture and Post-Prison Outcomes in an Era of Mass Incarceration" (PhD diss., Emory University, 2015), etd.library. emory.edu; Daniel P. Mears, Joshua C. Cochran, and William D. Bales, "Gender Differences in the Effects of Prison on Recidivism," *Journal of Criminal Justice* 40, no. 5 (2012): 370, doi: 10.1016/j.jcrimjus.2012.06.009.

5 George Jackson, *Soledad Brother: The Prison Letters of George Jackson* (Chicago: Lawrence Hill, 1970), 19.

6 Pendergrass and Hoke, *Six by Ten*, 188.

7 Billie Gomez, "Dear American Justice," American Prison Writing Archive, February 10, 2016.

8 This chapter's broad overview does not (and cannot in the allotted space) include writing from immigrant detention or military lockups.

9 Dan Berger, *Captive Nation: Black Prison Organizing in the Civil Rights Era* (Chapel Hill: University of North Carolina Press, 2014), xiii.

10 Craig Haney, C. Banks, and Phillip Zimbardo, "Interpersonal Dynamics in a Simulated Prison," *International Journal of Criminology* 1 (1973): 69–97. On the effects of prison work on prison staff, see Jaime Brower, "Correctional Officer Wellness and Safety Literature Review," US Department of Justice Office of Justice Programs Diagnostic Center, 2013, https://nicic.gov; and Dasha Lisitsina, "'Prison Guards Can Never Be Weak': The Hidden PTSD Crisis in America's Jails," *Guardian*, May 20, 2015, www.theguardian.com.

11 Elizabeth Hinton details how even social service supports, in the 1960s and beyond, were transformed into venues for surveillance and police contacts; see *From the War on Poverty to the War on Crime: The Making of Mass Incarceration in America* (Cambridge: Harvard University Press, 2016); see also Loïc Wacquant, *Punishing the Poor: The Neoliberal Government of Social Insecurity* (Durham: Duke University Press, 2009).

12 Wendy Sawyer and Peter Wagner, "The Whole Pie: 2020," Prison Policy Initiative, March 24, 2020, www.prisonpolicy.org.

13 "91 Percent of Americans Support Criminal Justice Reform," American Civil Liberties Union, November 16, 2017, www.aclu.org. At the same time, most Americans (64 percent) admit that they know little or nothing about prison conditions, such as the quality of health care; see "National Center for State Courts Poll # 2006-NCSC: Sentencing Attitudes," 2006, Princeton Survey Research Associates International, Roper Center for Public Opinion Research, Cornell University, Ithaca, https://ropercenter.cornell.edu.

14 "Highest and Lowest," World Prison Brief, www.prisonstudies.org.

15 On crime not as a result of social factors but as a justification for state-sponsored legal violence, see Christian Parenti, "Crime as Social Control," *Social Justice* 27, no. 3 (Fall 2000): 43–49; and Michel Foucault, *Power/Knowledge: Selected Interviews and Other Writings, 1972–1977* (New York: Pantheon, 1980), 47. On sinking crime rates since the early 1990s, see Laureen-Brooke Eisen, "America's Faulty Perception of Crime Rates," Brennan Center, March 16, 2016, www.brennancenter.org.

16 The National Advisory Commission on Criminal Justice Standards and Goals stated in 1973 that "there is overwhelming evidence that these institutions create crime rather than prevent it"; prisons and jails had racked up such "a shocking record of failure," the commission recommended stopping all prison construction and closing all juvenile facilities. "Task Force Report on Corrections" (Washington, DC: Government Printing Office, 1973), 358. On the inter-partisan politics of the punishment arms race, see Christian Parenti, *Lockdown America: Police and Prisons in the Age of Crisis* (New York: Verso, 2000); Jonathan Simon, *Governing through Crime: How the War on Crime Transformed American Democracy and Created a Culture of Fear* (New York: Oxford University Press, 2007); and Bruce Western, *Punishment and Inequality in America* (New York: Russell Sage Foundation, 2006). On the role of liberal initiatives in building the carceral state, see Naomi Murakawa, *The First Civil Right: How Liberals Built Prison America* (New York: Oxford University Press, 2014).

17 Quoted in Amy E. Lerman, *The Modern Prison Paradox: Politics, Punishment, and Social Community* (New York: Cambridge University Press, 2013), 14. Marc Mauer writes that "some of the data from that period [before mass-scale imprisonment] compares US *prison* rate, but by including jail data also (to make it comparable to other nations) US rate was roughly 1.5x higher than industrialized nations (and considerably higher than Scandinavia)." Personal email, July 29, 2022.

18 Wacquant, *Punishing the Poor.*

19 Shaila Dewan and Carl Hulse, "Republicans and Democrats Cannot Agree on Absolutely Anything. Except This," *New York Times*, November 14, 2018, www.nytimes.com.

20 Kevin H. Wozniak, "American Public Opinion about Prisons," *Criminal Justice Review* 39, no. 3 (2014): 305–24, doi: 10.1177/0734016814529968.

21 Quoted in Lerman, *Modern Prison Paradox*, 12; this is an opinion shared by the other witnesses to prison practice, prison officers. Lerman, 10, 132.

22 Danielle Kaeble and Mary Cowhig, "Correctional Populations in the United States," Bureau of Justice Statistics, April 2018, www.bjs.gov.

23 Kenneth E. Hartman, "The Trouble with Prison," in *Fourth City: Essays from the Prison in America*, ed. Doran Larson (East Lansing: Michigan State University Press, 2014), 181–85.

24 For example, Rhodes v. Chapman, 452 U.S. 337 (1981); Colin Dayan, *The Story of Cruel and Unusual* (Boston: MIT Press, 2007); Lerman, *Modern Prison Paradox*, 40.

25 Estimates run toward $300 billion. See Tara O'Neill Hayes, "The Economic Costs of the US Criminal Justice System," American Action Forum, July 16, 2020, www.americanactionforum.org.

26 Michelle Brown, *The Culture of Punishment: Prison, Society, and Spectacle* (New York: New York University Press, 2009), 5–14, 50–84; Rachel Barkow, *Prisoners of Politics: Breaking the Cycle of Mass Incarceration* (Cambridge: Belknap/Harvard University Press, 2019).

27 "The Trial Penalty: The Sixth Amendment Right to Trial on the Verge of Extinction and How to Save It," National Association of Criminal Defense Lawyers, July 10, 2018, www.nacdl.org; John Gramlich, "Only 2% of Federal Criminal Defendants Go to Trial, and Most Who Do Are Found Guilty," Pew Research Center, June 11, 2019, www.pewresearch.org.

28 Western, *Punishment and Inequality*, 31.

29 Colin Dayan, *The Law Is a White Dog: How Legal Rituals Make and Unmake Persons* (Princeton: Princeton University Press, 2011), 184.

30 Even when incarcerated people's bones are broken, the Supreme Court has made clear that there is no call for judicial review unless explicit *intent* to harm can be demonstrated, a standard nearly impossible to meet; see Dayan, *Story of Cruel and Unusual* and *Law Is a White Dog*, 192. For an example of prison staff facing negligible consequences for nearly fatal assault, see Tom Robbins, "Brutal Beating Wakes Attica's Ghosts," *New York Times*, February 28, 2015, www.nytimes.com.

31 Michael Sainato, "US Prison System Plagued by High Illiteracy Rates," *Observer*, July 18, 2017, https://observer.com; Lerman, in *Modern Prison Paradox* (161), notes that 50 percent of parolees are functionally illiterate.

32 As its permissions questionnaire states, the APWA reserves "the right to edit or reject work that advocates violence, names names in ongoing legal cases, or libels named individuals." This is done primarily in order to protect authors from retaliation.

33 Michelle Alexander, *The New Jim Crow: Mass Incarceration in the Age of Colorblindness* (New York: New Press, 2010), 234.

34 Marie Gottschalk, *Caught: The Prison State and the Lockdown of American Politics* (Princeton: Princeton University Press, 2016), 274.

35 John Gramlich, "5 Facts about Crime in the US," Pew Research Center, January 30, 2018, www.pewresearch.org.

36 Nils Christie, *Crime Control as Industry: Towards GULAGs, Western Style*, 2nd ed. (New York: Routledge, 1994), 42. The lessons from northern European prisons have for the past half century stood as evidence of population homogeneity's softening effects on punishment policy; in turn, as these nations grapple with large-scale migration, they also prove themselves unexceptional in the harshening effects of growing diversity; see, for example, Ellen Barry and Martin Selsoe Sorensen, "In Denmark, Harsh New Laws for Immigrant 'Ghettos,'" *New York Times*, July 1, 2018, www.nytimes.com.

37 John Gramlich, "From Police to Parole, Black and White Americans Differ Widely in Their Views of Criminal Justice System," Pew Research Center, May 21, 2019, www.pewresearch.org. See also Western, *Punishment and Inequality*; Simon, *Governing through Crime*; and Wacquant, *Punishing the Poor*.

38 Brown, *Culture of Punishment*, 201.

Chapter 1. The Prison as Idea and Practice

1 See Marie Gottschalk, *The Prison and the Gallows: The Politics of Mass Incarceration in America* (New York: Cambridge University Press, 2006). Gottschalk points out that at the time of the founding, one-quarter of all British immigrants to the colonies had come as transported felons, down from one-half in the seventeenth century (43). See also Michel Foucault, *Discipline*

and Punish, trans. Alan Sheridan (New York: Pantheon, 1977); and Michele Lise Tarter and Richard Bell, introduction to *Buried Lives: Incarcerated in Early America*, ed. Michele Lise Tarter and Richard Bell (Athens: University of Georgia Press, 2012).

2 Tarter and Bell, introduction, x; H. Bruce Franklin, *Prison Literature in America: The Victim as Criminal and Artist* (New York: Oxford University Press, 1989), xxii. Franklin's is still the only book-length history of writing by incarcerated people in the United States.

3 Jevon Jackson, "Does Prison Make People Worse? (The Education Question)," American Prison Writing Archive, August 16, 2017.

4 Upon such occasions, "which ought to show only the terrorizing power of the prince, there was a whole aspect of the carnival, in which rules were inverted, authority mocked and criminals transformed into heroes." Such scenes afforded the people the chance "to hear an individual who had nothing more to lose curse the judges, the laws, the government and religion." Foucault, *Discipline and Punish*, 60–61.

5 On the failures of the penal roadwork policy, see Michael Meranze, *Laboratories of Virtue: Punishment, Revolution and Authority in Philadelphia, 1790–1835* (Chapel Hill: University of North Carolina Press, 1996). On belief in the need for community sympathy, see Michael L. Frazer, *The Enlightenment of Sympathy: Justice and the Moral Sentiments in the Eighteenth Century and Today* (New York: Oxford University Press, 2010).

6 On "affective exchange," see Jodi Schorb, "Reading Prisoners on the Scaffold: Literacy in an Era of Disciplinary Spectacle," in Tarter and Bell, *Buried Lives*, 167. On "sympathetic identification," see Meranze, *Laboratories of Virtue*, 132.

7 Following the ideas of Italian jurist Cesare Beccaria, Rush also proposed fixed sentence lengths appropriate to each crime and criminal.

8 On the running contestation and struggle within penal planning and thinking, see Philip Goodman, Joshua Page, and Michelle Phelps, *Breaking the Pendulum: The Long Struggle over Criminal Justice* (New York: Oxford University Press, 2017). Their book counters penal histories that see neat pendular swings between rehabilitation and punishment. One problem with such clean distinctions is that rehabilitation itself is often coercive.

9 Benjamin Rush, *An Enquiry into the Effects of Public Punishments upon Criminals, and upon Society* (Philadelphia: Joseph James, 1787), 11, https://quod.lib.umich.edu.

10 Caleb Smith, *The Prison and the American Imagination* (New Haven: Yale University Press, 2009), 55.

11 "The prison assumed its place as both a site of discipline and a space of horror, enlightenment reform and uncanny dread. . . . It joined the world of the gothic to the century of light, evincing that ambiguous distance that structured the project of reformative incarceration itself. Images of horrible crypts haunted the Enlightenment project." Meranze, *Laboratories of Virtue*, 210.

12 On public perceptions of prison conditions, see Kevin H. Wozniak, "American Public Opinion about Prisons," *Criminal Justice Review* 39, no. 3 (2014): 305–24. On recidivism rates, see Eva Herscowitz, "US Recidivism Rates Stay Sky High," *Crime Report*, July 30, 2021, https://thecrimereport.org; and Matthew R. Durose, Alexia D. Cooper, and Howard N. Snyder, "Recidivism of Prisoners Released in 30 States in 2005: Patterns from 2005 to 2010—Update," Bureau of Justice Statistics, April 2014, www.bjs.gov.

13 Michelle Brown, *The Culture of Punishment: Prison, Society, and Spectacle* (New York: New York University Press, 2009), 5.

14 Rachel Barkow, *Prisoners of Politics: Breaking the Cycle of Mass Incarceration* (Cambridge: Belknap/Harvard University Press, 2019), 14.

15 Jodi Schorb, *Reading Prisoners: Literature, Literacy, and the Transformation of American Punishment, 1700–1845* (New Brunswick: Rutgers University Press, 2014), 8, 23.

16 Schorb, *Reading Prisoners*, 23.

17 Meranze, *Laboratories of Virtue*, 302, 303.

18 Meranze, *Laboratories of Virtue*, 205.

19 Meranze, *Laboratories of Virtue*, 217–23; Robert Perkinson, *Texas Tough: The Rise of America's Prison Empire* (New York: Macmillan, 2010), 67.

20 Caleb Smith, *Prison and the American Imagination*, 97–98.

21 Sarah Baumgartel et al., "Time-in-Cell: The Liman-ASCA 2014 National Survey of Administrative Segregation in Prison," Liman Program, Yale Law School Association of State Correctional Administrators, August 2015, https://law.yale.edu. On the effects of time in extreme isolation, see Lisa Guenther, *Solitary Confinement: Social Death and Its Afterlives* (Minneapolis: University of Minnesota Press, 2013); and Craig Haney, "Mental Health Issues in Long-Term Solitary and 'Supermax' Confinement," *Crime & Delinquency* 49, no. 1 (2003): 124–56, doi: 10.1177/0011128702239239; for reporting, including by people held in isolation, see Solitary Watch, https://solitarywatch.org.

22 Charles Dickens, "Philadelphia, and Its Solitary Prison," chap. 7 in *American Notes* (London: Chapman & Hall, 1842), 125–26, http://xroads.virginia.edu. On the numbers held in such confinement today, see Baumgartel et al., "Time-in-Cell."

23 Schorb, *Reading Prisoners*, 127–28.

24 Patrick Lyon, *The Narrative of Patrick Lyon, Who Suffered Three Months Severe Imprisonment in Philadelphia Gaol; on Merely a Vague Suspicion, of Being Concerned in the Robbery of the Bank of Pennsylvania: With His Remarks Thereon* (Philadelphia: Francis and Robert Bailey, 1799), 24, 72–73, Evans Early American Imprint Collection, https://quod.lib.umich.edu.

25 The battles between advocates for the Eastern and Auburn Plans—solitary versus congregate labor—were as heated, in one assessment, as "the contestation over slavery in the decades leading up to the Civil War." Goodman, Page, and Phelps, *Breaking the Pendulum*, 29, citing David Rothman, "Perfecting the

Prison: United States, 1789–1865," in *The Oxford History of the Prison: The Practice of Punishment in Western Society*, ed. N. Morris and D. J. Rothman (Oxford: Oxford University Press, 1997), 105–6. Auburn continues to operate and, other than bearing a storied history, is not exceptional among maximum-security prisons across New York State or the nation.

26 Austin Reed, *The Life and Adventures of a Haunted Convict*, ed. Caleb Smith (New York: Modern Library, 2016); Rebecca M. McLennan, *The Crisis of Imprisonment: Protest, Politics, and the Making of the American Penal State, 1776–1941* (Cambridge: Cambridge University Press, 2008), 128.

27 Perkinson, *Texas Tough*, 52.

28 Schorb, *Reading Prisoners*, 139.

29 Jennifer Graber, "Engaging the Trope of Redemptive Suffering: Inmate Voices in the Antebellum Prison Debates," *Pennsylvania History: A Journal of Mid-Atlantic Studies* 79, no. 2 (Spring 2012): 209–33, 227, doi: 10.1353/pnh.2012.0021.

30 William A. Coffey, *Inside Out; or, An Interior View of the New-York State Prison: Together with Biographical Sketches of the Lives of Several of the Convicts. By One Who Knows* (New York: J. Costigan, 1823).

31 William Joseph Snelling, *The Rat-Trap; or, Cogitations of a Convict in the House of Correction* (Boston: G. N. Thomson, Weeks, Jordan, 1837), 10.

32 Snelling, *Rat-Trap*, 19; "Pretrial Detention," Prison Policy Initiative, www.prisonpolicy.org; John Gramlich, "Only 2% of Federal Criminal Defendants Go to Trial, and Most Who Do Are Found Guilty," Pew Research Center, June 11, 2019, www.pewresearch.org.

33 Foucault, *Discipline and Punish*; Bruce Western, *Punishment and Inequality in America* (New York: Russell Sage Foundation, 2006); Loïc Wacquant, *Punishing the Poor: The Neoliberal Government of Social Insecurity* (Durham: Duke University Press, 2009); Michelle Alexander, *The New Jim Crow: Mass Incarceration in the Age of Colorblindness* (New York: New Press, 2010). This effect is not, of course, limited to prisons. Writers such as Horace Lane, in *The Wandering Boy*, Reed, Jack London, and testimony from young people of color today describe daily harassment by police on the streets. Horace Lane, *The Wandering Boy, Careless Sailor, and Result of Inconsideration: A True Narrative* (Skaneateles: Luther A. Pratt, 1839), 78–79, 178, 179, 211.

34 Reed, *Life and Adventures*, 149–50.

35 Reed, *Life and Adventures*, 150.

36 Reed, *Life and Adventures*, 148.

37 Reed, *Life and Adventures*, 149.

38 Reed, *Life and Adventures*, 144.

39 Reed, *Life and Adventures*, 175.

40 Quoted in Christie Thompson, "Five Things to Know about One of the Deadliest Federal Prisons," Marshall Project, May 31, 2022, www.themarshallproject.org.

41 McLennan, *Crisis of Imprisonment*, 3.

42 Foucault, *Discipline and Punish*, 232. The centuries-long talk and failure of prison reform are two of the historical grounds for impatience among prison abolitionists today (e.g., Critical Resistance, http://criticalresistance.org).

43 Graber, "Engaging the Trope of Redemptive Suffering," 227. The disconnection between reform-minded theory and actual practice was also evident in women's prisons. As Estelle B. Freedman points out, women found professional opportunities in prison administration due to the belief that women were particularly suited to oversee other women, yet "only with a heavy dose of traditional prison methods would women's work in the profession be considered legitimate." *Their Sisters' Keepers: Women's Prison Reform in America, 1830–1930* (Ann Arbor: University of Michigan Press, 1984), 58, 77.

44 McLennan, *Crisis of Imprisonment*, 66, 89; James J. Misrahi, "Factories with Fences: An Analysis of the Prison Industry Enhancement Certification Program in Historical Perspective," *American Criminal Law Review* 33, no. 2 (Winter 1996): 411–36. On the history and more recent debate on private sector involvement in penal practices, see Alexis M. Durham II, "Origins of Interest in the Privatization of Punishment: The Nineteenth and Twentieth Century American Experience," *Criminology* 27, no. 1 (February 1989): 107–40, doi: 10.1111/j.1745-9125.1989.tb00865.x.

45 Perkinson notes in *Texas Tough* that punishment was "inflicted to assert supremacy and debase prisoners" (129). Also like enslaved people, convict laborers were punished for failing to meet production quotas, while those who did meet such quotas saw them immediately raised; see McLennan, *Crisis of Imprisonment*, 121.

46 McLennan, *Crisis of Imprisonment*, 135.

47 Perkinson, *Texas Tough*, 69.

48 McLennan, *Crisis of Imprisonment*, 172.

49 McLennan, *Crisis of Imprisonment*, 86. The use of forced labor as punishment for crime was commonly accepted by the founders, including Rush. Timothy J. Flanagan writes that "work has been a feature of American corrections here since institutions have been used as a mechanism for correcting offenders." "Prison Labor and Industry," in *The American Prison: Issues in Research and Policy*, ed. Lynne Goodstein and Doris Layton MacKenzie (New York: Plenum, 1989), 139. On the origins of involuntary prison labor and the exception clause, see Patrick Rael, "Demystifying the 13th Amendment and Its Impact on Mass Incarceration," *Black Perspectives*, December 9, 2016, www.aaihs.org. On constitutional considerations of prison conditions, see Margo Schlanger, "The Constitutional Law of Incarceration, Reconfigured," *Cornell Law Review* 103, no. 2 (2018): 357, https://scholarship.law.cornell.edu.

50 Douglas A. Blackmon, *Slavery by Another Name* (New York: Anchor, 2009). See also *13th*, directed by Ava DuVernay (Netflix, 2016).

51 Michele Goodwin, "The Thirteenth Amendment: Modern Slavery, Capitalism, and Mass Incarceration," *Cornell Law Review* 104, no. 4 (May 2019): 899–990,

https://scholarship.law.cornell.edu; Jennifer Rae Taylor, "Constitutionally Unprotected: Prison Slavery, Felon Disenfranchisement, and the Criminal Exception to Citizenship Rights," *Gonzaga Law Review* 47, no. 2 (2011–2012): 365–92. For contemporary first-person testimony, see Amika Mota, "I Saved Lives as an Incarcerated Firefighter. To California, I Was Just Cheap Labor," *Guardian*, September 1, 2020, www.theguardian.com. See also the demands of the 2018 prison labor strike, "Prison Strike 2018," Incarcerated Workers' Organizing Committee, https://incarceratedworkers.org; and Janos Marton, "The Nationwide Prison Strike: Why It's Happening and What It Means for Ending Mass Incarceration," American Civil Liberties Union, August 21, 2018, www.aclu.org.

52 Matthew J. Mancini, *One Dies, Get Another: Convict Leasing in the American South, 1866–1928* (Columbia: University of South Carolina Press, 1996); Alex Lichtenstein, *The Political Economy of Convict Labor in the New South* (New York: Verso, 1996).

53 Perkinson, *Texas Tough*, 102. Perkinson includes a brief list of prison writing from this era (403, 108).

54 Perkinson, *Texas Tough*, 88–89.

55 David M. Oshinsky, *"Worse Than Slavery": Parchman Farm and the Ordeal of Jim Crow* (New York: Free Press, 1996), 56. This system operated under open legislative cognizance; the three major lessees of carceral labor in Mississippi were all state or federal legislators, including a former US senator who "founded the Ku Klux Klan" (Oshinsky 64). An equally deliberate effort to lock up young Black men is documented in Elizabeth Hinton's study of the rise of mass-scale incarceration in the 1970s, a policy fully supported and made possible by white liberals. *From the War on Poverty to the War on Crime: The Making of Mass Incarceration in America* (Cambridge: Harvard University Press, 2016), chap. 6.

56 Michael Tonry, *Thinking about Crime: Sense and Sensibility in American Penal Culture* (New York: Oxford University Press, 2004); Alexander, *New Jim Crow*; Wacquant, *Punishing the Poor*; Marc Mauer, *Race to Incarcerate* (New York: New Press, 2006); Western, *Punishment and Inequality*; Jonathan Simon, *Governing through Crime: How the War on Crime Transformed American Democracy and Created a Culture of Fear* (New York: Oxford University Press, 2007). Elizabeth Hinton documents the policy focus on criminalizing young Black urban men in the growing carceral state of the 1960s, *From the War on Poverty to the War on Crime*.

57 This included, as it does today, stripping the vote from people who have served their time. See "Voting Rights," Sentencing Project, www.sentencingproject.org, accessed April 23, 2021. Marc Howard notes that convict leasing better explains current practices than do practices in northern and western prisons. *Unusually Cruel: Prisons, Punishment, and the Real American Exceptionalism* (New York: Oxford University Press, 2017), 155.

58 See, for example, Delia Cabe, "Angola State Prison: A Short History," Knight Case Studies Initiative, Columbia University, https://ccnmtl.columbia.edu, accessed April 23, 2021.

59 Quoted in Oshinsky, *"Worse Than Slavery,"* 79.

60 McLennan, *Crisis of Imprisonment*, 124–25.

61 Franklin, *Prison Literature*, 134–35.

62 Franklin, *Prison Literature*, 137–38.

63 See "Prison Strike 2018"; and Marton, "Nationwide Prison Strike." This collective self-awareness presented perhaps its most high-profile manifestation in the 1971 Attica Rebellion; see "Attica Prison Liberation Faction, Manifesto of Demands 1971," https://libcom.org, January 6, 2012.

64 Franklin, *Prison Literature*, 135. This observation was made by Franklin before the discovery of Austin Reed's memoir.

65 Gerald Toole, *An Autobiography of Gerald Toole, the State's Prison Convict, Who Murdered Daniel Webster, Warden of the Conn State Prison, on the 27th of March, 1862* (Bibliolife Network), 17. Organized labor supported legal bans on the purchase of prison-made goods and labelling such goods as "prison made." E. T. Hiller, "Labor Unionism and Convict Labor," *Journal of the American Institute of Criminal Law and Criminology* 5, no. 6 (1914): 851–79, https://scholarlycommons.law.northwestern.edu; Perkinson, *Texas Tough*, 135.

66 W. E. B. Du Bois, *The Souls of Black Folk* (New York: Dover, 1994), 133. Du Bois is echoed by Albert Woodfox recalling his statement to other Black men in a Louisiana prison: "I was targeted because I was black. That's why I kept getting arrested." *Solitary: Unbroken by Four Decades of Solitary Confinement. My Story of Transformation and Hope* (New York: Grove, 2019), 92. See also Elizabeth A. Gaynes, "The Urban Criminal Justice System: Where Young + Black + Male = Probable Cause," *Fordham Urban Law Journal* 20, no. 3 (Spring 1993): 621–40, https://ir.lawnet.fordham.edu; and Alexander, *New Jim Crow*.

67 See Ibram X. Kendi, *Stamped from the Beginning* (New York: The Nation Press, 2016), 306. Indeed, northern prisons often bear greater racial disproportions than states in the South. Wisconsin's Black/white prison population ratio is three times that of Mississippi's. See the Sentencing Project's interactive national map, www.sentencingproject.org, accessed January 13, 2021.

68 Jack London, "The Tramp," in *The War of the Classes* (New York: Macmillan, 1905), 79–80 (also quoted in Franklin, *Prison Literature*, 139). Add to London's class analysis the growth of the current, mass-scale, racialized carceral state, and you have the basis for what sociologist Loïc Wacquant observed in 2000: the mirroring of the racial prison in the Black ghetto, and the racial ghetto in the mass prison. "The New 'Peculiar Institution': On the Prison as Surrogate Ghetto," *Theoretical Criminology* 4, no. 3 (2000): 377–89, doi: 10.1177/1362480600004003007.

69 Wendy Sawyer, "How Much Do Incarcerated People Earn in Each State?," Prison Policy Initiative, April 10, 2017, www.prisonpolicy.org.

70 In the 1870s, amid the consolidation of industrial methods inside, and the rise of labor organizations outside, imprisoned workers engaged in sabotage, arson, and self-maiming, as well as "well-disciplined labor strikes and slow-downs, and spontaneous riots and brawls." McLennan, *Crisis of Imprisonment*, 139; see also Perkinson, *Texas Tough*, 93, 131. It's worth note that the majority of incarcerated people in the North in these years were veterans of the Civil War: up to 90 percent in 1866 in certain institutions. McLennan, *Crisis of Imprisonment*, 140. Recent incarcerated strikers, from Attica to California to Georgia, mount demands remarkably like those of their predecessors. See Nicole Lewis, "What's Really Happening with the National Prison Strike?," Marshall Project, August 24, 2018, www.marshallproject.org.

71 McLennan, *Crisis of Imprisonment*, 221–22, 224. Once again, the introduction of education came simply as a stopgap to occupy imprisoned people and reduce public criticism. See Schorb, *Reading Prisoners*, 163.

72 Khalil Gibran Muhammad, *The Condemnation of Blackness: Race, Crime, and the Making of Modern Urban America* (Cambridge: Harvard University Press, 2011), 276–77; Laura I. Appleman, "Deviancy, Dependency, and Disability: The Forgotten History of Eugenics and Mass Incarceration," *Duke Law Journal* 68 (2018): 417, 419. Jonathan Simon writes, "Eugenic thinking pointed to serious crime as the product of a 'degenerate' minority ('the criminal') presumed likely to be violent and predatory in their criminality. For such minorities, the normal deterrence constraints of the law were presumably ineffectual, and reform was presumably impossible (or at least unlikely)." "'The Criminal Is to Go Free': The Legacy of Eugenic Thought in Contemporary Judicial Realism about American Criminal Justice," *Boston University Law Review* 100 (2020): 787.

73 McLennan, *Crisis of Imprisonment*, 194–95. On Progressive Era prison reforms, and their limits, see David J. Rothman, *Incarceration and Its Alternatives in 20th Century America* (Washington, DC: US Dept. of Justice, Law Enforcement Assistance Administration, National Institute of Law Enforcement and Criminal Justice, 1979), section 5, 33–44.

74 Jack London, "The Pen," in *The Road* (New York: Macmillan, 1907), 8–121.

75 Kate O'Hare, *In Prison* (New York: Knopf, 1923), 107.

76 Alexander Berkman, *Prison Memoirs of an Anarchist* (New York: Mother Earth, 1912), 242.

77 Berkman, *Prison Memoirs*, 241.

78 This includes a young man who Berkman claims is a descendent of Dr. Benjamin Rush.

79 O'Hare, *In Prison*, 158, 178; "Report on Penal Institutions Probation and Parole," National Commission on Law Observance and Enforcement, 1931.

80 Eugene V. Debs, *Walls and Bars: Prisons and Prison Life in the "Land of the Free"* (Chicago: Charles H. Kerr, 2000), 142, 39.

81 Debs, *Walls and Bars*, 174.

82 Debs, *Walls and Bars*, 186.

83 Franklin, *Prison Literature*, 161–62. Franklin quotes a 1930 article in *The Nation* by Miriam Allen de Ford: "Cells were searched all through San Quentin—not for narcotics or knives, but for manuscripts" (162).

84 William Andrew Todd, "Convict Lease System," *New Georgia Encyclopedia*, last modified July 17, 2020, www.georgiaencyclopedia.org.

85 Robert E. Burns, *I Am a Fugitive from a Georgia Chain Gang!* (New York: Vanguard, 1932), 57.

86 Anonymous, *Female Convict*, as told to Vincent Burns (New York: Macaulay, 1934). This book, sadly, is out of print. This passage is quoted in Franklin, *Prison Literature*, 169.

87 Goodman, Page, and Phelps, *Breaking the Pendulum*.

88 Jonathan Simon, "The 'Society of Captives' in the Era of Hyper-Incarceration," *Theoretical Criminology* 4, no. 3 (2000): 285–308, 287.

89 Perkinson, *Texas Tough*, 217–18.

90 Simon, "'Society of Captives,'" 287–88.

91 David Garland, *The Culture of Control: Crime and Social Order in Contemporary Society* (Chicago: University of Chicago Press, 2002), 37.

92 Garland, *Culture of Control*, 41.

93 Quoted in Goodman, Page, and Phelps, *Breaking the Pendulum*, 6. See also Donald Clemmer, "Observations on Imprisonment as a Source of Criminality," *Journal of Criminal Law and Criminology* 43, no. 3 (1950), article 6, scholarly-commons.law.

94 Garland, *Culture of Control*, 35.

95 Garland, *Culture of Control*, 3.

96 Mona Lynch, *Sunbelt Justice: Arizona and the Transformation of American Punishment* (Palo Alto: Stanford University Press, 2010); Heather Schoenfeld, *Building the Prison State: Race and Politics of Mass Incarceration* (Chicago: University of Chicago Press, 2018).

97 Goodman, Page, and Phelps, *Breaking the Pendulum*.

98 Malcolm Braly, *On the Yard* (New York: New York Review Books, 2002), 179. Braly spent many years inside San Quentin; he was threatened with return if he published the novel before completing parole (Braly, i).

99 Etheridge Knight, *The Essential Etheridge Knight* (Pittsburgh: University of Pittsburgh Press, 1986).

100 Woodfox, *Solitary*, 30. Such critiques of internal prison policy stood against a background of controversial judicial decisions—few so widely debated or condemned as the executions of Julius and Ethel Rosenberg. On this judicial history, see Jake Kobrick, "The Rosenberg Trial," Federal Judicial Center, Federal Judicial History Office, 2013, www.fjc.gov. On media coverage immediately preceding the trial, see Cherie Lewis, "Coverage of the Rosenberg Case: May 20–June 22, 1953," Association for Education in Journalism, 1976.

101 Craig Haney, "Riding the Punishment Wave: On the Origins of Our Devolving Standards of Decency," *Hastings Women's Law Journal* 9, no. 1 (1998): 27–78.

Today we can read stories of a mentally ill man literally scalded to death in a 160-degree shower (Derek Hawkins, "An Inmate Died after Being Locked in a Scalding Shower for Two Hours. His Guards Won't Be Charged," *Washington Post*, March 20, 2017); guards releasing rival gang members into a recreation cage and betting on who will survive (Tim Corwell, "Staged Fights, Betting Guards, Gunfire and Death for the Gladiators," *Independent*, August 21, 1996); and the commission of more sexual assault in prison than is reported against all American women over age twelve outside, half of which is committed by staff (Marie Gottschalk, *Caught: The Prison State and the Lockdown of American Politics* [Princeton: Princeton University Press, 2016], 137).

102 The causal priority of each of these and other factors continues to be debated. See Mauer, *Race to Incarcerate*; Wacquant, *Punishing the Poor*; Western, *Punishment and Inequality*; Alexander, *New Jim Crow*; Barkow, *Prisoners of Politics*; Brown, *Culture of Punishment*; Angela J. Davis, ed., *Policing the Black Man: Arrest, Prosecution, and Imprisonment* (New York: Pantheon, 2017); James Forman Jr., *Locking Up Our Own: Crime and Punishment in Black America* (New York: Farrar, Straus, Giroux, 2017); Garland, *Culture of Control*; Ruth Wilson Gilmore, *Golden Gulag: Prisons, Surplus, Crisis, and Opposition in Globalizing California* (Los Angeles: University of California Press, 2007); Gottschalk, *Prison and the Gallows*, and *Caught*; Amy E. Lerman, *The Modern Prison Paradox: Politics, Punishment, and Social Community* (New York: Cambridge University Press, 2013); John Pfaff, *Locked In: The True Causes of Mass Incarceration—and How to Achieve Real Reform* (New York: Basic Books, 2017); Simon, *Governing through Crime*; Christian Parenti, *Lockdown America: Police and Prisons in the Age of Crisis* (New York: Verso, 2000); Joshua Page, *The Toughest Beat: Politics, Punishment, and the Prison Officers Union in California* (New York: Oxford University Press, 2011); Hinton, *From the War on Poverty to the War on Crime*; and Naomi Murakawa, *The First Civil Right: How Liberals Built Prison America* (New York: Oxford University Press, 2014). All agree that racism was and continues to be a major driver of mass-scale incarceration, and that the policing, judicial, and prison practices that large-scale confinement entails would have been unimaginable if targeted against white people, let alone against white-collar crime.

103 See especially Hinton, *From the War on Poverty to the War on Crime*, 176, 317, 304–5; and Murakawa, *First Civil Right*.

104 Hinton, *From the War on Poverty to the War on Crime*, chap. 6.

105 Reuben Jonathan Miller, *Halfway Home: Race, Punishment, and the Afterlife of Mass Incarceration* (New York: Little Brown, 2021), 77.

106 John Irwin, quoted in Eric Cummins, *The Rise and Fall of California's Radical Prison Movement* (Stanford: Stanford University Press, 1994), 19. See also Dan Berger, *Captive Nation: Black Prison Organizing in the Civil Rights Era* (Chapel Hill: University of North Carolina Press, 2014).

107 Garrett Felber, "'Shades of Mississippi': The Nation of Islam's Prison Organizing, the Carceral State, and the Black Freedom Struggle," *Journal of American History*

105, no. 1 (June 2018): 71–95, doi: 10.1093/jahist/jay008; Berger, *Captive Nation*; Cummins, *Rise and Fall of California's Radical Prison Movement*.

108 Malcolm X and Alex Haley, *The Autobiography of Malcolm X* (New York: Grove, 1965), 170.

109 Deshawn Cooper, "Notes from the Underground," in *Fourth City: Essays from the Prison in America*, ed. Doran Larson (East Lansing: Michigan State University Press, 2014), 263.

110 Gottschalk, *Prison and the Gallows*, 175. On Black political organizing in prisons, and the roles of jails and prisons in the rising civil rights movement more generally, see Berger, *Captive Nation*.

111 Knight, *Essential Etheridge Knight*, 48.

112 Eldridge Cleaver, *Soul on Ice* (New York: Dell, 1968), 34–35. Despite this claim, Cleaver continued to cut a path of destruction among others, especially women: "Sexist attitudes and formulations among [Black Panther] party leadership were evidenced perhaps most starkly in the case of Eldridge Cleaver, who joined the party and became minister of information in 1967. Cleaver, a convicted rapist, wrote in his influential book *Soul on Ice* that he considered the rape of white women to be a revolutionary act, and that he 'practiced' on Black women to start. While this book was written before he entered the party, he never officially repudiated these views before joining." Ashley Farmer, Mary Phillips, Robyn C. Spencer, and Leela Yellesetty, "Women in the Black Panther Party: A Roundtable," *International Socialist Review*, no. 111 (2018–2019), https://isreview.org.

113 Smith, *Prison and the American Imagination*.

114 Cleaver, *Soul on Ice*, 34.

115 Meranze, *Laboratories of Virtue*, 20.

116 George Jackson, *Soledad Brother: The Prison Letters of George Jackson* (1970; reis. Chicago: Lawrence Hill, 1994), 27–28.

117 Jackson, *Soledad Brother*, 38.

118 Jackson, *Soledad Brother*, 4.

119 Berger, *Captive Nation*, 94.

120 See James Ridgeway and Jean Casella, "Prisoner Sent to Solitary Based on Reading Materials," Solitary Watch, June 16, 2010, https://solitarywatch.org.

121 Jackson, *Soledad Brother*, 27.

122 Keramet Reiter, *23/7: Pelican Bay Prison and the Rise of Long-Term Solitary Confinement* (New Haven: Yale University Press, 2018), 3. Supermax practice as well as its rationale were presaged in Jackson being at times welded into his cell.

123 See, for example, Michael M. O'Hear, "The Original Intent of Uniformity in Federal Sentencing," *University of Cincinnati Law Review* 74, no. 3 (Spring 2006): 749–818; and Berger, *Captive Nation*, 98. Berger offers a particularly incisive reading of *Soledad Brother* and of Jackson as a prison icon, organizer, and political influence on other incarcerated people.

124 Angela Y. Davis and Bettina Aptheker, eds., *If They Come in the Morning: Voices of Resistance* (New York: Third Press, 1971), 177. What Davis states as a political

fact echoes what David Oshinsky writes of Black people under convict leasing: People who had no hand in the making or the application of laws also "saw little reason to respect the law or look down upon those who were punished and sent to jail." Oshinsky, *"Worse Than Slavery,"* 131–32.

125 See, for example, Alexander, *New Jim Crow*; and Paul Butler, *Chokehold: Policing Black Men* (New York: New Press, 2017).

126 Jonathan Simon, *Mass Incarceration on Trial* (New York: New Press, 2013), chap. 1.

127 See Hinton, *From the War on Poverty to the War on Crime*, 207; and Kenneth C. Haas, "The Triumph of Vengeance over Retribution: The United States Supreme Court and the Death Penalty," *Crime, Law and Social Change* 21 (1994): 127–54, doi: 10.1007/BF01307908. Marc Howard describes the drastic reduction in state and federal parole, *Unusually Cruel*, chap. 6.

128 *Perry Mason* and *The Defenders* championed the heroic work of defense attorneys. Prison and crime films of the era, such as *The Defiant Ones* (1958), *Cool Hand Luke* (1967), *Bonnie and Clyde* (1967), and *Midnight Cowboy* (1969), offered sympathetic portraits of both petty and violent outlaws as fully, if often deeply flawed human beings. Since Clint Eastwood's "Dirty Harry" franchise (1971, 1973, 1976, 1983, 1988), the media backlash against Warren Court decisions has presented protections against unlawful violations as mere loopholes for the guilty and their conniving attorneys, while heroic prosecutors seek justice. In practice, prosecutors have usurped the power of judges to assess crime and determine punishments (and how much punishment will help them to reelection by white voters). These are now punishments determined in thirty-nine of forty cases not before a judge or jury but in plea bargains so impossible to refuse that innocent people will plead guilty to avoid losing in a courtroom where they cannot afford, and will not be afforded, adequate counsel. See William J. Stuntz, *The Collapse of American Criminal Justice* (Cambridge: Belknap/Harvard University Press, 2001). Emily Bazelon writes that "plea bargaining has become the silent engine of our criminal justice system." She quotes Justice Anthony Kennedy (who quotes Stuntz): plea bargaining "is not some adjunct to the criminal justice system; it is the criminal-justice system." *Charged: The New Movement to Transform American Prosecution and End Mass Incarceration* (New York: Random House, 2019), 138.

129 Vesla M. Weaver, "Frontlash: Race and the Development of Punitive Crime Policy," *Studies in American Political Development* 21 (Fall 2007): 230–65, doi: 10.1017/S0898588X07000211.

130 Hinton, *From the War on Poverty to the War on Crime*; Murakawa, *First Civil Right*; Wacquant, *Punishing the Poor*; Simon, *Governing through Crime*. Vesla Weaver offers evidence that the rise in crime rates that rationalized mass incarceration may have been only apparent; she points to the expansion and professionalization of crime reporting, the financial motivations for police to record more crime, the willingness of the media to stoke panic, and the baby-

boom rise in the number of young men in their prime crime-committing years. See Weaver, "Frontlash," 244–47. Fear was leveraged to raise public support for prison expansion.

131 Jeremy Travis and Bruce Western, "Poverty, Violence, and Black Incarceration," in Davis, *Policing the Black Man*, 314.

132 Marc Mauer, "The Endurance of Racial Disparity in the Criminal Justice System," in Davis, *Policing the Black Man*, 49. See also Muhammad, *Condemnation of Blackness*; and Kendi, *Stamped from the Beginning*.

133 Travis and Western, "Poverty, Violence, and Black Incarceration," 307.

134 On the long history of the link between state abandonment of the poor and harsher policing and penality, see Bernard E. Harcourt, *The Illusion of Free Markets: Punishment and the Myth of Natural Order* (Cambridge: Harvard University Press, 2011).

135 Simon, *Governing through Crime*.

136 Perkinson, *Texas Tough*, 323.

137 "The law treats man's conduct as autonomous and willed, not because it is, but because it is desirable to proceed as if it were." Ronald J. Allen, "Retribution in Modern Penal Law: The Principle of Aggravated Harm," *Buffalo Law Review* 25, no. 1 (October 1975): 1–35, 18, 23 (note 87), https://digitalcommons.law.buffalo.edu.

138 Gottschalk, *Prison and the Gallows*, 230.

139 Perkinson, *Texas Tough*, 328, 329, 343–49.

140 Jeremy Bentham, *An Introduction to the Principles of Morals and Legislation* (1791; reis. Kitchener: Batoche Books, 2000), 24.

141 "Occupational Employment and Wages, May 2021: Correctional Officers and Jailers," US Bureau of Labor Statistics, last modified March 31, 2022, www.bls.gov; Tracy Huling, "Building a Prison Economy in Rural America," in *Invisible Punishment: The Collateral Consequences of Mass Imprisonment*, ed. Marc Mauer and Meda Chesney-Lind (New York: New Press, 2002); Parenti, *Lockdown America*; Western, *Punishment and Inequality*.

142 Anne-Marie Cusac, *Cruel and Unusual: The Culture of Punishment in America* (New Haven: Yale University Press, 2009), 212.

143 Nils Christie, *Crime Control as Industry: Towards GULAGs, Western Style*, 2nd ed. (New York: Routledge, 1994), 42.

144 Gottschalk, *Prison and the Gallows*, 226.

145 See Beth E. Richie's study of how the institutionalization of harsher criminal justice responses to sexual assault on white women of means had the effect not only of supporting the rise of the prison state but of leaving Black women assault victims themselves more vulnerable to policing and incarceration. *Arrested Justice: Black Women, Violence, and America's Prison Nation* (New York: New York University Press, 2012), 104–5.

146 On what George Kateb characterizes as public assurance of the rightness of punishment based on racism, ethnocentrism, and "Protestant reading of the Jewish scriptures," see "Punishment and the Spirit of Democracy," *Social Research* 74,

no. 2 (Summer 2007): 269–306, 286, doi: 10.1353/sor.2007.0057. On staff unions, see Page, *Toughest Beat*.

147 Gottschalk, *Prison and the Gallows*, 226.

148 On dissenting judges' condemnation of the anti-rationalism in the use of victim impact statements, see Robert Ferguson, *Inferno: An Anatomy of American Punishment* (Cambridge: Harvard University Press, 2014), 83–84.

149 Gottschalk, *Prison and the Gallows*, 233. More cynically, Joe Shapiro calls this the era of the rise of "the vengeance-rights lobby" (quoted in Haney, "Riding the Punishment Wave," 70).

150 Lenore Anderson, *In Their Names: The Untold Story of Victims' Rights, Mass Incarceration, and the Future of Public Safety* (New York: New Press, 2022).

151 For the most comprehensive and reliable history of the Attica Uprising, see Heather Ann Thompson, *Blood in the Water: The Attica Prison Uprising of 1971 and Its Legacy* (New York: Pantheon, 2016).

152 After Attica, the refusal of the state to accept any responsibility included a full-scale and decades-long (and continuing) state cover-up after the massacre. See Malcolm Bell, *The Attica Turkey Shoot* (1985; reis. New York: Skyhorse, 2017); and Thompson, *Blood in the Water*.

153 To mark the event, John Lennon and Yoko Ono wrote a song including these lyrics:

> Rockefeller pulled the trigger
> That is what the people feel
> Attica state, attica state
> We're all mates with attica state
> Free the prisoners, jail the judges
> Free all prisoners everywhere. (ll. 9–14)

Source: "Attica State Lyrics," Lyrics.com, www.lyrics.com, accessed August 18, 2020.

154 Russel G. Oswald, "Statement by Commissioner Oswald," *New York Times*, September 14, 1971, www.nytimes.com. Attica was simply the best known of the dozens of prison uprisings in the early seventies. Again, see Berger, *Captive Nation*, 93.

155 Dan Berger attributes much of publishers' interest in searching out imprisoned writers to the popular success of *Soledad Brother*. *Captive Nation*, 119.

156 *Break de Chains of Legalized U.$. Slavery* (Durham: North Carolina Women's Prison Book Project, 1976).

157 John Oliver Simon and Leslie Simon, eds., *The Caged Collective: The Life and Death of the Folsom Prison Creative Writers' Workshop* (Berkeley: Aldebaran Review, 1978).

158 *Captive Voices, Echoes off the Walls III: An Anthology of Literary Works* (Paradise: Dustbooks, 1975).

159 Stephen Levine and Dovie C. Mathis, eds., *Death Row: An Affirmation of Life* (San Francisco: Glide, 1972).

160 Ross Firestone, ed., *Getting Busted: Personal Experiences of Arrest, Trial, and Prison* (New York: Douglas, 1970).

161 Davis and Aptheker, *If They Come in the Morning*.

162 Gordon Kirkwood-Yates and John Oliver Simon, eds., *Latitude Pain, Longitude Anger* (Berkeley: Aldebaran Review, 1976).

163 Kuwasi Balagoon, ed., *Look for Me in the Whirlwind: The Collective Autobiography of the New York 21* (New York: Random House, 1971).

164 Cynde Gregory and Jeanne Finley, eds., *My Light Comes Shining: Women's Writing from Albany County Jail* (Albany: Albany City Arts Office, 1978).

165 Karlene Faith, ed., *Soledad Prison: University of the Poor* (Palo Alto: Science and Behavior Books, 1975).

166 Jack Brown, *Monkey off My Back: An Ex-Convict and Addict Relates His Discovery of Personal Freedom* (Grand Rapids: Zondervan, 1971).

167 *Who Took the Weight? Black Voices from Norfolk Prison* (Boston: Little, Brown, 1972).

168 Robert E. Chinn, *Dig the Nigger Up—Let's Kill Him Again* (New York: Zebra/Scorpio Books, 1976).

169 Willie J. Williams, *A Flower Blooming in Concrete* (Detroit: Lotus Press, 1976).

170 H. Bruce Franklin, introduction to *Prison Writing in 20th-Century America*, ed. H. Bruce Franklin (New York: Penguin, 1998), 14.

171 In Joe Lockard's (to date) unpublished manuscript "Prison Writing Anthologies in the United States," the author notes five such titles published in the 1980s, including an important global anthology of women's prison writing, now out of print. Judith Scheffler, *Wall Tappings: An International Anthology of Women's Prison Writings, 200 to the Present* (New York: Feminist Press, 1986).

172 German Lopez, "Mass Incarceration in America, Explained in 22 Maps and Charts," *Vox*, October 11, 2016, www.vox.com.

173 Jack Henry Abbott, *In the Belly of the Beast* (reis. New York: Vintage, 1991), 14.

174 Robert F. Worth, "Jailhouse Author Helped by Mailer Is Dead," *New York Times*, February 11, 2002, www.nytimes.com.

175 See Michael Hames-García, *Fugitive Thought: Prison Movements, Race, and the Meaning of Justice* (Minneapolis: University of Minnesota Press, 2004), 103–4.

176 Assata Shakur, *Assata: An Autobiography* (Chicago: Lawrence Hill Books, 1987), 59–60.

177 Richie, *Arrested Justice*, offers the statistics on rates of sexual abuse of Black women before and their rates of filings against sexual abuse in prison (51–52); she makes plain how women's bodies—especially Black women's bodies—are treated as property of state institutions (53). The continuity of pre- and in-prison sexual abuse and exploitation (by male guards) is so common as to constitute a trope of women's prison testimony. See, for example, the personal narratives in *Inside This Place, Not of It: Narratives from Women's Prisons*, ed. Robin Levi and Ayelet Waldman (New York: Verso, 2011).

178 Shakur, *Assata*, 49–50. Given its politics, not to mention its author's continuing place on the FBI's most wanted list (see "Joanne Deborah Chesimard," Most Wanted Terrorists, Federal Bureau of Investigation, www.fbi.gov, accessed January 13, 2021), it is no accident that *Assata* was published by Lawrence Hill Books, the same press that published *Soledad Brother* and that specializes in progressive titles and "topics of interest to African Americans and other underrepresented groups" (see "Lawrence Hill Books," Imprints, Chicago Review Press, www.chicagoreviewpress.com, accessed June 23, 2020).

179 Michael Tonry, "Why Crime Rates Are Falling throughout the Western World," *Crime and Justice* 43 (2014); "The Curious Case of the Fall in Crime," *Economist*, July 20, 2013, www.economist.com. On US crime rates, see John Gramlich, "What the Data Says (and Doesn't Say) about Crime in the United States," Pew Research Center, November 20, 2020, www.pewresearch.org; and Vanessa Barker, "Explaining the Great American Crime Decline: A Review of Blumstein and Wallman, Goldberger and Rosenfeld, and Zimring," *Law and Social Inquiry* 35, no. 2 (Spring 2010): 489–516, doi: 10.1111/j.1747–4469.2010.01192.x.

180 Udi Ofer, "How the 1994 Crime Bill Fed the Mass Incarceration Crisis," American Civil Liberties Union, June 4, 2019, www.aclu.org.

181 This is a phrase that novelist Toni Morrison coined and that was often misread. See Daniel Arkin, "Toni Morrison Defended, Championed and Chastised Presidents," *NBC News*, August 6, 2019, www.nbcnews.com.

182 Amanda K. Cox, "Mumia Abu-Jamal," in *Encyclopaedia Britannica*, last updated April 20, 2022, www.britannica.com; Mumia Abu-Jamal, *We Want Freedom: A Life in the Black Panther Party* (Cambridge: South End Press, 2004).

183 "Mumia Abu-Jamal," Correspondents, Prison Radio, www.prisonradio.org, accessed June 3, 2022.

184 Jacqueline Conciatore, "Abu-Jamal Sues NPR to Force Broadcast of Commentaries," *Current*, April 8, 1996, https://current.org; Mumia Abu-Jamal, *Live from Death Row* (New York: Harper Collins, 1995).

185 Abu-Jamal, *Live from Death Row*, 16.

186 Mumia Abu-Jamal, "Teetering on the Brink: Between Death and Life," *Yale Law Journal* 100 (1991): 992–1003, doi: 10.2307/796712. Reprinted in Abu-Jamal, *Live from Death Row*, 3–18. The *McCleskey* case was essential to the continuing criminalization of Blackness since it effectively isolated the entire criminal legal system from charges of racism. See, for example, Murakawa, *First Civil Right*, 135.

187 See Freemumia.com, accessed August 12, 2022.

188 Jarvis J. Masters, *Finding Freedom: Writings from Death Row* (Junction City: Padma, 1997), 173.

189 Masters, *Finding Freedom*, 176.

190 Leonard Peltier, *Prison Writings: My Life Is My Sun Dance* (New York: St. Martin's, 1999), 151.

191 James Forman Jr., *A Place to Stand* by Jimmy Santiago Baca," National Book Foundation, www.nationalbook.org, accessed August 1, 2022.

192 Jimmy Santiago Baca, *A Place to Stand* (New York: Grove Atlantic, 2001), 5.

193 "DOCCS Fact Sheet," New York State Department of Corrections and Community Supervision, January 1, 2021, https://doccs.ny.gov.

194 "Incarceration Rates by Country 2022," World Population Review, https://world-populationreview.com, accessed February 12, 2022; "State-by-State Data," The Facts, Sentencing Project, www.sentencingproject.org, accessed February 12, 2022.

195 "State-by-State Data," The Facts, Sentencing Project, www.sentencingproject.org, accessed August 25, 2020.

196 Kenneth E. Hartman, *Mother California: A Story of Redemption behind Bars* (New York: Atlas, 2009), 31, 38, 71.

197 Kenneth E. Hartman, "The Trouble with Prison," in Larson, *Fourth City*, 181–85.

198 Lockard, "Prison Writing Anthologies in the United States."

199 Woodfox, *Solitary*, 59.

200 Marlon Peterson, *Bird Uncaged: An Abolitionist's Freedom Song* (New York: Bold Type Books, 2021), 159.

201 Keri Blakinger, *Corrections in Ink* (New York: St. Martin's, 2022), 215–16.

202 Compare comments by death camp survivor Primo Levi, when he describes the *musselmanner*, or walking dead—the "complete witnesses" to crushing conditions that, by definition, memoirists have survived and so can never fully articulate. *The Drowned and the Saved*, trans. Raymond Rosenthal (New York: Vintage, 1989), 83–84.

203 Donald J. Trump's 2016 campaign, inauguration speech, and presidency are salient here, and they stood in stark contrast to his signing the First Step Act, aimed at reducing prison numbers. This wider, de-escalating turn, however, may be turning again, as COVID-19 era violent crime rates spike in many cities; see Roni Caryn Rabin and Tim Arango, "Gun Deaths Surged during the Pandemic's First Year, the C.D.C. Reports," *New York Times*, May 10, 2022, www.nytimes.com.

204 "Responses to the COVID-19 Pandemic," Prison Policy Initiative, December 23, 2020, www.prisonpolicy.org.

205 James Lartey, "Trump Signs Bipartisan Criminal Justice Overhaul First Step Act into Law," *Guardian*, December 21, 2018, www.theguardian.com.

206 This history has also taken up only work that reached outside readers. Untouched here is the rich history of prison newspapers, which have circulated inside and often reached (and still do) readers outside. For the most comprehensive archive of such publications, see JSTOR's American Prison Newspapers, 1800–2020: Voices from the Inside, www.jstor.org.

207 Challenges do persist for this work. Only the privacy of legal mail is (in theory) protected. The main venue for the APWA call for essays is unevenly distributed across the country and has been successfully banned by at least one state. "Pub-

lisher Again Challenges Censorship of Publications by Florida DOC," *Prison Legal News*, August 10, 2021, www.prisonlegalnews.org. Mail access—in and out—is often unreliable, subject to the judgment and whims of mailroom staff. States are also banning paper mail altogether and having all hardcopy scanned electronically. Mia Armstrong, "Prisons Are Increasingly Banning Physical Mail," *Slate*, August 9, 2021, https://slate.com.

208 See the permissions questionnaire that all writers complete (linked at American Prison Writing Archive site, prisonwitness.org). All APWA search facets are based on the voluntary information offered by incarcerated writers. (The APWA represents incarcerated writers only as they choose to represent themselves.) Writers learn of the APWA through the newsletters of various prisoner-support organizations and a call for essays in *Prison Legal News* (*PLN*), a monthly magazine covering legislation and court decisions and offering investigative journalism on prison issues ("Prison Legal News," www.prisonlegalnews.org, accessed January 14, 2021). The reach of *PLN* is limited, however. See Prison Legal News v. Secretary, Florida Department of Corrections, No. 15–14220 (11th Cir. 2018). Writers who do contact the APWA are sent the permissions questionnaire and return it with their essays or poems. This assumes, of course, that prison regimes allow *PLN* in, and their writing to get out. Further obstacles are that writing materials generally come from prison commissaries that exploit people earning wages (if any) counted in pennies. The APWA has been supported by the division of Library and Technology Information Services, and the Office of the Dean of Faculty at Hamilton College, by major grants from the National Endowment for the Humanities and the Mellon Foundation, and by Johns Hopkins University, where it has been relocated after its creation, development, and growth at Hamilton College, starting in 2012.

Chapter 2. Defeating Retribution, Fighting Accountability, Manufacturing "Monsters"

Epigraphs: Solo, quoted in Megan Sweeney, "Solo's Life Narrative: Freedom for Me Was an Evolution, Not a Revolution," in *Incarceration and Race in Michigan: Grounding the National Debate in State Practice*, ed. Scott Lynn Orilla and Stokes Curtis (East Lansing: Michigan State University Press, 2020), 105; Roberto Carrasco Gamez, "My Name Is Mr. Roberto Carrasco Gamez," American Prison Writing Archive, March 15, 2018.

1 Kenneth C. Haas, "The Triumph of Vengeance over Retribution: The United States Supreme Court and the Death Penalty," *Crime, Law and Social Change* 21 (1994): 127–54, 133–34, doi: 10.1007/BF01307908. H. L. A. Hart also calls "primitive" the confusion of the retributive pain of criminal punishment with compensation to crime victims, in *Punishment and Responsibility: Essays in the Philosophy of Law*, 2nd ed. (New York: Oxford University Press, 2008), 235. John Stuart Mill calls such sentiments the "animal element" in any sense of justice, made proper only when felt as a collective social response to wrongdoing, in

Utilitarianism (1861), *Collected Works of John Stuart Mill* (Toronto: University of Toronto Press, 1969), 10: 250, 248. Whatever we call or theorize about retributive legal decisions, in such decisions, in George Kateb's words, "The will to punish seems to precede any theory of punishment"; Kateb further notes that such will is a "betrayal" of the spirit of a constitution set against the power of the state to condemn and calls today's politics in the United States "criminally violent." "Punishment and the Spirit of Democracy," *Social Research* 74, no. 2 (Summer 2007): 207, 281.

2 Monica M. Gerber and Jonathan Jackson identify in vengeance the emotional pleasure of knowing that incarcerated people suffer, with little or no care for proportionality. Their work locates revenge in the desire to dominate over out-groups, thus explaining an acceptance of today's denial of fair procedures, a fact that stands behind complacency with a racially disproportionate carceral system. While just deserts may be "about restoring balance in society as a whole," revenge is about the very victim-offender relationship that courts have for millennia sought to arbitrate. "Retribution as Revenge and Retribution as Just Deserts," *Social Justice Research* 26, no. 1 (August 2012): 63, 76–77, 78, doi: 10.2139/ssrn.2136237. Far from merely a populist impulse, a "vengeance-oriented philosophy" now dominates the criminal justice decisions of the Supreme Court: it is "victim-oriented, arbitrary, discriminatory, and not limited by considerations of proportionality." Haas, "Triumph of Vengeance," 137. Contrast this with Court decisions from 1949 to 1952, delegitimizing retribution as an aim of criminal law, seeking deterrence and rehabilitation rather than retaliation or vengeance. See Matthew Haist, "Deterrence in a Sea of Just Deserts: Are Utilitarian Goals Achievable in a World of Limiting Retributivism," *Journal of Criminal Law & Criminology* 99, no. 3 (Spring 2009): 798–99.

3 Quoted in Hart, *Punishment and Responsibility*, 164.

4 For a discussion of retributivist thinking in the same period in which it had taken precedence in penal practice, and of its failure to justify itself according to major theories of punishment, see Hugo Adam Bedau, "Retribution and the Theory of Punishment," *Journal of Philosophy* 75, no. 11 (November 1978): 601–20. Michele Cotton documents how states, after codifying the purposes of penal confinement in terms of utilitarian ends (rehabilitation, deterrence, and incapacitation), followed such codification with retributive practices. "Back with a Vengeance: The Resilience of Retribution as an Articulated Purpose of Criminal Punishment," *American Criminal Law Review* 37, no. 4 (2000): 1313–62.

5 Naomi Murakawa, *The First Civil Right: How Liberals Built Prison America* (New York: Oxford University Press, 2014), 19.

6 See Craig Haney, "The Psychological Impact of Incarceration: Implications for Post-Prison Adjustment," US Department of Health and Human Services, December 2001, https://aspe.hhs.gov. Haney's article confirms several of the major deleterious effects to which incarcerated writers testify. See also "Prisons Can Seriously Damage Your Mental Health," Prison Reform Trust, www.

prisonreformtrust.org.uk, accessed January 28, 2021. The stringent (and often arbitrary) conditions of post-release supervision further limit the chances of creating a break from the effects of incarceration. See David J. Harding et al., "Short- and Long-Term Effects of Imprisonment on Future Felony Convictions and Prison Admissions," *Proceedings of the National Academy of Science of the United States* 114, no. 42 (October 2017): 11103–8, doi: 10.1073/pnas.1701544114. Meredith Booker documents how the simple fact of incarceration drastically reduces lifetime earnings. "The Crippling Effect of Incarceration on Wealth," Prison Policy Initiative, April 26, 2016, www.prisonpolicy.org. In "Wounds from Incarceration That Never Heal," Tony N. Brown and Evelyn Patterson document how incarceration damages not only incarcerated people but their families. *New Republic*, June 28, 2016, https://newrepublic.com. This is an effect we will look at more closely in chapter 4.

7   Bryan Stevenson notes how the victim rights movement personalized criminal offense and helped to facilitate the transformation of a (purportedly) rehabilitative into a vengeance system. *Just Mercy: A Story of Justice and Redemption* (New York: Spiegel and Grau, 2015), 140–42. Others point to Ronald Reagan's explicit naming of victim vengeance as imprisonment's central purpose. Philip Goodman, Joshua Page, and Michelle Phelps, *Breaking the Pendulum: The Long Struggle over Criminal Justice* (New York: Oxford University Press, 2017), 104. See also Marie Gottschalk, *The Prison and the Gallows: The Politics of Mass Incarceration in America* (New York: Cambridge University Press, 2006), 226.

8   For an argument supporting this view, see Robert Blecker, *The Death of Punishment: Searching for Justice among the Worst of the Worst* (New York: St. Martin's, 2013); and "Making Prisons Prisons Again: A Solution to Overcrowding That the Left Really Doesn't Want to Talk About," editorial, *Law Enforcement Today*, September 3, 2022, www.lawenforcementtoday.com.

9   John Gardner, introduction to Hart, *Punishment and Responsibility*, xli.

10   The most influential expression of this view is in Immanuel Kant, *The Philosophy of Law*, trans. W. Hastie (1887; reis. Clark: Law Book Exchange, 2007), 195–204. Kant's retributivist thinking appears deeply ironic today, however, seated as it is in the belief that retribution—punishment proportionate to the crime—is an act of respect for the human dignity of the perpetrator: retribution acknowledges the perpetrator as a self-determining person, and thus subject to the consequences of their chosen actions, and not as a mere means toward other ends (such as public safety via deterrence). Immanuel Kant, *The Metaphysics of Morals*, trans. Mary Gregor (New York: Cambridge University Press, 1996), 6: 33, 104–5. As Arthur Shuster writes, "In this sense, to punish a person would be to pay him the highest compliment, whereas to let him off the hook would be to condemn him as childish, irresponsible, and something less than a full human being." Arthur Shuster, "Kant on the Role of the Retributive Outlook in Moral and Political Life," *Review of Politics* 73, no. 3 (Summer 2011): 425–48. See also Thomas E. Hill, "Kant on Wrongdoing, Desert, and Punishment," *Law*

and Philosophy 18, no. 4 (1999): 407–41. Dignity, as we will see, is precisely what punishment that is disproportionate, arbitrary, and generic degrades.

11 John Locke, *An Essay Concerning Human Understanding*, ed. Peter H. Nidditch (1700; reis. New York: Oxford University Press, 1975), 27, 346. Also quoted and discussed in Colin Dayan, *The Law Is a White Dog: How Legal Rituals Make and Unmake Persons* (Princeton: Princeton University Press, 2011), 89.

12 There are currently 439 essays in the APWA that include the term "human being"; the great majority describe prison staff attitudes and practices that challenge that status.

13 John Gardner notes that without the substantial support of utilitarian ends (i.e., deterrence and reform), retribution is mere retaliation. Introduction to Hart, *Punishment and Responsibility*, xxxi. Kevin Carlsmith documents that those who say they support deterrence are neither more nor less sensitive to deterrent effects than those who support retribution. "On Justifying Punishment: The Discrepancy between Words and Actions," *Social Justice Research* 21, no. 2 (September 2008): 121, doi: 10.1007/s11211-008-0068-x.

14 Court decisions have for decades deferred to prison administrators to decide what rights and remedies incarcerated people can exercise or seek, to the point that, as Sharon Dolovich writes, "prison officials can violate constitutional rights if they can show that doing so facilitates running the prison." "Forms of Judicial Deference in Prison Law," *Prison Legal News*, January 2013, www.prisonlegal-news.org. See also "Recent Trends in Corrections and Prisoners' Rights Law," in *Correctional Theory and Practice*, ed. Clayton A. Hartjen and Edward E. Rhine (Belmont: Wadsworth, 1992), 119–38, www.ojp.gov. For a recent instance of judicial deference, see Prison Legal News v. Secretary, Florida Department of Corrections, No. 15–14220 (11th Cir. 2018). The Prison Litigation Reform Act of 1996 set severe restrictions on incarcerated people seeking legal remedies in federal court. See "No Equal Justice: The Prison Litigation Reform Act in the United States," Human Rights Watch, June 16, 2009, www.hrw.org; and "Know Your Rights: The Prison Litigation Reform Act (PLRA)," American Civil Liberties Union, last updated November 2002, www.aclu.org. The result of such court and legislative decisions is a system in which, as Michel Foucault writes, "justice no longer takes responsibility for the violence that is bound up with its practice." *Discipline and Punish: The Birth of the Prison*, trans. Alan Sheridan (New York: Vintage, 1995), 9.

15 I am thinking here specifically of the list of the criminogenic effects and "pains of imprisonment" described in Gresham Sykes's classic study, *The Society of Captives: A Study of a Maximum Security Prison* (1958; reis. Princeton: Princeton University Press, 2007). Haggerty and Bucerius look at problems in the critical literature since 1958 that expands Sykes's list of pains and thus risks a ranking of pains in which some appear unworthy of address, without upsetting the common assumption that imprisonment is (and should be) painful, and without suggesting paths toward fundamental change; Kevin D. Haggerty and

Sandra Bucerius, "The Proliferating Pains of Imprisonment," *Incarceration* 1, no. 1 (2020): 1–16, doi: 10.1177/2632666320936432. Attending to the defeat of the four cardinal carceral aims avoids ranking while taking none of imprisoned people's pains lightly; it also points to specific needs for reform/transformation/abolition without depending on sympathy with incarcerated people—except as an aggregate of corroborating witnesses—or assuming that imprisonment should not present challenges to the imprisoned.

16 The difference, as George Kateb points out, is that state punishment is voluntary "while many violent crimes do not lend themselves to that description." "Punishment and the Spirit of Democracy," 291.

17 Andrew Jackson Smith, "Mass Producing Mentally Ill Citizens in America's Prisons," in *Fourth City: Essays from the Prison in America*, ed. Doran Larson (East Lansing: Michigan State University Press, 2014), 232. Also in the American Prison Writing Archive, September 16, 2015.

18 On the application of such rational actor theory to criminal justice, see "Rational Choice Theory," Criminology Theories, Criminal Justice, http://criminal-justice.iresearchnet.com, accessed August 1, 2020. Wendy Brown reminds us that "theory is not just the opposite of application, but carries the impossibility of application. As a meaning-making enterprise, theory depicts a world that does not quite exist, that is not quite the world we inhabit." *Edgework: Critical Essays on Knowledge and Politics* (Princeton: Princeton University Press, 2005), 80. Translation across this "not quite," bridged by political rhetoric and its application, has provided both the causal connection to and the distance between rational actor theory and disastrous penal policy. More broadly, as Hart reminds us, "'Theories' of punishment are not like scientific theories, which posit what can be shown true pending counter evidence. Punishment 'theories' are moral claims, what should be done." *Punishment and Responsibility*, 71–72.

19 Jonathan Simon, *Mass Incarceration on Trial* (New York: New Press, 2013), chap. 1. Simon notes the effects of high-profile serial killings on public images of lawbreakers.

20 Stevenson, *Just Mercy*, 15; see also Danielle Sered, *Until We Reckon: Violence, Mass Incarceration, and a Road to Repair* (New York: New Press, 2019). See also Anne-Marie Cusac, *Cruel and Unusual: The Culture of Punishment in America* (New Haven: Yale University Press, 2009), 14.

21 John Vance, "Labelling Theory," American Prison Writing Archive, August 16, 2017.

22 Jamel Lamont Brown, "Learning to Grow inside a Prison Cell," American Prison Writing Archive, November 10, 2014.

23 Willie Bailey III, "My Own Prison," American Prison Writing Archive, October 21, 2016.

24 In turn, boards of parole commonly dismiss even those who have served decades and have racked up pages of successful programming, education, volunteer achievements, and prison work records: "When denying parole,"

writes Jeffrey Lane from Ohio, "the board often cites one of their catchalls, 'the serious nature of the crime,' as their reason." Jeffrey D. Lane, "Disparity in Ohio Prisons, a Discourse for the Greater Public Good," American Prison Writing Archive, October 24, 2016. From Michigan, George N. Hall writes that "no one is the same person he or she was decades in the past, not even murderers. The prisoner's behavior, while incarcerated, is the measure by which it should be determined whether he or she should be considered for release, not the behavior for which the prisoner is incarcerated." "Who Is Nonviolent?," American Prison Writing Archive, May 28, 2019. See also Alexis Watts and Edward E. Rhine, "Parole Board Held in Contempt after Failing to Follow State's Parole Release Laws," Robina Institute, https://robinainstitute.umn.edu, accessed January 22, 2021; Beth Schwartzapfel, "How Parole Boards Keep Prisoners in the Dark and behind Bars," *Washington Post*, July 11, 2015, www.washingtonpost.com; and Harding et al., "Short- and Long-Term Effects of Imprisonment."

25 Daniel Perry, "As I Write This First Hand Account . . . ," American Prison Writing Archive, May 13, 2014.

26 Perry, "As I Write."

27 Robert Morales, "The New Death Penalty," American Prison Writing Archive, October 22, 2016.

28 Irma Rodriquez, "Irma Rodriquez," in *Inside This Place, Not of It: Narratives from Women's Prisons*, ed. Robin Levi and Ayelet Waldman (London: Verso, 2011), 208.

29 Robert Saleem Holbrook, "From Public Enemy to Enemy of the State," American Prison Writing Archive, May 30, 2008.

30 "Report to the United Nations on Racial Disparities in the US Criminal Justice System," Sentencing Project, April 19, 2018, www.sentencingproject.org; "Demographic Differences in Sentencing," United States Sentencing Commission, November 14, 2017, www.ussc.gov.

31 The latter fact indicates why it is no accident that inside prison social order, those who have harmed children can be attacked for any or no reason at all. See Michael Beverley, "A Perspective on Prison," in Larson, *Fourth City*, 24–31. Also included in American Prison Writing Archive, October 24, 2016. Murakawa attributes prison riots in part to imprisoned people's awareness of sentencing disparities. *First Civil Right*, 95–96.

32 Kenneth E. Hartman, "The Trouble with Prison," in Larson, *Fourth City*, 181.

33 Rachel Barkow, *Prisoners of Politics: Breaking the Cycle of Mass Incarceration* (Cambridge: Belknap/Harvard University Press, 2019), 1–3. Barkow points out that the resulting laws tend to be overly broad; the label of sex offender makes this particularly clear: this title includes adults who rape children, the child who pulls down a schoolmate's pants as a prank, and the eighteen-year-old lover of a sixteen-year-old high school sweetheart (24, 35). Criminologist Frank Zimring has called mandatory minimum sentencing "a temper tantrum masquerading as an act of government." Quoted in Emily Bazelon, *Charged: The New Movement*

to Transform American Prosecution and End Mass Incarceration (New York: Random House, 2019), 63.

34 Barkow, *Prisoners of Politics*, 35–37. Carlsmith makes plain that such high-profile and rabble-rousing punishment measures, once applied, rarely deliver what people recognize as justice. "On Justifying Punishment."

35 Barkow, *Prisoners of Politics*, 29.

36 Jameel Sykes, "Incarcerated . . . ," American Prison Writing Archive, May 5, 2014.

37 Lincoln Allen Keith, "Shaved," American Prison Writing Archive, March 17, 2018.

38 Lenore Anderson makes evident that this specificity of punishment was created to avenge monied white victims, ignores others, and lands largely on poor nonwhite people. *In Their Names: The Untold Story of Victims' Rights, Mass Incarceration, and the Future of Public Safety* (New York: New Press, 2022).

39 Elaine Scarry notes that pain is something we know with absolute certainty, and also is perfectly incommunicable. *The Body in Pain: The Making and Unmaking of the World* (New York: Oxford University Press, 1983), 4. Hart observes what is equally incontestable: there are no units of measure of "wickedness" or of suffering. *Punishment and Responsibility*, 161. While these facts should inspire parsimony in punishment, they have instead offered open license for the "punishment wave" described by Craig Haney in "Riding the Punishment Wave: On the Origins of Our Devolving Standards of Decency," *Hastings Women's Law Journal* 9, no. 1 (1998): 27–78.

40 Erving Goffman, *Asylums: Essays on the Condition of the Social Situation of Mental Patients and Other Inmates* (New York: Vintage, 1961).

41 Kenneth E. Hartman, "Searching for the Beautiful Prison," American Prison Writing Archive, October 21, 2016.

42 Frederike Funk, Victoria McGeer, and Mario Gollwitzer, "Get the Message: Punishment Is Satisfying if the Transgressor Responds to Its Communicative Intent," *Personality and Social Psychology Bulletin* 40, no. 8 (2014): 986–97, doi: 10.1177/0146167214533130. Funk et al.'s work is based on controlled experiments; these conclusions, however, are confirmed in Danielle Sered's years of restorative justice work. See Sered, *Until We Reckon*.

43 For counterexamples of restorative justice-in-prison programs, see "Restorative Justice," Insight Prison Project, www.insightprisonproject.org, accessed July 28, 2020; and "Resources," Restorative Justice Exchange, http://restorativejustice. org, accessed July 28, 2020.

44 Cited in Sered, *Until We Reckon*, 29. At best, studies of victim satisfaction with current criminal procedures and outcomes bear mixed results—a weak basis for mass-scale incarceration. See M. Kunst, L. Popelier, and E. Varekamp, "Victim Satisfaction with the Criminal Justice System and Emotional Recovery: A Systematic and Critical Review of the Literature," *Trauma, Violence, & Abuse* 16, no. 3 (October 2008): 336–58, doi: 10.1177/1524838014555034; Malini Laxminarayan

et al., "Victim Satisfaction with Criminal Justice: A Systematic Review," *Victims & Offenders: An International Journal of Evidence-Based Research, Policy, and Practice* 8, no. 2 (2013): 119–47, doi: 10.1080/15564886.2012.763198; Robert C. Davis and Barbara E. Smith, "Victim Impact Statements and Victim Satisfaction: An Unfulfilled Promise?," *Journal of Criminal Justice* 22, no. 1 (1994): 1–12, doi: 10.1016/0047-2352(94)90044-2.

45 In a widely cited essay on punishment as an expressive act, Joel Feinberg writes,

> It is much easier to show that punishment has a symbolic significance than to say exactly what it is that punishment expresses. At its best, in civilized and democratic countries, punishment surely expresses the community's strong disapproval of what the criminal did. Indeed it can be said that punishment expresses the judgment (as distinct from any emotion) of the community that what the criminal did was wrong. I think it is fair to say of our community, however, that punishment generally expresses more than judgments or disapproval; it is also a symbolic way of getting back at the criminal, of expressing a kind of vindictive resentment. To any reader who has in fact spent time in a prison, I venture to say, even Professor Gardner's strong terms—"hatred, fear, or contempt for the convict"—will not seem too strong an account of what imprisonment is universally taken to express. Not only does the criminal feel the naked hostility of his guards and the outside world—that would be fierce enough—but that hostility is self-righteous as well. His punishment bears the aspect of legitimized vengefulness.

"The Expressive Function of Punishment," *Monist* 49, no. 3 (July 1965): 402–3, doi: 10.5840/monist196549326.

46 Dayan, *Law Is a White Dog*, 4, 20, 32, xii. See also Stanley Cohen and Laurie Taylor, *Escape Attempts: The Theory and Practice of Resistance in Everyday Life*, 2nd ed. (New York: Routledge, 1992), 37.

47 Sered, *Until We Reckon*, 91, 93. That punishment should in fact communicate to the transgressor is implicit everywhere in retributive theory, as when Feinberg asks, "Could not the state do this job [condemn an action] without punishment? Perhaps, but when it speaks by punishing, its message is loud, and sure of getting across." "Expressive Function of Punishment," 408.

48 Victoria Sanchez, "Victoria Sanchez," in Levi and Waldman, *Inside This Place, Not of It*, 179.

49 Robert Cannon Jr., "Beyond the Wall," American Prison Writing Archive, September 26, 2018.

50 Stephen Long, "A Prisoner's Essays," American Prison Writing Archive, October 17, 2016.

51 Sered, *Until We Reckon*, 3–4, 67. It is thus little wonder that recidivism rates run upwards of 75 percent within five years of release. Matthew R. Durose, Alexia D. Cooper, and Howard N. Snyder, "Recidivism of Prisoners Released in 30 States in 2005: Patterns from 2005 to 2010—Update," Bureau of Justice Statistics, April 2014, www.bjs.gov.

52 Donald Hairgrove, "A Single Unheard Voice," American Prison Writing Archive, April 4, 2016.

53 John Russel Bossé, "I Have to Write of My Condition When I Am Safely Distanced from It," American Prison Writing Archive, June 11, 2014.

54 Eric Martin Hassel, "Waiting Room 16," American Prison Writing Archive, June 15, 2018.

55 Jevon Jackson, "Does Prison Make People Worse? (The Education Question)," American Prison Writing Archive, August 16, 2017.

56 Christopher Balmer, "Finding Appreciation," American Prison Writing Archive, October 24, 2016.

57 Angel Ayala, "I'm a 32-Year-Old California Prisoner Serving a 137-Years-to-Life Sentence," American Prison Writing Archive, June 15, 2018.

58 Lee Whitt, "Boxed In . . . ," American Prison Writing Archive, October 25, 2016.

59 John Pfaff, *Locked In: The True Causes of Mass Incarceration—and How to Achieve Real Reform* (New York: Basic Books, 2017), 14.

60 W. E. Roberts, "452 Words on Incarceration," American Prison Writing Archive, March 15, 2018.

61 Jacob Barrett, "Prison Culture," American Prison Writing Archive, October 17, 2022.

62 Ebony Delaney, "Safety and Security," American Prison Writing Archive, June 15, 2018.

63 James Africa, "Institutionalized Part 2/ Let Us Break Men in Our Image," American Prison Writing Archive, February 28, 2018.

64 Prison Vitality, "Man versus Beast," American Prison Writing Archive, January 30, 2015.

65 K. D. Welch, "The Void Exitsance!," American Prison Writing Archive, June 29, 2015.

66 Jeremy Pinson, "Life in Solitary Confinement," American Prison Writing Archive, February 24, 2016.

67 Amy Benjamin, "No Excuses. Reasons," American Prison Writing Archive, August 25, 2014.

68 Andrew Jackson Smith, "Adaptive Core Curriculum for Prisoners," American Prison Writing Archive, February 6, 2014.

69 See the description of Swedish criminal sanctions at "Sanctions," Kriminal Varden, www.kriminalvarden.se, accessed January 25, 2021.

70 On the history of perpetual punishment and its common occurrence today, see Christopher Seeds, *Death by Prison: The Emergence of Life without Parole and Perpetual Confinement* (Oakland: University of California Press, 2022).

71 Darrel Limbocker, "Prison Is a Place," American Prison Writing Archive, March 15, 2018.

72 Linda Kay Stermer, "How Long Is Long Enough?," American Prison Writing Archive, September 25, 2018.

73 Durose, Cooper, and Snyder, "Recidivism of Prisoners." See also F. T. Cullen, C. L. Jonson, and D. S. Nagin, "Prisons Do Not Reduce Recidivism: The High Cost of Ignoring Science," *Prison Journal* 91, no. 3 (2011): 48S-65S, doi: 10.1177/0032885511415224. Another major driver of returns to prison is overly restrictive and often arbitrarily enforced parole conditions. Jake Horowitz, "Policy Reforms Can Strengthen Community Supervision," Pew Research Center, April 23, 2020, www.pewtrusts.org; Sharon Brett, "No Contact Parole Restrictions: Unconstitutional and Counterproductive," *Michigan Journal of Gender & Law* 18, no. 2 (2012), https://repository.law.umich.edu; Victoria Edwards, "Parole Rules, Meant to Protect the Public, Can Make Reentry Hard," *City Limits*, May 23, 2017, https://citylimits.org.

74 Donald Hairgrove, "A Day in Life," American Prison Writing Archive, April 4, 2016.

75 Billie Gomez, "Dear American Justice," American Prison Writing Archive, February 10, 2016.

76 Haney, "Riding the Punishment Wave," 32.

77 Derrick Starks, "Neuroplasticity inside the Ghetto," American Prison Writing Archive, May 18, 2018.

78 Robert Mark Pitts, "My Nervousness," American Prison Writing Archive, March 16, 2018.

79 Phillip V. Smith II, "A Weekend in the Hills," American Prison Writing Archive, June 15, 2018.

80 Uhuru B. Rowe, "My Appeal to Citizens of Conscience," American Prison Writing Archive, October 28, 2016.

81 Francis L, "America's Succubus: The Nightmare of the Criminal Justice System in the United States," American Prison Writing Archive, June 15, 2018.

82 See "Time-in-Cell: A 2021 Snapshot of Restrictive Housing Based on a Nationwide Survey of US Prison Systems," Arthur Liman Center for Public Interest Law, Yale University, September 8, 2022. This number is down by half since 2015; Alison James, Jessa Wilcox, and Ram Subramanian, "Solitary Confinement: Common Misconceptions and Emerging Safe Alternatives," Vera Institute of Justice, May 2015, www.vera.org.

83 C. F. Villa, "California Elegy," American Prison Writing Archive, October 22, 2016. The potential consequences of experiences like Villa's were shown in 2013, when a man released directly from SHU in the Colorado prison system killed its director. John Dannenberg, "Systemic Changes Follow Murder of Colorado Prison Director," *Prison Legal News*, July 10, 2014, www.prisonlegalnews.org. See also Anjali Tsui, "Does Solitary Confinement Make Inmates More Likely to Reoffend?," PBS, April 18, 2017, www.pbs.org.

84 Travis Cunningham, "Benevolence," American Prison Writing Archive, September 25, 2018.

85 Patrick Lexis, "Where Should I Start?," American Prison Writing Archive, January 16, 2019.

86 Stephan Darris, "A Brief Summary of the Demise of the Colorado Dept. of Corrections and Poor Drug Offender Reform," American Prison Writing Archive, April 28, 2014.

87 Karter K. Reed, "The Psychology of Prison," American Prison Writing Archive, October 23, 2016.

88 James Lawson-Wilson, "Today I Received an Outlet for the Thoughts That Are with Me Every Waking Moment," American Prison Writing Archive, September 26, 2018.

89 Josef Michael Jensen, "Where Am I Going?," American Prison Writing Archive, March 16, 2018.

90 India Porter, "My Story," American Prison Writing Archive, October 24, 2016.

91 See D. Manderson, "Athena's Way: The Jurisprudence of the Oresteia," *Law, Culture and the Humanities* 15, no. 1 (2019): 253–76, doi:10.1177/1743872116642146. "The trilogy thus ends with the cycle of retributive bloodshed closed and supplanted by the rule of law and the justice of the state." Editors of the Encyclopaedia Britannica, "Oresteia," *Encyclopaedia Britannica*, last modified June 29, 2011, www.britannica.com. After decades of tough-on-crime, victim-vengeance politics and practice, a return to a belief that the elected district attorney represents not only victims but the whole community now marks the recent rise of "progressive" DAs; see, for example, Martin Kuz, "Los Angeles' New DA Redefines What 'People's Lawyer' Does (Q&A)," *Christian Science Monitor*, January 21, 2021, www.csmonitor.com.

92 Peter Wagner and Bernadette Rabuy, "Following the Money of Mass Incarceration," Prison Policy Initiative, January 25, 2017, www.prisonpolicy.org.

93 A man who goes by the nickname Corner Store, quoted in Shane Bauer's *American Prison* (New York: Penguin, 2018), 141.

Chapter 3. Defeating Rehabilitation, Prison Resistance, and Transformation

Epigraphs: "Sheri Dwight," in *Inside This Place, Not of It: Narratives from Women's Prisons*, ed. Robin Levi and Ayelet Waldman (New York: Verso, 2011), 54; David Jones, "Inside Story," *Prison Journalism Project Newsletter* 2, no. 6 (June 15, 2021), https://prisonjournalismproject.org.

1 See, for example, James Q. Wilson, *Thinking about Crime* (1975; reis. New York: Basic Books, 2013).

2 On the adoption of harm as penal aim, see Todd R. Clear, *Harm in American Penology: Offenders, Victims, and Their Communities* (Albany: State University of New York Press, 1994); Craig Haney, "Riding the Punishment Wave: On the Origins of Our Devolving Standards of Decency," *Hastings Women's Law Journal* 9, no. 1 (1998): 27–78; and Angela J. Davis, ed., *Policing the Black Man: Arrest, Prosecution, and Imprisonment* (New York: Pantheon, 2017).

3 Gresham M. Sykes, studying prison culture in the late 1950s, recognized that "these tasks are not easily balanced in a coherent policy," and that, in the end, the public's major concern remains "the prevention of escapes and disorders"; the result is that talk of rehabilitation continues largely for public consumption. *The Society of Captives: A Study of a Maximum Security Prison* (1958; reis. Princeton: Princeton University Press, 2007), 12, 39, 34.

4 That is, through imposing harsher conditions and sentences to avoid the political charge of being "soft on crime." See, for example, Jonathan Simon, *Governing through Crime: How the War on Crime Transformed American Democracy and Created a Culture of Fear* (Oxford: Oxford University Press, 2007); and Rachel Barkow, *Prisoners of Politics: Breaking the Cycle of Mass Incarceration* (Cambridge: Belknap/Harvard University Press, 2019).

5 On headline sentencing, see, for example, Breanna Edwards, "Alabama Man Has Been Serving a Life Sentence for the Last 38 Years for Stealing $9," *Essence*, December 23, 2019, www.essence.com; on recidivism rates of up to 76 percent, see Matthew R. Durose, Alexia D. Cooper, and Howard N. Snyder, "Recidivism of Prisoners Released in 30 States in 2005: Patterns from 2005 to 2010," Bureau of Justice Statistics, April 2014, https://bjs.ojp.gov; on headline-making murder, see, for example, Derek Hawkins, "An Inmate Died after Being Locked in a Scalding Shower for Two Hours. His Guards Won't Be Charged," *Washington Post*, March 20, 2017, www.washingtonpost.com.

6 From my reading in prison witness from the United States, the Middle East, Africa, and Asia, this sense of shock and confusion in the face of prison practices is nearly singular to American prison writing and reveals just how deeply Americans have been led to believe that prisons operate under the rule of law. Such shock even appears in the work of writers who come to prison with fully evolved critiques of American criminal justice; see, for example, Assata Shakur's *Assata: An Autobiography* (Chicago: Lawrence Hill Books, 1987), esp. 10. In "Broken beyond Repair," Anthony Grasso offers a historical debunking of the idea that rehabilitative thinking ever effectively countered the prison's punitive intent. He writes that, in the Progressive Era, "by accepting the existence of born criminals, rehabilitative penology put the onus for reform exclusively on individuals, disregarded social and economic factors contributing to crime, and absolved the state of any duty to reform so-called incorrigibles" (395); even educational offerings served to sort the redeemable from such "incorrigibles," who would be confined indefinitely (397). More broadly, then as today, "The logic of rehabilitation not only dismisses the structural factors that cause crime but also ignores how incarceration creates obstacles to reform that can offset the benefits of rehabilitation" (403). He concludes that "a full revival of rehabilitative penology in today's political and intellectual climates will only exacerbate the punitive instincts that built this institutional and ideological landscape" (403). Anthony Grasso, "Broken beyond Repair: Rehabilitative Penology

and American Political Development," *Political Research Quarterly* 70, no. 2 (June 2017): 394–407, doi: 10.1177/1065912917695189. Philip Goodman writes in a similar vein as he counters the notion that rehabilitation and punishment are extremes in a back-and-forth movement: "The pendulum analogy is simply inadequate—it overstates the coherence of the poles and it understates the extent to which, at the local level, the same forces may be at work across time and across various penal regimes." Philip Goodman, "'Another Second Chance': Rethinking Rehabilitation through the Lens of California's Prison Fire Camps," *Social Problems* 59, no. 44 (November 2012): 453, doi: 10.1525/sp.2012.59.4.437. A major aim of this chapter is to see beyond current horizons. As much as we might want to see sudden reductions in prison numbers and changes in thinking, hundreds of thousands of people will remain in prison for cumulative millennia before more conclusive hope can be offered. Emerging directly from first-person experience of rehabilitative efforts, failures, absences, and sporadic successes, the testimony in this chapter offers not only implicit and explicit critiques and recommendations regarding existing practice, but more quickly realized specific and holistic visions and possible paths beyond the prison's past and current punitive instincts.

7   Lisa Guenther, "Reading Plato on Death Row," American Prison Writing Archive, June 20, 2016.

8   Michael L. Owens, "Prisons Were Created to Punish, Deter, and Rehabilitate," American Prison Writing Archive, March 16, 2018.

9   See "Thomas Mott Osborne's Within Prison Walls," New York Correctional History Society, www.correctionhistory.org, accessed June 14, 2022.

10 Sykes, *Society of Captives*, 11.

11 Julilly Kohler-Hausmann, "Unmaking the Rehabilitative Ideal," in *Getting Tough: Welfare and Imprisonment in 1970s America* (Princeton: Princeton University Press, 2017).

12 Kohler-Hausmann, "Unmaking the Rehabilitative Ideal," 215, 218. See also Marie Gottschalk, *The Prison and the Gallows: The Politics of Mass Incarceration in America* (New York: Cambridge University Press, 2006), 37–38. Gottschalk characterizes the 1971 report *Struggle for Justice* from the American Friends' Service Committee as "the starkest and best known expression of liberal disillusionment with indeterminate sentences and the rehabilitative model" (38).

13 Quoted in Kohler-Hausmann, "Unmaking the Rehabilitative Ideal," 219. And men with pride, such as George Jackson, claimed that incarcerated people were waking up, no longer cowed by the illusion of parole, as early as 1970. *Soledad Brother: The Prison Letters of George Jackson* (1970; reis. Chicago: Lawrence Hill, 1994), 26.

14 The work of Francis T. Cullen, Bonnie S. Fisher, and Brandon K. Applegate strongly suggests that the public may well be open to such change since it simply is not as punitive as lawmakers claim; at worst, punitiveness among the Ameri-

can people is "mushy" (8) since that public is ready to accept criminal responses that serve utilitarian ends. "Public Opinion about Punishment and Corrections," *Crime and Justice* 27 (2000): 1–79, doi: 10.1086/652198.

15   Guenther, "Reading Plato on Death Row."

16   Ruth Wilson Gilmore, *Golden Gulag: Prisons, Surplus, Crisis, and Opposition in Globalizing California* (Los Angeles: University of California Press, 2007), 14. According to the Bureau of Labor Statistics, corrections officers and jailers alone account for 405,870 jobs in the United States; these are in addition to the thousands more employed to contract, build, and maintain prisons; supply them; work inside as administrators, counselors, clergy; and outside on contracts for food, medical care, phone services, and so forth. "Occupational Employment and Wages, May 2020: Correctional Officers and Jailers," United States Bureau of Labor Statistics, www.bls.gov, accessed July 21, 2021. For a broad overview of those who profit from prisons, see Daniel A. Rosen, "The Punishment Economy: Winners and Losers in the Business of Mass Incarceration," *Prison Legal News*, May 2021, 1–11. See also Michelle Chen, "Who Profits from Our Prison System?," *Nation*, August 9, 2018, www.thenation.com.

17   Marquis Gilliam, "Your True Character Is Revealed," American Prison Writing Archive, September 26, 2018.

18   Nicholas A. Hale, "First Off I Would Like to Give You," American Prison Writing Archive, June 18, 2020.

19   James Bauhaus, "Parole Farce Continues," American Prison Writing Archive, February 10, 2017.

20   Amanda C. Gatlin, "Choices," American Prison Writing Archive, March 15, 2018.

21   Ricky Pendleton, "My Voice through the Prison Walls," American Prison Writing Archive, August 16, 2017.

22   Daniel Hagen, "A.D.C. the Beast," American Prison Writing Archive, March 16, 2018. Also from Arkansas, Charles A. Brownell sees a system motivated by the desire to generate profits, including from the programs purported to be about reform. "Prison Reform and Rehabilitation," American Prison Writing Archive, May 28, 2019.

23   Manitas, "No Place for Redemption," American Prison Writing Archive, October 17, 2016.

24   Paul S. Johnson, "Jails & Prisons," American Prison Writing Archive, May 23, 2019.

25   Charles Brooks Sr., "Harsh Reality," American Prison Writing Archive, October 18, 2016.

26   Michael Flores, "America's Sustainable Civil War," American Prison Writing Archive, January 16, 2019.

27   James Lawson-Wilson, "Broken," American Prison Writing Archive, September 26, 2018.

28   Burl Corbet, "A View from the Bottom," American Prison Writing Archive, March 16, 2018.

29 Enysia Rosado, "Works of Art," American Prison Writing Archive, October 28, 2019.

30 James Barstad, "In 1974, When I Was Nine Years Old," American Prison Writing Archive, August 16, 2017.

31 Mary Ann Jalomos, "Texas Is an Institutionalized Industry," American Prison Writing Archive, October 12, 2017.

32 April Dawn Pineda, "As of Today July 31st 2017," American Prison Writing Archive, July 31, 2017.

33 Nashay M. Ziegler-Wurtz, "Corrections Is Generally Considered the," American Prison Writing Archive, October 28, 2019.

34 India Porter, "My Story," American Prison Writing Archive, October 24, 2016.

35 Fredrick M. T. Pearson, "A Peek on the Inside," American Prison Writing Archive, June 18, 2020.

36 Shaka Senghor, *Writing My Wrongs: Life, Death, and Redemption in an American Prison* (New York: Convergent Books, 2016), 178.

37 SKS Heruglyphx Maga Neteru, "Political Education Deprived," American Prison Writing Archive, September 27, 2018.

38 Steven A. DeLogé, "A Speed Trap in a Small Midwestern Town," American Prison Writing Archive, November 3, 2017.

39 Paul J. Kiser, "Example?," American Prison Writing Archive, July 5, 2018.

40 Kareem Davenport, "Society's Outlook on Prisoners," American Prison Writing Archive, June 18, 2020.

41 The most commonly cited work that lawmakers and prison officials used to justify dismantling rehabilitation programs is Robert Martinson, "What Works?—Questions and Answers about Prison Reform," *National Affairs*, Spring 1974, www.nationalaffairs.com. Martinson's work has long since been critiqued for its problematic methodology; it also offers a more optimistic view of prison programming than was claimed. See, for example, Philip Goodman, Joshua Page, and Michelle Phelps, *Breaking the Pendulum: The Long Struggle over Criminal Justice* (New York: Oxford University Press, 2017), 106–7; and Elizabeth Hinton, *From the War on Poverty to the War on Crime: The Making of Mass Incarceration in America* (Cambridge: Harvard University Press, 2016), 243–45.

42 Cesar A. Avila, "The Stress of Limitations in Rehabilitation," American Prison Writing Archive, March 16, 2018. Fellow Californian Ken Hartman seconds Avila's reading of staff attitudes as "the perfect dodge to responsibility: We would run these rehabilitative programs, but the inmates just won't cooperate. The gangs destroy anything good we try to do. The inmates are not capable of anything positive. These are the well-rehearsed excuses that play well to a public conditioned to assume that prisoners are, in fact, irredeemably recalcitrant, gang members who live to sow destruction and are all, simply, bad. . . . It is a question of economics. The fewer of us, the smaller the empire." Kenneth E. Hartman, "What Is and What Should Be," American Prison Writing Archive, October 21, 2016. Also writing from California, Marlon Blacher

sees what could, is not, and should be done, and thus what the second-largest state prison system in the nation—a system that includes rehabilitation in its title—is perpetrating: "fraud." "СДСЯ? (part 1)," American Prison Writing Archive, October 15, 2016.

43 Meagan Adams, "An American Epidemic," American Prison Writing Archive, May 28, 2018.

44 L. Mack-Lemdon, "The R.T.P.PC.SA.P&H Saga," American Prison Writing Archive, June 18, 2020. The danger of such slippage into a security mindset among treatment professionals was seen by the late Norwegian criminologist Nils Christie: "Christie underlines that in using the Self Supply Model [i.e., prison staff rather than 'importing' outside professionals] there is a serious danger that the different professional groups too strongly subordinate themselves to the prisons' security systems." Torfinn Langelid, "The Sharing of Responsibility in the Rehabilitation of Prisoners in Norway: The Import-Model in Theory & Practice," *Journal of Correctional Education* 50, no. 2 (June 1999): 53.

45 Tommy Lee Dean, "These Days Has the Colorado Department of Corrections," American Prison Writing Archive, November 3, 2017. Evan Ebel killed the director of the CDOC shortly after his release in 2014; changes have since been made, as Dean notes, in CDOC release procedures. See John Dannenberg, "Systemic Changes Follow Murder of Colorado Prison Director," *Prison Legal News*, July 10, 2014, www.prisonlegalnews.org.

46 Jon R. Morgan, "Age, Nothing but an IDOC #," American Prison Writing Archive, September 25, 2018.

47 Joseph R. Dickey, "Prison Reform," American Prison Writing Archive, June 18, 2020.

48 Vincent Calamia, "My Name Is Vincent Calamia," American Prison Writing Archive, December 15, 2017.

49 These are programs delivered by outside volunteers, at no cost to prisons or the state, as is the case for higher education programs inside. (In the section below on helpful programming, I mark when programs mentioned are volunteer or facility-based). Alternatives to Violence, noted by several witnesses in this chapter, started in prison and has expanded to schools and communities; see AVP at "About Us," Alternatives to Violence, https://avpusa.org, accessed July 21, 2021.

50 Dean Faiello, "Metanoia," American Prison Writing Archive, October 24, 2016.

51 Tom J. Orton, "Utah Society and Corrections Effectively Teach Felons," American Prison Writing Archive, December 18, 2018.

52 A. Whitfield, "It Could Be Me," in *Fourth City: Essays from the Prison in America*, ed. Doran Larson (East Lansing: Michigan State University Press, 2014), 60–62.

53 Stacy Shaw, "Finding Freedom inside of Prison," American Prison Writing Archive, June 15, 2018.

54 George Whitham, "Friendship," in Larson, *Fourth City*, 40.

55 Michael Arreygue, "Fate?," American Prison Writing Archive, October 15, 2016.

56 Corey John Richardson, "How Some Men Find Love," in Larson, *Fourth City*, 41.

57 Levert Brookshire III, "Cell Block Society Post-Release Master Plan: Protecting Life First 18 Months Re-Evaluation," American Prison Writing Archive, October 15, 2016.

58 Albert Woodfox, *Solitary: Unbroken by Four Decades of Solitary Confinement. My Story of Transformation and Hope* (New York: Grove, 2019), 329–30.

59 Arline Lawless, "Descriptions of Sources of Stress, and Ways of Copin," American Prison Writing Archive, March 16, 2018.

60 Donald Hairgrove, "A Day in Life," American Prison Writing Archive, April 4, 2016.

61 Josef M. Jensen, "The Power of Honesty and Forgiveness," American Prison Writing Archive, March 16, 2018.

62 Shariff Ingram, "I Am Writing of My Experiences in Prison," American Prison Writing Archive, November 2, 2017.

63 Christopher Balmer, "Control Your Own Future," American Prison Writing Archive, October 24, 2016.

64 Laura L. Purviance, "Hello, My Name Is Laura," American Prison Writing Archive, June 15, 2018.

65 Rosado, "Works of Art."

66 Among the submissions received for *Fourth City*, out of which the APWA emerged, essays directed at young people and incarcerated peers were so plentiful that they made up one of the eleven categories of subject matter that organized the book. See the essays in that volume under "Kite Out."

67 In fact, drugs, alcohol, or both are part of most criminal histories. See "Principles of Drug Abuse Treatment for Criminal Justice Populations," National Institute on Drug Abuse, last modified August 3, 2021, www.drugabuse.gov; Lawrence A. Greenfeld, "Alcohol and Crime," Bureau of Justice Statistics, April 5, 1998, https://bjs.ojp.gov; and Christopher S. Wren, "Drugs or Alcohol Linked to 80% of Inmates," *New York Times*, January 9, 1998, www.nytimes.com.

68 Sheldon D. Bush, "My Name Is Sheldon Bush," American Prison Writing Archive, November 2, 2017.

69 Keith Burley, "A Definition of Freedom," American Prison Writing Archive, February 10, 2016.

70 J. D. Fransden, "Being of Light: Meditation and Transcendence inside Administrative Segregation," American Prison Writing Archive, October 23, 2016.

71 Abraham Hagos, "A Prisoners Manifesto on Rehabilitation," American Prison Writing Archive, October 23, 2016.

72 Intelligent Allah, "Bread and Water Vegan: Struggling for Health and Humanity inside Prison," American Prison Writing Archive, October 24, 2016.

73 William Smith Bey, "In the 2016 Race, Former Felon Votes Also Matter," American Prison Writing Archive, October 18, 2016.

74 Robert Saleem Holbrook, "From Public Enemy to Enemy of the State," American Prison Writing Archive, May 30, 2008.

75 SKS Heruglyphx Maga Neteru, "Political Education Deprived."

76 Jack Henry Abbott, *In the Belly of the Beast: Letters from Prison* (New York: Vintage, 1981), 94.

77 See Sykes, *Society of Captives*, 76.

78 James Same, "Doing Prison, One Day at a Time," American Prison Writing Archive, June 18, 2020.

79 Jamil Hayes, "Coping with Prison," American Prison Writing Archive, October 28, 2019.

80 Dennis J. Sierra, "Writing to My Inner Child," American Prison Writing Archive, October 28, 2019.

81 Tony Enis, "Least Likely Places," American Prison Writing Archive, February 3, 2020.

82 James L. Griffin, "For Years I Wanted To," American Prison Writing Archive, January 16, 2019.

83 This is most consequentially expressed in the decisions of parole boards, whose reasoning is opaque, and that often deny release based on the "nature of the crime," no matter how long ago or the age at which it was committed. See Beth Schwartzapfel, "How Parole Boards Keep Prisoners in the Dark and behind Bars," *Washington Post*, July 11, 2015, www.washingtonpost.com; Jorge Renaud, "Grading the Parole Release Systems of All 50 States," Prison Policy Initiative, February 26, 2019, www.prisonpolicy.org; and Doran Larson, "What's Justice Got to Do with It?," *Prison Legal News*, September 2020, www.prisonlegalnews.org.

84 This locating of the past as a reference point for, rather than a hindrance to, moving forward echoes H. L. A. Hart's recommendation that the crime should be attended to only as one "symptom" among others of the character that confinement should guide toward a better future. *Punishment and Responsibility: Essays in the Philosophy of Law*, 2nd ed. (New York: Oxford University Press, 2008), 160.

85 Claims that prison programming was ineffective helped to dismantle such programs. The classic source is D. Lipton, R. Martinson, and J. Wilks, *The Effectiveness of Correctional Treatment—A Survey of Treatment Evaluation Studies* (Westport: Praeger, 1975). As Jerome G. Miller notes of this report's aftermath, "On January 18, 1989, the abandonment of rehabilitation in corrections was confirmed by the US Supreme Court. In *Mistretta v. United States*, the Court upheld federal 'sentencing guidelines' which removed rehabilitation from serious consideration when sentencing offenders. Defendants will henceforth be sentenced strictly for the crime, with no recognition given to such factors as amenability to treatment, personal and family history, previous efforts to rehabilitate oneself, or possible alternatives to prison." "The Debate on Rehabilitating Criminals: Is It True That Nothing Works?," *Washington Post*, March 1989, reprinted by the Prison Policy Initiative, www.prisonpolicy.org.

86 Prison facilities can take credit simply for allowing volunteers to come inside, which requires staff to conduct added gate checks and some added paperwork.

Prisons also take credit for hosting volunteer programs in their reports to state authorities.

87 This distinction can appear vague at times. As noted, prisons host volunteer programs but do not directly support them or provide personnel; higher education programs, for example, may be run through a state college or university, but faculty are decidedly not department of corrections employees. They are designated as facility volunteers, even when paid by their employing educational institutions.

88 Higher education programs are generally delivered by faculty paid by their home institutions; I mark them as voluntary because no facility funding is provided.

89 John Robert Sweat, "A Selfie Criminal Autopsy," American Prison Writing Archive, October 23, 2016.

90 Until 1994, a mere 1 percent of all Pell grants supported around 350 college programs in prisons across the country. See Wendy Sawyer, "Since You Asked: How Did the 1994 Crime Bill Affect Prison College Programs?," Prison Policy Initiative, August 27, 2019, www.prisonpolicy.org. Since Pell is an entitlement program, this 1 percent did not reduce any funding available to non-incarcerated students. The crime bill that banned eligibility was sponsored and "shepherded" through Congress by then Delaware senator Joe Biden. Madison Pauly, "Biden Won't Say if He Still Stands by His Crime Bill's Ban on Pell Grants for Prisoners," *Mother Jones*, June 11, 2019, www.motherjones.com.

91 Adam Roberts, "Better Living through Editing," American Prison Writing Archive, June 16, 2018.

92 Mick Whitlock, "A Vision for the Future," American Prison Writing Archive, August 25, 2010.

93 See, for example, Danielle Dirks, "Sexual Revictimization and Retraumatization of Women in Prison," *Women's Studies Quarterly* 32, nos. 3–4 (Fall–Winter 2004): 102–15; M. E. Karlsson and M. J. Zielinski, "Sexual Victimization and Mental Illness Prevalence Rates among Incarcerated Women: A Literature Review," *Trauma, Violence, & Abuse* 21, no. 2 (2020): 326–49, doi: 10.1177/1524838018767933. For first-person narratives of such abuse and retraumatization, see the testimonies in Levi and Waldman, *Inside This Place, Not of It*.

94 Sylvia Boykin, "Addendum to #32392 Commutation Application," American Prison Writing Archive, October 25, 2016.

95 The website for State Correctional Institute-Chester describes its treatment program as "a collaborative effort between the Pennsylvania Department of Corrections and Community Education Centers, Inc. (CEC). This collaboration has been formed to rehabilitate inmates with a history of substance abuse. The treatment program is operated by Community Education Centers, Inc." "SCI Chester," State Prisons, Pennsylvania Department of Corrections, www.cor.pa.gov, accessed July 22, 2021. This facility has been the subject of efforts to reform prison operations on a Scandinavian model. See Katie Meyer, "One of Pa.'s

Prison Units Is About to Go Scandinavian," WHYY, October 10, 2019, https://whyy.org.

96 Jy'Aire Smith-Pennick, "I Hate to Admit It, but Prison Is a Blessing in Disguise," Marshall Project, June 10, 2021, www.themarshallproject.org. Elsewhere, Smith-Pennick writes, "But prisons didn't change me; I transformed myself, by standing still, soul searching, developing healthier habits and taking advantage of the programs I have access to. I simply refuse to waste any more time." He also declares himself a prison "abolition[ist]"; in "How I Went from Gangster to Geek," Marshall Project, February 4, 2022, www.themarshallproject.org.

97 Graham also offers a cautionary tale regarding what he saw happen when a program he initiated was taken over by the state DOC:

> Early in my incarceration I started a prisoner-operated restorative justice program called the Whole Heart Project of St. Cloud. It was the first restorative justice program in Minnesota that was ran this way, and the focus was on fostering a greater sense of community within the prison walls, searching for ways to contribute to the community outside of the walls, and learning more beneficial ways to break the cycle of crime and violence. Since the program was voluntary and prisoner-ran, the goals were adhered to and there was a marked focus upon self-improvement by the participants. The institution responded by shipping all of the original participants to different institutions and co-opting the program in favor of a type that is overseen by a prison administration hierarchy. The results of this have been mixed. There have been some improvements in the ability to facilitate drives to fundraise for causes assisting the greater community, and more money for such efforts is being made now than under prisoner's direction. On the other hand, the majority of Restorative justice programs offered do not have as many conscientious, driven people at their helms. . . . The staff responsible for operating those programs have done a lot to hamper the operation of restorative justice outside of community fundraising. . . . Their membership is plagued by distrust, infighting over direction, dissatisfaction with the program, and a general lack of understanding of restorative justice principles. In short, while the programs like Alternatives to Violence and Power of People have strengthened over the years, the restorative justice program has flirted with becoming largely a fundraising mechanism of the victim services unit. The aim of seeing transformative social justice integrated into the prison system is increasingly a thing dependent upon the availability and time constraints of outside volunteers rather than an institution supported, prisoner-driven effort. If the funding and logistical support available to the hybrid restorative justice program were made available to the Power of People and AVP programs the resources could have a much greater impact both within the prison and in the greater community at large.

"A Minnesota Experience: Qualitative Analysis of Minnesota Department of Corrections Policy," American Prison Writing Archive, March 17, 2018.

Michael Willie comments on the challenges incarcerated people can face when they try to create the programming they need.

> When you volunteer for a club and start getting into the nuts and bolts of it all, you learn that it's not uncommon to be working on a worthy and beneficial project only to be shot down at the last moment. Chain of command works that way. I remember a mentor's word of advice to me of starting my volunteer work.
>
> "Keep asking. They can't say no forever because our forever will be way past their forever. Their forever is retirement."

From "Murderers' Ball," in *As I Hear the Rain: 2019 Prison Writing Awards Anthology* (New York: PEN America, 2019), 228.

98 Danielle Sered highlights the failure of incarceration to serve victims. *Until We Reckon: Violence, Mass Incarceration, and a Road to Repair* (New York: New Press, 2019). Lenore Anderson documents this as well as how criminal justice practices further victimize crime victims. *In Their Names: The Untold Story of Victims' Rights, Mass Incarceration, and the Future of Public Safety* (New York: New Press, 2022).

99 Bobby Bostic, "In the Garden," American Prison Writing Archive, June 16, 2018.

100 Judith, "LiT-uPP Is a Transformational Program," American Prison Writing Archive, March 17, 2018.

101 Steven F. Lomas, "Meditation," in Larson, *Fourth City*, 108.

102 Eve Mazzarella, "The Redemptive Power of Yoga," American Prison Writing Archive, January 16, 2019.

103 Keith A. Deaton, "A Little Bit of Sunshine," American Prison Writing Archive, May 28, 2018.

104 Diana Waggy, "Inspiration," American Prison Writing Archive, February 24, 2010.

105 Fredrick Sledge, "What Makes a Difference?," American Prison Writing Archive, November 3, 2017.

106 Anthony Brunetti, "The Causes and Correction of the Criminal Mind," American Prison Writing Archive, October 23, 2016. Brunetti's crediting of staff respect for the effectiveness of programming is echoed by Terry Allen Kupers in a chapter titled "A Rehabilitative Attitude": "If prisoners have the opportunity to interact with staff in relations of mutual respect, and if staff offer choices that make prisoners feel that they still have some agency even though they are prisoners, then those prisoners' chances of succeeding when they return to the community will be much improved." Kupers attributes the success of a hunger strike by men inside California's notorious Pelican Bay State Prison to their "foster[ing] respect in all participants, the officers, the courts, the administrators, legislators, and all the various gangs and cliques

in prison." *Solitary: The Inside Story of Supermax Isolation and How We Can Abolish It* (Oakland: University of California Press, 2017), 174.

107 Bev Jaynes, "A Look In on the Prison Performing Arts Theater and Poetry Classes," American Prison Writing Archive, November 2, 2017.

108 Ni Nermirttan, "I Would First Like to Express My Gratitude," American Prison Writing Archive, March 28, 2010.

109 Lee Whitt, "A Lonely World," American Prison Writing Archive, October 25, 2016.

110 Dickey, "Prison Reform."

111 Zachary Smith, "Another Ineffective Prison Reform Plan," American Prison Writing Archive, June 16, 2018.

112 Daniel Pirkel, "America's Criminal Justice System: Rehabilitation or Criminalization?," American Prison Writing Archive, September 27, 2018. Pirkel specifically recommends motivation through "good time" and "earned time": credits to reduce total sentence lengths as a reward for constructive behavior, including program participation. See, for example, "The First Step Act of 2018: Earned Time Credits," Sentencing Resources, Defender Services Office, November 2019, www.fd.org; "Earned Time Credit," Prison Fellowship, www.prisonfellowship.org, accessed July 23, 2021.

113 Kenneth E. Hartman, "The Absent Voice of Prisoners," American Prison Writing Archive, October 22, 2016.

114 Darnell Lane, "Rehabilitation Is Lost in Our Era of Mass Incarceration," American Prison Writing Archive, January 21, 2019.

115 Decades after ineligibility was set in place in 1994, Second Chance Pell revived federal tuition funding in prisons on a competitive, experimental basis during the Obama administration; the program—on a selected and still experimental basis—continues. Congress has since decided that qualified people inside can resume receiving Pell tuition supports in 2023. See "A Monumental Shift: Restoring Access to Pell Grants for Incarcerated Students," Vera Institute, March 2021, www.vera.org.

116 Mathew Lucas Ayotte, "From the Ground Up," American Prison Writing Archive, October 28, 2019.

117 Mick Whitlock, "A Practical Approach to Prison Reform," American Prison Writing Archive, February 23, 2010.

118 There is ample evidence of the financial benefits to the public of college-in-prison programs, as well as of their transformational human effects. See, for example, Lois M. Davis et al., "Evaluating the Effectiveness of Correctional Education," RAND Corporation (2013), doi: 10.7249/RR266; Freeman A. Hrabowski III and Jeremy Robbi, "The Benefits of Correctional Education," *Journal of Correctional Education* 53, no. 3 (September 2002): 96–99; and "Benefits of Prison Education," Northwestern Prison Education Program, Northwestern University, https://sites.northwestern.edu, accessed July 23, 2021. It is no accident that education is also a strong barrier against a first incarceration. See, for ex-

ample, Lance Lochner and Enrico Moretti, "The Effect of Education on Crime: Evidence from Prison Inmates, Arrests, and Self-Reports," *American Economic Review* 94, no. 1 (March 2004): 155–89.

119 Christopher D. Ridley, "Education & Recidivism," American Prison Writing Archive, March 16, 2018.

120 Randall L. Cole, "The Power of Education," in Larson, *Fourth City*, 260–61.

121 Daniel Pirkel, "Transforming the Prisoner Culture," American Prison Writing Archive, November 14, 2017. The program mentioned was inspired by a model in Louisiana's notorious Angola Prison (a former slave plantation). See "About," Prison Initiative, Calvin University, https://calvin.edu, accessed July 23, 2021.

122 Davis et al., "Evaluating the Effectiveness of Correctional Education."

123 See, for example, Jon Marcus, "In Era of High Costs, Humanities Come under Attack," Hechinger Report, March 7, 2013, www.hechingerreport.org.

124 Mikhail Markhasev, "Why a Philosophy Major Is Necessary for Prisoners," American Prison Writing Archive, October 28, 2019.

125 Deshawn Cooper, "Notes from the Underground," in Larson, *Fourth City*, 264. Contrast Cooper's pride with Kenneth A. Barr's despair in neighboring New Jersey: "What do you do when there is no hope for redemption? What do you do when there is no light at the end of the tunnel and you realize that you will die in the place that you hate most? Or what do you do when the only thing that you will be remembered for is the worst thing that you ever did?" "Hello, My Name Is," American Prison Writing Archive, September 26, 2018. (Barr writes from the same prison that Gresham Sykes describes in *The Society of Captives*.)

126 Lilah Burke, "After the Pell Ban," *Inside Higher Education*, January 27, 2021, www.insidehighered.com.

127 This was, admittedly, a consciously provocative title, and I welcomed the push-back from incarcerated thinkers noted below.

128 Drew Leder and the Jessup Correctional Institution Scholars, "The Enlightened Prison," in *The Beautiful Prison*, ed. Doran Larson; series editor Austin Sarat, *Studies in Law, Politics, and Society*, vol. 64 (Bingley: Emerald, 2014).

129 Hartman has since been released.

130 Reprinted in the American Prison Writing Archive as Kenneth E. Hartman, "Searching for the Beautiful Prison," October 21, 2016. In another essay, Hartman makes five practical recommendations for changing prison culture and practice: "1, End the use of demeaning prison uniforms; 2, Open access to local communities so that people outside do not see incarcerated people through a veil of fear and fantasy; 3, Let people inside and out cross over to volunteer their skills, knowledge, and labor to better all communities and people; 4, Restore support for higher education in prison; and 5, Reward positive behavior. This is really the heart of the matter and the crux of the problem." "5 Positive Steps to Reform Prisons," American Prison Writing Archive, December 9, 2013.

131 Whitt, "A Lonely World."

132 "While the system may cost billions of dollars, have a negligible impact on crime, and be inexplicable from an outside perspective, it is sustaining livelihoods, supporting communities, and growing careers—things that people are not willing to easily relinquish." Heather Schoenfeld, *Building the Prison State: Race and Politics of Mass Incarceration* (Chicago: University of Chicago Press, 2018), 211.

Chapter 4. Containment and Incapacitation's Collateral Effects

Epigraphs: Asar Imhotep Amen, "Punishment, Revenge, and Torture: The Heart of America's Criminal 'Justice' System," American Prison Writing Archive, May 24, 2019; Shaka Senghor, *Writing My Wrongs: Life, Death, and Redemption in an American Prison* (New York: Convergent Books, 2016), 229.

1 H. L. A. Hart, *Punishment and Responsibility: Essays in the Philosophy of Law*, 2nd ed. (New York: Oxford University Press, 2008), 173, ftnt 20.

2 Daniel M. Leeds et al., "Incarcerated Adults with Dependent Children," Program for the International Assessment of Adult Competencies, February 2020, https://piaacgateway.com; Lauren E. Glaze and Laura M. Maruschak, "Parents in Prison and Their Minor Children," United States Bureau of Justice Statistics, August 2008, https://bjs.ojp.gov. Even a short time in jail or prison can become grounds for losing parental rights; see Eli Hager and Anna Flagg, "How Incarcerated Parents Are Losing Their Children Forever," Marshall Project, December 2018, www.themarshallproject.org.

3 Michael McLaughlin et al., in "The Economic Burden of Incarceration in the US," estimate the costs to families of incarceration in the hundreds of billions. Institute for Advancing Justice Research and Innovation, Washington University of St. Louis, October 2016. As Saneta deVuono-Powell et al. write, "Nearly 2 in 3 families (65%) with an incarcerated member were unable to meet their family's basic needs"; "Poverty, in particular, perpetuates the cycle of incarceration, while incarceration itself leads to greater poverty." "Who Pays? The True Cost of Incarceration on Families," Ella Baker Center for Human Rights, Forward Together, Research Action Design, September 2015, http://whopaysreport.org. See also Kristin Turney, Jason Schnittker, and Christopher Wildeman, "Those They Leave Behind: Paternal Incarceration and Maternal Instrumental Support," *Journal of Family and Marriage* 74, no. 5 (2012): 1149–65, doi: 10.1111/j.1741-- 3737.2012.00998.x.

4 "High rates of removal of parent-aged residents from poor communities set off a series of effects that destabilize the capacities of those communities to provide informal social control." Todd R. Clear, "The Effects of High Imprisonment Rates on Communities," *Crime and Justice* 37, no. 1 (2008): 117; see also 102, doi: 10.1086/522360. Incarceration "disrupts" the "life course" of the incarcerated, "the partners and children of former inmates . . . and the public safety . . . of communities." Bruce Western, Leonard Lopoo, and Sara McLanahan, "Incarceration and the Bonds between Parents in Fragile Communities," in *Imprison-*

ing America, ed. Mary Patillo, David Weiman, and Bruce Western (New York: Russell Sage Foundation, 2004), 41. Indeed, concentrated incarceration has been shown to degrade even the physical health of targeted communities. James C. Thomas and Elizabeth Torrone, "Incarceration as Forced Migration: Effects on Selected Community Health Outcomes," *American Journal of Public Health* 96, no. 10 (2006): 1–5, doi: 10.2105/AJPH.2005.081760.

5 Bruce Western and Becky Pettit, "Incarceration and Social Inequality," *Daedalus* 139, no. 3 (Summer 2010): 18, doi: 10.1162/daed_a_00019. Todd Clear confirms, "Imprisonment has grown to the point that it now produces the very social problems on which it feeds." *Imprisoning Communities: How Mass Incarceration Makes Disadvantaged Communities Worse* (New York: Oxford University Press, 2007), 3. Bruce Western, Becky Pettit, and Josh Guetzkow write of a deepening cycle in which incarceration exacerbates inequality, increasing crime. "Black Economic Progress in the Era of Mass Incarceration," in *Invisible Punishment: The Collateral Consequences of Mass Imprisonment*, ed. Marc Mauer and Meda Chesney-Lind (New York: New Press, 2002), 165–80.

6 David Roodman writes that "the crux of the matter is that tougher sentences hardly deter crime, and that while imprisoning people temporarily stops them from committing crime outside prison walls, it also tends to increase their criminality after release." "The Impacts of Incarceration on Crime," September 25, 2017, SSRN, doi: 10.2139/ssrn.3635864. "The possibility of improved public safety through increased incarceration is by now exhausted, and, long term, [it] increases crime." Western and Pettit, "Incarceration and Social Inequality," 17; Bruce Western, *Homeward: Life in the Year after Prison* (New York: Russell Sage Foundation, 2018), 178; Don Stemen, "Reconsidering Incarceration: New Directions for Reducing Crime," *Federal Sentencing Reporter* 19, no. 4 (April 2007): 221–33, doi: 10.1525/fsr.2007.19.4.221. While criminal behavior drops naturally with age, imprisonment appears to retard that effect; see Clear, *Imprisoning Communities*, 37, see also 10, 31, on prison's criminogenic effects; "Study Finds Increased Incarceration Has Marginal-to-Zero Impact on Crime," Equal Justice Initiative, August 7, 2017, https://eji.org.

7 On the effects of incarceration on families, see Turney, Schnittker, and Wildeman, "Those They Leave Behind"; and Christopher Wildeman, Jason Schnittker, and Kristin Turney, "Despair by Association? The Mental Health of Mothers with Children by Recently Incarcerated Fathers," *American Sociological Review* 77, no. 2 (February 2012): 216–43, doi: 10.1177/0003122411436234. On the layering of concentrated incarceration upon communities of concentrated disadvantage, see Robert J. Sampson and Charles Loeffler, "Punishment's Place: The Local Concentration of Mass Incarceration," *Daedalus* 19, no. 3 (Summer 2010): 20–31, doi: 10.1162/daed_a_00020; and Robert J. Sampson, "Criminal Justice Processing and the Social Matrix of Adversity," *Annals of the American Academy of Political and Social Science* 651 (January 2014): 296–301, doi: 10.1177/0002716213502936. This concentration is particularly hard felt by chil-

dren; see Christopher Wildeman, "Parental Imprisonment, the Prison Boom, and the Concentration of Childhood Disadvantage," *Demography* 46, no. 2 (May 2009): 265–80, doi: 10.1353/dem.0.0052. As Bruce Western observes, "The prison steps in where the welfare state has failed." *Homeward*, 61.

8 Melissa Noel and Cynthia Najowski, "When Parents Are Incarcerated, Their Children Are Punished, Too," *American Psychological Association* 50, no. 8 (September 2019): 33, www.apa.org. See also "Incarcerated Parents and Their Children: Trends 1991–2007," Sentencing Project, February 2009, www.sentencingproject.org. A dozen states have legislation that seeks to mitigate the damaging effects of incarceration on children, though nearly all of these states are unable to make these efforts as effective as we might hope. See Emma Peyton Williams, "How 12 States Are Addressing Family Separation by Incarceration— and Why They Can and Should Do More," Prison Policy Initiative, February 27, 2023, www.prisonpolicy.org.

9 Susan Phillips and Barbara Bloom, "In Whose Best Interest? The Impact of Changing Public Policy on Relatives Caring for Children with Incarcerated Parents," *Child Welfare* 77 (1998): 531–41. The literature on the destructive short- and long-term effects on children of parental incarceration is extensive. See, for example, Amanda Geller et al., "Beyond Absenteeism: Father Incarceration and Child Development," *Demography* 49, no. 1 (February 2012): 49–76, doi: 10.1007/s13524-011-0081-9; Kristin Turney and Rebecca Goodsell, "Parental Incarceration and Children's Wellbeing," *Future of Children* 28, no. 1 (Spring 2018): 147–64, doi: 10.1353/foc.2018.0007; Kristin Turney, "Stress Proliferation across Generations? Examining the Relationship between Parental Incarceration and Childhood Health," *Journal of Health and Social Behavior* 55, no. 3 (2014): 302–19, doi: 10.1177/0022146514544173; Kristen Turney and A. R. Haskins, "Falling Behind? Children's Early Grade Retention after Paternal Incarceration," *Sociology of Education* 87, no. 4 (2014): 241–58, doi: 10.1177/0038040714547086; Holly Foster and John Hagan, "Incarceration and Intergenerational Social Exclusion," *Social Problems* 54, no. 4 (November 2007): 399–433, doi: 10.1525/ sp.2007.54.4.399; and Christopher Wildeman, "Parental Incarceration, Child Homelessness, and the Invisible Consequences of Mass Imprisonment," *Annals of the American Academy of Political and Social Science* 651 (January 2014): 74–96, doi: 10.1177/0002716213502921. Thomas E. Lengyl has estimated the cost-benefit ratio of incarcerating parents at 7 to 1. *Spreading the Pain: The Social Costs of Incarcerating Parents* (New York: Healing the Divide, 2006). The cost of simple phone calls to maintain family ties can be either prohibitive or devastating to family budgets. Clint Smith, "The Lines of Connection," *Atlantic*, July 29, 2021, www.theatlantic.com. Gwen Rubinstein and Debbie Mukamal look at how the restrictions imposed on releasees from drug convictions punish their loved ones by barring housing, food, and other forms of state support for the poor. "Welfare and Housing—Denial of Benefits to Drug Offenders," in Mauer and Chesney-Lind, *Invisible Punishment*, 37–49.

10 On the damage done to relationships and marriage prospects, see Kristin Turney, "Liminal Men: Incarceration and Relationship Dissolution," *Social Problems* 62, no. 4 (November 2015): 499–528, doi: 10.1093/socpro/spv015; and John H. Laub, Daniel S. Nagin, and Robert J. Sampson, "Trajectories of Change in Criminal Offending: Good Marriages and the Desistance Process," *American Sociological Review* 63, no. 2 (1998): 225–38, doi: 10.2307/2657324. Incarceration can reduce marriage rates in targeted communities by 20–40 percent, while marriage reduces criminal activity; Western, Lopoo, and McLanahan, "Incarceration and the Bonds between Parents in Fragile Communities," 40, 42. On parenting, see Clear, "Effects of High Imprisonment Rates"; Annie E. Casey Foundation, "Children of Incarcerated Parents, a Shared Sentence," April 2016, www.aecf.org; Megan Comfort, *Doing Time Together: Love and Family in the Shadow of the Prison* (Chicago: University of Chicago Press, 2008); and Audrey Beck et al., "Partnership Transitions and Maternal Parenting," *Journal of Marriage and Family* 72 (2010): 219–33, doi: 10.1111/j.1741-3737.2010.00695.x. This weakening of parental bonds takes place despite research showing that contact with children reduces future criminal behavior among the incarcerated. D. J. Martinez and J. Christian, "The Familial Relationships of Former Prisoners: Examining the Link between Residence and Informal Support Mechanisms," *Journal of Contemporary Ethnography* 38, no. 2 (2009): 201–24, doi: 10.1177/0891241608316875. On employment prospects, see Devah Pager, "The Mark of a Criminal Record," *American Journal of Sociology* 108, no. 5 (March 2003): 937–75, doi: 10.1086/374403; and Devah Pager, *Marked: Race, Crime, and Finding Work in an Era of Mass Incarceration* (Chicago: University of Chicago Press, 2009). By thus reducing employment prospects, felony records deepen poverty for whole communities; Harry J. Holzer, Steven Raphael, and Michael A. Stoll, "Will Employers Hire Former Offenders," in Patillo, Weiman, and Western, *Imprisoning America*, 205–46. On all of the above, see Western and Pettit, "Incarceration and Social Inequality"; Bruce Western, *Punishment and Inequality in America* (New York: Russell Sage Foundation, 2006); Donald Braman, *Doing Time on the Outside: Incarceration and Family Life in America* (Ann Arbor: University of Michigan Press, 2004); and Meredith Booker, "The Crippling Effect of Incarceration on Wealth," Prison Policy Initiative, April 26, 2016, www.prisonpolicy.org.

11 Western and Pettit, "Incarceration and Social Inequality," 17; Western, *Punishment and Inequality*, 168. David S. Kirk and Robert J. Sampson show that arrest alone can increase subsequent criminal activity. "Juvenile Arrest and Collateral Educational Damage in the Transition to Adulthood," *Sociology of Education* 86, no. 1 (January 2013): 36–62, doi: 10.1177/0038040712448862. On the delegitimizing effects on law of concentrated incarceration, see Tom R. Tyler and Jeffrey Fagan, "Legitimacy and Cooperation: Why Do People Help the Police Fight Crime in Their Communities?," *Ohio State Journal of Criminal Law* 231 (2008), doi: 10.2139/ssrn.887737; and Clear, *Imprisoning Communities*, 89. James Forman Jr.

describes how distrust in police and law not only increases crime but degrades those non-state community norms and structures that reduce crime. "Children, Cops, and Citizenship: Why Conservatives Should Oppose Racial Profiling," in Mauer and Chesney-Lind, *Invisible Punishment*, 150–62.

12 Important work has been based in interviews and surveys. See, for example, Amy Lerman and Vesla Weaver, *Arresting Citizenship: The Democratic Consequences of American Crime Control* (Chicago: University of Chicago Press, 2014); Todd R. Clear, Dina R. Rose, and Judith A. Ryder, "Incarceration and the Community: The Problem of Removing and Returning Offenders," *Crime & Delinquency* 47, no. 3 (2001): 335–51, doi: 10.1177/0011128701047003003.

13 See, for example, "About Us," Legal Services for Prisoners with Children, https:// prisonerswithchildren.org, accessed July 1, 2022; All of Us or None (@AOUON), Facebook, accessed July 1, 2022; Clear, *Imprisoning Communities*, chap. 6; and James Forman Jr., *Locking Up Our Own: Crime and Punishment in Black America* (New York: Farrar, Straus, Giroux, 2017).

14 Donald Braman, "Families and Incarceration," in Mauer and Chesney-Lind, *Invisible Punishment*, 135.

15 This is a real problem since an apparent lack of interest in parental contact (an interest made much more difficult to prove from behind bars) can be grounds for losing parental rights. Samantha-Rae Tuthill, "Can a Parent Lose Their Right to a Child While in Prison?," Lawinfo, February 18, 2021, www.lawinfo.com.

16 Julius Kimya Humphrey Sr., "So I Can Hear You Call Me Father," American Prison Writing Archive, May 23, 2019.

17 Tracy Lee Kendall, "Daddy's Gone: Parenting behind Bars," American Prison Writing Archive, January 18, 2016.

18 Andrew R. Sumahit Jr., "Incarcerated Father," American Prison Writing Archive, February 10, 2010.

19 Tafari Tai, "Circumstances of Incarceration," American Prison Writing Archive, August 12, 2016.

20 Ken Sherman, "Here Is Another Brief Overview into the Drastic Conditions . . . ," American Prison Writing Archive, October 23, 2016.

21 Larry R. Carter, "Grandaddy, Come Home," American Prison Writing Archive, June 3, 2019.

22 Romell Winters, "Our Families Are Victims Too!," American Prison Writing Archive, October 18, 2016.

23 Linda Field, "Life without Children," American Prison Writing Archive, November 3, 2017.

24 Assata Shakur, *Assata: An Autobiography* (Chicago: Lawrence Hill Books, 1987), 257–58.

25 Corey J. Richardson, "Father Alert," American Prison Writing Archive, January 13, 2018.

26 Ruth Askew Brelsford, "I Get Up at 4:30," American Prison Writing Archive, March 17, 2018.

27 Nolaw97, "Visitations in Prison," American Prison Writing Archive, August 15, 2017.

28 Arline Lawless, "Descriptions of Sources of Stress, and Ways of Copin," American Prison Writing Archive, March 16, 2018.

29 Kali Yuga Vikalpa, "The Lesser of Two Hells," American Prison Writing Archive, October 28, 2018.

30 Shane Bell, "4 Year Old Nephew Travels across the State to Visit, but Is Denied by Prison Staff," American Prison Writing Archive, August 25, 2017.

31 Senghor, *Writing My Wrongs*, 215. This distribution of prisons in rural regions is not based on any penological rationale but the desire to spread jobs into these regions, often giving these regions added political power. See Jacob Whiton, "In Too Many American Communities, Mass Incarceration Has Become a Jobs Program," Brookings, June 18, 2020, www.brookings.edu; "Prison Gerrymandering Project," Prison Policy Initiative, www.prisonersofthecensus.org, accessed September 27, 2021; Tracy Huling, "Building a Prison Economy in Rural America," in Mauer and Chesney-Lind, *Invisible Punishment*, 197–213.

32 Shaye E., "Six Months before My Release," American Prison Writing Archive, June 18, 2020.

33 Lee Novinger, "Many Women Are Dying Here," American Prison Writing Archive, January 16, 2019.

34 Linda Kay Stermer, "How Long Is Long Enough?," American Prison Writing Archive, September 25, 2018.

35 Herukhuti, "Life without Parole Is the Death Penalty, within Genocide," American Prison Writing Archive, October 20, 2016.

36 Justin Case, "Just in Case You Did Not Know," American Prison Writing Archive, July 11, 2018. The study cited confirms Justin Case's claims: see McLaughlin et al., "Economic Burden of Incarceration."

37 Harold Caprers, "Open Letter to My Peers," American Prison Writing Archive, January 16, 2019.

38 Rufus Andrew Phelps III, "Hello, I Am Writing in Response," American Prison Writing Archive, August 16, 2017.

39 Sebastian O'Neal, "I First Came to Prison," American Prison Writing Archive, January 16, 2019.

40 The American Pharaoh, "Jungle Creed," American Prison Writing Archive, June 18, 2020.

41 Jeffrey Jason Gardner, "Profiteering from Crime and Prisons," American Prison Writing Archive, March 16, 2018.

42 Peter Padilla, "American Prison Writing Archive Is," American Prison Writing Archive, March 16, 2018.

43 Ronald Marshall, "An Appeal to Families of Incarcerated Loved Ones," American Prison Writing Archive, September 27, 2015.

44 Alice G. Bingner, "My Introduction to District Court," American Prison Writing Archive, June 18, 2020.

45 States do not explicitly deny such considerations, but presentencing reports are much more focused on risk of re-offense, damage to victims, and defendant capacity for reform. They are also of questionable accuracy and suffer no scrutiny, unlike trial evidence. See "A Proposal to Ensure Accuracy in Presentence Investigation Reports," *Yale Law Journal* 91, no. 6 (1982): 1225–49, https://doi.org/10.2307/796052; and Douglas A. Berman, "Foreword: Beyond Blakely and Booker: Pondering Modern Sentencing Process," *Journal of Criminal Law and Criminology* 95, no. 3 (2005): 653–88.

46 Anastasia Bogomolova, "Mass-Incarceration—What Is It Costing Us and Our Children?," American Prison Writing Archive, December 1, 2017.

47 Kenneth Fitzgerald Nixon, "Dear Mr. Unwilling and Reluctant Witness," American Prison Writing Archive, March 16, 2018.

48 In addition to the community damage noted above by critics and the incarcerated, these communities suffer what Amy Lerman and Vesla Weaver call "arrested citizenship"; whole demographics—particularly young Black men without high school education—have become second-class citizens, unable to vote, find jobs, support families, or exercise basic rights or engage with state power other than under the thumb of law enforcement; see *Arresting Citizenship*.

49 Romell Winters, "Like Father, Like Son?," American Prison Writing Archive, March 16, 2018.

50 Peter Mehmel, "A Hidden Cost," American Prison Writing Archive, March 16, 2018.

51 Amy Benjamin, "No Excuses. Reasons," American Prison Writing Archive, August 25, 2014.

52 See, for example, Western, *Punishment and Inequality*.

53 Rahasheem Brown, "The Mentality of an Incarcerated Criminal! Part One," American Prison Writing Archive, October 19, 2016.

54 Victor Andrew Apodaca Sr., "I Am Despised in Our Communities," American Prison Writing Archive, March 16, 2018.

55 Richard Hall, "If You Will Not Stand Up for Your Own Humanity . . . Who Will?," American Prison Writing Archive, October 21, 2016.

56 Anonymous, "Mother-Daughter in Prison," in *Fourth City: Essays from the Prison in America*, ed. Doran Larson (East Lansing: Michigan State University Press, 2014), 117.

57 Running Water, "Prison or Kids: It's Not a Joke," in Larson, *Fourth City*, 116.

58 Isaiah M. Thomas, "It Was July 18th, and All I Knew Was That Today," American Prison Writing Archive, June 23, 2019.

59 Lacino Hamilton, "#Incarcerated Lives Matter," American Prison Writing Archive, October 23, 2016.

60 Michael Rippo, "A Brief Deconstruction of America's Leviathan," American Prison Writing Archive, October 24, 2016. The Blackstone ratio: "Better that ten guilty persons escape than that one innocent suffer." "Blackstone Ratio," Oxford Reference, www.oxfordreference.com, accessed September 3, 2021.

61 Maurice Harris, "A Transformation: Prisoners to Peace Ambassadors," American Prison Writing Archive, October 21, 2016.

62 Timothy J. Muise, "Media Fear Factor and a Dangerous Overreaction," American Prison Writing Archive, October 23, 2016.

63 Daniel S. Throop, "The Island Effect: Social Marooning in Corrections as Extra-Judicial Punishment," American Prison Writing Archive, June 18, 2020.

64 Darin Bufalino, "Thanksgiving Day 2014," American Prison Writing Archive, October 23, 2016.

65 Jesse Campbell III, "Economic Slavery," American Prison Writing Archive, March 16, 2018.

66 Robbie Switzer Green, "The Reentry Movement Is Long Overdue," American Prison Writing Archive, January 21, 2019.

67 Tandy Marshall, "A Professor Once Asked Me," American Prison Writing Archive, November 2, 2017.

68 Ty Evans, "The Political Cause of Overcrowded Prisons: Dysfunctional Political Systems, Not Crime, Cause Mass Incarceration," American Prison Writing Archive, October 23, 2016.

69 Alice G. Bingner, "Corrections: An Exercise in Futility," American Prison Writing Archive, June 18, 2020.

70 Edward C. Shelley, "I Am Currently Incarcerated," American Prison Writing Archive, November 2, 2017.

71 Mark T. Wayne, "The Fallacies of Incarceration," American Prison Writing Archive, January 21, 2019.

72 Richard S. Gross, "I Block," American Prison Writing Archive, June 18, 2020.

73 His essay does not account for the efforts by imprisoned people to resist carceral conditions and maintain their humanity, which we saw in the previous chapter. But his work implies what effort is required by those who do seek constructive self-transformation.

74 Ivan Kilgore, "The Deceptions of Crime and Punishment in American Society," American Prison Writing Archive, October 22, 2016.

75 Brad Carney, "The Vertical Neighborhood from Hell," American Prison Writing Archive, February 5, 2016.

76 Tshombe Amen, "Release Date . . . ," American Prison Writing Archive, October 15, 2016.

77 Andrae L. Bridges, "My Name Is Andrae L. Bridges," American Prison Writing Archive, October 23, 2016.

78 Robert Cannon Jr., "Beyond the Wall," American Prison Writing Archive, September 26, 2018.

79 Dewayne L. Harris (a.k.a., Min Khalil Shabazz Muhammad), "What Is a Washington State Inmate," American Prison Writing Archive, June 18, 2020.

80 Grey Ghost, "The Conclusion," American Prison Writing Archive, January 16, 2019.

81 Shakkir T. Mujahid, "The Debriefing Proposal," American Prison Writing Archive, March 16, 2018.

82 Christopher Buckham, "Super-Masculinity," American Prison Writing Archive, June 15, 2018.

83 Daniel Rogers, "My Experience as a Prisoner . . . ," American Prison Writing Archive, April 13, 2016.

84 James Lawson-Wilson, "Today I Received an Outlet for the Thoughts That Are with Me Every Waking Moment," American Prison Writing Archive, September 26, 2018.

85 Christopher Balmer, "Never-Ending Fight," American Prison Writing Archive, December 24, 2014.

86 Tandy Marshall, "A Day before My 18th Birthday," American Prison Writing Archive, February 21, 2017.

87 B. C. Murray, "Alone," American Prison Writing Archive, May 23, 2019.

88 Ryan M. Moser, "Breaking the Cycle," American Prison Writing Archive, September 25, 2018.

89 Christopher John Velthuysen, "My Possible Parole," American Prison Writing Archive, January 16, 2019.

90 Jason A. Daugherty, "My Greatest Fear," in Larson, *Fourth City*, 268–69.

91 Tracy Glenn, "A Criminal End," American Prison Writing Archive, March 25, 2014.

92 See "Confined and Costly: How Supervision Violations Are Filling Prisons and Burdening Budgets," Council of State Governments Justice Center, June 18, 2019, https://csgjusticecenter.org; Edward McKinley, "Technical Parole Violations Cost State at Least $683M as Offenders Locked Up," *Albany Times-Union*, March 11, 2021, www.timesunion.com; and Alexi Jones, "Correctional Control 2018: Incarceration and Supervision by State," Prison Policy Initiative, December 2018, www.prisonpolicy.org.

93 Valjean Royal, "Post-Release Programs and Gender Variant People," in Larson, *Fourth City*, 275–76. Royal's essay was written eight years before the Supreme Court's 2020 decision barring LGBT discrimination in the workplace. See Michael D. Shear, "Gorsuch, Conservative Favorite Appointed by Trump, Leads Way on Landmark Decision," *New York Times*, June 15, 2020, www.nytimes.com.

94 Connie Gibbs, "Recidivism: The Need for Transitioning Guidance," in Larson, *Fourth City*, 270–71.

95 Ronald Marshall, "Combatting the Circumstances and Nature of Recidivism," American Prison Writing Archive, September 27, 2015. The disenfranchisement that the formerly incarcerated suffer also diminishes the electoral power of the neighborhoods where they return—communities unlikely to enjoy much of lawmakers' attention in any case. See Marc Mauer, "Mass Imprisonment and the Disappearing Voters," in Mauer and Chesney-Lind, *Invisible Punishment*, 50–58;

Lerman and Weaver, *Arresting Citizenship*, esp. chap. 8; and Christopher Uggen and Jeff Manza, "Lost Voices: The Civic and Political Views of Disenfranchised Felons," in Patillo, Weiman, and Western, *Imprisoning America*, 165–204.

96 Brendon Smith, "Mass Incarceration and Unjustice and Discrimination in the United States Court System," American Prison Writing Archive, May 28, 2018. This reading of a New Jim Crow is at the heart of Michelle Alexander's book by the same name (New York: New Press, 2010). See also Lerman and Weaver, *Arresting Citizenship*; and Western, *Homeward*.

Chapter 5. Defeating Deterrence

Epigraphs: Jennifer Battles, "What Is Life Like in an Alabama Prison?," American Prison Writing Archive, February 3, 2021; Brian McCarn, "Scarred the Effects of Institutionalization," American Prison Writing Archive, October 24, 2016.

1 Sampson and Laub write that "holding age constant and allowing individual heterogeneity in age effects, we found that when in a state of marriage, the propensity to crime was lower for the same person than when not in marriage. Similar results were found for military service and steady employment." People who choose to change their behavior must also meet opportunities to support such change: "Choice alone without structures of support, or the offering of support alone absent a decision to desist, however inchoate, seems destined to fail." Robert J. Sampson and John H. Laub, "A Life-Course View of the Development of Crime," *Annals of the American Academy of Political and Social Science* 602 (2005): 18, 43, doi: 10.1177/0002716205280075.

2 Despite evidence that these rates are going down, they remain troublingly high. See "Recidivism Rates: What You Need to Know," Council on Criminal Justice, September 1, 2021, https://counciloncj.org. Criminologists distinguish general deterrence, in which broad knowledge of the consequences of crime causes people in general to desist from criminal acts, from specific deterrence, the actual experience of criminal sanctions leading individuals to the decision to desist from committing additional illegal acts. As we have seen and will read of further in this chapter, incarceration itself fails to inspire specific deterrence, and general deterrence is effective only for those who have clear, viable choices in their methods of survival. As Susan Burton reflects in her memoir on carceral involvement, "You had to have decent options in order to make good decisions, and from my vantage point, I saw few opportunities for my life." *Becoming Ms. Burton* (New York: New Press, 2017), 50.

3 Daniel S. Nagin notes that "the great majority of studies point to a criminogenic effect of the prison experience on subsequent offending"; people show little understanding of the risks or penalties of apprehension, thus diminishing general deterrence. "Deterrence: A Review of the Evidence by a Criminologist for Economists," *Annual Review of Economics* 5 (2013): 93–94, 95.

4 "There is little evidence of a specific deterrent effect arising from the experience of imprisonment compared with the experience of noncustodial sanctions such

as probation. Instead, the evidence suggests that reoffending is either unaffected or increased." Daniel S. Nagin, "Deterrence in the Twenty-First Century," *Crime and Justice* 42, no. 1 (2013): 201, doi: 10.1146/annurev-economics-072412-131310. Eighteenth-century jurist Cesare Beccaria writes on this point.

> One of the greatest curbs on crimes is not the cruelty of punishments, but their infallibility. . . . The certainty of a punishment, even if it be moderate, will always make a stronger impression than the fear of another which is more terrible but combined with the hope of impunity; even the least evils, when they are certain, always terrify men's minds.

Cesare Beccaria, *On Crimes and Punishments*, trans. Henry Paolucci (1764; reis. New York: Macmillan, 1986), quoted in Raymond Paternoster, "How Much Do We Really Know about Criminal Deterrence?," *Journal of Criminal Law and Criminology* 100, no. 3 (2010): 769, doi: 10.2307/25766109. There can be even less deterrent effect, of course, when few people know the legal penalties for their acts.

5 Raymond Paternoster and Shawn Bushway note that "a commitment to a criminal identity and criminal life becomes more understandable . . . when viewed in the context of the stock of conventional alternatives available to many criminal offenders." "In sum, desistance from crime is not easy; in fact, it is exceedingly difficult, and many who embark on the path of self-change fail and do so repeatedly." "Desistance and the 'Feared Self': Toward an Identity Theory of Criminal Desistance," *Journal of Criminal Law and Criminology* 99, no. 4 (Fall 2009): 1122, 1133, doi: 10.1177/0093854816651905.

6 See Michael Tonry, "The Mostly Unintended Effects of Mandatory Penalties: Two Centuries of Consistent Findings," *Crime and Justice* 38, no. 1 (2009): 65–114, doi: 10.1086/599368; Marc Mauer, *Race to Incarcerate* (New York: New Press, 2006); John Pfaff, *Locked In: The True Causes of Mass Incarceration—and How to Achieve Real Reform* (New York: Basic Books, 2017); Mona Lynch, *Sunbelt Justice: Arizona and the Transformation of American Punishment* (Palo Alto: Stanford University Press, 2010), 148–49; and Heather Schoenfeld, *Building the Prison State: Race and Politics of Mass Incarceration* (Chicago: University of Chicago Press, 2018), 211, 336, ftnts 28, 29. H. L. A. Hart observes that, in the case of capital punishment, there is no evidence that such punishment deters or that its abolition increases crime; indeed, the evidence suggests just the reverse. *Punishment and Responsibility: Essays in the Philosophy of Law*, 2nd ed. (New York: Oxford University Press, 2008), 83, 88; Anthony N. Doob and Cheryl Marie Webster, "Sentence Severity and Crime: Accepting the Null Hypothesis," *Crime and Justice* 30 (2003): 143–95. "Being held in juvenile detention facilities," Michaela Soyer's study observes, "did not teach teenagers how to stay away from crime in a complex environment that would inevitably draw them back to their old life." "The Role of Agency in the Desistance Process," in *A Dream Denied: Incarceration, Recidivism, and Young Minority Men in America* (Los Angeles: University of California Press, 2016), 95.

7 John H. Laub and Robert J. Sampson, *Shared Beginnings, Divergent Lives: Delinquent Boys to Age 70* (Cambridge: Harvard University Press, 2003), 291 (includes citation of multiple studies confirming this point); Don Stemen, "The Prison Paradox: More Incarceration Will Not Make Us Safe," Vera Institute of Justice, July 2017, www.vera.org; Joseph Margulies, "Why Prisons Are Criminogenic," *Justicia*, January 3, 2022, https://verdict.justia.com. On how successfully juvenile facilities transform children into serious criminal offenders, see Keri Blakinger and Maurice Chammah, "They Went to Prison as Kids. Now They're on Death Row," Marshall Project, February 1, 2022. Marc Howard points out that recidivism increased amid growing prison admissions. *Unusually Cruel: Prisons, Punishment, and the Real American Exceptionalism* (New York: Oxford University Press, 2017), 98–99.

8 Laub and Sampson, *Shared Beginnings*, 291; John H. Laub and Robert J. Sampson, "Understanding Desistance from Crime," *Crime and Justice* 28 (2001): 1–69, doi: 10.1086/652208. H. L. A. Hart observes that punishment that is or is perceived to be disproportionate also risks flouting morality and "bringing law into contempt." *Punishment and Responsibility*, 25.

9 Pager's specific focus is employment prospects: "Research consistently shows that finding quality steady employment is one of the strongest predictors of desistance from crime. . . . The fact that a criminal record severely limits employment opportunities—particularly among blacks—suggests that these individuals are left with few viable alternatives." Devah Pager, "The Mark of a Criminal Record," *American Journal of Sociology* 108, no. 5 (March 2003): 961, doi: 10.1086/374403. See also Christopher Uggen, "Work as a Turning Point in the Life Course of Criminals: A Duration Model of Age, Employment, and Recidivism," *American Sociological Review* 65, no. 4 (2000): 529–46, doi: 10.2307/2657381; and Laub and Sampson, *Shared Beginnings*, 47, 181.

10 Supportive relationships are a major deterrent to crime—relationships that incarceration strains or breaks. Laub and Sampson write,

> In our view, more than being identified by a single trait like poor verbal intelligence or low self-control or even a series of static traits, the persistent offender, to the extent this term has meaning, seems devoid of linking structures at each phase of the life course, especially involving relationships that can provide nurturing, social support, and informal social control.

Laub and Sampson, *Shared Beginnings*, 280. See also Kristin Turney, "Liminal Men: Incarceration and Relationship Dissolution," *Social Problems* 62, no. 4 (November 2015): 499–528, doi: 10.1093/socpro/spv015; on the range of difficulties prison time presents to released people seeking to desist from crime, see Marieke Liem, *After Life Imprisonment: Reentry in the Era of Mass Incarceration* (New York: New York University Press, 2016); and Bruce Western, *Homeward: Life in the Year after Prison* (New York: Russell Sage Foundation, 2018).

11 Bobby G. Wheeler, "Monuments to Stupidity," American Prison Writing Archive, June 30, 2018.

12 Daniel Pirkel, "America's Criminal Justice System: Rehabilitation or Criminalization?," American Prison Writing Archive, September 27, 2018.

13 See, for example, Robert H. Stensrud, Dennis D. Gilbride, and Robert M. Bruinekool, "The Childhood to Prison Pipeline: Early Childhood Trauma as Reported by a Prison Population," *Rehabilitation Counseling Bulletin* 62, no. 4 (2019): 195–208, doi: 10.1177/0034355218774844; Marco Sarchiapone et al., "Association between Childhood Trauma and Aggression in Male Prisoners," *Psychiatry Research* 165, nos. 1–2 (2009): 187–92, doi: 10.1016/j.psychres.2008.04.026; and Merih Altintas and Mustafa Bilici, "Evaluation of Childhood Trauma with Respect to Criminal Behavior, Dissociative Experiences, Adverse Family Experiences and Psychiatric Backgrounds among Prison Inmates," *Comprehensive Psychiatry* 82 (2018): 100–107, doi: 10.1016/j.comppsych.2017.12.006. For a broad exposé on the cruelly destructive effects of juvenile incarceration, see Nell Bernstein, *Burning Down the House: The End of Juvenile Prison* (New York: New Press, 2014). This is a particular concern among incarcerated people simply because so many enter the system as children and so many others witness the incarceration of children; on the numbers, see Wendy Sawyer, "Youth Confinement: The Whole Pie," Prison Policy Initiative, December 19, 2019, www.prisonpolicy.org.

14 Lasan Bellamy, "How Long-Term Incarceration Effected Me as a Juvenile," American Prison Writing Archive, August 16, 2017.

15 Meagan Adams, "An American Epidemic," American Prison Writing Archive, May 28, 2018.

16 Curtis Lee Walker, "Juvenile Justice," American Prison Writing Archive, January 21, 2019.

17 Quoted in Bernstein, *Burning Down the House*, 69.

18 Garmon Coats, "Level III," American Prison Writing Archive, June 18, 2020.

19 Charles A. Brownell, "Frozen in Time," American Prison Writing Archive, February 3, 2021.

20 Prince, "Some Things Make You Laugh Make You Cry—Fight for Justice," American Prison Writing Archive, October 27, 2017.

21 Frans Sital, "What System!?," American Prison Writing Archive, October 24, 2016.

22 Christopher Hallum, "Twenty-One Years, Finally Done," American Prison Writing Archive, March 16, 2018.

23 Chanell Burnette, "When All Hope Is Lost," American Prison Writing Archive, May 23, 2019.

24 The Lone Wolf, "Life without Parole Is Torture," American Prison Writing Archive, August 1, 2014. The number of life and virtual life sentences (50-plus years) is not trivial; see Ashley Nellis, "Still Life: America's Increasing Use of Life and Long Term Sentences," Sentencing Project, May 3, 2017, www.sentencing-

project.org; and Marc Mauer and Ashley Nellis, *The Meaning of Life: The Case for Abolishing Life Sentences* (New York: New Press, 2018).

25 Michael H. Murphy, "Solitary's Terrible Toll," American Prison Writing Archive, November 2, 2017.

26 Richard S. Gross, "I Block," American Prison Writing Archive, June 18, 2020.

27 Daniel Lee Harris, "Bang! The Door Goes Shut," American Prison Writing Archive, March 16, 2018.

28 T. L. Maynard, "Chances and Choices," American Prison Writing Archive, June 18, 2020.

29 Compare, for example, Primo Levi's *Survival in Auschwitz* (New York: Simon and Schuster, 1995); a similar struggle to maintain self-respect and personal dignity is also pervasive in American slave narratives; see, for example, Yuval Taylor, ed., *I Was Born a Slave: An Anthology of Classic Slave Narratives*, vol. 1 (Chicago: Lawrence Hill Books, 1999).

30 Ivan Kilgore, "The Rhetoric of Imprisonment and the Reality of the Cage," American Prison Writing Archive, October 22, 2016.

31 McCarn, "Scarred."

32 Amy Buckley, "Mississippi Prison Insanity," American Prison Writing Archive, November 2, 2017.

33 Cole Onstad, "Prison Life," American Prison Writing Archive, May 24, 2019.

34 Jay C. Miller, "The Lost Boys of Prisontonia," American Prison Writing Archive, May 24, 2019.

35 Michael L. Owens, "Prisons Were Created to Punish, Deter, and Rehabilitate," American Prison Writing Archive, March 16, 2018.

36 James Castrillo, "Every Morning," in *Fourth City: Essays from the Prison in America*, ed. Doran Larson (East Lansing: Michigan State University Press, 2014), 280.

37 Dexter Henderson, "The Purpose of This Letter," American Prison Writing Archive, June 15, 2018.

38 Allen Ramer, "Criminality: A State of Mind," American Prison Writing Archive, October 22, 2016.

39 Don Cox, "The Life of a Texas Prisoner," American Prison Writing Archive, June 15, 2018.

40 Joseph E. Jones, "Fallacies of the FIRST STEP Act and the Flaws of Prison Reform," American Prison Writing Archive, June 18, 2020.

41 Mikell McCall, "Education," American Prison Writing Archive, June 18, 2020.

42 Felton L. Matthews Jr., "Home: An Essay on Prison Pre-Release Anxiety and Post Traumatic Stress Disorder," American Prison Writing Archive, February 9, 2020.

43 Ryan S. King, Marc Mauer, and Tracy Huling, "Big Prisons, Small Towns: Prison Economics in Rural America," Sentencing Project, February 2003, www.sentencingproject.org; David Walker, "Prisons: A Cautionary Tale of Rural Economic Development," in *Sustainable Development Policy and Administration*, ed.

Gedeon M. Mudacumura, Desta Mebratu, and M. Shamsul Haque (New York: Routledge, 2016).

44 Paul Keller, "Here Is My Submission," American Prison Writing Archive, August 16, 2017.

45 Michael Beverley, "A Perspective on Prison," in Larson, *Fourth City*, 26.

46 Cynthia L. Wallace, "Staff as a Whole Create the Pressure Cooker Environment," American Prison Writing Archive, June 15, 2018.

47 Shariff Ingram, "I Often Wonder How Differently," American Prison Writing Archive, March 16, 2018.

48 Amber Rose, "A Voice from Inside," American Prison Writing Archive, June 18, 2020.

49 Shree Agrawal, "Sources of Stress in Prison," American Prison Writing Archive, March 15, 2018.

50 Anna Vanderford, "Gargle, Rinse, Repeat," American Prison Writing Archive, September 25, 2018.

51 Benjamin Boyce, "I Did 340 Pushups a Day," Marshall Project, January 28, 2021.

52 Charles Brooks Sr., "The Rideout," American Prison Writing Archive, October 23, 2016.

53 Newman N. Kage, "Manners & Respect," American Prison Writing Archive, June 10, 2021.

54 Chanell Burnette, "The Red, Unfortunate, and Blue," American Prison Writing Archive, June 10, 2021.

55 Steven A. DeLogé, "A Speed Trap in a Small Midwestern Town," American Prison Writing Archive, November 3, 2017.

56 Timothy D. V. Bazrowx, "The Razor Ribbon Retribution," American Prison Writing Archive, November 12, 2017.

57 B. C. Murray, "Who Benefits from Prison?," American Prison Writing Archive, September 25, 2018.

58 Buckley, "Mississippi Prison Insanity."

59 Sabrina, "I Have Been Incarcerated Here at FMWCC," American Prison Writing Archive, November 2, 2017.

60 David W. Mason, "Crossing Over," American Prison Writing Archive, February 3, 2021.

61 Bobby G. Wheeler, "Does the Public Need Crime?," American Prison Writing Archive, January 21, 2019.

62 Reese S. Wilson, "Non Multa Sed Multam: Quality, Not Quantity," American Prison Writing Archive, June 20, 2016.

63 Steven Lazar, "Over the Past Thirty Years," American Prison Writing Archive, June 15, 2018.

64 Don White, "Prison Life, Geez, Where to Begin," American Prison Writing Archive, October 15, 2016.

65 MarQui Clardy Sr., "Over-Sentencing and Over-Incarceration: The Dehumanization of Criminal Justice," American Prison Writing Archive, December 20, 2018.

66 Mutope Dugma, "Institutionalized Racism Perpetuate Racial Hatred, Not Just Hatred towards Other Races, but Hatred towards Certain Characteristic within Ones Own Race," American Prison Writing Archive, October 17, 2016.

67 "The prison," Bruce Western writes, "steps in where the welfare state has failed." Western, *Homeward*, 61.

68 Robert W. Warrington, "The Most Important Essay I've Ever Written: A Recidivism Solution," American Prison Writing Archive, September 16, 2015.

69 Asar Imhotep Amen, "Punishment, Revenge, and Torture: The Heart of America's Criminal 'Justice' System," American Prison Writing Archive, May 24, 2019.

70 John Gargano, "Smoke and Mirrors," American Prison Writing Archive, October 20, 2016.

71 Kenneth E. Hartman, "Paying with Time," American Prison Writing Archive, October 21, 2016.

72 See, for example, Kahlil Gibran Muhammad, *The Condemnation of Blackness: Race, Crime, and the Making of Modern Urban America* (Cambridge: Harvard University Press, 2011); and Michelle Alexander, *The New Jim Crow: Mass Incarceration in the Age of Colorblindness* (New York: New Press, 2010).

73 Asar I. Amen, "Black Lives Have Never Mattered in the United States of America and Never Will: A 'Modern'-Day Slaves Perspective," American Prison Writing Archive, October 21, 2016.

74 Kevin Sawyer, "The Rehabilitation Fallacy," American Prison Writing Archive, August 16, 2017.

75 Rain Man, "Rain Man," American Prison Writing Archive, June 18, 2020.

76 Darnell Lane, "Rehabilitation Is Lost in Our Era of Mass Incarceration," American Prison Writing Archive, January 21, 2019.

Conclusion

Epigraphs: Derek R. Trumbo, "Why Write about Life in Prison?," *Slate*, February 22, 2022, https://slate.com; Jo-Ann Mayhew, "Corrections Is a Male Enterprise," *Journal of Prisoners on Prisons* 1, no. 1 (1988), www.jpp.org.

1 Angela Y. Davis, *Are Prisons Obsolete?* (New York: Seven Stories Press, 2003), 21.

2 In the final chapter to Marc Howard's anatomy of the exceptional cruelty of US penal and judicial systems—in comparison with European practice—he lists evidence for such positive changes. (He also quotes Marie Gottschalk's observation that reformers are still badly outgunned by the powers behind the status quo.) See chapter 9 of *Unusually Cruel: Prisons, Punishment, and the Real American Exceptionalism* (New York: Oxford University Press, 2017). Some states that are closing prisons are repurposing them for socially constructive use. See Nicole D. Porter and Ayanna Lyons, "Repurposing Correctional Facilities to Strengthen Communities," Sentencing Project, August 11, 2022, www.sentencingproject.org.

3 Mariame Kaba, *We Do This 'til We Free Us: Abolitionist Organizing and Transforming Justice* (Chicago: Haymarket, 2021), 118. See also Heather Schoenfeld,

Building the Prison State: Race and Politics of Mass Incarceration (Chicago: University of Chicago Press, 2018), 236. On the challenges faced by very recently elected progressive district attorneys, see, for example, Taylor Romine, "Boudin Opponent Named to Replace Him as San Francisco District Attorney," CNN, July 7, 2022, www.cnn.com; and Jamiles Lartey, "New Orleans Battled Mass Incarceration. Then Came the Backlash over Violent Crime," Marshall Project, July 6, 2022, www.themarshallproject.org.

4 Bruce Western, *Homeward: Life in the Year after Prison* (New York: Russell Sage Foundation, 2018), xiv.

5 See, for example, Mary Ellen Flannery, "The School-to-Prison Pipeline: Time to Shut It Down," National Education Association, January 5, 2015, www.nea.org.

6 Tihanne Mar-Shall, "The Poverty to Prison Pipeline," *Law Journal for Social Justice*, March 29, 2021; Adam Looney and Nicholas Turner, "Work and Opportunity before and after Incarceration," Brookings, March 14, 2018, www.brookings.edu.

7 Ashly Marie Yamat, "The Foster-Care-to-Prison Pipeline," *Justice Policy Journal* 17, no. 2 (Fall 2020), www.cjcj.org.

8 Seth J. Prins et al., "School Health Predictors of the School-to-Prison Pipeline: Substance Use and Developmental Risk and Resilience Factors," *Journal of Adolescent Health* 70 (2022): 463–69, jahonline.org.

9 M. E. Onah, "The Patient-to-Prisoner Pipeline: The IMD Exclusion's Adverse Impact on Mass Incarceration in United States," *American Journal of Law and Medicine* 44, no. 1 (March 2018): 119–44, doi: 10.1177/0098858818763818; PMID: 29764321; "Mental Health," Prison Policy Initiative, August 10, 2022, www.prisonpolicy.org.

10 Corey Michon, "Uncovering Mass Incarceration's Literacy Disparity," Prison Policy Initiative, April 1, 2016, www.prisonpolicy.org; Natalie Pate, "The Path to Prison Is Often Paved by Illiteracy. Yet Many Prisoners Aren't Being Taught to Read," *Salem Statesman Journal Sun*, August 7, 2022.

11 Robert H. Stensrud, Dennis D. Gilbride, and Robert M. Bruinekool, "The Childhood to Prison Pipeline: Early Childhood Trauma as Reported by a Prison Population," *Rehabilitation Counseling Bulletin* 62, no. 4 (July 2019): 195–208; Hannah Green, "Criminalizing Trauma," Society for Family Policy and Practice, August 10, 2022, APA.org.

12 This work is supported by a generous grant from the Mellon Foundation, which has also enabled transfer of the APWA from its original home at Hamilton College to Johns Hopkins University, under the co-directorship of myself and Hopkins political science professor Vesla Weaver. See Rachel Wallach, "American Prison Writing Archive Moves to Johns Hopkins," *Hub* (Johns Hopkins University), June 15, 2022, https://hub.jhu.edu.

13 For examples of seriously engaged first-person testimony to criminal legal practices, see, again, Amy Lerman and Vesla Weaver, *Arresting Citizenship: The Democratic Consequences of American Crime Control* (Chicago: University of Chicago Press, 2014); Todd R. Clear, Dina R. Rose, and Judith A. Ryder, "Incarceration and

the Community: The Problem of Removing and Returning Offenders," *Crime & Delinquency* 47, no. 3 (2001): 335–51, doi: 10.1177/0011128701047003003; Reuben Jonathan Miller, *Halfway Home: Race, Punishment, and the Afterlife of Mass Incarceration* (New York: Little, Brown, 2021); and Issa Kohler-Hausman, *Misdemeanorland: Criminal Courts and Social Control in an Age of Broken Windows Policing* (Princeton: Princeton University Press, 2019).

14 Horace Engdahl, preface to *Witness Literature: Proceedings of the Nobel Centennial Symposium*, December 4–5, 2001 (Stockholm: World Scientific, 2002), ix.

15 Doran Larson, "Prison Writer as Witness: Can DH Read for Social Justice?" *Digital Humanities Quarterly* 15, no. 3 (2021), www.digitalhumanities.org.

16 Members of another, major category of first-person witnesses to American incarceration—prison staff and administrators—rarely write or speak of their experience, under the pressures of professional investments in the status quo and a code of silence.

17 An additional project of the Prison Witness Collective is subject tagging of all APWA essays. This work will allow readers to select threads of essays on the topics that incarcerated people commonly write about.

18 Marie Gottschalk, *Caught: The Prison State and the Lockdown of American Politics* (Princeton: Princeton University Press, 2016), 137.

19 Such issues have been addressed by scholars and others. On the political views of imprisoned and formerly imprisoned people, for example, see Christopher Uggen and Jeff Manza, "Lost Voices: The Civil and Political Views of Disenfranchised Felons," in *Imprisoning America: The Social Effects of Mass Incarceration*, ed. Mary Patillo, David Weiman, and Bruce Western (New York: Russell Sage Foundation, 2004); and Nicole Lewis, "How Do Your Political Views Compare to Those of People behind Bars?," Marshall Project, November 3, 2020, www.themarshallproject.org. My argument is that such work could be more widespread and its results more broadly disseminated among the general public and key decision makers.

20 Research in the field of prison writing is still relatively new and often stops short of using such writing to address concrete practices or as a main source of legal or political theorizing (rather than as a subject of academic literary study). For examples of such efforts, see Barbara Harlow, *Resistance Literature* (New York: Methuen, 1987); Michael Hames-García, *Fugitive Thought: Prison Movements, Race, and the Meaning of Justice* (Minneapolis: University of Minnesota Press, 2004); Jason Haslam, *Fitting Sentences: Identity in Nineteenth- and Twentieth-Century Prison Narratives* (Toronto: University of Toronto Press, 2005); Dylan Rodríguez, *Forced Passages: Imprisoned Radical Intellectuals and the US Prison Regime* (Minneapolis: University of Minnesota Press, 2006); and the many texts written or edited by Joy James.

21 Leuner, Kirstyn J., Koehler, Catherine, and Larson, Doran, (2022) "Activist Bibliography as Abolitionist Pedagogy in the American Prison Writing Archive," *Criticism* 64, no. 3 (2022).

22 These classes take up no theory; we do not read prison abolitionist writers (other than those in the Archive). I start from the assumption that incarcerated people can make their own case and offer ample theorization.

23 This includes juveniles; see Nell Bernstein, *Burning Down the House: The End of Juvenile Prison* (New York: New Press, 2014), 148.

24 Robert Cover, *Narrative, Violence, and the Law: The Essays of Robert Cover*, ed. Martha Minow, Michael Ryan, and Austin Sarat (Ann Arbor: University of Michigan Press, 1992), 203.

25 The closest thing to such considerations are presentence investigation reports; these, however, focus primarily on culpability and potential for reform, not on what incarceration will do to a convicted person. These reports are also often inaccurate and negatively affect sentencing, any carceral treatment, and reentry. They generally require no statement on what a prison sentence will mean to convicted people's futures, families, or communities. See "A Proposal to Ensure Accuracy in Presentence Investigation Reports," *Yale Law Journal* 91, no. 6 (1982): 1225–49, doi: 10.2307/796052; and Douglas A. Berman, "Foreword: Beyond Blakely and Booker: Pondering Modern Sentencing Process," *Journal of Criminal Law and Criminology* 95, no. 3 (2005): 656–57. "In the case Gregg v. United States (1969), the Supreme Court held, 'there are no formal limitations on [presentencing report] contents, and they may rest on hearsay and contain information bearing no relation whatever to the crime with which the defendant is charged.'" "The History of the Pre-Sentence Investigation Report," Center on Juvenile and Criminal Justice, January 1, 2008, www.cjcj.org.

26 As Bryan Stevenson has famously stated, "We have a system of justice that treats you better if you're rich and guilty than if you're poor and innocent." "Bryan Stevenson Talks to Oprah about Why We Need to Abolish the Death Penalty," Equal Justice Initiative, August 3, 2022, https://eji.org.

27 Horace Engdahl, "Introductory Remarks," in *Witness Literature*, 4.

28 Within ten years of its inception, the American Prison Writing Archive had posted the equivalent of over 41 percent of the word count of all known North American slave narratives, which were produced over the course of over 150 years. Imprisoned people are not barred by law from gaining literacy, as was the case under slavery, but the print equivalent of over forty-six and a half volumes the size of the book project out of which the APWA emerged, *Fourth City* (a 338-page, ten-by-seven-inch textbook-format essay collection) is testament to the breadth of will among caged people to reach people outside.

29 Similar effects are widely evidenced, of course, in the witness literatures of slavery and the Holocaust.

30 Jodi Schorb, *Reading Prisoners: Literature, Literacy, and the Transformation of American Punishment, 1700–1845* (New Brunswick: Rutgers University Press, 2014), 127.

31 Rebecca McLennan, *The Crisis of Imprisonment: Protest, Politics, and the Making of the American Penal State, 1776–1941* (New York: Cambridge University Press, 2008), 221–24.

32 Dan Berger, *Captive Nation: Black Prison Organizing in the Civil Rights Era* (Chapel Hill: University of North Carolina Press, 2014), 93.

33 "Prison Strike 2018," Incarcerated Workers' Organizing Committee, https://incarceratedworkers.org; Janos Marton, "The Nationwide Prison Strike: Why It's Happening and What It Means for Ending Mass Incarceration," American Civil Liberties Union, August 21, 2018, www.aclu.org. Such strikes arguably helped to push recent ballot measures to bar forced prison labor. Victoria Law, "Forced Prison Labor Was Also on the Ballot," *Nation*, November 10, 2022, www.thenation.com.

34 See "Rebecca Ginsburg Receives Immroth Award," American Library Association, March 17, 2020, www.ala.org.

35 Matthew Friedman, "Just Facts: As Many Americans Have Criminal Records as College Diplomas," Brennan Center, November 17, 2015, www.brennancenter.org. Full citizenship has also been diminished by felony disenfranchisement of millions of potential voters.

36 In a book that documents how the city of Los Angeles historically used (and uses) jails not to control crime but to criminalize nonwhite people and control its racial profile, Kelly Lytle Hernández writes what applies as well to the nation.

> L.A's addiction to punishment has denied dignity and opportunity to millions while also bankrupting our ability to invest in the services essential for community progress. Generations of Black and Brown people, given no real economic choices, have paid with their health, their freedom, and their lives.

City of Inmates: Conquest, Rebellion, and the Rise of Human Caging in Los Angeles, 1777–1965 (Chapel Hill: University of North Carolina Press, 2017), 214.

37 See, for example, Jerry Kang, "Trojan Horses of Race," *Harvard Law Review* 118, no. 5 (March 2005): 1489–1593.

38 Marc Mauer, *Race to Incarcerate* (New York: New Press, 2006), chap. 10; Michelle Brown, *The Culture of Punishment: Prison, Society, and Spectacle* (New York: New York University Press, 2009); Rachel Barkow, *Prisoners of Politics: Breaking the Cycle of Mass Incarceration* (Cambridge: Belknap/Harvard University Press, 2019); R. C. Gomes and L. F. Williams, "Race and Crime: The Role of the Media in Perpetuating Racism and Classism in America," *Urban League Review* 14, no. 1 (Summer 1990): 57–70; Elizabeth Sun, "The Dangerous Racialization of Crime in US News Media," *American Progress*, August 29, 2018, www.americanprogress.org.

39 Kaba, *We Do This 'til We Free Us*, 95; Davis, *Are Prisons Obsolete?* On the concrete effects today of so-called carceral reforms, see Maya Schenwar and Victoria Law, *Prison by Any Other Name: The Harmful Consequences of Popular Reforms* (New York: New Press, 2021).

40 Local, state, and national organizations can be found in the Prison Activist Research Center directory, www.prisonactivist.org.

41 On the selective, racially biased, and pathologizing readings of crime statistics, see Khalil Gibran Muhammad, *The Condemnation of Blackness: Race, Crime, and the Making of Modern Urban America* (Cambridge: Harvard University Press, 2011); and Elizabeth Hinton, *From the War on Poverty to the War on Crime: The Making of Mass Incarceration in America* (Cambridge: Harvard University Press, 2016).

42 Hinton, *From the War on Poverty to the War on Crime*; Naomi Murakawa, *The First Civil Right: How Liberals Built Prison America* (New York: Oxford University Press, 2014); Bruce Western, *Punishment and Inequality in America* (New York: Russell Sage Foundation, 2006); Loïc Wacquant, *Punishing the Poor: The Neoliberal Government of Social Insecurity* (Durham: Duke University Press, 2009); Christian Parenti, *Lockdown America: Police and Prisons in the Age of Crisis* (New York: Verso, 2000).

43 A number of commentators have observed that the needed reductions in prison populations cannot be achieved merely by the release of those convicted of nonviolent, nonsexual, non-serious crimes. See Dana Goldstein, "How to Cut the Prison Population by 50 Percent," Marshall Project, March 4, 2015, www.themarshallproject.org; and Alexi Jones, "Reforms without Results: Why States Should Stop Excluding Violent Offenses from Criminal Justice Reforms," Prison Policy Initiative, April 2020, www.prisonpolicy.org.

44 These include penalties short of incarceration, and, more ambitiously, exercise of restorative justice. See, for example, Judy C. Tsui, "Breaking Free of the Prison Paradigm: Integrating Restorative Justice Techniques into Chicago's Juvenile Justice System," *Journal of Criminal Law and Criminology* 104, no. 3 (2014): 635–66; Danielle Sered, *Until We Reckon: Violence, Mass Incarceration, and a Road to Repair* (New York: New Press, 2019); and Lenore Anderson, *In Their Names: The Untold Story of Victims' Rights, Mass Incarceration, and the Future of Public Safety* (New York: New Press, 2022), esp. part 5.

45 Horace Engdahl, "Introductory Remarks," in *Witness Literature*, 9.

46 See Sharon Dolovich, "Forms of Deference in Prison Law," *Federal Sentencing Reporter* 24, no. 4 (2012): 245–59, doi: 10.1525/fsr.2012.24.4.245.

47 Keramet Reiter, *23/7: Pelican Bay Prison and the Rise of Long-Term Solitary Confinement* (New Haven: Yale University Press, 2018), 5–6.

48 Anderson, *In Their Names*, 273.

INDEX

AA/NA meetings, 118
Abbott, Jack Henry, 43–44, 113
Abu-Jamal, Mumia, 46; in *Yale Law Journal*, 47
accountability, 76, 84–85; of prison administrators, 70; in prison practice, 88; of prison staff, 200; retribution relation to, 57
action, mindset relation to, 115–16
Adams State University, 123
addiction, 72, 160, 218; IDOC relation to, 202
administrators, of prisons, 16, 242n43; accountability of, 70; constitutional rights relation to, 6–7, 230, 258n14; visitation affected by, 152; as witness, 295n16
Aeschylus, 85
affirmative penal action, 62
Alexander, Michelle, 8, 9
Alternative to Violence Program (A.V.P.), 118–19, 122, 270n49
American Indian Movement, 48
American Prison Writing Archive (APWA), 8, 235n2 (Preface), 238n32, 271n66, 296n28; banning of, 254n207; justice in, 231; in PLN, 255n208; public presentation of, 227–28; teachers using, 221–22; as witness, 54, 218–19, 221–22
An American Radical (Rosenberg), 50–51
Anderson, Lenore, 41, 231
Angola State Prison, 51
anti-violence programs, 100, 118–19, 122, 270n49

Apology of the Death of Socrates (Plato), 133
APWA. *See* American Prison Writing Archive
Arizona, incarceration rate in, 49
Arkansas, Eastern faiths in, 124
arrested citizenship, 284n48
Assata (Shakur), 44–45, 146–47, 253n178
Attica Rebellion, 37, 41–42, 251n153
Auburn Correctional Facility, in New York State, 17–18, 19, 240n25
Auburn Plan, 20, 23, 240n25
Autobiography of Malcolm X (X), 33, 34
A.V.P. *See* Alternative to Violence Program

Baca, Jimmy Santiago, 48–49
Bank of America, 156
barbaric punishment, 7
Barkow, Rachel, 63
beautiful prison, 134–35
Beccaria, Cesare, 287n4
Becoming Ms. Burton (Burton), 51
Bell, Richard, 13
Bentham, Jeremy, 39–40
Berger, Dan, 3
Berkman, Alexander, 24, 25–26
Betts, Dwayne R., 50
Biden, Joe, 39, 273n90
Bird Uncaged (Peterson), 52
Black civil rights, 140
Black Lives Matter, 140, 221
Black Panther Party, 34, 112, 248n112

constitutional rights, prison administrators' relation to, 6–7, 230, 258n14

containment, 138, 173, 176; children affected by, 141–42, 145–49, 161–62, 181–82; desistance affected by, 185; family affected by, 162–64, 181–82; institutionalization from, 139; parental responsibilities affected by, 142–44, 166; poverty affected by, 159–60; reentry affected by, 179–80; suffering relation to, 216; victims relation to, 140–41

conviction rates, 176

convict laborers, 242n45, 243n55, 244n65, 245n70

convict leasing, 243n57; of Black people, 21–22, 248n124; in Georgia, 27

Cornell Prison Education Program (CPEP), 119–20

corporal punishment, 19

Corrections in Ink (Blakinger), 52

costs, of incarceration, 153–57, 170, 256n6; taxes relation to, 169, 202–3

Cover, Robert, 223

COVID-19: crime rates during, 5, 9; violent crime during, 216, 254n203

CPEP. *See* Cornell Prison Education Program

CPS. *See* Certified Peer Specialist

creative writing courses, 43, 118

crime, 236n16, 245n72, 272n84; identity relation to, 288n5; incarceration relation to, 167–68, 171, 216–17; marriage relation to, 287n1; parole boards relation to, 272n83; poverty relation to, 27–28, 208–9; private interest relation to, 210; public consciousness of, 40, 207–8; punishment relation to, 39, 60–62, 63, 66, 78, 86, 287n4; rehabilitation relation to, 266n6; sentences relation to, 61, 279n6; state violence relation to, 38; survival relation to, 184, 199; trauma relation to, 41

crime rates, 4–5, 46, 249n130; communities' relation to, 184–85; during COVID-19, 5, 9; incarceration relation to, 11, 49; tough-on-crime rhetoric relation to, 53

crime survivors, rehabilitation preferred by, 66

criminal behavior, of ex-felons, 140, 177–78

criminal conviction, poverty relation to, 23–24

criminalization: of children, 217–18; race relation to, 184

criminal justice industry, 86, 136–37, 203

criminal legal system: degradation of, 183–84; in democracy, 222; public consciousness of, 225–27; racism in, 253n186; reform to, 140, 216; scholarship on, 219–20, 221

cruelty, 79, 102

culture, in prison, 277n130; institutionalization relation to, 194–95; masculinity in, 174–75; prison staff relation to, 200–201; rehabilitation affected by, 195–96

Cuomo, Mario, 39

Cusac, Anne-Marie, 40

Davis, Angela, 37, 215, 227

Dayan, Colin, 7, 67

death penalty, race relation to, 47

death row, 89, 91

Debs, Eugene, 24, 26

degradation, 25–26; of criminal legal system, 183–84; desistance affected by, 185; humanity relation to, 57; identity relation to, 67; punishment relation to, 87

dehumanization, 67, 108; dignity relation to, 192–93; identity relation to, 63–64; numbing relation to, 69; personality affected by, 81; reform affected by, 180; resistance to, 74, 89; retribution relation to, 57, 58, 85–86; testimony to, 230

institutionalization, 69, 137, 193–94; from containment, 139; family affected by, 180; prison culture relation to, 194–95; survival relation to, 73; trauma relation to, 199

Intense Meth Program (IMT), 95

In the Belly of the Beast (Abbott), 43

Irwin, John, 32

isolation, 15–16, 175–76. *See also* solitary confinement

Jackson, George, 35–37, 41, 90

Jim Crow, 181, 212

Johns Hopkins University, 294n12

Johnson, Lyndon, 39

JPay, 156

judges, 235n2 (Introduction); mandatory minimum sentences effect on, 91; witness effect on, 223

judicial system, vengeance relation to, 40–41

Judith, 123, 124–25

justice, 47; in APWA, 231; money relation to, 103; pain relation to, 6, 40, 65; in policies, 213; restorative, 129, 274n97, 298n44; suffering relation to, 6, 57, 138, 215; violence in, 258n14

juvenile offenders, 186–87, 288n6. *See also* children

Kaba, Mariame, 216

Kant, Immanuel, 257n10

Kariakou, John, 51

Kateb, George, 255n1

Kerman, Piper, 50

Kids and Kin, 121

Knight, Etheridge, 31, 34

Kohler-Hausmann, Julilly, 90

KunQuest, Quntos, 52

labor strikes, 245n70

law and order rhetoric, in politics, 5, 31–32. *See also* tough-on-crime rhetoric

law enforcement, 138–39. *See also* police; policing

Law Enforcement Assistance Administration, of Johnson, 39

lawmakers, 5, 136, 226, 228–30; communities' relations to, 286n95; pain relation to, 10; rehabilitation relation to, 92; sentences relation to, 184; victims relation to, 66, 86

Law & Order (television show), 7

Lawrence Hill Books, 253n178

Leder, Drew, 134–35

legal training, prison witness in, 224, 229

Lennon, John, 251n153

LGBT discrimination, 286n93

Liddy, G. Gordon, 43

The Life and Adventures of a Haunted Convict (Reed), 18–19

lifetime earnings, 256n6

Little, Malcolm. *See* X, Malcolm

lived experience, in testimony, 12

Live from Death Row (Abu-Jamal), 46

Lockard, Joe, 50

Locke, John, 58

Locked In (Pfaff), 208

Lock Up (television show), 7

London, Jack, 23, 24, 25

loneliness, suicide relation to, 75

Los Angeles, 297n36

love: humanity relation to, 105–6; meditation relation to, 110–11

Lynch, Mona, 30

Lyon, Patrick, 16–17, 26

mail access, 254n207

Mailer, Norman, 43–44

mandatory minimum sentences, 93, 260n33; crime relation to, 208; judges affected by, 91

Man's Search for Meaning (Frankl), 101

marriage, 281n10, 287n1

masculinity, in prison culture, 174–75

ABOUT THE AUTHOR

DORAN LARSON is Edward North Professor of Literature at Hamilton College. He led a writing workshop inside Attica Correctional Facility from 2006 to 2016 and has organized two college-in-prison programs in New York State. Author of *Witness in the Era of Mass Incarceration* and editor of *Fourth City: Essays from the Prison in America*, he founded at Hamilton College, and now co-directs, with Vesla Weaver, the Mellon-supported American Prison Writing Archive at Johns Hopkins University.